THE RIGHT TO PARODY

In *The Right to Parody: Comparative Analysis of Copyright and Free Speech*, Amy Lai examines the right to parody as a natural right in free speech and copyright, proposes a legal definition of parody that respects the interests of rights-holders and accommodates the public's right to free expression, and describes mechanisms to ensure that parody will best serve this purpose. Combining philosophical inquiry with robust legal analysis, the book draws upon examples from the United States, Canada, the United Kingdom, France, and Hong Kong. While it caters to scholars in intellectual property and constitutional law, as well as free speech advocates, it is written in a non-specialist language designed to appeal to any reader interested in how the boom in online parodies and memes relates to free speech and copyright.

Amy Lai has a background in law and literature and was educated at the University of Cambridge and the University of British Columbia.

The Right To Parody

COMPARATIVE ANALYSIS OF COPYRIGHT AND FREE SPEECH

AMY LAI

CAMBRIDGE
UNIVERSITY PRESS

CAMBRIDGE
UNIVERSITY PRESS

University Printing House, Cambridge CB2 8BS, United Kingdom

One Liberty Plaza, 20th Floor, New York, NY 10006, USA

477 Williamstown Road, Port Melbourne, VIC 3207, Australia

314–321, 3rd Floor, Plot 3, Splendor Forum, Jasola District Centre,
New Delhi – 110025, India

79 Anson Road, #06–04/06, Singapore 079906

Cambridge University Press is part of the University of Cambridge.

It furthers the University's mission by disseminating knowledge in the pursuit of
education, learning, and research at the highest international levels of excellence.

www.cambridge.org
Information on this title: www.cambridge.org/9781108427388
DOI: 10.1017/9781108688949

First published 2019

Printed and bound in Great Britain by Clays Ltd, Elcograf S.p.A.

A catalogue record for this publication is available from the British Library.

ISBN 978-1-108-42738-8 Hardback

Contents

Contents

Preface and Acknowledgments

Four years ago, the "Umbrella Revolution" broke out in Hong Kong. Glued to the Internet, I was bewildered and angered by what happened in the place that I once called home, while feeling fortunate and relieved to have settled in one of the most civilized nations in the world. Yet the ripples of the revolution and its suppression were felt across Vancouver and many Canadian cities. After all, Canada, far from a paradise, is by no means immune to corruption. Tyranny takes many forms. Like many welcoming and tolerant societies, Canada has produced great leaders, educators, and thinkers. At the same time, it has served as a breeding ground for the power-hungry, the deceitful, and the (wilfully) ignorant to spread lies, to bully, and to ostracize the upright and clear-headed for not kowtowing to them and for calling them out.

My frustration and cynicism, caused by what I read, witnessed, and experienced, have been channeled in positive and constructive ways. Four years later, all those sleepless nights, struggles, and tears have borne fruit. Looking back, I could not help but realize how privileged I was to be able to write and complete my dissertation, which reflects my hard work, my beliefs, and my spirit, in my adopted home, and to turn it into a book.

***

I am deeply grateful to Professor Graham Reynolds and Professor Joost Blom of the University of British Columbia for their kindness, diligence, patience, knowledge, and keen insights into the topic.

My gratitude also goes to former Dean Mary Anne Bobinski, Professors Joseph Liu, Mary Chapman, Shigenori Matsui, Robert Howell, Paul Quirk, and Jon Festinger, among others. I deeply appreciate Rozalia Mate for her support especially when I felt isolated and was in tears.

I am also indebted to the Centre for International Governance Innovation (CIGI) for its offer of fellowships. My unforgettable 2017 summer at the University of Waterloo, including memories of the magnificent CIGI building, inspiring exchanges with my colleagues at the Centre, and lovely Canada geese, would not have been possible without them.

Words could not express my surprise when I received an offer from Cambridge University Press in August 2017 – well before I finished the dissertation – to publish this book. My deep gratitude goes to Matthew Gallaway, senior editor at the New York office, for having faith in my work, as well as the anonymous readers for their constructive feedback. The editorial team of Cambridge was an additional joy in this nostalgic journey.

Finally, I am forever indebted to my family members, who instilled in me the proper values and inspired me to become a decent human being with integrity. National and cultural identities are products of circumstances and are often fluid and arbitrary. Families, which are based on love, are genuine.

***

After the tear gas dispersed and the smoke subsided, Hong Kong reverted to its usual state of superficial harmony and drunkenness. Many sober people stopped worshipping celebrities and authority figures who had chosen to sell their souls, lost respect for people whom they once looked up to, and "unfriended" some "friends" both on Facebook and in real life. Surprisingly, feelings of disillusionment and loss can be tremendously liberalizing. Old, shaky relationships can end in an instant. At any time, new and genuine ones are cultivated on shared visions, values, and experiences.

Bertrand Russell once said: "The trouble with the world is that the stupid are cocksure and the intelligent are full of doubt." It is my wish that my work will inspire intelligent people to speak up and to parody. I hereby dedicate this book to all people out there who have integrity, who help to uphold the rule of law, and who stand up to evil and tyranny.

The Dog and the Wolf

A gaunt Wolf was almost dead with hunger when he happened to meet a house-dog who was passing by. "Ah, Cousin," said the Dog. "I knew how it would be; your irregular life will soon be the ruin of you. Why do you not work steadily as I do, and get your food regularly given to you?"

"I would have no objection," said the Wolf, "if I could only get a place."
"I will easily arrange that for you," said the Dog; "come with me to my master and you shall share my work."

So the Wolf and the Dog went towards the town together. On the way there the Wolf noticed that the hair on a certain part of the Dog's neck was very much worn away, so he asked him how that had come about.

"Oh, it is nothing," said the Dog. "That is only the place where the collar is put on at night to keep me chained up; it chafes a bit, but one soon gets used to it."

"Is that all?" Said the Wolf. "Then good-bye to you, Master Dog."

"BETTER STARVE FREE THAN BE A FAT SLAVE."

Aesop, "The Dog and the Wolf." *Fables*, retold by Joseph Jacobs. Vol. XVII, Pt. 1. The Harvard Classics. New York: P.F. Collier & Son, 1909–14; Bartleby.com, 2001. http://www.bartleby.com/17/1/.

The laws and materials in this book are updated to the end
of October 2018.

Introduction

By the time I'm in the studio recording my parody,
10,000 parodies of that song are on YouTube.[1]

Over the past decades, an increasing number of Western jurisdictions have recognized "parody" as a fair use/fair dealing defense or exception in their copyright laws. They have done so either through their courts, which determined that parody is protected within existing defenses, or through their legislatures, which have explicitly added exceptions or fair dealing categories to their copyright laws. In 1994, for instance, the United States Supreme Court recognized parody as fair use in its landmark decision *Campbell v. Acuff-Rose Music, Inc.*[2] In Canada, the Copyright Modernization Act of 2012 expands the fair dealing doctrine by permitting the use of copyrighted materials to create a parody or satire, provided that the use is "fair."[3] The Copyright Directive of the European Union, enacted in 2001 to implement the WIPO Copyright Treaty and to harmonize aspects of copyright law across Europe, provides that Member States might exempt from copyright a "use" of a protected element "for the purpose of caricature, parody or pastiche."[4] In late 2014, the United Kingdom finally took up the "caricature, parody or pastiche" exception through legislative reform.[5]

---

[1] Gary Graff, *Weird Al Ponders Lady Gaga Parody*, REUTERS (June 23, 2010), https://uk.reuters.com /article/music-us-weirdal/weird-al-ponders-lady-gaga-parody-idUKTRE65M0LQ20100623 (last visited Oct. 10, 2017).

[2] Campbell v. Acuff-Rose Music, Inc., 510 U.S. 569 (1994).

[3] *See* Copyright Modernization Act, S.C. 2012, c. 20, s. 21 (Can.).

[4] Article 5(3) of the Copyright Directive allows Member States to establish copyright exceptions to the art. 2 reproduction right and the art. 3 right of communication to the public "for the purpose of caricature, parody or pastiche," among others. The Copyright Directive 2001/29/EC (2001), arts. 3, 5(3).

[5] Clive Coleman, *Parody Copyright Laws Set to Come into Effect*, BBC NEWS (Oct. 20, 2014), www.bbc .com/news/entertainment-arts-29408121 (last visited Oct. 10, 2017); Copyright, Designs and Patents Act, 1988, s. 30A (U.K.).

To date, few Asian jurisdictions have recognized a fair use or fair dealing exception in the form of parody, but things may change in the future.[6] In response to an upsurge of parodic works on the Internet since the beginning of the twenty-first century, the Hong Kong government introduced the Copyright (Amendment) Bill 2011 that criminalized the communication of copyrighted works on the Internet but did not provide for a parody exception.[7] Due to vehement opposition from the public, Bill 2011 was withdrawn, and the revised Bill, introduced in 2014, was shelved after further opposition from the public and some members of the legislature.[8]

The prevalence of parodies in the media and in everyday life and the increasing recognition of parody as a fair use/fair dealing defense or exception in copyright jurisprudences raise the question of whether parodying copyrighted works should be regarded more affirmatively as a right, rather than an exception or something to be exempted from copyright protection. The affirmation of creating parodies as a right leads to further questions concerning the nature and scope of this right and how it should be protected – whether through copyright law's internal mechanisms, or with the help of a solution external to the copyright regime. As the number of jurisdictions exempting parody from copyright protection has continued to increase, while others are proposing to include it in their laws, discussion of these issues is overdue.

This book aims to examine several questions. First, should the right to parody constitute part of the core freedom of expression of a normative copyright regime? Scholars who advocate a parody defense or exception generally emphasize the significance of parody as a form of cultural expression and as a potential source of innovation and growth.[9] This book will adopt a far more affirmative stance, by arguing that parody is a right in both the free speech and the copyright contexts. Second, if parodying copyrighted works is a right, what should be the scope of this right, and how should the law accommodate and protect it? This book will propose that a broad legal definition of parody should be adopted by statutes and courts. It will also argue that courts should look beyond the copyright regime for an

---

[6]   In India, the Kerala High Court coined the term "counter drama" to describe a parodic work that criticized the original, and holding it as fair use in *Civic Chandran v. Ammini Amma* (1996). Japan has not recognized such an exception, but advocates have been pushing for change. Latitude for Japanese parodists is nonetheless narrowed considerably due to the refusal of courts to tolerate infringements of moral rights. Susan Wilson & Cameron J. Hutchison, *A Comparative Study of "Fair Use" in Japanese, Canadian and US Copyright Law*, 41 HOSEI RIRON 224, 251–52, 276–78 (2009).

[7]   *E.g.*, Koon-Ho Justin Lam, *Copyright (Amendment) Bill 2014 – The Return of Creativity Suppression?* HONG KONG LAW BLOG (Oct. 15, 2014), http://hklawblog.com/2014/10/15/copyright-amendment-bill -2014-the-return-of-creativity-suppression/ (last visited Oct. 10, 2017).

[8]   *Id.*

[9]   *E.g.*, Kris Erickson, Martin Kretschmer & Dinusha Mendis, *Copyright and the Economic Effects of Parody: An Empirical Study of Music Videos on the YouTube Platform and an Assessment of the Regulatory Options*, CREATE WORKING PAPER NO. 4 (Jan. 1, 2013), www.create.ac.uk/publications/ copyright-and-the-economic-effects-of-parody/ (last visited Oct. 10, 2017); Ian Hargreaves, *Digital Opportunity: A Review of Intellectual Property and Growth*, UNITED KINGDOM INTELLECTUAL PROPERTY OFFICE (May 2011), at 5.37, http://orca.cf.ac.uk/30988/1/1_Hargreaves_Digital% 20Opportunity.pdf (last visited Oct. 10, 2017).

external solution to safeguard the right to parody, by drawing upon the free speech or the freedom of expression doctrine as they apply the parody defense or exception.

The book will combine philosophical inquiries with legal analyses in its examination of the rights to free speech and parody. Regarding the first question, it will draw upon natural law theories to argue that the right to free speech is a universal right, and expressing oneself through parodies is an exercise of this right. It will then discuss the nature of copyright from both natural rights and utilitarian perspectives, to illuminate how the right to parody copyrighted works, like the right to parody in the free speech context, is also a universal right that should be accommodated by copyright law.

Regarding the second question, the book will draw upon natural rights and utilitarian perspectives to define the scope of the right to parody. It will contend that the right to free speech is more fundamental than copyright. A broad legal definition of parody, which includes works targeting the originals as well as those that direct their criticism or commentary towards something else, accommodates more speech and is preferable to narrow definitions. However, parodies must not adversely impact the interests of rights-holders by serving as market substitutes for the original works or their derivatives. Although it is often appropriate for a legislature to take the responsibility to guarantee rights and to define these rights by statute, rather than calling on courts to assert their own judgments based entirely on notions of higher law, this chapter will argue that courts can and should also apply the parody defense or exception with reference to the free speech doctrine, to ensure that lawful speech would not be suppressed for the sake or under the pretext of copyright protection.

The book will then employ five case studies – the United States, Canada, the United Kingdom, France, and Hong Kong – to elucidate its arguments for a broad definition of parody and for courts to apply the parody defense or exception with reference to the free speech/freedom of expression doctrine. It will study how the free speech jurisprudences of these jurisdictions have been informed by the natural law, and how the proposed parody defense or exception would serve to bring their copyright jurisprudences, which have been influenced by utilitarianism, and/or a narrow conception of natural rights privileging the authors' over the users' rights, more in line with their free speech jurisprudences. Studies of these jurisdictions will also reveal the usefulness of the free speech/freedom of expression doctrine as an external mechanism in safeguarding parodists' speech freedom. If this external solution should be insufficient to protect free speech, then internal solutions, such as amending the moral rights provisions in relation to parody in copyright statutes, would serve to create the needed breathing space for free speech.

Undoubtedly, there exists a substantial body of research on the parody defense or exception. Examples include Richard Posner's papers that explain the right to parody from a law and economics perspective,[10] and Carys Craig's papers that

---

[10] Richard Posner, *When Is Parody Fair Use?* 21 J. LEGAL STUD. 67 (1992).

advocate for the expansion of the fair use/fair dealing doctrine to accommodate more derivative works through the lenses of feminist legal criticism.[11] Posner endorses only a very narrow definition of parody, whereas Craig neither discusses parody and satire, nor explains whether they both should be considered fair use/fair dealing. Further, the endorsement of relatively broad definitions of parody by most, if not all, scholars has been informed by instrumentalism and/or practical considerations. The novelty of this book lies in its employment of natural law theories, along with utilitarian perspectives, to explore the right to parody. It was deeply inspired by Robert Merges' book, *Justifying Intellectual Property*, which is described as a "landmark" and "a new Bible" in intellectual property law, and which draws upon Locke, Rawls, and Kant to argue that IP rights are based on a solid ethical foundation and are property rights, not incentives or conventions.[12] While Merges' pioneering book does not examine the right to parody, this book does.

Although there are works examining the relationship between copyright and free speech, including Jonathan Griffiths' and Uma Suthersanen's *Copyright and Free Speech: Comparative and International Analyses* (2005),[13] and that between free speech and parody, such as Joseph Liu's article *Copyright and Breathing Space*,[14] this will be the first book-length study of copyright, parody, and free speech.

One may wonder why this book targets the significance of the parody defense or exception in the context of copyright law, while this defense is equally, if not more, important in protecting free speech in other areas of law, one example being defamation law. Examining the parody defense or exception in copyright law by no means diminishes its significance in other areas of law. Defamation laws, by protecting the right to express opinions, also safeguard the right to express opinions through parodies. In contrast, copyright laws that do not accommodate the right to parody copyrighted works may allow valuable ideas to be suppressed for the sake or under the pretext of copyright protection. Not only would free speech be suppressed, but parody as a long-standing art form and a popular form of expression would decline. The book nevertheless by no means shuts out defamation laws from its legal analyses. Given that an examination of the free speech jurisprudence of each jurisdiction will constitute a significant part of its thesis, defamation laws, along with other speech restrictions, will be brought into the discussion to the extent that they are relevant to the arguments.

---

[11]   Carys J. Craig, *Reconstructing the Author-Self: Some Feminist Lessons for Copyright Law*, 15 Am. U. J. GENDER SOC. Pol'y & L. 207 (2007); Carys Craig, *Locke, Labour, and Limiting the Author's Right: A Warning against a Lockean Approach to Copyright Law*, 28 QUEEN'S L.J. 1 (2002).

[12]   ROBERT MERGES, JUSTIFYING INTELLECTUAL PROPERTY (2012). *See* reviews by Harvard law professor Henry E. Smith and Dennis Crouch of PatentlyO.com, which can be found on the Harvard University Press website: www.hup.harvard.edu/catalog.php?isbn=9780674049482 (last visited Oct. 10, 2017).

[13]   JONATHAN GRIFFITHS & UMA SUTHERSANEN (EDS.) COPYRIGHT AND FREE SPEECH: COMPARATIVE AND INTERNATIONAL ANALYSES (2005).

[14]   Joseph Liu, *Copyright and Breathing Space*, 30 COLUM. J. ARTS & L. 101 (2007).

One may also query the choice of jurisdictions in this comparative study. The jurisdictions in this book were carefully chosen with a view to engage the theoretical core in a meaningful manner. The United States has a long history of judicial decisions holding that parody is a defense to copyright infringement. On the other hand, the parody exceptions were not included in Canadian and British statutes until recently. A similar exception has yet to be included in Hong Kong's copyright law due to strong opposition from the public. The parody exception has been recognized in French copyright jurisprudence since 1957, long before the EU Copyright Directive took effect, although the author's moral right is also greatly valued in this civil law jurisdiction. The different free speech and moral rights traditions have/will strongly influence(d) the interpretations and applications of the parody exceptions in these jurisdictions.

Finally, one may also query whether the right to parody is truly a natural right, given that the right to free speech is hardly enjoyed in all jurisdictions over the world. Clearly, this book aims to explain what laws on free speech and parody should be like, rather than describe what these laws currently are. Hence, the mere fact that the right to free speech is severely restricted in some authoritarian nations by no means invalidates or diminishes the force of the argument that the right to parody is natural and inherent in all people. In fact, the enshrinement of freedom of expression in many national constitutions testifies to its being a value to which every nation aspires or at least pays lip services. In addition, because this work aims to propose a normative standard safeguarding the right to parody, it relies heavily upon natural law theory, despite the fact that copyright laws of the selected jurisdictions seem to be driven more by utilitarianism than by natural rights. Regardless of the changes that the copyright laws of these (or any other) jurisdictions will undergo in the future, the proposed model will continue to serve as a yardstick against which new laws should be measured.

OUTLINE

The book is divided into two parts. Part I, which forms its theoretical core, will argue that the right to parody should constitute part of the core freedom of expression of a normative copyright regime. Chapter 1 will describe the ancient origins of free speech and its significance in the development of Western democracies. The chapter will then draw upon writings by John Milton, John Locke, John Rawls, and Immanuel Kant to examine the right to free speech or freedom of expression as a natural, universal right subject to restrictions necessary for the respect of the rights or reputations of others and the protection of national security and public order. From ancient times, people have exercised this natural right by expressing themselves through parodies. Controls on parody in authoritarian and dictatorial regimes are tacit acknowledgment of its important role in democracies and its power in bringing social change.

Chapter 2 will explain why parodying copyrighted works is also a natural, universal right, and describe the extent to which copyright law should accommodate and protect the right to parody. It will study the nature of copyright from both natural law and utilitarian perspectives. Whether copyright is a natural right or a conventional right, it should give way to the more fundamental right to free speech when conflicts between them arise. The relative importance of these two rights justifies a broad legal definition of parody encompassing works that target the original works and those that criticize or comment on something else, as long as they would not likely serve as market substitutes for their original works or their derivatives. The public's right to parody, moreover, should not conflict with the author's moral rights. Given the fundamental nature of speech freedom, courts should also apply the parody defense or exception, which is internal to copyright law, with reference to the free speech doctrine, a mechanism external to the copyright regime, to ensure that lawful speech would not be suppressed for the sake/ under the pretext of copyright protection.

Part II will examine each of the selected jurisdictions to further the argument that the proposed parody defense or exception would serve to properly balance rights-holders' and parodists' interests. Each of its five chapters will roughly follow the same structure. First, they will examine how the jurisdiction's free speech tradition has been informed by the natural law tradition and how the right to parody is a natural right. A subsequent section will then explain how the copyright jurisprudence of the jurisdiction has been informed by utilitarianism and/or a propertized conception of copyright. The same section will then illuminate how the proposed exception would help to bring its copyright system in line with its free speech tradition. A final section will then employ hypothetical example(s) to explain that courts should ideally apply the parody defense or exception with reference to the free speech or freedom of expression doctrine. Failing that, courts should seek internal solutions to safeguard the right to parody.

Chapter 3 will study the parody defense in American copyright law. It will trace the history of the parody fair use defense and study the flawed parody/satire dichotomy created by the U.S. Supreme Court, according to which works not directing at least part of their criticisms or commentaries against the originals do not qualify as fair use. The chapter will then justify the parody definition encompassing both "parody" and "satire" and the prioritization of the "market substitution" factor over the other three factors in the fair-use analysis. It will also look at cases in which courts erroneously found "satirical" works to be unfair, and illuminate how the proposed parody definition would have enabled courts to properly balance the interests of different parties. The chapter will then turn to the importance of the First Amendment doctrine in ensuring that copyright law would not become less protective of free speech than defamation law, and that rights-holders who aim to use copyright law to suppress lawful speech – including those who have lost defamation suits involving parodies of copyrighted materials – would not likely succeed.

Chapter 4 will study the "parody" and "satire" fair dealing exceptions in Canada's Copyright Modernization Act. It will argue that a propertized conception of fair dealing, the influence of American case law, and the very meaning of "satire" itself may work together to influence how Canadian courts define the scope of protection offered by these exceptions. Hence, courts may find that "satirical" works do not pass the second-stage fairness analysis and are unfair dealings even though they would not harm the owners' interests. A broad parody exception would better serve to balance the interests of both parties by reducing any influence of a propertized conception of fair dealing and by leading courts to focus on the market substitution factor. Although the Supreme Court of Canada held that courts can interpret provisions of the Copyright Act in light of Charter values only in circumstances of "genuine ambiguity," a broadened parody exception might create circumstances of "genuine ambiguity," which would entitle courts to apply the exception by engaging with the Charter to balance freedom of expression with the Act's objectives.

Chapter 5 will study the parody exception introduced into British copyright law in 2014. It will argue that "parody" in the new exemption "for the purpose of caricature, parody or pastiche" will be broad enough to cover a wide range of works, and its "humor" requirement will not be difficult to fulfill. Hence, this parody exception promises to align the British copyright jurisprudence with its freedom of expression jurisprudence. Yet the moral rights provisions in the statute present a potential hindrance to free speech, while the public interest doctrine, narrowly circumscribed in *Ashdown v. Telegraph Group Ltd.*, will prevent courts from applying the parody exception in a way that best serves the public's interests. Nonetheless, courts could enhance the protection of artistic and political speech through an internal solution – emphasizing the nature of the defendant's use factor. Furthermore, should *Ashdown* be overruled, or the European Court of Justice's decision in *Deckmyn v. Vandersteen* be followed, courts could apply the parody exception with reference to a broadened public interest doctrine to enable parodies to survive moral rights challenges.

Chapter 6 will look at France, the only civil law jurisdiction in this book, whose copyright system is considered to be more oriented towards the protection of authorial property than their counterparts in other jurisdictions. While its Intellectual Property Code does not have the equivalent of the American fair-use or Canadian/British fair-dealing doctrines, it provides for a parody exception. Despite potential moral right challenges in a copyright jurisprudence oriented towards the protection of authors' rights, this parody exception, as interpreted by French courts, is generally in keeping with the freedom of expression tradition. Further, because France is a Member State of the EU, courts there can draw upon the freedom of expression doctrine in both domestic and European laws to safeguard the right to parody. Should domestic courts deny parody exceptions for works that would not harm the author's moral rights and commercial interests, parodists can appeal to the European Court of Human Rights, which would then apply art. 10 of the European Convention to provide more room for free expressions in the form of parodies.

Chapter 7 will look at the parody exception in Hong Kong's Copyright (Amendment) Bill 2014. After offering a socio-political account for the upsurge of parodic works in Hong Kong's social media since year 2000, it will explain how a parody exception would help to foster its creative industries and promote a critical political culture. However, neither the "parody, satire, caricature, and pastiche" exception in the Bill, nor a scholar's suggestion that the law should not distinguish between these genres, would best serve these purposes. Furthering Part I's argument, the chapter will contend that a broad parody exception should replace "parody" and "satire," but be distinguished from both "caricature" and "pastiche," which, unlike parody, need not contain any criticism or commentary. As free speech continues to decline in Hong Kong, this doctrine could not be relied upon as an external safeguard for the parodist's right to expression. An internal solution – providing an exception to the author's integrity right to object to derogatory treatment in the form of parody – would serve to provide more space for free speech.

WHAT'S IN A NAME?

The concluding chapter will ask: Can "parody" be called by any other name and still serve its function? On a related note, if the most vital factor that determines the fairness of the use or dealing is whether the new work would harm the interests of the rights-holder by substituting for the underlying work in the market, is the "parody" exception or defense even necessary in copyright law? By reiterating its ancient origins, its presences in different cultures throughout the centuries, and the significant role that it has played in fostering criticisms and commentaries, this book will conclude that "parody" should not be called by any other name as its serves its legal function to safeguard this important right. After all, names carry tremendous power.

PART I

1

The Natural Right to Free Speech and Parody

A society that takes itself too seriously risks bottling up its tensions and treating every example of irreverence as a threat to its existence. Humour is one of the great solvents of democracy. It permits the ambiguities and contradictions of public life to be articulated in non-violent forms. It promotes diversity. It enables a multitude of discontents to be expressed in a myriad of spontaneous ways. It is an elixir of constitutional health.[1]

The right to freedom of speech is a fundamental right, and parody is an exercise of this right. This chapter will unfold the story of free speech by journeying from Ancient Greece and Rome, through Renaissance Europe and early modern England, to late eighteenth-century France and America, where speech freedom was secured in different bills of rights and declared as a fundamental liberty in major revolutions. The chapter will then illuminate how free speech is a fundamental right through the lenses of natural law, which also has its origins in ancient Greece, by examining the writings of Milton, Locke, Rawls, and Kant. The right to parody thus stems from this natural right. Controls on parodic expression throughout history have acknowledged its potential power to bring social change. Speaking through parodies is also essential to self-fulfillment, the pursuit of truth, and democratic governance.

I. THE ORIGINS OF FREE SPEECH

The ancient Greek city-state of Athens was the first society in recorded history to embrace the notions of freedom and democracy.[2] The term "democracy" originates

---

[1] This quotation originated from Laugh It Off Promotions CC v. South African Breweries International (Finance) BV t/a Sabmark International and Another [2005] ZACC 7, para. 110, a decision of the Constitutional Court of South Africa, www.saflii.org/za/cases/ZACC/2005/7.html. Justice Dikgang Moseneke, handing down a unanimous judgment, held that T-shirt maker Laugh It Off had not infringed South African Breweries' trademark with the message on its T-shirts by replacing "America's lusty, lively beer, Carling Black Label beer, enjoyed by men around the world" with "Black Labour White Guilt, Africa's lusty lively exploitation since 1652, no regard given worldwide."

[2] KURT A. RAAFLAUB, *Aristocracy and Freedom of Speech in the Greco-Roman World*, IN FREE SPEECH IN CLASSICAL ANTIQUITY 58 (I. Sluiter & Ralph Mark Rosen, eds., 2004).

from the Greek word *dēmokratía*, meaning the "rule of the people," which was founded on *demos* (people) and *krátos* (power or rule).[3] For Athenians to participate in their own government, *isegoria*, or the equality of speaking rights, was complemented by *parrhesia*, which refers to open and candid speech in private and public life.[4] Athenians eulogized *parrhesia*, most frequently translated as "free speech," "freedom of speech," or "frank speech," as a practice allowing them to express an egalitarianism that not only rejected hierarchy, but also freed them from the restraints of a reverence for superiors or the past, so that they could move forward to create a new order.[5] Although *parrhesia* did not carry the idea of individual freedom as it is understood today, it did encapsulate the freedom that enables people to choose their own governments and rulers.[6] In sum, *parrhesia*, or free speech, was one of the key egalitarian foundations and participatory principles of the democratic regime of the Athenians.[7]

Unsurprisingly, the significance of *parrhesia* in democratic Athens is revealed in the writings of Greek philosophers. Socrates, the great advocate of free speech, identified equality and resistance to hierarchy as the essential attributes of a democratic regime.[8] The Assembly, the primary forum for political decisions, was a place where all citizens, irrespective of social and economic status, could "deliberate on something concerning the governance of the city" (*poleos dioikeseos*), and where "carpenter, bronze worker, shoemaker, merchant, shop-owner, rich, poor, noble, lowly born" could stand up and participate in the deliberations.[9] Socratic *parrhesia*, or the freedom to say whatever one wants so long as it is in accordance with the truth, became a significant part of his student Plato's political

---

3   ROBERT HARGREAVES, THE FIRST FREEDOM: A HISTORY OF FREE SPEECH 5 (2002); Robert W. Wallace, *Power to Speak – and Not to Listen – in Ancient Athens*, IN FREE SPEECH IN CLASSICAL ANTIQUITY 221 (I. Sluiter & Ralph Mark Rosen, eds., 2004).

4   *Id.*

5   ARLENE W. SAXONHOUSE, FREE SPEECH AND DEMOCRACY IN ANCIENT ATHENS 40, 86 (2008).

6   MOSES FINLEY, in DEMOCRACY: ANCIENT AND MODERN 116 (1988), contends that in ancient Athens there were "no theoretical limits to the power of the state, no activity … in which the state could not legitimately intervene provided that decision was taken properly … Freedom meant the rule of law and participation in decision making process, not the possession of inalienable rights." HARGREAVES, *supra* note 3, at 5–6; *see* WALLACE, *supra* note 3, at 227; SAXONHOUSE, *supra* note 5, at 23.

7   There were limits to free speech in ancient Athens. For example, playwrights had to observe the laws relating to impiety, even when writing comedies. In addition, Athenian historian Thucydides identifies the problems of practicing *parrhesia* in democratic decision-making in his *Assemblies*, one major issue being that speakers did not always speak truthfully. SAXONHOUSE, *supra* note 5, at 131.

8   *Id.* at 48.

9   *Id.* at 94, *citing* CYNTHIA FARRAR, THE ORIGINS OF DEMOCRATIC THINKING: THE INVENTION OF POLITICS IN CLASSICAL ATHENS (1988). For many generations, the trial of Socrates, who was charged with "corrupting the young" and impiety, has served as a symbol of the violation of freedom of expression, which poses the difficult question of how to reconcile the democratic freedoms of Athens with his execution. Some affirm that Athens was a fundamentally tolerant regime and that the trial was an aberration. Hargreaves approaches the issue from a different perspective, by contending that the death of Socrates is "the first and plainest example of how a democracy may be diminished when it dispenses with the freedom of expression," and how a "truly free spirit is likely to fall victim to the tyranny of the majority as he is of a single dictator." HARGREAVES, *supra* note 3, at 21.

ideals.[10] Aristotle, a student of Plato, further compared the Assembly to a potluck dinner, where each participant could contribute and benefit other citizens through the wisdom of many.[11]

The Roman Empire had no word that corresponds to the Greek word *parrhesia*. The Latin term *libertas*, meaning liberty, did not refer to free speech in the way Athenians would have understood it.[12] The Roman Senate and senior statesmen were the only citizens to whom the right to political discussion was formally granted.[13] Although ordinary citizens could vote in the Roman assemblies, they had no formal right to make their voices heard.[14] Yet neither the non-existence of a specific term for free speech, nor the reluctance of the elite class to extend this right to the public, indicated a lack of awareness among ordinary people that speaking freely was an important part of their freedom. Thus, they often found ways and opportunities to vent their opinions and even influence those of the Senate.[15]

Following the decline of the Roman Empire, Europe entered the Dark Ages. During this period, the Catholic Church, which became the most powerful force in medieval life, withheld from the populace their freedom of conscience and freedom of speech.[16] By the fifteenth century, however, its authority was undermined by a new generation of Renaissance humanists who spoke out against the Church and the State. They included Desiderius Erasmus, a Dutch Catholic priest and theologian who satirized the corrupt practices of the Catholic Church;[17] Niccolo Machiavelli, the Italian historian and philosopher who looked to the founding and early years of the ancient Roman Republic to develop a theory of free speech based on the dangers of repression;[18] and Martin Luther, the German priest and key figure in the Protestant Reformation.[19] The spread of heresy was facilitated by the invention of the printing press.[20]

The struggle for speech freedom continued throughout the Enlightenment period despite the regulation and control of the press by the Roman Catholic Church and state governments. In England, for example, freedom of speech was secured in Parliament through the Bill of Rights in 1689.[21] In 1695, the Licensing of the Press Act ("the Licensing Act"), through which the Crown exerted its prerogative power to control the press, was rejected by the

---

[10]   MARLEIN VAN RAALTE, *Socratic Parrhesia and Its Afterlife in Plato's Laws*, IN FREE SPEECH IN CLASSICAL ANTIQUITY 305, 310 (I. Sluiter & Ralph Mark Rosen, eds., 2004).

[11]   SAXONHOUSE, *supra* note 5, at 150, *citing* ARISTOTLE, POLITICS, bk III, CH. 2.

[12]   RAAFLAUB, *supra* note 2, at 54; HARGREAVES, *supra* note 3, at 22.

[13]   HARGREAVES, *supra* note 3, at 23; RAAFLAUB, *supra* note 2, at 55.

[14]   SUSAN WILTSHIRE, GREECE, ROME AND THE BILL OF RIGHTS 116 (1992).

[15]   RAAFLAUB, *supra* note 2, at 55–56.

[16]   HARGREAVES, *supra* note 3, at 39–41.

[17]   *Id.* at 41–45.

[18]   SAXONHOUSE, *supra* note 5, at 31–32.

[19]   HARGREAVES, *supra* note 3, at 45–49.

[20]   *Id.* at 50–53.

[21]   *Id.* at 111; Bill of Rights (Act) 1689 (England) 1688 c.2.

Commons.[22] In fact, the American Revolution was triggered in part by Britain's attempt to impose stamp duties on printed materials in its American colonies.[23] Although the American Constitution of 1789 made no mention of free speech, in response to calls for greater constitutional protection for individual liberties, its Bill of Rights was ratified in 1791, and the First Amendment states: "Congress shall make no law ... abridging the freedom of speech, or of the press."[24] The ideals of the American Revolution accordingly inspired the Declaration of the Rights of Man and of the Citizen in France, where, until the revolution, censorship had been universal, and freedom of speech granted at the discretion of the monarch.[25] Passed in 1789, Article XI of the Declaration identifies free speech and the liberty of the press as the most precious rights of man.[26]

II. THE NATURAL RIGHT TO FREE SPEECH

What is natural law, and why should a natural-law approach be used to illuminate the fundamental nature of the right to free speech? From natural-law perspectives, the act of positing law can and should be guided by higher principles that are universal, immutable, and discoverable by reason – principles that also offer yardsticks against which to measure positive law.[27] According to natural-law legal theory, "the authority of legal standards necessarily derives, at least in part, from considerations having to do with the moral merit of those standards."[28] To discuss the right to free speech, which has long been recognized as a fundamental right, one therefore

[22] Under the Licensing Act, established in 1662, all books were required to be licensed either by the Archbishop of Canterbury or the Bishop of London. *Id.* at 93. One should note that the lapse of the Act did not signify the end of censorship. In the twenty years afterwards, the government explored other means of regulating the press, including the 1712 Stamp Act, which imposed a tax on all printed papers, pamphlets and advertisements. Besides rules that forbade the reporting of debates in Parliament, the common law crime of seditious libel was used against authors and printers throughout the eighteenth century, through which courts placed the stability of the State over the freedom of the press. *Id.* at 113–17.

[23] *Id.* at 115.

[24] *Id.* at 175; U.S. CONST. amend. I.

[25] *Id.* at 154; *citing* Déclaration des Droits de l'Homme et du Citoyen de 1789 [Declaration of the Rights of Man and of the Citizen (August 1789)] (Fr.).

[26] These freedoms died in the Reign of Terror four years later and were not revived until after the overthrow of Napoleon. *Id.* at 167.

[27] RAYMOND WACKS, PHILOSOPHY OF LAW: A VERY SHORT INTRODUCTION 15, 22 (2006).

[28] Natural-law legal theory is to be distinguished from (though not independent of) natural-law moral theory, according to which "the moral standards that govern human behavior are, in some sense, objectively derived from the nature of human beings and the nature of the world." KENNETH EINAR HIMMA, *Natural Law*, INTERNET ENCYCLOPEDIA OF PHILOSOPHY, www.iep.utm.edu/natlaw/ (last visited Mar. 30, 2018). For instance, John Finnis's naturalism is both an ethical theory and a theory of law, according to which the purpose of moral principles is to give ethical structure to the pursuit of equally valuable basic goods, and the purpose of the law is to facilitate "the common good" of a community through authoritative rules that solve coordination problems arising in connection with the pursuit of these basic goods. *Id.*; *see* originally JOHN FINNIS, NATURAL LAW AND NATURAL RIGHTS 276 (1980).

should draw upon natural-law perspectives, which dictate what laws are just laws and what forms these laws should take, rather than law and economics or any instrumentalist perspectives.

Like free speech, natural law has its origins in ancient Athens.[29] Natural law then became a major tenet of Stoic philosophy during the Hellenistic age,[30] and exerted a profound influence over the Roman legal doctrine of *jus naturale*.[31] Although during the middle ages the Catholic Church appropriated the pagan idea of natural law for Christian purposes,[32] it was secularized again by the Enlightenment humanists in the seventeenth century, who contended that nature's laws and what are good and bad are discernible by human reason, and therefore do not require a God or gods to confirm their validity.[33] However conservative these views concerning universal principles may seem, since the Enlightenment period they have been employed by revolutionaries in their attempts to overthrow regimes considered to have trampled upon individuals' natural rights.[34]

Whereas natural-law ethics provide guidance for one's actions, such that one will pursue the good such as life and knowledge, natural rights define a moral "space" over which one has sole jurisdiction or liberty to act according to the good, and within which no other people may rightfully interfere.[35] The writings by Milton, Locke, Rawls, and Kant illustrate that the right to free speech is a natural right.

A. *John Milton's* Areopagitica

Although both free speech and natural law originated in ancient Greece, no ancient Greek philosophers directly applied natural law to the concept of *parrhesia*, let alone defended free speech as a natural right. Interestingly, though, Milton's *Areopagitica*:

---

[29] Both Plato and Aristotle demanded that human laws conform to a natural and rationally discernable standard of justice that transcends local customs or conventions. WACKS, *supra* note 27, at 11.

[30] The Stoics, following Aristotle, believed that human beings are born with a self-awareness that leads them towards self-preservation, a capacity to distinguish good from bad, and a development of laws of thought and ethics that apply to all people at all time and in all places. WILTSHIRE, *supra* note 14, at 14.

[31] *The Digest* (also called the *Pandects*), a major source of Roman law compiled at the behest of the emperor Justinian between AD 530 and 533, holds that there are three sorts of laws: the law of the state, *ius civile*, which expresses the interests of a particular community; the law of nations, *ius gentium*; and the law of nature, *ius naturale*, which corresponds to "that which is always good and equitable." For Romans, natural law served as the means of adapting laws peculiar to a particular locale or a legal system for an international or transnational civilization. *Id.* at 20–22.

[32] According to St. Thomas Aquinas, the Dominican scholar who reconciles Aristotelian with Christian views of life, the Eternal Law is known only to God, but men can discover and participate in the Eternal Law through the light of reason, and he calls this participation the Natural law. WACKS, *supra* note 27, at 12–13; WILTSHIRE, *supra* note 14, at 35–37.

[33] In his influential work *De Jure Belli ac Pacis*, Hugo de Groot, or Grotius, asserts that even if God did not exist, natural law would have the same content. WACKS, *supra* note 27, at 16; WILTSHIRE, *supra* note 14, at 69.

[34] WACKS, *supra* note 27, at 17.

[35] Randy E. Barnett, *A Law Professor's Guide to Natural Law and Natural Rights*, 20 HARV. J.L. & PUB. POL'Y 655, 668–69 (1997).

A *Speech for the Liberty of Unlicenc'd Printing* (1644), considered to be "the most eloquent plea for a free press ever penned,"[36] and "the foundational essay of the free speech tradition,"[37] uses ancient Athens as its model for free speech by making frequent allusions to this city and its authors. Its title was derived from Areopagus, the hill to the west of the Acropolis where the Athenian council gathered to give their advice to the *polis*.[38] "Areopagitica" was also the title of ancient Greek orator Isocrates' speech, which invoked virtues embodied in the judges sitting on the Areopagus in the early fifth century BC, and which Isocrates found lacking among Athenians of his own time.[39] By naming his essay about free press after Isocrates' speech, Milton thus suggested that the sought-after virtues would only flourish when people enjoy the freedom to offer their views in print.[40] In addition, the epigraph of Milton's essay originated from Greek playwright Euripides' *Suppliant Women*, which states that "this is true liberty where free born men, having to advise the people, may speak free."[41] Through this quotation, Milton thus asserts that free speech is a right to which all free-born men are entitled.[42]

Areopagitica was first addressed to the English Parliament, which, at the height of the English Civil War, instituted a regime of prior censorship through the Licensing Order of 1643, requiring every book and pamphlet, and other written materials, to be approved by the government before it could be printed.[43] Central to *Areopagitica*, which Milton published without official approval in 1644, is the belief that prior censorship is evil. It dampens the ability to reason, removes moral choice, and obstructs the pursuit of truth, which is necessarily intertwined with falsehood but which benefits by confronting it: "Let her [Truth] and Falsehood grapple; whoever knew Truth put to the worse, in a free and open encounter."[44] Not only does Milton compare such forms of censorship to murder,[45] but he also regards a good book as

---

36 HARGREAVES, *supra* note 3, at 100.

37 VINCENT BLASI, Milton's Areopagitica and the Modern First Amendment, YALE LAW SCHOOL LEGAL SCHOLARSHIP REPOSITORY OCCASIONAL PAPERS, Paper 6 (1995), at 1, http://digitalcommons.law.yale.edu /cgi/viewcontent.cgi?article=1007&context=ylsop_papers (last visited Oct. 10, 2017).

38 HARGREAVES, *supra* note 3, at 99.

39 SAXONHOUSE, *supra* note 5, at 20.

40 *Id.*

41 *Id.*; HARGREAVES, *supra* note 3, at 99; *citing* JOHN MILTON, AREOPAGITICA (1644), www.saylor.org/site/ wp-content/uploads/2012/08/ENGL402-Milton-Aeropagitica.pdf (last visited Oct. 10, 2017).

42 HARGREAVES, *supra* note 3, at 99; SAXONHOUSE, *supra* note 5, at 20.

43 MILTON, *supra* note 41.

44 Milton argued that reading impious material is not dangerous because "[t]o the pure, all things are pure." He further contrasts the classical, enlightened tradition of the Greeks and Romans with the censorship tradition imposed by the Catholic Church and the Spanish Inquisition. Although Greece and Rome condemned libelous materials, neither embraced censorship. It was not until after the year 800 that the Roman Catholic Church implemented a censorship policy, which became increasingly stringent in Spain and Italy during the fifteenth century and was endorsed by the Council of Trent that ended in 1563. By then, "no Book, pamphlet, or paper" could be printed unless "approv'd and licenc't under the hands of 2 or 3 glutton Friers." *Id.*

45 "[W]ho kills Man kills a reasonable creature, Gods Image; but hee who destroyes a good Booke, kills reason it selfe, kills the Image of God, as it were in the eye. Many a man lives a burden to the Earth;

possessing "a potencie of life."[46] Destroying it is not "slaying of an elemental life, but strikes at that ethereal and fifth essence, the breath of reason itself, slays an immortality rather than a life."[47] England should learn from the Greeks and Romans, who punished blasphemous and libelous writing, but would not require all authors to submit their works for prior approval. Hence, it should allow unrestricted printing and only punish those who abuse this freedom.[48]

Areopagitica inspired numerous writers, including early Enlightenment thinker John Locke. In his essay, Milton made it quite clear that the liberty of unlicensed printing was not meant to be universal.[49] It was Locke, writing in the late seventeenth century, who proved to be a more coherent defender of toleration, hence a more ardent supporter of free thought and expression.[50] If Milton's advocacy for freedom of expression mainly draws upon the truth-seeking argument,[51] then John Locke's espousal of free speech focuses as much on individual autonomy and self-government as on the "marketplace" argument.[52]

B. John Locke: Freedom of Conscience, Individual Autonomy, and Self-Government

Locke elevates the position of individual rights by asserting that they are not granted by any superior authority, but are inalienable rights with which people are naturally endowed, in his *Two Treatises on Government, An Essay Concerning Human Understanding*, and *A Letter Concerning Toleration*.[53] The influence of these writings, all published in 1689, was far-reaching. They were crucial to the establishment of the English Bill of Rights, which secured freedom of speech and of elections for members of

---

but a good Booke is the pretious life-blood of a master spirit, imbalm'd and treasur'd up on purpose to a life beyond life." *Id.*

[46] *Id.*

[47] *Id.*

[48] *Id.*

[49] According to Milton, toleration extends to "many," but not all. Catholics were arguably excluded from toleration for political as well as religious reasons, the latter including the alleged superstitious nature of Catholicism: "Yet if all cannot be of one mind, as who looks they should be? this doubtles is more wholsome, more prudent, and more Christian that many be tolerated, rather then all compell'd. I mean not tolerated Popery, and open superstition, which as it extirpats all religions and civill supremacies, so it self should be extirpat, provided first that all charitable and compassionat means be us'd to win and regain the weak and the misled: that also which is impious or evil absolutely either against faith or maners no law can possibly permit, that intends not to unlaw it self: ..." *Id.*

[50] Like Milton, Locke objected to prepublication censorship. After the Licensing Act was renewed in 1693, he developed his objections to licensing in a Memorandum to the Parliament, although his major objection to the Act had more to do with monopolies than with censorship. HARGREAVES, *supra* note 3, at 111.

[51] Alon Harel, *Freedom of Speech*, THE ROUTLEDGE COMPANION TO THE PHILOSOPHY OF LAW 601–02 (Andrei Marmor, ed. 2015).

[52] *Id.* at 603.

[53] WILTSHIRE, *supra* note 14, at 76, 79.

Parliament.[54] In addition, many have traced the phrase "Life, Liberty, and the pursuit of Happiness" in the American Declaration of Independence to Locke's assertion that every person has a natural right to defend his "Life, Health, Liberty, or Possessions."[55]

A *Letter Concerning Toleration* is deemed to provide "the seventeenth century's most intellectually persuasive justification for the right to free speech" after Milton's *Areopagitica*.[56] At first glance, Locke's espousal of free speech is not obvious. He contends that the liberty of conscience is an inalienable right, and that the power of the government "consists only in outward force" and cannot compel moral behavior, which "consists in the inward persuasion of the mind."[57] In *An Essay Concerning Human Understanding*, he affirms that reason persuades people and leads them towards the truth: without reason, their opinions were "but the effects of chance and hazard, of a mind floating at all adventures without choice, and without direction."[58] Political and religious leaders, who are in no superior position to grasp the truth than people with reasoning capacities, have no right to force their opinions on them, nor would such attempts do any good.[59] Freedom of conscience is the precursor and progenitor of freedom of speech. Moreover, the right to speak freely is arguably implied in the freedom from coercion and the liberty to reason and to pursue what one considers the truth.[60]

Locke's espousal of the right to free speech is also implied in his endorsement of a limited government in *Second Treatise of Government*. This government, which people form by a social contract to preserve their natural rights to life, liberty, and property, can be overthrown by the same people when it becomes unjust or authoritarian.[61] It follows that freedom of speech, along with the freedom of action, is a necessary tool to keep check on the government to ensure that it would not assume a role independent of the welfare of those who have contracted together to create it.[62]

---

[54] HARGREAVES, *supra* note 3, at 110.

[55] *See, e.g.*, ROSS J. CORBETT, THE LOCKEAN COMMONWEALTH (2009); MICHAEL P. ZUCKERT, THE NATURAL RIGHTS REPUBLIC (1996); THOMAS L. PANGLE, THE SPIRIT OF MODERN REPUBLICANISM (1988).

[56] HARGREAVES, *supra* note 3, at 104.

[57] JOHN LOCKE, A LETTER CONCERNING TOLERATION (1689), https://socserv2.socsci.mcmaster.ca/econ/ugcm/3ll3/locke/toleration.pdf (last visited Oct. 10, 2017).

[58] JOHN LOCKE, AN ESSAY CONCERNING HUMAN UNDERSTANDING, ch. XVII (1689), http://enlightenment.supersaturated.com/johnlocke/BOOKIVChapterXVII.html (last visited Oct. 10, 2017).

[59] "For there being but one truth . . . what hope is there that more men would be led into it if they had no rule but the religion of the court and were put under the necessity to quit the light of their own reason, and oppose the dictates of their own consciences, and blindly to resign themselves up to the will of their governors and to the religion which either ignorance, ambition, or superstition had chanced to establish in the countries where they were born?" LOCKE, *supra* note 57.

[60] HARGREAVES, *supra* note 3, at 109.

[61] JOHN LOCKE, SECOND TREATISE OF GOVERNMENT, chs. XVII–XVIX (1689), www.earlymoderntexts.com/assets/pdfs/locke1689a.pdf (last visited Oct. 10, 2017).

[62] SAXONHOUSE, *supra* note 5, at 22.

C. John Rawls: Free Speech, Equal Participation, and Democracy

Twentieth-century philosopher John Rawls takes up the Lockean idea of social contract in his book *A Theory of Justice* by setting up a hypothetical situation, called the "original position," in which "free and equal" persons come together to agree on the moral principles of justice that regulate their social and political relations.[63] Calling his conception "justice as fairness," he seeks to create an agreement situation that would be fair among all the parties to this hypothetical social contract.[64] Hence, the principles that the parties agree upon, and whatever laws or institutions are required by the principles, would also be fair.[65]

Rawls regards "freedom of speech and assembly" as one of the "basic liberties" under his first principle, the "Principle of Equal Liberty," thus making an even more direct connection between free speech and the democratic system than Locke does.[66] Yet his conceptual priority to freedom of conscience claims an ancestor in Locke's works. Defining it as "religious and moral freedom," or the freedom to honor one's "religious or moral obligations," Rawls further identifies "the equal liberty of conscience" as the only principle that people in the original position can acknowledge and adopt to regulate the liberties of citizens in regard to their fundamental, religious, moral, and philosophical interests.[67] Under this principle, people would not take chances with their liberty by permitting the dominant religious or moral doctrines to persecute or to suppress the less dominant ones, or to subject their freedom to the calculus of social interests.[68] Freedom of conscience and freedom of speech and assembly are subsumed under a "principle of [equal] participation," which requires that all citizens have an equal right to take part in, and to determine the outcome of, the constitutional process that establishes the laws of their society.[69]

In his Preface to the revised edition of *A Theory of Justice*, Rawls further contends that the basic rights and liberties "guarantee equally for all citizens the social conditions essential for the adequate development and the full and informed exercise of their two moral powers – their capacity for a sense of justice and their capacity for a conception of the good."[70] If Rawls' conception of the good carries the ideas of self-development and self-realization,[71] then these ideas constitute an even more important component of Immanuel Kant's theory of free speech.

---

[63] JOHN RAWLS, A THEORY OF JUSTICE 11, 13 (1971).
[64] *Id.* at 12–13, 16–17.
[65] *Id.* at 11–22.
[66] *Id.* at 61, 225; *see* HAREL, *supra* note 51, at 607–08.
[67] RAWLS, *supra* note 63, at 205–07.
[68] *Id.* at 207.
[69] *Id.* at 221–22.
[70] JOHN RAWLS, A THEORY OF JUSTICE vii (Revised ed., 1999).
[71] In *Political Liberalism*, Rawls explains that a conception of the good includes "a conception of what is valuable in human life." Normally it consists "of a more or less determinate scheme of final ends, that is, ends [goals] that we want to realize for their own sake, as well as attachments to other persons and loyalties to various groups and associations." JOHN RAWLS, POLITICAL LIBERALISM 19–20 (3D ED., 2005).

D. Emmanuel Kant: Enlightenment, Self-Development, and Self-Realization

Generally considered to be a moral theorist, Kant is rightly deemed "the most forceful exponent of natural-law theory in modern days" because he upholds the objective validity of fundamental moral and political principles.[72] Kant's theory of justice is thus identical with what is generally known as the natural law.[73] A prime example is his "Categorical Imperative," which identifies objectively justifiable moral principles that must apply in the same way to all rational beings without exception. His first formulation of the Categorical Imperative rests upon a principle of universality: "The first principle of morality is, therefore, act according to a maxim which can, at the same time, be valid as universal law. – Any maxim which does not so qualify is contrary to morality."[74]

Kant's defense of freedom of speech combines an autonomy-based argument with his strong conviction that free speech is congenial to the self-development and self-realization of individuals.[75] The formation and expression of beliefs do not involve intersubjective agreement and do not in themselves hinder other people's freedom. Hence, they do not give rise to moral grounds for public regulation or coercive laws, which would diminish personal freedom and autonomy, and therefore are appropriate only when they are necessary to preserve and promote human freedom.[76]

Kant further argues that free speech is a right essential for personal development as much as for a healthy and functional society. In his essay, "What is Enlightenment?", he notes that for "enlightenment," or "a human being's emergence from his self-incurred minority [or childhood]," to take place, "nothing is required but freedom . . . namely, freedom to make public use of one's reason in all matters," meaning "that use which someone makes of it as a scholar before the entire public of the world of

---

[72] A.P. D'ENTRÈVES, NATURAL LAW: AN INTRODUCTION TO LEGAL PHILOSOPHY 110 (2d ed., 1970). It should be noted, however, that Kant's writings, which hold that rightness comes before goodness, does not completely adhere to what is known as the "paradigmatic natural law view," according to which "(1) the natural law is given by God; (2) it is naturally authoritative over all human beings; and (3) it is naturally knowable by all human beings"; "(4) the good is prior to the right, that (5) right action is action that responds nondefectively to the good." According to Mark Murphy, the views of many writers are easily called natural law views, even though they do not share all of these paradigmatic positions, and there is "no clear answer to the question of when a view ceases to be a natural law theory, though a nonparadigmatic one, and becomes no natural law theory at all." The Natural Law Tradition in Ethics, STANFORD ENCYCLOPEDIA OF PHILOSOPHY, https://plato.stanford.edu/entries/nat ural-law-ethics/ (last visited Mar. 30, 2018).

[73] John Ladd's Introduction *in* IMMANUEL KANG & LADD, THE METAPHYSICAL ELEMENTS OF JUSTICE: PART I OF THE METAPHYSICS OF MORALS xviii (2d ed., 1965).

[74] IMMANUEL KANT, GROUNDING FOR THE METAPHYSICS OF MORAL: WITH ON A SUPPOSED RIGHT TO LIE BECAUSE OF PHILANTHROPIC CONCERNS 30 (James Ellington, trans., 3d ed., 1993). Kant's second formulation of the Categorical Imperative bears the most relevance to his theory of rights and justice: "Act in such a way that you always treat humanity, whether in your own person or in the person of any other, never simply as a means, but always at the same time as an end." *Id.* at 36.

[75] HAREL, *supra* note 51, at 606.

[76] IMMANUEL KANT, KANT: THE METAPHYSICS OF MORALS 30 (Mary Gregor, trans. & ed., 1996).

readers."[77] Outlawing free speech therefore makes enlightenment impossible and denies people their right of humanity.[78] Enlightenment takes place on both the personal and the state levels. His *Theory and Practice* defends free speech in the form of freedom of the press, which serves as the ultimate safeguard of the people's rights. "[F]reedom of the pen" is the only right that people have against the sovereign by speaking out against unjust or defective laws and policies. To outlaw this freedom would deny the ruler the vital information that he needs to act as the representative of the people, thus bringing him "in contradiction with himself."[79]

E. Free Speech and Its Natural Limits

Although the right to speak is a natural right, it is not without limits. These philosophers' writings indicate that this right does not entitle the speaker to threaten national security, disregard public morals, or make defamatory remarks. To a lesser extent, their writings also suggest that no one should have the right to make hate speech, which attacks people on the basis of such attributes as race, religion, or gender.

By stressing the role of the sovereign state, Locke, Rawls, and Kant all indicate that national security is one of the constraints to which freedom of speech should be subject. According to Locke, because people cannot secure their lives, health, liberties, and properties for themselves in a state of nature, they give up part of their natural freedom and enter into a binding commitment to a majority-rule society, which, unlike nature, provides a law, a judge, and an executive working "to no other end, but the peace, safety, and public good of the people."[80] Rawls likewise asserts that "an effective sovereign, or even the general belief in his efficacy, has a crucial role" even in the best society, in order to protect the basic rights of the people, to assign them basic duties, and to "guide men's conduct for mutual advantage."[81] Kant argues for the primacy of the legal system, which constrains both the power of the sovereign and citizens' unruly desires, and which must be morally acceptable to all and based upon the "Universal

---

[77] Immanuel Kant, *An Answer to the Question: What Is Enlightenment?* (1798), IN IMMANUEL KANT, PRACTICAL PHILOSOPHY 17–19 (Mary Gregor, Trans. & ed., 1996).

[78] *See id.*

[79] "[F]reedom of the pen," Kant writes, is "the sole palladium of the people's rights. For to want to deny them this freedom is not only tantamount to taking from them any claim to a right with respect to the supreme commander (according to Hobbes), but is also to withhold from the latter – whose will gives order to the subjects as citizens only by representing the general will of the people – all knowledge of matters that he himself would change if he knew about them and to put him in contradiction with himself ..." IMMANUEL KANT, THEORY AND PRACTICE (1793), http://users.sussex.ac.uk/~sefdo/tx/tp2 .htm (last visited Oct. 10, 2017).

[80] LOCKE, *supra* note 61, ch. XI.

[81] RAWLS, *supra* note 63, at 238.

Principle of Justice."[82] These theorists all espouse, to various extents, civil disobedience as a means to protest unjust laws.[83] Yet advocating for and engaging in
civil disobedience with the aim of changing policies or laws does not undermine
the importance of the sovereignty or national security.

Another constraint on free speech is public morality. Although none of these
writers comments directly on the relationship between free speech and public
morality, their concerns for public morality indicate that it should pose
a constraint on free speech in circumstances where expressions violate community
standards. Locke, contending that the state exists not to enforce public morality but
to protect people's rights, nonetheless labels certain forms of conduct as moral vices
and sets out standards concerning how people should treat their fellow beings.[84]
Rawls, whose principle of equal liberty seems to exclude moral paternalism, does not
formally or explicitly commit to the view that morals laws are inevitably unjust.[85]
Kant's principle of right holds that the state should not impede the "external freedom" of an individual, "provided he does not infringe upon that freedom of
others."[86] Kant nonetheless argues in several places that the proper role of the
political sovereign should uphold a "feeling for propriety" among the public by
regulating or outlawing certain practices.[87] Hence, speech that violates public
morality should be restricted.

The right to free speech does not entitle speakers to make defamatory remarks.
The idea of self-ownership in Locke's famous pronouncement, "every man has
a 'property' in his own 'person,'" suggests that reputation is an aspect of identity
cultivated through effort and a piece of property that deserves protection.[88] For
Rawls, almost all expressions are significant to the exercise of one's rational capacity
to judge and shape the structure of one's society as a free and equal citizen. Yet "libel

[82] ROGER J. SULLIVAN, AN INTRODUCTION TO KANT'S ETHICS 11–12 (3D ED., 1997).

[83] According to Locke, because the government derives its authority from the people, a government that
      fails to discharge its fundamental duties delegitimizes itself and justifies people's rebellion against it.
      In Rawls's account of civil disobedience, protesters are entitled to break the law when policymakers do
      not respect the principles of justice governing free and equal persons. RAWLS, *supra* note 70, at 364–65.
      Although whether Kant supports civil disobedience may seem dubious, scholars generally agree that
      he at least supports a passive form of it. *See, e.g.*, MICHAEL ALLEN, CIVIL DISOBEDIENCE IN GLOBAL
      PERSPECTIVE: DECENCY AND DISSENT OVER BORDERS 108, 110 (2017); David Cummiskey, *Justice and
      Revolution in Kant's Political Philosophy*, IN RETHINKING KANT VOLUME I217–40 (Pablo Muchnik ed.,
      2008).

[84] In A LETTER CONCERNING TOLERATION, Locke contrasts errors in religious opinions with moral vices,
      including prostitution and malice, criticizing the enforcers of religious orthodoxy for placing their
      emphasis on the former while permitting the latter without chastisement. LOCKE, *supra* note 57.

[85] Rawls says that "justice as fairness requires us to show that modes of conduct interfere with the basic
      liberties of others or else violate some obligation or natural duty before they can be restricted." RAWLS,
      supra note 63, at 291.

[86] KANT, *supra* note 76.

[87] Kant argues that the state should regulate "begging, uproar in the streets, stenches, and public
      prostitution" and even outlaw the public professions of atheism, to preserve the "moral sense" of
      the public. *Id.* at 100.

[88] LOCKE, *supra* note 61, ch. V § 27.

and defamation of private persons (as opposed to political figures)" bear "no significance at all for the public use of reason to judge and regulate the basic structure, and it is in addition a private wrong . . . ."[89] According to Kant, a person's innate right to freedom carries a duty to "[b]e an honorable human being . . . asserting one's worth as a human being in relation to others."[90] One's reputation, moreover, "is an innate external belonging" that originally belongs only to the person. Therefore, it must not be subject to manipulation by others who use it as "a mere means for others" in pursuit of their own ends.[91]

Would any of these philosophers have endorsed laws prohibiting hate speech? Although freedom of expression is a fundamental liberty under Rawls' first principle, this freedom should not extend to advocacy against the fundamentals of justice, as in speech advocating for the exclusion or subordination of certain groups.[92] Locke and Kant, who lived several centuries ago, have been criticized for what are considered to be racism and sexism in their writings.[93] Yet their beliefs in individual freedom and autonomy arguably would have made them supporters of hate speech laws. As explained, Locke's idea of freedom of speech is tied to his belief in individual autonomy. He also believes that the government should protect people's "Life, Health, Liberty, or Possessions." Therefore, to the extent that one's exercise of freedom of speech may adversely impact the health or autonomy of one's fellows, as in hate speech, it should be prohibited. Likewise, Kant contends that all human beings, being free and equal members of a shared moral community, should always act in such a way that they would be willing for there to be a general law that everyone else should do the same in the same situation.[94] In addition, people have the "perfect duty" not to use themselves or others "merely as a means to an end."[95] Because hate speech is abusive and exploitative, people have the moral duty not to make hate speech. This further implies that hate speech should also be prohibited by law.

F. Natural Law vs. Economic Perspectives

Can freedom of speech be explained by other theories? This subsection argues that the law and economics framework by Richard Posner can supplement natural-law perspectives in justifying the right to free speech. In his well-cited article, "Free

---

[89] RAWLS, *supra* note 63, at 336.

[90] KANT, *supra* note 77, at 392.

[91] KANT, *supra* note 76, at 76.

[92] Jeremy Waldron, *What Does a Well-Ordered Society Look Like?*, 2009 HOLMES LECTURES AT HARVARD LAW SCHOOL (Oct. 5–7, 2009), at 4, www.law.nyu.edu/sites/default/files/ECM_PRO_063313.pdf (last visited Oct. 10, 2017).

[93] E.g., Julie K. Ward, *The Roots of Modern Racism*, THE CRITIQUE (Sep.–Oct. 2016), www.thecritique .com/articles/the-roots-of-modern-racism/ (last visited Oct. 10, 2017).

[94] Refer to the first formulation of Kant's categorical imperative. KANT, *supra* note 74, at 30.

[95] This is the second formulation of Kant's categorical imperative. *Id.* at 36.

Speech in an Economics Perspective," Posner proposes to build on the free-speech formula that Judge Learned Hand used in *United States v. Dennis*.[96] Judge Hand's formula determines the constitutionality of a regulation limiting freedom of speech, by asking "whether the gravity of the 'evil' [i.e., if the instigation sought to be prevented or punished succeeds], discounted by its improbability, justifies such invasion of free speech as is necessary to avoid the danger."[97] Posner expands and refines the formula by decomposing the cost of regulation into its two principal components: value, or the social loss from suppressing valuable information, and error, or the legal-error costs incurred in trying to distinguish the information that society desires to suppress from valuable information.[98] Posner further discounts value to present value, to reflect the fact that the harm from allowing dangerous speech to continue may not be incurred for some years.[99] Accordingly, he uses his formula to justify different laws regulating free speech. Defamatory statements are regulated because they are statements of facts with low values and legal-error costs, but would cause great harms to the reputations of the defamed persons, especially if they are private persons and not public figures.[100] The formula also applies to the regulation of obscene materials which may be offensive only by community standards, because moving the offensive materials to more discreet locations only leads to a slight diminution of their value to consumers, and close substitutes can be found for strictly prohibited materials.[101] As for national security laws, subversive ideas will not likely do great harm to nations with stable political institutions, which therefore have less need to regulate subversive speech than relatively unstable institutions do.[102]

Posner aptly challenges the common perception that political speech has more value than other forms of speech. He identifies serious problems with placing political speech at the top of a hierarchy of speech values because of the "historically and logically close connection between free elections and other institutions of democratic government, on the one hand, and freedom of speech and the press on the other."[103] First, there is no clear distinction between political speech and

---

[96]   Richard Posner, *Free Speech in an Economics Perspective*, 20 SUFFOLK U. L. REV. 1 (1986).

[97]   *Id.* at 8; *citing* United States v. Dennis, 183 F.2d 201, 212 (2d Cir. 1950), aff'd, 341 U.S. 494 (1951). In symbols, the speech should be regulated only if $B < PL$, where B is the cost of the regulation (including any loss from suppression of valuable information), P is the probability that the speech sought to be suppressed will do harm, and L is the magnitude (social cost) of the harm. *Id.*

[98]   Posner adds that value is a function of the size of the actual and potential audience for the speech in question and of the decrease in audience brought about by the challenged regulation. *Id.*

[99]   With these adjustments, the *Dennis* formula becomes $V + E < P \times L/(1 + i)n$, where V stands for "value," E for "error," n for the number of periods between the utterance of the speech and the resulting harm, and i for an interest or discount rate which translates a future dollar of social cost into a present dollar. *Id.*

[100]   *Id.* at 42–43.

[101]   *Id.* at 44–45.

[102]   *Id.* at 32.

[103]   *Id.* at 9.

other speech.[104] Second, even if eliminating all political speech would be more harmful than eliminating all art, all advertising, or even all scientific debate, "a limited abridgment of political speech may be less harmful than a more sweeping abridgment of nonpolitical speech."[105] Finally, political freedom cannot be shown to be more important than economic freedom, and political monopolies may not be worse than government-imposed economic monopolies, restrictions, and exclusions.[106] Thus, political speech should not be considered more valuable than "economic" speech, "broadly defined to include all speech that enhances individual welfare and therefore embracing artistic expression (including even the most vulgar entertainment) and scientific inquiry."[107] In fact, Posner's refusal to prioritize one form of expression over another has seemingly inspired him to apply his formula to politically subversive expressions and pornographic and obscene materials alike, and to balance the costs of regulating such expressions against their harms in a convincing manner.

As laudable as Posner's debunking of the hierarchy of speech values is, his economic perspective could at best supplement and will remain subordinate to the natural-law perspectives in justifying speech freedom. First, in seeking to define what are valuable and harmful to the audience and society, one cannot rely solely on economics but must also appeal to reason. For example, the moral reason against criminal solicitation – not harming or exploiting other people – is arguably as strong as any economic rationale against it. Likewise, demands for equality, liberty, and autonomy, all natural-law principles, are equally compelling reasons as effective governance, an economic rationale, for granting the right to free speech to all people. Second, by defining value in his formula as the social loss from suppressing valuable information, Posner accords to speech values that are primarily, if not solely, social. He contends that utterances by individuals with very small actual and potential audiences have only limited values. In doing so, he neglects the possibility that those expressions, as well as the mere act of making them, may carry tremendous values to individuals. Hence, he emphasizes the role of free speech in promoting a marketplace of ideas and democratic governance, while overlooking its related role in safeguarding and encouraging individual autonomy and self-development, which are embraced by Locke and Kant. In short, his economic framework is by no means a holistic one, and falls short of natural-law free speech theories.

G. International Recognition of Freedom of Speech

The recognition of the right to free speech in major international conventions further testifies to its fundamental nature and its significance to democratic societies

---

[104] *Id.* at 10.
[105] *Id.*
[106] *Id.*
[107] *Id.*

and the autonomy of individuals. At its first session in 1946, the General Assembly of the United Nations affirmed "freedom of information," or "the right to gather, transmit and publish news anywhere and everywhere without fetters," as "a fundamental human right" and "the touchstone of all the freedoms to which the United Nations is consecrated."[108] In 1948, two human rights declarations, the American Declaration on the Rights and Duties of Men and the United Declaration of Human Rights (UDHR), were adopted. Both state that every person has the right to freedom of opinion and expression, which is limited by the rights, security and welfare of others.[109] Although the UDHR does not specifically provide for prohibitions on hate speech or incitement to hatred, its Article 7 provides for equal protection for all against discrimination and incitement to discrimination.[110] The International Covenant on Civil and Political Rights (ICCPR), adopted in 1966, combines the statements of rights and responsibilities in its Article 19, which states that "[e]veryone shall have the right to hold opinions without interference" and "the right to freedom of expression," the exercise of which may be subject to certain restrictions as provided by law and are necessary, "[f]or respect of the right or reputations of others," and "[f]or the protection of national security or of public order (ordre public), or of public health or morals."[111] Article 19 has been referred to as the "core of the Covenant and the touchstone for all other rights guaranteed therein," bridging the civil and political dimensions of the Covenant by reflecting a liberal conception of society that prioritizes the "marketplace of ideas," or the right of each person to choose form their opinions in complete freedom from indoctrination and repression.[112] Its Article 20(2) also places an obligation on States Parties to prohibit hate speech.[113]

Similar provisions on freedom of expression and information are found in regional treaties. One example is Article 10 of the European Convention on Human Rights, which, like the ICCPR, sets forth the parameters for legal restrictions "in the

---

[108] U.N. Doc. A/RES/59/1 (Dec. 14, 1946).

[109] The American Declaration, Art. 4 states that "[e]very person has the right to freedom of investigation, of opinion, and of the expression and dissemination of ideas, by any medium whatsoever." According to the UDHR, Art. 19, "[e]veryone has the right to freedom of opinion and expression," which includes "freedom to hold opinions without interference and to seek, receive and impact information and ideas through any media and regardless of frontiers." The American Declaration, Art. 28, provides that "[t]he rights of man are limited by the rights of others, by the security of all, and by the just demands of the general welfare and the advancement of democracy." The UDHR, Art. 30 specifies that nothing in the Declaration "may be interpreted as implying for any State, group or person any right to engage in any activity or to perform any act aimed at the destruction of any of the rights and freedoms set forth herein." Universal Declaration of Human Rights (Dec. 10, 1948), Arts. 19, 30; American Declaration on the Rights and Duties of Men (May 2, 1948), Arts. 4, 28.

[110] UDHR, Art. 7.

[111] International Covenant on Civil and Political Rights (Dec. 16, 1966), entered into force (Mar. 23, 1976), Art. 19.

[112] *Id.*

[113] Art. 20(2) of the ICCPR provides: "Any advocacy of national, racial or religious hatred that constitutes incitement to discrimination, hostility or violence shall be prohibited by law."

interests of national security, territorial integrity or public safety, for the prevention of disorder or crime, for the protection of health or morals, for the protection of the reputation or rights of others, for preventing the disclosure of information received in confidence, or for maintaining the authority and impartiality of the judiciary."[114] The American Convention on Human Rights, Article 13, provides "the right to freedom of thought and expression," which "shall not be subject to prior censorship but shall be subject to subsequent imposition of liability" to ensure "respect for the rights or reputations of others" and "the protection of national security, public order, or public health or morals."[115] The African Charter of Human and Peoples Rights, Article 9, grants every individual the right to receive information and the right to express and disseminate opinions "within the law."[116] The 2004 Revised Arab Charter on Human Rights, Article 32, "guarantees the right to information and to freedom of opinion and expression," among others, but provides that "such rights and freedoms shall be exercised in conformity with the fundamental values of society and shall be subject only to such limitations as are required to ensure respect for the rights or reputation of others or the protection of national security, public order and public health or morals."[117]

Pursuant to these conventions and treaties, international courts have agreed in principle that freedom of expression must be guaranteed not only for the dissemination of expressions, information, and ideas that are favorably received or considered inoffensive or indifferent, but also for those that shock, disturb, or offend the state or any members of the population.[118] Though skeptical of limiting freedom of expression or the public's right to information, they have recognized national governments' extensive measures to prohibit or sanction speech that incites violence, insurrection, or armed resistance.[119] They have also held that public morality legitimizes censorship on artistic expressions in some cases.[120] In addition, they

[114] European Convention for the Protection of Human Rights and Fundamental Freedoms (Nov. 4, 1950), entered into force Sep. 3, 1953, Art. 10.

[115] American Convention on Human Rights (Nov. 22, 1969), entered into force July 18, 1978, Art. 13.

[116] African Charter on Human and Peoples' Rights (June 27, 1981), entered into force Oct. 21, 1986, Art. 9.

[117] Arab Charter on Human Rights (Sep. 15, 1994), revised May 22, 2004, entered into force Mar. 15, 2008, Art. 32.

[118] See, e.g., Fressoz & Roire v. France, app. no. 29183/95 (Eur. Ct. H.R. 1999); Handyside v. United Kingdom, app. no. 5493/72 (Eur. Ct. H.R. 1976).

[119] For example, in Halis v. Turkey, the Turkish government imprisoned a journalist who expressed positive opinion in a book review about aspects of the Kurdish separatist movement for violating the Turkish Prevention of Terrorism Act. The European Court of Human Rights found that the measures undertaken by the Government had the legitimate aim of protecting national security and public safety, although the conviction and sentence of the journalist were disproportionate and violated the journalist's right to freedom of expression. Halis v. Turkey, app. no. 30007/96 (Eur. Ct. H.R. 2005).

[120] For instance, in Olmedo-Bustos et al. v. Chile, the Inter-American Court of Human Rights found that Chile had failed to meet its obligations under the American Convention when it refused to permit *The Last Temptation of Christ* to be shown in Chile. Olmedo-Bustos et al. v. Chile, app. no. 73-C (I/A Court H.R. 2001). In contrast, the European Court of Human Rights in Otto-Preminger-Institut v. Austria upheld the ban and seizure of a film deemed offensive to the Catholic majority of a community. Otto-Preminger-Institut v. Austria, app. no. 13470/87 (Eur. Ct. H.R. 1994).

have acknowledged the right to reputation in defamation cases, while prioritizing freedom of expression over the preservation of reputation where matters of public concern are involved.[121] Finally, courts have put much weight on the contextual factor in assessing whether expressions would or had incite(d) hatred and whether their censorship would constitute a breach of the right to freedom of expression.[122]

III. THE NATURAL RIGHT TO PARODY

If the right to free speech is a natural right, then isn't making parodies, a form of speech, also a natural right, subject to the same restrictions? An in-depth discussion of the meaning of "parody" will be provided in Chapter 2, which will compare different definitions and propose a working legal definition that properly balances owners' and users' rights. A more general definition is provided at this juncture to justify the right to make parodies as a natural right.

The *Oxford English Dictionary* defines "parody" as a "composition in prose or verse in which the characteristic turns of thought and phrase in an author or class of authors are imitated in such as a way as to make them appear ridiculous."[123] The *American Heritage Dictionary* defines a parody as a "literary or artistic work that imitates the characteristic style of an author or a work for comic effect or ridicule."[124] While they do not agree on whether a parody may only use the original as its target, or may mimic the original in order to criticize or comment on something else, they both identify the imitation of the original work or author as parody's essential characteristic.[125] As literary scholar Simon Dentith says, all language use involves imitation. Given that "all written utterances situate themselves in relation to texts that precede them and are in turn alluded to or repudiated by texts that follow," parody is "one of the many forms of intertextual allusion out of which texts are produced."[126]

As in free speech and natural law, one can trace the origin of parody in ancient Greece. Different forms of parody were dominant in ancient Greek culture. The Greek term *parodia* generally refers to a mock-heroic poem, one written in epic Homeric style but with a trivial or "low" topic, although travesty poems with "high" topics but written in "low" styles could also be found, notably in the satyr

---

[121] E.g., Incal v. Turkey, app. no. 41/1997/82 (Eur. Ct. H.R. 1998); Zana v. Turkey, app. no. 18954/91 (Eur. Ct. H.R. 1997).

[122] In Incal, the court found a breach of the right to freedom of expression, stating that, "the Court does not discern anything which would warrant the conclusion that Mr Incal was in any way responsible for the problems of terrorism in Turkey, and more specifically in İzmir." para. 58.

[123] THE OXFORD ENGLISH DICTIONARY 247 (2d ed., 1989).

[124] THE AMERICAN HERITAGE DICTIONARY 1317 (5th ed., 2006).

[125] Chapter 2 will explain why parody should be broadly defined by the law and why a work appropriating an original work to criticize or comment on something other than the original may also be considered a parody.

[126] SIMON DENTITH, PARODY 5 (2000).

plays.[127] According to Aristotle's *Poetics*, Hegemon of Thasos, a near contemporary of Aristophanes (450–388 BC), invented parody and authored such mock-epics as the *Gigantomachia*, or *Battle of the Giants*.[128] One source goes further back in time and identifies Hipponax of Ephesus of the sixth century BC as the real inventor and first author of parody.[129] Nonetheless, *parodia* does not refer merely to mock-epic. It was more frequently used by Greek and subsequent Roman writers to refer to "a more widespread practice of quotation, not necessarily humorous, in which both writers and speakers introduce allusions to previous texts."[130] For example, the relatively well-known comic plays of Aristophanes are full of parodic allusions to tragedian Euripides (480–406 BC).[131] The parodic form did not vanish after the fall of the Greek Empire: it has persisted, through the middle ages to modern and postmodern times, in literatures, popular culture, and everyday life.[132]

Because parody is a form of speech, the right to parody, like free speech, is essential to all the principles underlying speech freedom discussed in this chapter. Given that free speech and democracy originated in ancient Greece, where authors enjoyed much freedom despite attacks from some public officials, the proliferation of parodic forms in ancient Greek culture was perhaps not a pure coincidence. One may even attribute the profusion of parodic forms to the legends about the Olympian Gods, the scandalous incidents of which provided ample opportunities for parody.[133]

Parodies enable authors to articulate their ideas and symbolic values in dramatic manners. Unsurprisingly, authors of parodies and satires often fell victim to dictatorial governments in different periods of history. For instance, the "Bishops' Ban" in Elizabethan England prohibited the printing of satires, and demanded that the published works of authors including John Marston, Gabriel Harvey and Thomas Nashe, many of which made abundant use of parody to critique society, be burned.[134] In Nazi Germany, Werner Finck,

---

[127] *Id.* at 40, 42. An example of the former, and the only *parodia* that still survives today, is the *Batrachomyomachia*, or the *Battle of the Frogs and Mice*, written by an anonymous author during the time of Alexander the Great. Euripides' *Cyclops*, a parody of the Cyclops episode in Homer's *Odyssey*, is an example of the latter. *Id.* at 40–42.

[128] According to Fred Householder, "not only words but phrases and lines are borrowed from Homer" in Hegemon's works. Margaret A. Rose, Parody: Ancient, Modern and Post-modern 12 (1993).

[129] For example, Hipponax's *Hexameters* contains a parodic evocation of more serious epic openings such as Homer's call to the Muse in the opening of the *Odyssey* ("Tell me, O Muse, of the man of many devices, who wandered full many ways after he had sacked the sacred citadel of Troy."). *Id.* at 16.

[130] Dentith, *supra* note 126, at 10.

[131] *Id.* at 39.

[132] *See, e.g.*, Dentith, *supra* note 126; Rose, *supra* note 128.

[133] Dentith, *supra* note 126, at 10.

[134] Marston's *The Metamorphosis of Pigmalion's Image and Certaine Satyres* (1598), which imitates Ovid and the Satires of Juvenal to satirize society, was one of the banned works. Geoffrey Miles, Classical Mythology in English Literature: A Critical Anthology 358 (Geoffrey Miles ed.,

a famous cabaret actor and author with a gift for parody and satire, was imprisoned in a concentration camp for six weeks for attempting to ridicule the State and the party.[135] Nobel Prize-winning Italian playwright and actor Dario Fo, who frequently employed the parodic method to criticize his government as well as the Catholic Church, was censored, banned from television, and briefly jailed by the government for his subversive messages.[136] In Chile, members of the Grupo Aleph, a local theatre group, were jailed after performing a parody on the 1973 Chilean coup d'état, and then forced to go into exile by the military government that sought to control the media.[137] More recently, a popular television anchor in China was suspended from his job at the state broadcaster for making a parody of an old song to insult Mao Zedong, former chairman of the Chinese Communist Party, at a private gathering.[138]

Controls on parody throughout history, such as in the form of censorship, have tacitly acknowledged its potential power to bring about social change.[139] Hence, scholars and critics have remarked how parody could spur the public to engage in the democratic process by holding up the most powerful institutions and individuals in society to sardonic scrutiny.[140] It is not only in developed nations that parodic works are regarded as promoting the fundamental values underlying the constitutionally protected right to freedom of expression.[141] The importance of parody in promoting democratic values has been recognized, for instance, in post-apartheid South Africa, where freedom of "the press and other media" and "freedom of artistic creativity" are constitutionally entrenched rights.[142] After a long

---

1999). Debora Shuger has called this ban, issued by the Archbishop of Canterbury and the Bishop of London in 1599, "the most sweeping and stringent instance of early modern censorship." Debora Shuger, *Civility and Censorship in Early Modern England*, IN CENSORSHIP AND SILENCING: PRACTICES OF CULTURAL REGULATION 89 (Robert C. Post ed., 1998).

[135] TYLER T. OCHOA, *Dr. Seuss, The Juice and Fair Use: How the Grinch Silenced a Parody*, 45 J. COPYRIGHT SOC'Y U.S.A. 546, 560 (1997).

[136] The arrest took place in 1973 in Sardinia, Italy, after Fo refused to allow the police into his theater. MICHAEL BILLINGTON, *Dario Fo: A Theatrical Jester Who Made Us Laugh in the Face of Tragedy*, THE GUARDIAN (Oct. 13, 2016), www.theguardian.com/stage/2016/oct/13/dario-fo-theatrical-jester-dies-aged-90 (last visited Oct. 10, 2017).

[137] KEITH RICHARDS, POP CULTURE LATIN AMERICA!: MEDIA, ARTS, AND LIFESTYLE 121–22 (2005).

[138] Fujian Bai, the anchor, sang "Taking Tiger Mountain by Strategy," a revolutionary opera produced during the Chinese Cultural Revolution, while interjecting the lyrics with his comments to suggest that China had "suffered enough" under Mao Zedong. *China TV Anchor Bi Fujian to Be Punished for Mao Insult*, BBC NEWS (Aug. 10, 2015), www.bbc.com/news/world-asia-china-33844095 (last visited Oct. 10, 2017).

[139] MARGARET A. ROSE, PARODY/META-FICTION 133–34 (1979).

[140] E.g., *id.*; GRAHAM REYNOLDS, *Necessarily Critical? The Adoption of a Parody Defence to Copyright Infringement in Canada*, 33 (2)MANITOBA L.J. 243, 246 (2009).

[141] For example, the Supreme Court of Canada held that parodies can be seen as promoting the fundamental values underlying the constitutionally protected right to freedom of expression, "including the search for political, artistic and scientific truth, the protection of individual autonomy and self-development, and the promotion of public participation in the democratic process." RJR MacDonald Inc. v. Canada (Attorney General) [1995] 3 S.C.R. 199, para. 72 (SCC).

[142] CONST. S. Africa, Art. 16(1).

period during which thoughts and ideas were banned, South African academics have come to discover "a regenerative and often deeply subversive element that is constantly challenging power and formulating different means of expression through new forms."[143] Expressed through parody and related forms, this subversive tendency would serve to strengthen their democracy.[144] As a South African judge remarked, the law must protect these new forms "whether the humour is expressed by mimicry in drag, or cartooning in the press, or the production of lampoons on T-shirts."[145]

Parodies should not be banned as long as they are not defamatory or obscene, do not threaten national security, and are not hate speech. Yet the values of parodies do not solely lie in democratic governance. In fact, parodies need not contain overly political messages. Kant's writings have illuminated how the values underlying free expression encompass not only participation in political processes and self-government, but also individual autonomy and self-fulfillment. Even Posner has warned against a hierarchy of speech values, and emphasized that cultural expressions have as many values as political ones. As one scholar remarks, the purpose of democratic society is to promote individual welfare which, in conjunction with the principle of equality, leads to the right to express beliefs and opinions. In addition, "the proper end of man is the realization of his character and potentialities as a human being ... [and] every man – in the development of his own personality – has the right to form his own beliefs and opinions ... [and] the right to express these beliefs and opinions."[146] It can be argued further that self-realization or self-fulfillment may be the only real value served by freedom of expression in that the value of democracy was based upon the value of self-realization.[147] In this light, political parodies are not inferior to parodies for building cultures or for personal expression and fulfillment. The two are not all that different in terms of purposes and values. They, and the values that they serve, reinforce each other.

* * *

---

[143] JUDITH FEBRUARY & RICHARD CALLAND, *Satire Must Be Encouraged*, IOL NEWS (Aug. 2, 2013), www.iol .co.za/news/satire-must-be-encouraged-1.1557050#.VGWUg5PF8dN (last visited Oct. 10, 2017).

[144] Milton argued that reading impious material is not dangerous because "[t]o the pure, all things are pure." He further contrasts the classical, enlightened tradition of the Greeks and Romans with the censorship tradition imposed by the Catholic Church and the Spanish Inquisition. Although Greece and Rome condemned libelous materials, neither embraced censorship. It was not until after the year 800 that the Roman Catholic Church implemented a censorship policy, which became increasingly stringent in Spain and Italy during the fifteenth century and was endorsed by the Council of Trent that ended in 1563. By then, "no Book, pamphlet, or paper" could be printed unless "approv'd and licenc't under the hands of 2 or 3 glutton Friers." *Id.*

[145] Laugh It Off Promotions CC, *supra* note 1, para. 108.

[146] THOMAS I. EMERSON, *Toward a General Theory of the First Amendment*, 72 YALE L.J. 877, 879 (1963).

[147] *See* MARTIN H. REDISH, *The Value of Free Speech*, 130 U. PA. L. REV. 591 (1982).

The right to parody, like the right to free speech, therefore is a natural right. Yet parodies appropriate preexisting materials, inside and outside of the public domain. Chapter 2 will proceed to examine the right to create parodies in the copyright context from different philosophical traditions. It will argue that freedom of speech is more fundamental than the right to intellectual property. This carries significant implications regarding how parody should be legally defined and how conflicts between the right to parody and copyrights in parodied materials should be reconciled under the law.

2

The Natural Right to Parody Copyrighted Works

Many definitions of parody have paid insufficient attention to its ancient heritage.[1]

The right to parody is a natural right in the copyright context. This chapter will survey various literary sources, scholarly views, and dictionary definitions of parody to arrive at its proper legal definition. It will also examine the nature of copyright by drawing upon different philosophical perspectives, and contend that whether deemed a natural right or an incentive to stimulate the production of works, copyright is by no means absolute. Hence, an author's or owner's rights in their works accommodate the public's right to free speech by parodying their works. These philosophical traditions, according to which the right to free speech is more fundamental than property and intellectual rights, also lend support to a broad, speech-friendly definition of parody as a work that draws upon preexisting work(s) to criticize or comment on it/them, or that directs its criticism or commentary towards something else.

This broad exemption for parody is likely more economically efficient than the narrow one endorsed by law and economics research. Nonetheless, not all works falling within the proposed definition of parody should be considered fair uses or fair dealings, or otherwise be exempted from protection. The importance of property and intellectual property rights suggests that a parody must not harm the interests of the author/copyright owner by displacing the original work in the market or, from a utilitarian perspective, must not disincentivize the author.

Parodies falling within the proposed definition and fulfilling the above conditions would not violate an author's moral rights of attribution and integrity. Because the right to parody is a natural right in both the free speech and the copyright contexts, to ensure that copyright would not become a pretext for suppressing free speech, courts should apply the parody exception by drawing upon the free speech/freedom of expression doctrine.

---

[1] MARGARET ROSE, PARODY: ANCIENT, MODERN AND POSTMODERN 5 (1993).

I. DEFINING "PARODY": SOURCES, DEFINITIONS AND VIEWS

Writers exercise their right to free speech through parodies. Parodies, moreover, are often creative expressions. This is true of Hegemon of Thasos' first parody in ancient Athens, or Werner Finck's performances poking fun at the Nazi regime, or the former television anchor's mockery of a deceased Chinese Communist leader. Yet what should be the scope of this right, and how should "parody" be defined?

As Dentith puts it, "the discussion of parody is bedevilled by disputes over definition," due to "the antiquity of the word parody," "the range of different practices to which it alludes," and "differing national usages."[2] As Chapter 1 has explained, Aristotle uses *parodia* to refer to a "narrative poem, of moderate length, in the meter and vocabulary of epic poems, but treating a light, satirical, or mock-heroic subject." But this is not the only meaning of the word. *Parodia* was more frequently used by Greek and subsequent Roman writers to refer to "a more wide-spread practice of quotation, not necessarily humorous, in which both writers and speakers introduce allusions to previous texts."[3] Currently, the *Oxford English Dictionary* defines "parody" as a "composition in prose or verse in which the characteristic turns of thought and phrase in an author or class of authors are imitated in such as a way as to make them appear ridiculous."[4] The *Cambridge Dictionary* defines it as "writing, music, art, speech, etc. which intentionally copies the style of someone famous or copies a particular situation, making the features or qualities of the original more noticeable in a way that is humorous."[5] The *American Heritage Dictionary* describes it as a "literary or artistic work that imitates the characteristic style of an author or a work for comic effect or ridicule."[6] All of these definitions emphasize parody's imitation of a preexisting work.

Two issues arise out of these definitions of "parody." The first issue concerns the subject of the parody. Neither the description in *Poetics*, nor the definition in the *American Heritage Dictionary*, clearly indicates whether the original text or character is the subject of a parody. In fact, Greek comedian Aristophanes (c.450–388 BC) made parodic allusions to tragedian Euripides (c.480–406 BC) both to comment on his fellow playwright and his works, and to reflect on the society of his time.[7] In contrast, the definitions in the *Oxford* and *Cambridge English Dictionaries* indicate that a parody targets the original. The second issue is whether the parody contains comic intent. Although all of these definitions mention elements of comedy, humor, or ridicule, whether a parody is comical or not can be highly subjective.

---

2   SIMON DENTITH, PARODY 6 (2002).
3   *Id.* at 10.
4   THE OXFORD ENGLISH DICTIONARY 247 (2d ed. 1989).
5   THE CAMBRIDGE DICTIONARY (2017), http://dictionary.cambridge.org/dictionary/english/parody (last visited Oct. 10, 2017).
6   THE AMERICAN HERITAGE DICTIONARY 1317 (5th ed. 2006).
7   DENTITH, *supra* note 2, at 39.

Regarding the first issue, scholars have divided numerous conceptions of parody[8] into two major groups according to the subjects of their critiques. The first group, which have been referred to as a "target" parodies,[9] are based upon the "popular perception of parody and the standard dictionary definition" that conceives of parody as a "specific work of humorous or mocking intent, which imitates the work of an individual author or artist, genre or style, so as to make it appear ridiculous."[10] The second group of parodies, which have been described as "weapon" parodies,[11] are based upon the conception that the critique need not be performed at the "expense of the parodied text,"[12] and can instead target something other than the work itself, such as "artistic traditions, styles ... genres" or society.[13] In addition, some parodies "merely hint at the text, assuming their audience to be familiar with it," while others "both present the text and comment upon it at the same time."[14]

Numerous scholars, including Linda Hutcheon and Simon Dentith, have endorsed the broad definition of "parody" that encompasses both "target" and "weapon" parodies.[15] In fact, the original meaning of *parodia* supports this broad definition. In his article "The Basis of Ancient Parody," F. J. Lelievre notes that an ambiguity is found in the prefix "para," which can be translated to mean both "nearness" and "opposition," conveying the respective meanings of "consonance and derivation" and "transgression, opposition, or difference," and that "in compounds a synthesis of these two forces may sometimes be found."[16] Margaret A. Rose cites the *Oxford English Dictionary*, which describes "para" as "having had the sense as a preposition of 'by the side of,' 'beside,' 'whence alongside of, by, past, beyond,

---

8   For instance, Margaret A. Rose in her book *Parody: Ancient, Modern and Post-Modern* conducts a survey of the works of such authors as Aristotle, Ben Jonson, Friedrich Nietzsche, Mikhail Bakhtin, Susan Sontag, Michel Foucault, Jacques Derrida, Martin Amis, and Umberto Eco, and identifies thirty-seven conceptions of parody. ROSE, *supra* note 1, at 280–283; *see* Graham Reynolds, *Necessarily Critical? The Adoption of a Parody Defence to Copyright Infringement in Canada*, 33(2) MANITOBA L.J. 243, 245 (2009).

9   Michael Spence, *Intellectual Property and the Problem of Parody*, 114 LAW Q. REV. 594, 594 (1998).

10 Ellen Gredley & Spyros Maniatis, *Parody: A Fatal Attraction? Part 1: The Nature of Parody and its Treatment in Copyright*, 19 EUR. I.P. REV. 339, 341 (1997).

11 Spence, *supra* note 9, at 594.

12 LINDA HUTCHEON, A THEORY OF PARODY: THE TEACHINGS OF TWENTIETH-CENTURY ART FORMS 6 (1985).

13 Spence, *supra* note 9.

14 *Id.* at 595.

15 Simon Dentith offers an inclusive account of parody, referring it to a "range of cultural practices which are all more or less parodic," hence "any cultural practice which provide a relatively polemical allusive imitation of another cultural production or practice." He further explains that the direction of attack can vary: a parody can serve as a "rejoinder, or mocking response to the word of another," "[b]ut many parodies draw upon the authority of precursor texts to attack, satirize, or just playfully to refer to elements of the contemporary world" or "some new situation to which it can be made to allude." DENTITH, *supra* note 2, at 9.

16 Rose, *supra* note 1, at 8, 48; *citing* F. J. Lelievre, The Basis of Ancient Parody, *in* GREECE AND ROME 66 (1954).

etc.'; in addition, 'in composition it had the same senses with such cognate adverbial ones as 'to one side, aside, amiss, faulty, irregular, disordered, improper, wrong,' also expressing 'subsidiary relation, alteration, perversion, simulation.'"[17] As Rose notes, such an ambivalence towards the target entails "not only a mixture of criticism and sympathy for the parodied text, but also the creative expansion of it into something else."[18] Rose convincingly argues that if *parodia* can "laugh both at and with its target,"[19] then there is no reason why "parody" should be narrowly defined to refer only to works that target the originals but not something else.[20]

Regarding comic intent, scholars have different opinions on whether a parody needs to be comical. Rose, defining parody as the "comic refunctioning of performed linguistic or artistic material," notes that "comic intent" has been a characteristic of parody since its earliest appearance in history.[21] In contrast, Hutcheon contends that "the continuing and unwarranted inclusion of ridicule in its definition has trivialised the form."[22] She asserts that "what is remarkable about modern parody is its range of intent – from the ironic and playful to the scornful and ridiculing."[23] Likewise, Spence observes that some parodies exploit the disjunction between the parody and the text to comic effect, while others do not.[24] Ellen Gredley and Spyros Maniatis go further to argue that parodies may be characterized by "admiration and reverence."[25] Indeed, not only is the presence of comic intent highly subjective, but an overemphasis on this element also risks overlooking parody's other valuable functions. On the other hand, a broad definition of parody encompassing works with different intents helps to resolve a related issue of whether a parody needs to be critical of the original text, its characters, or anything. Neither the definitions of *parodia*, nor those of parody in various dictionaries, mention critique at all. Given that parodies perform different functions, one would be hard pressed to argue that comic or critical intent is a necessary attribute of parody.

Through surveying literary sources, dictionary definitions, and scholarly views, this chapter has taken the position that a parody draws upon an existing work either to criticize or comment on the original, or direct its criticism or commentary towards

---

[17] *Id.* at 48.

[18] *Id.* at 51.

[19] *Id.* at 52.

[20] As Chapter 3 will explain, the U.S. Supreme Court adopted a narrow definition of parody, and labeled works that target something else "satire." Although the Federal Court of Canada in United Airlines, Inc. v. Cooperstock adopted a broad definition of parody, Chapter 4 will explain that a broadly defined parody category should replace the parody/satire dual categories in the current statute.

[21] Rose, *supra* note 1, at 25.

[22] Gredley & Maniatis, *supra* note 10, at 339.

[23] HUTCHEON, *supra* note 12, at 6.

[24] Spence, *supra* note 9, at 595.

[25] Gredley and Maniatis use as an example the parody of *The Wizard of Oz* by *Star Wars*. Indeed, an essay that studies the influences of *The Wizard of Oz* on *Star Wars* is published on the official *Star Wars* website. Bryan Young, *The Cinema behind* Star Wars: The Wizard of Oz, STAR WARS (Jan. 18, 2016), www.starwars.com/news/the-cinema-behind-star-wars-the-wizard-of-oz (Oct. 10, 2017).

something else, and need not be overly humorous or critical. The following sections will examine how the right to parody is justified from various philosophical perspectives, which further lend support to a broad, speech-friendly legal definition of parody as a work that draws upon preexisting work(s) to criticize or comment on it/them or that directs its criticism or commentary towards something else.

II. COPYRIGHT AND THE NATURAL RIGHT TO PARODY

That one possesses a natural right to parody copyrighted works may not be as intuitive as the belief that one enjoys a natural right to parody in the free speech context. This section will draw upon the works of natural law philosophers discussed in Chapter 1, along with utilitarian approaches, to explain that copyright, whether considered to be a natural right or an incentive to promote the creation of new works, is by no means absolute. Hence, the owner's copyright accommodates the public's right to free speech by parodying the copyrighted work.

A. Locke's Labor Theory of Acquisition and Provisos

Locke played a pivotal role in the enactment of the first Copyright Act in Britain. In the late 1690s, Parliament desired to eliminate the abuses of the Licensing Act, which was enforced by the Stationers' Company, a guild of printers given the exclusive power to print and censor literary works.[26] Embittered by the printers' power to prevent the publication of books without their prior permission, Locke presented a memorandum to the Commons, in which he attacked the monopoly of the Stationers' Company and proposed a limited property right for authors in their books.[27] At his urging, the Commons rejected the Licensing Act when it came up for renewal and appointed a committee to "prepare and bring in a Bill for the better regulation of Printing and Printing presses."[28] In 1709, Parliament enacted the Statute of Anne, or the Copyright Act of 1709, which granted publishers of books legal protection for fourteen years with the commencement of the statute, and twenty-one years of protection for any book already in print.[29] At the expiration of the first fourteen-year copyright term, the copyright re-vested in its author, if he or she were still alive, for a further term of fourteen years.[30]

---

[26] ROBERT HARGREAVES, THE FIRST FREEDOM: A HISTORY OF FREE SPEECH 111 (2002).

[27] "I know not why a man should not have liberty to print whatever he would speak and to be answerable for the one just as he is for the other if he transgresses the law in either," Locke wrote in this memorandum to the House of Commons. He proposed that authors' property rights in their works would be recognized for fifty years after publication or fifty to seventy years post-mortem. *Id.*

[28] *Id.* at 112.

[29] *Id.*

[30] *Id.; The Statute of Anne: The First Copyright Statute (1709)*, JEREMY NORMAN & CO., INC., HISTORY OF INFORMATION, www.historyofinformation.com/expanded.php?id=3389 (last visited Oct. 10, 2017).

Although Locke's other works do not discuss copyright, his labor theory of acquisition can be interpreted to endorse not only authors' rights in their works, but also users' rights to parody copyrighted works. In his *Second Treatise of Government*, Locke holds that people have a natural right of property in their bodies and own the labor of their bodies as well as the fruits of that labor.[31] Therefore, annexing or mixing one's labor with resources found in the common gives rise to property rights or legitimate claims to ownership, as long as "there is enough and as good left for others."[32] Alfred Yen extends Locke's labor theory to include the natural right to one's intellectual labor and the creations of such labor.[33] Robert Merges contends that Locke's labor theory applies equally well or even better to intellectual property than to real property. Drawing a parallel between the public domain and the state of nature, Merges argues that "fresh appropriation from a background of unowned or widely shared material," implied in Locke's work, is much more common today in the world of intellectual property than in the world of tangible assets.[34] In addition, if labor is relevant in establishing physical property rights, it plays a larger and more prominent role in establishing intellectual property rights.[35] Indeed, Locke, by describing his own work as labor, impliedly acknowledges a labor-based property claim to the product of writing.[36]

What about parodying copyrighted works? According to the Charity Proviso in Locke's *First Treatise of Government*, properties are given by God for the maintenance and development of the human race and therefore not a source of absolute power.[37] Hence, destitute people are entitled to assets for survival, even if those assets are otherwise legitimately held by other owners.[38] According to Merges, if intellectual property rights get in the way of "survival and sustenance," then such rights have to give way to the destitute.[39] Because those in "cultural destitution" do not have as strong a claim on the properties of better-off people for facilitating cultural

---

[31] "Though the earth, and all inferior Creatures, be common to all men, yet every man has a Property in his own Person." "The Labour of his Body, and the Work of his Hands, we may say, are properly his." John Locke, Second Treatise of Government, ch. V, § 27 (1689), *available at* http://press-pubs .uchicago.edu/founders/documents/v1ch16s3.html (last visited Oct. 10, 2017).

[32] *Id.*

[33] Alfred C. Yen, *Restoring the Natural Law: Copyright as Labor and Possession*, 51 Ohio St. L.J. 517, 523 (1990).

[34] Robert Merges, Justifying Intellectual Property 32 (2011).

[35] *Id.* at 33.

[36] *Id.*

[37] *Id.* at 61–63. "God, the Lord and Father of all, has given no one of his children such a property in his peculiar portion of the things of this world, but that he has given his needy brother a right to the surplusage of his goods; so that it cannot justly be denied him, when his pressing wants call for it; and therefore no man could ever have a just power over the life of another by right of property in land or possessions;" John Locke, First Treatise of Government, ch. 4, § 42 (1689), www.nlnrac.org/ear lymodern/locke/documents/first-treatise-of-government (last visited Oct. 10, 2017).

[38] Merges, *supra* note 34, at 61–63.

[39] Examples include cases where IP rights intersect with issues of human health, such as patents for AIDS drugs. *Id.* at 64.

developments, a balancing of rights becomes necessary.[40] Adam Mossoff's affirmation that human flourishing goes beyond pure "survival and sustenance" offers a more direct endorsement of parody. Just as Lockean labor can be physical or intellectual, Mosoff argues, Locke puts equal weight on economical, moral, and intellectual values.[41] Following Mosoff's logic, authors' rights in the fruits of their intellectual labor should accommodate creative appropriations of their works for the sake of human flourishing. Parodying copyrighted materials would be a good example.

Carys Craig criticizes the natural law approach to copyright. She attacks the Lockean approach from an internal perspective by arguing that granting property rights to ideas goes against two of Locke's very own Provisos. It violates his Sufficiency Proviso, which demands that there be "enough, and as good" left in the common for others, as well as his No-Spoilage (waste prohibition) Proviso, according to which people should not take from the common more than they can use.[42] From an external perspective, Craig argues, the Lockean approach prioritizes the rights of copyright-holders over those of the users, hence favoring commodification over communication and public interest.[43]

Granting property rights to ideas need not violate Locke's Provisos or prioritize owners' rights over public interests. In fact, the Provisos, by calling for the accommodation of users' rights, indicate that authors' and owners' rights can and should coexist with those of users. Wendy Gordon, for example, cites Locke's Sufficiency Proviso both to affirm that authors have property rights in their works and to resolve the conflicts between creative laborers and the public.[44] According to this Proviso, individuals have a right to homestead private property by working on nature, but they can do so only "at least where there is enough, and as good, left in common for others."[45] Applying this to the intellectual common, Gordon interprets the Proviso in an "individualized" way to mean that latecomers on the cultural scene should be free to use existing works, as long as prohibiting the latecomers' uses would make them worse off individually than they would have been if the original creators had not produced these works.[46] Gordon proposes to enforce this Proviso through the "liability rule," under which latecomers or borrowers offer reasonable royalty damage awards to the original creators or obtain compulsory licenses from them, and the "stowaway" approaches, which look into the latecomers' motive(s) in using

---

[40] *Id.* at 64–65.

[41] Adam Mossoff, *Saving Lock from Marx: The Labor Theory of Value in Intellectual Property*, 29 Soc. Phil. & Pol'y 283, 309–16 (2012).

[42] Carys Craig, *Locke, Labor, and Limiting the Author's Right: A Warning against a Lockean Approach to Copyright Law*, 28 Queen's L.J. 1, 23–30, 30–36 (2002).

[43] *Id.* at 40–48.

[44] Wendy J. Gordon, *A Property Right in Self-Expression: Equality and Individualism in the Natural Law of Intellectual Property*, 102 Yale L.J. 1533 (1993).

[45] Locke, *supra* note 31, § 27 (1689), *available at* http://press-pubs.uchicago.edu/founders/documents/v1ch16s3.html (last visited Oct. 10, 2017).

[46] *Id.* at 1570.

the copyrighted works.[47] Gordon does not mention parodies. However, by offering
something new to society through parodies, parodists arguably prove that they are
not free-riders who aim solely to take advantage of the creators and have no interest
in providing benefits to the public.

Benjamin Damstedt acknowledges the importance of the No-Spoilage Proviso in
constructing a Lockean theory of intangible properties. According to this Proviso,
people were given the world "for their benefit, and the greatest Conveniencies of
Life they were capable to draw from it," and so must strive for the optimal, "best" use
of the resources.[48] Intellectual property can promote the "wasteful overappropria-
tion" of resources: because intangible goods are non-rivalrous and "divisible without
limit," and the creation of an intangible good produces "an unlimited number of
intangible units," laborers would not be able or willing to convert all units into
money.[49] Justified taking can be seen as a good way to police waste prohibition.[50]
Admittedly, it may be difficult to identify the point where waste begins to occur.
Merges contends that so long as someone gets some use out of the concept, it has not
been wasted, and the fact that some people would have liked to use it at a reduced
price or for free is irrelevant.[51] Damstedt, on the other hand, defines Lockean waste
more broadly as something that occurs where "a unit of a product of labor is not put
to any use."[52] Limiting the ability of users to obtain copies of the intangible good
therefore leads to waste.[53] Following Damstedt's reasoning, to ensure productive
uses of intangible copyrighted resources, users are entitled to appropriate these
resources in ways that would benefit society without harming the owners.
Parodying copyrighted works would be a good example, and prohibiting such
a use would constitute waste.

To the extent that Locke's labor theory can extend to copyright, his Provisos
further justify the users' right to parody copyrighted works to serve the common
good. The idea that property rights and, by extension, intellectual property rights are
not absolute and should accommodate users' right to parody copyrighted works can
also be derived from Rawls' writing.

B. *Rawls' Personal Possessions and Theory of Distributive Justice*

Whereas Rawls recognizes the right to freedom of speech as a fundamental
liberty, both intellectual property rights and the right to parody copyrighted
works can be inferred from his theory of justice. As the Chapter 1 has

---

[47]   *Id.* at 1573.
[48]   LOCKE, *supra* note 31, § 31.
[49]   Benjamin G. Damstedt, *Limiting Locke: A Natural Law Justification for the Fair Use Doctrine*, 112
       YALE L.J. 1179, 1183 (2003).
[50]   *Id.* at 1196.
[51]   MERGES, *supra* note 34, at 58.
[52]   Damstedt, *supra* note 49, at 1194–95.
[53]   *Id.* at 1195.

explained, Rawls' first principle states that each person has "an equal right to the most extensive total system of equal basic liberties."[54] The right to "personal property," which only allows "a sufficient material basis for a sense of personal independence and self-respect," constitutes an essential part of individual liberty.[55] Merges argues for a fundamental right to intellectual property within the Rawlsian framework by expanding the definition of "personal possessions" to include creative works, which are often more personal than many types of property.[56] Because individual autonomy fostered by private property forms an indispensable part of a fair, well-ordered society, Rawls' conception of property as basic liberty evolving out of the "original position" should be broadened to include intellectual property rights.[57]

Rawls' principle of difference further justifies the potential income inequalities created by an intellectual property system, which enables creative professionals and right owners to profit from their works. The principle of difference justifies social and economic inequalities to the extent that they are both "attached to offices and positions open to all under conditions of fair equality of opportunity," and that they serve "the greatest benefit of the least-advantaged."[58] Reasonable people behind the "veil of ignorance" would agree to include intellectual property rights as a basic liberty and the apparent inequalities caused by the intellectual property system, as long as opportunities to participate as creative professionals are open and equal to all, and their works would benefit society in general.[59]

Merges is at pains to point out that even if intellectual property should be recognized as a basic liberty, it is not absolute in the Rawlsian framework. He divides every intellectual property right into two components: the "inviolable individual contribution" or "deserving core" of the work, which represents "the act of individual will" deserving protection, and the "periphery," which owes its origins to social forces and situational advantages and which society can claim by way of redistributive policies.[60] In doing so, Merges justifies authors' strong claims to their works and redistributions of some of the proceeds earned from those works to the public.[61] The line between the two components is murky because distinguishing the "periphery" from the "core" does not seem easy. Unsurprisingly, Merges also identifies fair use, which allows access to and use

---

54 JOHN RAWLS, A THEORY OF JUSTICE 61, 225 (1971).
55 *E.g.*, JOHN RAWLS, POLITICAL LIBERALISM 298 (3d ed. 2005); *see* SAMUEL FREEMAN, RAWLS 50 (2007); SAMUEL FREEMAN, THE CAMBRIDGE COMPANION TO RAWLS 67 (2003).
56 MERGES, *supra* note 34, at 117.
57 *Id.* at 364.
58 RAWLS, *supra* note 54, at 266.
59 MERGES, *supra* note 34, at 111, 128.
60 *Id.* at 121.
61 *Id.* at 122.

of copyrighted works, as one form of "redistribution."[62] It follows that the right to parody copyrighted works should form part of the Rawlsian distributive scheme.

C. *Kant's Inalienable Personal Right and Universal Principle of Right*

Kantian theory of property justifies the right to parody copyrighted works from a personality-based natural rights perspective. Kant contends that land and, by extension all properties, was originally possessed in common.[63] Yet it would be a violation of people's freedom to deprive them of the freedom to use objects in rational pursuit of their goals and to dispose freely of objects in their physical possession.[64] The desire to control objects thus leads to the concept of property, which society translates into operation.[65] Potential conflicts arise when different people exercise their freedom to claim properties and/or their property claims conflict with other freedoms. According to Kant's "Universal Principle of Right," an individual's expression of freedom must coexist with expressions of freedom by other people.[66] Hence, one's claim to property of an object can be rightfully established only when it is consistent with other people's freedom "in accordance with a universal law."[67]

Whereas Kant considers property right a natural right, it is a little less clear whether he deems intellectual property a property right. Kant contends in an essay he published in 1785 that a book's author has an "inalienable right (*ius personalissimum*) always himself to speak through anyone else, the right, that is, that no one may deliver the same speech to the public other than in his (the author's) name."[68] Whereas some consider *"ius personale"* to be a mere personal right but not a property right, others argue that authors' expressions of their desires through their works

---

[62] Merges identifies three stages of redistribution: "1) the initial grant of rights; (2) the deployment stage of works covered by IP rights; and (3) the time period after profits have been earned from sale of IP-covered works." At stage 2, rules permit third-party use of and access to a creative work, including fair use in copyright law, experimental use in patent law, and nominative or nontrademark use in trademark law. *Id.* at 128–29.

[63] PAUL GUYER, KANT ON FREEDOM, LAW, AND HAPPINESS 253 (2000), *citing* IMMANUEL KANT'S THE METAPHYSICS OF MORALS, PART I, DOCTRINE OF RIGHT, § 13, 6: 262 (1797), which states that the original possession of land can only be "possession in common because the spherical surface of the earth unites all the places on its surface."

[64] GUYER, *supra* note 63, at 279.

[65] *Id.* at 236.

[66] "Any action is right if it can coexist with everyone's freedom in accordance with a universal law, or if on its maxim the freedom of choice of each can coexist with everyone's freedom in accordance with universal law." The universal law of right is "to act externally so that the free use of your choice can coexist with the freedom of everyone in accordance with a universal law." *Id.* at 240–41, *citing* KANT, *supra* note 63, § 6: 230, 231.

[67] *Id.*, *citing* KANT, *supra* note 63, § 6: 231.

[68] Immanuel Kant, *On the Wrongfulness of Unauthorized Publication of Books*, § 8: 82 (1785), *in* IMMANUEL KANT, PRACTICAL PHILOSOPHY 31.

provide sufficient grounds for a theory of intellectual property rights.[69] Merges, in seeking to establish a solid ethical foundation for intellectual property, makes the argument that Kant's vision of lone individuals struggling to establish durable claims of property to objects for self-actualization and autonomy readily translates into authors expressing their ideas through their works and claiming property rights to these works.[70] Certainly, others have a duty to respect claims of authorship. However, under the Universal Principle of Right, rights granted to enhance human freedom must not be so broad as to interfere with other people's freedom. Kant arguably would not deny people the freedom to appropriate copyrighted works to express themselves. Far from that, because creative endeavors like writing parodies are examples of self-actualization, parodists are entitled to claim the new works as their own.

Some may argue that Kant's theory lends itself more readily to the moral rights doctrine than to the right to parody. Indeed, Kant's view that works are expressions of authors' identities and extensions of their personhood lends support to their inalienable rights in their works, so that they enjoy the moral rights, for instance, to identify as authors of their works, and to prevent excessive criticisms of them.[71] The moral rights doctrine is nonetheless compatible with the right to parody in the Kantian framework. A parody need not violate the "integrity" of the original as long as it stands as a new work. Kant contends in his 1785 essay that a book serves as a vehicle for authorial speech and a communication from publisher to public in the name of the author.[72] He thus compares the unauthorized publication of the author's text to compelling the author to speak against his or her will.[73] However, if the new work is modified to the extent that it would be wrong to attribute it to the author, then it can rightfully be published in the new author's name.[74] Hence, Kantian theory of rights justifies both the moral rights doctrine and the right to parody copyrighted works.

---

[69] See, e.g., Riccardo Pozzo, *Immanuel Kant on Intellectual Property*, 29(2) TRANS/FORM/AÇÃO 11, 12 (2006); MERGES, *supra* note 34, at 71.

[70] MERGES, *supra* note 34, at 71.

[71] See, e.g., Roberta Rosenthal Kwall, *"Author-Stories:" Narrative's Implications for Moral Rights and Copyright's Joint Authorship Doctrine*, 75 S. CAL. L. REV. 1, 19 (2001), *citing* IMMANUEL KANT, ESSAYS AND TREATISES ON MORAL, POLITICAL, AND VARIOUS PHILOSOPHICAL SUBJECTS (William Richardson ed. & trans., 1798).

[72] KANT, *supra* note 68, § 8: 81, *in* KANT, PRACTICAL PHILOSOPHY 30.

[73] "This right of the author is, however, not a right to a thing, namely to the copy (for the owner can burn it before the author's eyes), but an innate right in his own person, namely, to prevent another from having him speak to the public without his consent, which consent certainly cannot be presumed because he has already given it exclusively to someone else." *Id.* § 8: 86, *in* KANT, PRACTICAL PHILOSOPHY 35.

[74] *Id.* § 8: 86–87, *in* KANT, PRACTICAL PHILOSOPHY 35.

D. *Natural Law and Relational Authorship*

As explained, Craig's critique of the natural law approach fails to appreciate that the Lockean theory accommodates parodic works. Elsewhere, her reconstruction of the "author-self" readily reconciles with and complements the natural rights perspectives on parody. Craig rightly critiques the current copyright regime for propertizing and individualizing authorial activity.[75] Drawing upon relational feminism, she envisages the author as a "relational" self, who always works within a community and a network of social relations and discourses through "reinterpretation, recombination, . . . and transformation."[76] Craig argues that the individualization of authorship should give way to a communicative approach emphasizing its participatory and dialogic nature.[77] To foster creativity among all parties, the normative copyright regime should focus less on authors' entitlement to their works, and more on ways to structure relations among authors and between authors and the public.[78]

Craig does not go further to describe the kinds of derivative works that should be accommodated by her idea of "relational authorship." Yet her vision is in line with natural law perspectives: the Lockean Provisos, the Rawlsian distributive scheme, and Kant's Universal Principle of Right and Craig's idea of authorship all indicate that authors' rights in their works accommodate users' right to parody copyrighted works.

E. *The Right to Parody from Utilitarian Perspectives*

Other philosophers do not consider intellectual property rights, or even property rights, to be natural rights inherent in all people. Scottish philosopher David Hume, for example, contends that humans have no primary instinct to recognize private property, which would have had no purpose where resources are abundant. Where goods are scarce and portable and disputes over them are inevitable, they establish property rights to reward them for their work and keep society in good order.[79] Hence, all conceptions of justice regarding property are

---

[75] Carys J. Craig, *Reconstructing the Author-Self: Some Feminist Lessons for Copyright Law*, 15 J. GENDER, SOC. POL'Y & L. 207 (2007).

[76] *See id.* at 263, 265.

[77] Craig's approach would also have gained support from other scholars such as Martha Woodmansee and Carla Hesse, who illuminate how romantic authorship is a construct borne of historical and social circumstances, hence impliedly subjecting it to deconstruction. *See* Martha Woodmansee, *The Genius and the Copyright: Economic and Legal Conditions of the Emergence of the "Author,"* 17(4) EIGHTEENTH-CENTURY STUDIES 425 (1984); Carla Hesse, *The Rise of Intellectual Property, 700 B.C.–A.D. 2000: An Idea in the Balance*, 131 DAEDALUS 26 (2002).

[78] *See* Craig, *supra* note 75, at 263–64.

[79] DAVID HUME, A TREATISE OF HUMAN NATURE, bk 3, pt 2, § 2 (1740), www.earlymoderntexts.com/assets/pdfs/hume1740book3.pdf (last visited Oct. 10, 2017).

founded solely on how useful the convention of property is to society.[80] Deeming private property a creature of human convention, Hume would have recognized intellectual property also as a convention to enable authors to reap benefits from their creations rather than as a form of property.[81]

Jeremy Bentham, who advanced the idea of utilitarianism, likewise describes property as a pure creature of law.[82] Following his "fundamental axiom," according to which "it is the greatest happiness of the greatest number that is the measure of right and wrong," the most correct course of action is the one that produces the greatest net benefits.[83] John Stuart Mill similarly contends that " . . . property is only a means to an end, not in itself an end."[84] The moral worth of actions is to be judged in terms of the consequences of those actions. Considering property rights to be a means to a social good, both endorse the patent institution which, by setting time-limited monopoly rights, incentivizes authors to invent new products before their works eventually make their way into the public domain to be freely enjoyed by all.[85]

Utilitarian perspectives on property and intellectual property, being largely indifferent to questions of individual rights, seem to be a far cry from their natural law counterparts, although the justification of intellectual property as a basic liberty and incomes for creative professionals in the Rawlsian scheme can be seen as partly utilitarian. Unsurprisingly, the right to property has remained one of the most controversial human rights in terms of its existence and interpretation. Though recognized in Article 17 of the Universal Declaration of Human Rights (UDHR), Article 1 of Protocol No. 1 to the European Convention on Human Rights, as well as Article 21 of the American Convention on Human Rights, it is nowhere to be found in the International Covenant on Civil and Political Rights (ICCPR) or the International Covenant on Economic, Social and Cultural Rights (ICESCR).[86]

[80] "Thus, the rules of equity or justice [regarding property] depend entirely on the particular state and condition in which men are placed, and owe their origin and existence to that utility, which results to the public from their strict and regular observance." DAVID HUME, AN ENQUIRY CONCERNING THE PRINCIPLES OF MORALS, § 3 (1751), www.earlymoderntexts.com/assets/pdfs/hume1751.pdf (last visited Oct. 10, 2017).

[81] *See, e.g.*, Hector L. MacQueen, *Law and Economics, David Hume and Intellectual Property*, in ARGUMENT AMONGST FRIENDS: TWENTY-FIVE YEARS OF SCEPTICAL ENQUIRY 9–14 (Nick Kuenssberg ed., 2010); Arnold Plant, *The Economic Theory Concerning Patents for Inventions*, 1(1) ECONOMICA 30 (1934).

[82] As Bentham put it, "Property and law are born together, and die together. Before laws were made there was no property; take away laws, and property ceases." JEREMY BENTHAM, THEORY OF LEGISLATION 111–13 (1802) (C.K. Ogden, ed. & Richard Hildreth, trans. 1931).

[83] Jeremy Bentham, *A Comment on the Commentaries and a Fragment on Government*, IN THE COLLECTED WORKS OF JEREMY BENTHAM 393 (J. H. Burns & H. L. A. Hart, eds. 1977).

[84] JOHN STUART MILL, PRINCIPLES OF POLITICAL ECONOMY AND SOME OF THEIR APPLICATIONS TO SOCIAL PHILOSOPHY 138 (1875).

[85] Ulf Petrusson, *Patent and Open Access in the Knowledge Economy*, IN THE STRUCTURE OF INTELLECTUAL PROPERTY LAW 62 (Annett Kur & Vytautas Mizaras, eds. 2011).

[86] Universal Declaration of Human Rights, Art. 17; European Convention for the Protection of Human Rights and Fundamental Freedoms, Protocol No. 1, Art. 1; American Convention on Human Rights, Art. 21.

Similarly, the right to intellectual property is not found in all international conventions. It is not covered in the ICCPR, but both Article 27 of the UDHR and Article 15 of the ICESCR stipulate that everyone has the right to "the protection of the moral and material interests resulting from any scientific, literary or artistic production of which he is the author."[87] Further, the European Court of Human Rights has interpreted "the peaceful enjoyment of his possessions" in the European Convention to include intellectual properties.[88]

Regardless of whether intellectual property right should be regarded as a fundamental right, utilitarian theories on intellectual property are no different than natural law counterparts in that they accommodate parodies of works that fall under copyright protection and have not yet entered the public domain. The right to parody is built into natural law theories. In a utilitarian framework, parodies should be allowed as long as they do not defeat the purpose of the copyright system by harming the incentives of authors, or, in Bentham's words, by reducing the net benefits generated by authors' works.

III. JUSTIFICATIONS FOR A BROAD PARODY DEFINITION

Although both copyright and the right to parody copyrighted works are justified from different philosophical perspectives, the foregoing theories on property alone do not indicate whether a narrow or a broad legal definition of parody is preferable. This chapter has already evaluated different definitions of parody, and contended that a broad, speech-friendly definition of parody is preferable to a narrow one. Arguably, this broad definition is further bolstered by the above philosophical traditions due to the relative importance of speech freedom and property and intellectual property rights.

Locke's writings indicate that free speech and property rights are equally important. His endorsement of a limited government to preserve people's natural rights to "Life, Health, Liberty, or Possessions" in *Two Treatises on Government* indicates that both liberty and possessions are inalienable rights with which people are naturally endowed. His discussions of the liberty of conscience and expression in *A Letter Concerning Toleration* and *An Essay Concerning Human Understanding* are balanced by his labor acquisition theory in his *Second Treatise of Government*.

By contrast, Rawls considers free speech to be more fundamental than property. The freedom of speech is one of the basic liberties under his first principle. Although the right to "personal property" constitutes an essential part of individual liberty, an

---

[87] UDHR, Art. 27; International Covenant on Economic, Social and Cultural Rights, Art. 15 (Dec. 16, 1966), entered into force Jan. 3, 1976.

[88] E.g., Dima v. Romania, app. no. 58472/00 (Eur. Ct. H.R. 2005); Melnychuk v. Ukraine, app. no. 28743/03 (Eur. Ct. H.R. 2005); Anheuser-Busch Inc. v. Portugal [GR], app. no. 73049/01 (Eur. Ct. H.R. 2007).

absolute right to unlimited private property is excluded from the first principle.[89] Further, property rights are not desirable for their own sake, but are restrained by justice as fairness, enabling citizens to act from the principles of justice and to pursue their own conception of the good.[90] In addition, the idea of a property-owning democracy mandates a widespread dispersal of property and a redistribution of wealth against a background of fair equality of opportunity under the difference principle.[91] For Rawls, therefore, not only is freedom of speech more fundamental to property rights, but it is the former that guarantees citizens the social conditions to pursue justice and what is of value to them.[92]

Kant, like Rawls, considers the freedom of expression to be more fundamental than property right and any right that an author has in his or her work. Freedom of speech, which is crucial to the enlightenments of both society and individual, is an "innate" right, "that which belongs to everyone by nature, independently of any act that would establish a right."[93] This is distinguished from an "acquired" right, "for which such an act is required,"[94] and of which the right to property is an example.[95] Kant's 1785 essay further indicates that an author's personal right (be it a property right or not) in his or her work should give way to other people's right to parody it. Describing a published book as the vehicle of its author's speech, and a communication from publisher to public in the name of the author, he contends that a new work can rightfully be published in the modifier's name if it has altered the original to such an extent that it can longer be attributed to the original's author.[96] Following his logic, any right of the original author in his or her work should give way to the parodist's freedom of expression, as long as the latter alters the original work sufficiently to make it a new one. Clearly, to satisfy this criterion, the new work need not criticize the old work itself, but can direct its criticism or commentary towards something else.

From natural law perspectives, the view that speech rights are more important than property/intellectual property rights thus calls for a broad legal definition of parody because it accommodates more speech than a narrow one. The same conclusion can be reached by using a utilitarian framework. In fact, the utilitarian view that the rights to property and intellectual property are mere conventional rights makes an even stronger argument for a broad definition. The bottom line is that the parodies, however broad and accommodating, must not harm the incentives of authors.

[89] E.g., Freeman (2007), *supra* note at 55; Freeman (2003), *supra* note at 55.

[90] Rawls, *supra* note 55, at 19.

[91] Rawls, Justice as Fairness: A Restatement 66, 176 (2001); Rawls, *supra* note 54, at 67, 164, 302.

[92] Rawls, A Theory of Justice: A Revised Edition xii (1999).

[93] Immanuel Kant, Kant: The Metaphysics of Morals 63 (Mary Gregor, trans. & ed. 1996).

[94] *Id.*

[95] *See id.*

[96] Kant, *supra* note 68, § 8: 86–87, *in* Kant, Practical Philosophy 35.

IV. LAW AND ECONOMICS PERSPECTIVES AND INADEQUACIES

Thus far, this chapter has justified copyright and the right to parody from natural law and utilitarian perspectives. As the previous chapter has explained, the natural law framework offers a model for positive law. Merges asserts that the works of Locke, Rawls, and Kant provide excellent grounding in the "first principles of property," by placing equal emphases upon the importance of property to a fair society and the limits and constraints on property rights.[97] Economic efficiency, though an important goal of any area of law, is a "second-order goal" or a "midlevel principle," hence not an adequate foundational or normative principle.[98]

Yet economic efficiency is not to be brushed aside. This section therefore reviews the major research conducted on copyright and parody from law and economic perspectives[99] to assess if they are in line with the perspectives employed in this chapter.

The law and economics research on copyright and parody has provided theoretically and empirically inadequate justifications for a narrow parody exception. Richard Posner and William Landes employ a cost-benefit analysis to explain how the various copyright doctrines can be understood as attempts to promote economic efficiency. They argue that the costs of voluntary exchanges between copyrightholders and users in some cases are so high relative to their benefits that fair uses of copyrighted materials are justified.[100] One example is parody, which they value as a highly effective form of criticism.[101] In a different article, Posner points out that because authors may object to their works being criticized, and so may charge high fees for uses, parody, which is otherwise a "taking" and a prima facie infringement, should be fair use.[102] Nonetheless, the exemption for parodies should be narrowly confined to cases where the parody uses the borrowed work as a target. The exemption should not apply to cases where the borrowed work is used as a weapon to criticize something else, in which case it becomes a "satire," to which the author would not normally object. Thus, satires should not be exempted.[103]

Posner's narrow definition of parody is based upon the flawed assumption that authors and copyright owners would be inclined to prohibit derivative works that

---

[97]   MERGES, *supra* note 34, at 10, 13.

[98]   *Id.* at 6.

[99]   Posner clarifies that utilitarianism and economics are not the same thing. Utilitarianism holds that "the moral worth of an action, practice, institution, or law is to be judged by its effect in promoting happiness ... aggregated across all inhabitants ... of 'society'." Normative economics holds that it is judged by "its effect in promoting "welfare," or wealth maximization, distinguishable in ethically significant ways from the utilitarian ideal." Richard A. Posner, *Utilitarianism, Economics, and Legal Theory*, 8(1) J. LEG. STUD. 103, 104–05 (1979).

[100] William M. Landes & Richard A. Posner, *An Economic Analysis of Copyright Law*, 18 J. LEG. STUD. 325, 357 (1989).

[101] *Id.* at 359.

[102] Posner, *When Is Parody Fair Use?* 21 J. LEG. STUD. 67, 67–69 (1992).

[103] *Id.* at 71.

target their original works, but not those that criticize or comment on something else. Market evidence shows that copyright owners are not necessarily averse to licensing parodies.[104] In addition, even assuming that owners have less reason to prohibit the public from using their works as "weapons" against third-parties, they may still refuse to grant licenses to writers of these "weapons," due to their fear that their own works would not be shielded from criticism.[105] Because artistic works have multilayered meanings open to different interpretations, those making broad criticisms of society may end up criticizing the originals, at least from readers' perspectives.[106] In any case, owners may charge exorbitant fees for using their works for broad social criticisms.[107] Hence, it may not be in society's interest to insist that the public obtain prior approval from owners before using their works for such purposes.[108] Finally, because broad social criticism is arguably more valuable than the criticism of an individual work, satires or "weapon" parodies that make broad social commentaries may have an even stronger claim than "target" parodies to fulfilling the role that fair use or fair dealing was intended to play.[109]

Law and economics research, by considering the above factors, may very well find that a broad exemption for parody is more economically efficient than a narrow one, and that the law should provide for a broad definition of parody. Regardless, as in the case of free speech, law and economics should play a supplementary role to the natural law approach, according to which positive law should stand the test of reason, and which guarantees that what economic analyses find efficient are founded upon reason.

V. PRIORITIZING THE MARKET SUBSTITUTION FACTOR

A speech-friendly definition of parody, which encompasses works criticizing or commenting the originals and/or something other than the originals, is preferable to a restricted one. Requirements that the work be humorous or critical should also

---

[104] Juli Wilson Marshall & Nicholas J. Siciliano, *The Satire/Parody Distinction in Copyright and Trademark Law – Can Satire Ever Be a Fair Use?*, ABA Section of Litigation/ Intellectual Property Litigation Committee Roundtable Discussion Online, https://apps.americanbar.org /litigation/committees/intellectual/roundtables/0506_outline.pdf, at 5 (last visited Oct. 10, 2017). Keller and Tushnet note that "[t]he fundamental premise that copyright owners will not create or license parodies of their works is belied by market evidence." Examples include numerous artists granting "Weird Al" Yankovic a license to parody original songs, and Dimension Films creating the parody film *Scary Movie* based upon another Dimension Films movie, *Scream*. Bruce P. Keller & Rebecca Tushnet, *Even More Parodic Than the Real Thing: Parody Lawsuits Revisited*, 94 Trademark Rep. 979 (2004).

[105] Amy Lai, *Copyright Law and Its Parody Defense: Multiple Legal Perspectives*, 4 N.Y.U. J. Intell. Prop. & Ent. L. 311, 330 (2015).

[106] *Id.*

[107] *Id.*

[108] *Id.*

[109] Tyler T. Ochoa, *Dr. Seuss, the Juice and Fair Use: How the Grinch Silenced a Parody*, 45 J. Copyright Soc'y U.S.A. 546, 611–12 (1998).

be abandoned. It does not follow that all works that fall within this definition should be fair uses or dealings, or be exempted from copyright protection. What other condition(s) should be met? That the parody should not compete with or substitute for the original or its derivatives in the market can also be gleaned from the writings of these philosophers.

Although the right to free speech is more important than intellectual property right, the right to property is still fundamental from natural law perspectives and provides incentives to create in the utilitarian framework. Because property right is fundamental in the Lockean sense, the right to parody copyrighted works implied by Locke's Provisos should carry the condition that the parody does not impinge on the property of the original's author (or, by implication, reduce the money that he earns in exchange for the property.[110]) The same condition can be inferred from Rawls' distributive scheme.

Kant offers even more insights into what form parodies should take so that they do not infringe the authors' rights. As explained, Kant contends that a new work can rightfully be published in the modifier's name if altered to such an extent that it can no longer be attributed to the author.[111] In other words, no writer should take the original, change it slightly, and then pass it off as his or her own work. Arguably, a parodic work that fulfills Kant's criterion would be sufficiently different from the original and would not serve as its market substitute.

Hence, even though parodies – or any fair use or fair dealing exception – may harm the authors' interests in various ways, such as by casting their original works in a negative light and thereby reducing their sales, they should not reduce their incomes by competing with their originals or derivatives in the market. On both the parody definition and the market substitution constraint, the natural law perspectives therefore converge with their utilitarian counterparts. Parodies that do not impinge on the rights of the originals' authors by substituting for their works would not likely disincentivize them. The market substitution constraint thus reconciles two fundamental rights in natural law perspectives and fulfills the goal of copyright in the utilitarian framework.

What are the implications of the proposed parody exception and the market substitution factor? A work that draws upon an existing literature or television show or borrows its well-defined character, either to criticize or comment on the work or the character or to direct its criticism or commentary against something else, would qualify as fair use or fair dealing, as long as the new work would not directly compete with the original or its derivatives. Indeed, that an idea and the expression

---

[110] Locke describes the evolution of the money system, in which men exchange perishable goods produced by them for imperishable money: "And thus came in the use of money, some lasting thing that men might keep without spoiling, and that by mutual consent men would take in exchange for the truly useful, but perishable supports of life." LOCKE, *supra* note 31, § 47, *available at* http://press-pubs.uchicago.edu/founders/documents/v1ch16s3.html (last visited Oct. 10, 2017).

[111] Kant, *supra* note 68, § 8: 86–87, *in* KANT, PRACTICAL PHILOSOPHY 35.

of the idea can be so tied together in some cases that it becomes difficult to distinguish protected expressions from unprotected ideas – good examples being common visual and cultural references[112] – further weighs in favor of this broad exemption and the market substitution factor. A parodist who inadvertently borrowed what may be considered a copyrighted expression, such as a visual or cultural reference, would not be liable for infringement, as long as the parody does not displace demands for the original or its derivatives. This would be true even if the parody does not target the borrowed expression, or does not even use it for any critical or commentary purpose.

VI. PARODISTS' FREEDOM OF SPEECH V. AUTHORS' MORAL RIGHTS

Moral rights are nonetheless independent of economic or property rights. At this juncture, one must take a second look at the moral rights doctrine touched upon in an earlier section on Kant, to further examine why the broad parody exception not only would not lead to moral rights violations, but also necessitates the narrow circumscription of authors' rights to integrity of their works.

As the earlier section has emphasized, a parody, being a new piece of work, does not violate the author's inalienable rights in the underlying work.[113] Concerning the moral right of attribution, the success of a parody depends in part on its ability to invoke the underlying work which, along with its author, tends to be well-known among the intended audience. As such, rather than violating the author's "right to claim authorship of" or to be acknowledged as the creator of the original work,[114] it would impliedly recognize this right.

What about integrity right? Though inspired by an older work, a parody is a new work that does not violate the author's right to integrity of the underlying work. The right to integrity is defined as the right of the author "to object to any distortion, mutilation or other modification of, or other derogatory action in relation to, the said work, which would be prejudicial to his honor or reputation."[115] By their ordinary meanings, to "distort" means to "pull or twist out of shape," whereas to "mutilate" means to "inflict a violent and disfiguring injury on" something.[116] To "modify" means to "make partial or minor changes to

---

[112] *See, e.g.,* Leslie A. Kurtz, *Copyright: The Scènes à Faire Doctrine,* 41 FLA. L. REV. 79 (1989); *see also* Tyler T. Ochoa, *Origins and Meanings of the Public Domain,* 28 U. DAYTON L. REV. 215, 219 n.24, 254 (2002).

[113] The other moral rights, including the rights of disclosure (to publish the work anonymously or pseudonymously), are not at issue here, because a parody is based upon a work that is already published.

[114] Berne Convention for the Protection of Literary and Artistic Works, Art. 6*bis*(1) (Sep. 9, 1886, as amended in Brussels on June 26, 1948).

[115] *Id.*

[116] Definitions of "Distort" and "Mutilate" *in* THE OXFORD DICTIONARY (2017), https://en .oxforddictionaries.com/definition/distort; https://en.oxforddictionaries.com/definition/mutilate (last visited Oct. 10, 2017).

(something)."[117] A parody, due to its imitative nature and critical or commentary purpose, almost invariably modifies or changes the original work in minor ways, although distortion or mutilation may be relatively uncommon. Arguably, it is not "prejudicial" to the author's "honor or reputation" if it does not defame the author. In view of the importance of speech freedom, as long as the parody's "distortion, mutilation or other modification of, or other derogatory action" in relation to the underlying work does not defame its author, it does not violate the author's integrity right.

VII. APPLYING THE PARODY EXCEPTION

Although it is often appropriate for a legislature to take the responsibility to guarantee rights and to define these rights by statute, rather than calling on courts to assert their own judgments based entirely on notions of higher law, courts can and should apply a broad parody exception in a way that enhances free expression. Because the right to parody is a natural right in both the free speech and the copyright contexts, courts should draw upon the free speech doctrine when applying the parody exception in copyright disputes. This would further ensure that the right to parody is safeguarded and that lawful expressions are not suppressed for the sake or under the pretext of copyright protection.

Although a normative copyright regime should accommodate the right to free speech and parody, as can be gleaned through the lenses of different philosophical traditions, the conflict between copyright and speech rights exists. This external conflict, as some scholars note, has been internalized as part of copyright law in the form of the idea/expression dichotomy and the fair uses/dealings.[118] By examining how best to accommodate the public's right to parody without compromising copyright-holders' interests, this chapter has focused on the internal sphere. Yet carving out a broad parody exception that accommodates as much speech as possible would not be adequate to safeguard the right to parody: due to the external origin of this conflict, courts should apply the exception with reference to the free speech doctrine.

* * *

This chapter has argued that the right to parody is a natural right and that a broad exemption for parody can accommodate this right. This leads to other questions: Is the parody exception proposed in this chapter compatible with international

---

[117] Definition of "Modify" *in* THE OXFORD DICTIONARY (2017), https://en.oxforddictionaries.com/defini tion/modify (last visited Oct. 10, 2017).

[118] *E.g.,* Michael D. Birnhack, *Acknowledging the Conflict between Copyright Law and Freedom of Expression,* TEL AVIV UNIV. L. FACULTY PAPERS (2008), at 26–29, www.academia.edu/23547708/ Acknowledging_the_Conflict_between_Copyright_Law_and_Freedom_of_Expression_under_th e_Human_Rights_Act (last visited Oct. 10, 2017); Joseph Liu, *Copyright and Breathing Space,* 30 COLUM. J. L. & ARTS 101, 103–04 (2007).

conventions? If so, to what extent do the parody exceptions in different jurisdictions meet the standard proposed in this chapter?

The proposed parody exception would have to pass the three-step test, first established by Article 9(2) of the Berne Convention for the Protection of Literary and Artistic Works in 1967, and later transplanted into the Agreement on Trade-Related Aspects of Intellectual Property Rights (TRIPS).[119] Article 13 of the TRIPS Agreement requires that all members of the World Trade Organization provide strong protection for intellectual property rights, stating that "[m]embers shall confine limitations and exceptions to exclusive rights to certain special cases which do not conflict with a normal exploitation of the work and do not unreasonably prejudice the legitimate interests of the rights-holder."[120] The test's "open-ended" nature, which allows the TRIPS Agreement to evolve as intellectual property continues to develop, and individual jurisdictions to tailor their exceptions to their own culture and needs, has been noted.[121] Whether the parody exception passes the three-step test depends upon the meanings of such words as "special," "normal," and "unreasonably."

The proposed parody exception should readily meet the second and third criteria. An exception to a right conflicts with a "normal exploitation of the work" only if the uses allowed by the exception lead to economic competition between users and rights-holders, and thereby deprive the latter of significant or tangible commercial gains.[122] Likewise, an exception would "unreasonably prejudice" the legitimate interests of rights-holders only if it "causes or has the potential to cause," "an unreasonable loss of income to the rights-holder."[123] The proposed exception would easily meet the second and third criteria because of its prioritization of the market substitution factor. Works conforming to the proposed definition would not

[119]   Berne Convention for the Protection of Literary and Artistic Works, Art. 9(2) (Sep. 9, 1886, as amended in Stockholm on July 14, 1967).

[120]   Agreement on Trade-Related Aspects of Intellectual Property Rights, Art. 13 (Marrakesh, Morocco, Apr. 15, 1994). The three-step test is also incorporated into the WIPO Copyright Treaty (Article 10), several EU copyright directives, and several bilateral agreements. *E.g.*, *The Three-Step Test*, ELECTRONIC FRONTIER FOUNDATION, www.eff.org/files/filenode/three-step_test_fnl.pdf, at 2 (last visited Oct. 10, 2017).

[121]   *E.g.*, Martin Senftleben, *The International Three-Step Test: A Model Provision for EC Fair Use Legislation*, 1(2) J. INTELL. PROP., INFO. TECH. & E-COM. L. 67, 69 (2010); SUSY FRANKEL & DANIEL J. GERVAIS, ADVANCED INTRODUCTION TO INTERNATIONAL INTELLECTUAL PROPERTY 67 (2016).

[122]   Christophe Geiger, Daniel J. Gervais & Martin Senftleben, *The Three-Step-Test Revisited: How to Use the Test's Flexibility in National Copyright Law*, 29 AM. UNI. INT'L L. REV. 581, 594 (2014); Roger Knights, *Limitations and Exceptions under the "Three-Step-Test" and in National Legislation Differences Between the Analog and Digital Environments*, WORLD INTELLECTUAL PROPERTY ORGANIZATION'S REGIONAL WORKSHOP ON COPYRIGHT AND RELATED RIGHTS IN THE INFORMATION AGE (May 22–24, 2001), at 5, www.wipo.int/edocs/mdocs/copyright/en/wipo_cr_mow_01/wipo_cr_mow_01_2.pdf (last visited Oct. 10, 2016).

[123]   Geiger, Gervais & Senftleben, *supra* note 122, at 16–17, *citing* Report of the WTO Panel, United States – Section 110(5) of the US Copyright Act, June 15, 2000, WTO Document WT/DS160/R, para. 6.227, 6.229, www.wto.org.

likely cause unreasonable or significant harm to the rights-holders by competing with the underlying works and any future derivatives in the market.

The proposed parody exception should also satisfy the first part of the three-step test. While the vaguely-worded first criterion may seem challenging, its ambiguity should work in favor of the proposed exception. "Certain" may mean that the exceptions should be clearly defined (hence legal "certainty"),[124] or that they should be for specific purposes (only be made in "certain" specific cases).[125] "Special case" may mean that the exception must be narrow in "scope and reach" and must apply to limited circumstances.[126] "Special case" may also mean that the purpose for which the exception is made must be justified by a clear reason of public policy or other "special" circumstances.[127] The advent of the Internet has certainly facilitated the creation and dissemination of parodies, which have become very common and less "special." Yet the parody exception, the scope of which being clearly defined by the law, would serve specific purposes of accommodating free speech and fostering creative works. Undoubtedly, these are both public policy objectives. Hence, the proposed parody exception is compatible with the three-step test.

To what extent do the current laws accommodate the right to parody? Part II of the book will explore five jurisdictions and illuminate how their free speech jurisprudences are informed by the natural law tradition. Their copyright jurisprudences, nonetheless, have been driven by utilitarianism and/or a narrow conception of natural rights that privilege authors' or copyright-holders' interests over those of users. Their current parody exceptions are not the most conducive to the promotion of free speech and creativity. Thus, each of the chapters will explain how the proposed parody exception will help to bring these copyright systems in line with their free speech traditions by accommodating free expressions without harming the rights-holders' interests.

---

[124] *Id.* at 14, *citing* Report of the Panel, *supra* note 123, para. 6.108.

[125] Knights, *supra* note 122, at 4, *citing* SAM RICKETSON, THE BERNE CONVENTION FOR PROTECTION OF LITERARY AND ARTISTIC WORKS 482 (1987).

[126] Geiger, Gervais & Senftleben, *supra* note 122, at 593, *citing* Report of the Panel, *supra* note 124, para. 6.112.

[127] Knights, *supra* note 122.

PART II

3

The Parody/Satire Dichotomy in American Law

Only one thing is impossible for God: To find any sense in any copyright law on the planet.[1]

In literature imitations do not imitate.[2]

Part I of this book has argued that the right to free speech is a natural right. Indeed, the right to free speech in the United States, protected by the First Amendment in the Constitution, was informed by the natural law. The right to parody is an exercise of this natural right. The U.S. Supreme Court in *Campbell v. Acuff-Rose Music, Inc.* nonetheless provided for a parody defense that was driven by both utilitarianism and natural rights perspectives privileging the interests of copyright-holders over those of the public, and that set up a parody/satire dichotomy according to which works not directing at least part of their criticisms or commentaries against the originals do not qualify as fair use. The broad parody defense proposed in Part I would help to bring the American copyright jurisprudence more in line with its free speech tradition by protecting the right to parody without hurting the incentives or interests of rights-holders.

This chapter will study the history of free speech in the United States, as well as the parody tradition in American culture. It will then examine the Supreme Court's creation in *Campbell* of a parody/satire dichotomy, and justify the importance of a broad parody defense despite the liberalization of fair use in recent years. The broad parody defense would not be weakened by moral rights challenges under the current law. It would also better accommodate free expressions in the form of parodies, while properly balancing the interests of rights-holders with those of the public.

As Part I has argued, courts apply the broad parody defense by drawing upon the First Amendment doctrine, a mechanism external to the copyright regime, to further

---

[1] MARK TWAIN, MARK TWAIN'S NOTEBOOK 381 (Albert B. Paine ed., 1935).
[2] MARK TWAIN, MORE MAXIMS OF TWAIN 8 (1927).

align the copyright system with the free speech jurisprudence. This can be accomplished by shifting the burden of proof from defendants to plaintiffs, and by analogizing copyright to defamation to ensure that non-defamatory works would not be suppressed for the sake or under the pretext of copyright protection. Money damages, instead of injunctions, should also be issued where necessary, so that free expressions would not be directly banned.

I. FREE SPEECH AND THE RIGHT TO PARODY IN AMERICA

The First Amendment of the U.S. Constitution, which states that "Congress shall make no law ... abridging the freedom of speech, or of the press,"[3] serves as the guarantor of free speech in the nation. The Founding Fathers of America, or leading government officials of the period when its political institutions were created and shaped, agreed that free speech was one aspect of the freedom stemming from the inalienable rights to "Life, Liberty and the Pursuit of Happiness" to which all human beings are entitled, according to the Declaration of Independence.[4] James Madison, one of the founders who later became the Fourth President of the United States, asserted that the right to free speech was one of the "natural rights, retained" in his introduction of the Bill of Rights to the first Congress.[5] Thomas Paine similarly distinguished natural rights, which may not be alienated by the government, from civil rights, which are created by government.[6] Although free speech was defended as a fundamental natural right,[7] it was also appreciated as a means to other freedoms in founding documents.[8] In addition, both as a natural right and as a right that is highly useful to society, it was never confined to speech about political matters.[9]

The nationalization of free speech in American history was nonetheless a long and arduous journey. The ratification of the Bill of Rights in 1791 was soon followed by major national free speech controversies concerning the 1798 Sedition Act,

---

[3] U.S. CONST. amend. I.
[4] Thomas West defines this period as roughly between 1765 and 1820. Thomas West, *Free Speech in the American Founding and in Modern Literalism*, 21 SOC. PHIL. & POL'Y 310, 314–15 (2004).
[5] *Id.* 320.
[6] *Id.* at 321.
[7] Legal scholar John McGinnis notes that "free speech is not simply or even principally a means for sustaining a particular form of government; to the contrary, protecting free speech and other property rights is the end for which government is constituted." *Id.* at 321.
[8] For example, the Mass Declaration of Rights, 1780, Art. 41 states: "The liberty of the press is essential to the security of freedom in a state: it ought not, therefore, to be restrained in this commonwealth." The New Hampshire Declaration of Rights, 1783, Art. 22 states: "the liberty of the press is essential to the security of freedom in a state; it ought, therefore, to be inviolably preserved." *Id.* 321–22.
[9] *Id.* at 322.

antislavery speech, and antiwar speech during the Civil War.[10] These struggles were crucial to the drafting of the Fourteenth Amendment, ratified in 1868, which provides that persons born in the nation are American citizens and that "no state shall ... abridge the privileges or immunities of citizens of the United States; nor shall any state deprive any person of life, liberty, or property without due process of law."[11] Previously, the Supreme Court in *Barron v. Baltimore* (1833) held that the Bill of Rights applied only to the federal government, and that states were free to enforce statutes that restricted its enumerated rights.[12] In *Gitlow v. New York* (1925), the court relied upon the due process clause of the Fourteenth Amendment to hold that almost every provision of the Bill of Rights applies to both the federal and the state governments.[13] The Fourteenth Amendment, or the "second" Bill of Rights, thus requires states to respect freedoms of speech, press, religion and assembly articulated in the First Amendment.[14]

Under Justice Earl Warren, the Supreme Court of the mid- to late-twentieth century took an expansive stance towards the First Amendment.[15] Hence, free speech was treated as presumptively protected constitutional value during this period.[16] Although the later courts lack the Warren Court's enthusiastic commitment to free speech, they have adhered to the rule that the government cannot regulate the content of speech unless specific exceptions apply. In *Cohen v. California* (1971), Justice Harlan, citing *Whitney v. California* (1927), emphasized that the constitutional right of free expression is a "powerful medicine" and operates to protect a marketplace of ideas.[17] Associate Justice Thurgood Marshall explained in *Police Department of Chicago v. Mosley* (1972) that "the government has no power to restrict expression because of its message, its ideas, its subject matter, or its content" under the First Amendment.[18] It continued:

> To permit the continued building of our politics and culture, and to assure self-fulfillment for each individual, our people are guaranteed the right to express any thought, free from government censorship. The essence of this forbidden censorship is content control. Any restriction on expressive activity because of its content would completely undercut the "profound national commitment to the

---

[10] Michael K. Curtis, Free Speech, The People's Darling Privilege: Struggles for Freedom of Expression in American History 3 (2000).

[11] *Id.*

[12] *Id.* at 10.

[13] Gitlow v. N.Y., 268 U.S. 652 (1925).

[14] *Id.*

[15] Bernard Schwartz, The Warren Court: A Retrospective 72 (1996).

[16] *Id.* at 70, 76 & 79.

[17] Cohen v. Cal., 403 U.S. 15, 24 (1971); *citing* Whitney v. Cal., 274 U.S. 357, 375–77 (1927).

[18] Police Dept. of Chi. v. Mosley, 408 U.S. 92, 95 (1972).

principle that debate on public issues should be uninhibited, robust, and wide-open."[19]

Hence, a law that inhibits freedom of speech must have an important and compelling interest to do so and must be narrowly tailored to serve that interest.[20]

Although the limits of free speech were not explicitly stated in the federal Constitution or in any of the early state constitutions, the idea that free speech is not freedom for licentious speech was implicit in the very concept of freedom.[21] Later, the limits were made explicit. The principal kinds of injurious speech recognized by the Founders included "personal libel" (speech that injures an individual), "seditious libel" (speech that injures the government), and speech that injures public health or the moral foundations of society.[22] One predominant view of personal libel in the founding era deemed it a kind of personal injury no different from assault or rape, while another view looked at instances of libel "as breaches of the peace, and as much resembling challenges to fight."[23] Seditious libel was considered injurious on the rationale that there can be no fundamental right to turn the people against the government that secures their rights and liberties.[24] Regarding public morality, Washington's Farewell Address in 1796 stated that "virtue or morality is a necessary spring of popular government," and speech or conduct injuring public morals must be subject to governmental control.[25]

Free speech has nonetheless become a presumptively protected value, and the government cannot regulate its content unless specific exceptions apply. The above exceptions, therefore, have been narrowly circumscribed by courts over the years. Despite the recognition of "seditious libel" as injurious speech in the founding era, the government has not attempted to punish criticism of its officials or policies, except when it is deemed to threaten national security in times of war.[26] Over the past decades, it has also made great progress in the protection of dissent in wartime. The principle that speech cannot constitutionally be prohibited unless it is intended to and/or likely to incite imminent lawless action has largely withstood the pressure of the war on terrorism.[27] Meanwhile, most limits on obscenity and pornography

---

[19] *Id.* at 95–96.
[20] Most cases dealing with content-based restrictions were decided in favor of the defendants instead of the government. One "rare" exception was Burson v. Freeman, 504 U.S. 191, 206, 211 (1992), which involved a Tennessee state law prohibiting election campaigning within 100 feet of a building housing a polling place. Justice Harry Blackmun wrote that the case, which involved a "content-based restriction on political speech," required strict scrutiny and the 100-feet limit was "narrowly tailored" to serve the "compelling interest" in preserving the secrecy of the ballot.
[21] West, *supra* note 4, at 325.
[22] *Id.*
[23] *Id.* at 327–28.
[24] *Id.* at 329–30.
[25] *Id.* at 339–40.
[26] Geoffrey R. Stone, *Free Speech and National Security*, 84 IND. L.J. 939, 941–42, 944, 949 (2009).
[27] *Id.* at 953–55.

have also been removed.[28] Although obscene material is not protected by the First Amendment, the Court, acknowledging "the inherent dangers of undertaking to regulate any form of expression," laid down a test that a work must pass to be "obscene" and legitimately subject to state regulation.[29] As a result, most pornographic materials have remained protected.[30] In addition, at the height of the civil rights movement in the 1960s, the Supreme Court radically changed the common law of defamation that privileged the rights of plaintiffs and put publishers at a severe disadvantage,[31] by holding that public officials cannot recover for defamation unless they could show that defendants had acted with "actual malice," defined as "knowledge that the information was false" or as harboring "reckless disregard of whether it was false or not."[32] This standard was soon extended to cover "public figures,"[33] although the standard for private individuals is understandably lower.[34] While many countries prohibit hate speech, or inflammatory speech targeting people on the basis of such attributes as race, religion, or gender, only speech that poses an imminent danger of unlawful action may be restricted and punished in the United States.[35]

Because governmental control over the content of the print media is mild and the Internet is largely unregulated, people have been able to express and publish their thoughts freely. Works that the government once considered to be too "obscene" to be published or sold, and whose bans were later lifted by courts on First Amendment grounds, include not only world-renowned Irish author James Joyce's *Ulysses*,[36] but also works that are perhaps less well-known, such as *Fanny Hill*,[37] *Howl*,[38] and *Naked Lunch*.[39] Books still get banned. Yet this usually happens when organizations, such as church groups, schools, and public libraries remove certain books on the

---

[28] E.g., West, *supra* note 4, at 383; Phyllis Schlafly, *The Morality of First Amendment Jurisprudence*, 31 HARV. J. L. & PUB. POL'Y 95 (2008).

[29] Miller v. Cal., 413 U.S. 15, 39 (1973).

[30] Schlafly, *supra* note 28, at 95.

[31] Russell L. Weaver & David F. Partlett, *Defamation, Free Speech, and Democratic Governance*, 50 N.Y. L. SCH. L. REV. 57, 65–66 (2006).

[32] N.Y. Times Co. v. Sullivan, 376 U.S. 254, 280 (1964).

[33] Curtis Publishing Co. v. Butts, 388 U.S. 130 (1967).

[34] In Gertz v. Robert Welch, Inc., 418 U.S. 323 (1974), the Supreme Court held that actual malice not necessary for defamation of a private person if negligence is present.

[35] The Supreme Court ruled in Brandenburg v. Ohio, 395 U.S. at 447 that "The constitutional guarantees of free speech and free press do not permit a state to forbid or proscribe advocacy of the use of force, or of law violation except where such advocacy is directed to inciting imminent lawless action and is likely to incite or produce such action." The *Brandenburg* test has not been seriously challenged.

[36] In 1934, the U.S. Court of Appeals for the Second Circuit ruled that the book was not obscene, thus allowing it to be published in the United States: United States v. One Book Entitled Ulysses by James Joyce, 72 F.2d 705 (2d Cir. 1934); THE JAMES JOYCE CENTRE (Feb. 21, 2014), http://jamesjoyce.ie/day-21-february/ (last visited Oct. 10, 2017).

[37] JONATHON GREEN & NICHOLAS J. KAROLIDES, ENCYCLOPEDIA OF CENSORSHIP 346 (2005).

[38] Lydia Hailman King, *"Howl" Obscenity Prosecution Still Echoes 50 Years Later*, FIRST AMENDMENT CENTER (Oct. 3, 2007), www.firstamendmentcenter.org/%E2%80%98howl%E2%80%99-obscenity-prosecution-still-echoes-50-years-later/ (last visited Oct. 10, 2017).

[39] GREEN & KAROLIDES, *supra* note 37, at 370–71.

grounds that their sexual, political, or religious content is inappropriate for children.[40]

Parodies are commonly found in American culture and society. One example is nineteenth-century poet Edgar Allen Poe, who parodied earlier genres and authors, and whose own works became popular targets of imitation by later writers.[41] Mark Twain frequently parodied, among other things, English detective fiction to critique European manners, artifacts, and culture.[42] The writing of parodies was also encouraged in the early twentieth century by such periodicals as *The New Yorker*.[43] Over the past few decades, the parodic form has been employed in postmodern American literature to question and problematize the realist/modernist notions of the self and reality, and frequently used as a political counter-discourse by African American writers.[44] During the 2016 Presidential Election, Republican nominee (and current President) Donald Trump's most iconic piece of campaign apparel, a baseball cap emblazoned with his slogan "Make America Great Again," was parodied in different ways. One example was cartoonist Mike Luckovich's caricature in which Trump wears a white cap with the slogan "Make American White Again," an obvious attempt to mock him for what was considered to be his white supremacy.[45] Because parodies like these are neither obscene nor defamatory, and do not threaten national security, it is only fair that they are protected by the law. To suppress these expressions would have been unconstitutional.

II. THE RIGHT TO PARODY IN AMERICAN COPYRIGHT LAW

Certainly, the written law does not guarantee conditions that enable the exercise of free speech.[46] Even though the First Amendment makes outright bans of the controversial writings impossible, literary works may be suppressed by public or private parties. Bad reviews, withdrawals of support, and threats of litigation are some of the methods.[47] Copyright law can become a powerful weapon to suppress

---

[40]   *Id.* at 57–58.

[41]   *Parodying Poe*, Harry Ransom Centre, University of Texas at Austin, www.hrc.utexas.edu/educator/ modules/poe/parodying/ (last visited Oct. 10, 2017).

[42]   *E.g* ., JAMES E. CARON, MARK TWAIN, UNSANCTIFIED NEWSPAPER REPORTER 9 (2008); Don L. F. Nilsen, *Detective Fiction*, IN THE MARK TWAIN ENCYCLOPEDIA 214 (J. R. LeMaster & James D. Wilson, eds. 1993).

[43]   KATHLEEN KUIPER, PROSE: LITERARY TERMS AND CONCEPTS 178 (2012).

[44]   GENE A. JARRETT, REPRESENTING THE RACE: A NEW POLITICAL HISTORY OF AFRICAN AMERICAN LITERATURE 127–60 (2011).

[45]   Caricature by AJC Mike Luckovich (political cartoons from *The Atlanta Journal-Constitution's* Pulitzer Prize winner), www.myajc.com/rf/image_lowres/Pub/p6/MyAJC/2015/08/25/Images/photos .medleyphoto.8015971.jpg (last visited Oct. 10, 2017).

[46]   LAURA STEIN, SPEECH RIGHTS IN AMERICA: THE FIRST AMENDMENT, DEMOCRACY, AND THE MEDIA 1 (2007).

[47]   Kit O'Connell, *US Still Bans, Suppresses Books Despite that First Amendment*, MINTPRESS NEWS (June 29, 2015), www.mintpressnews.com/us-still-bans-suppresses-books-despite-the-forbidden-bookshelf/207064/ (last visited Oct. 10, 2017).

parodies, many of which may be based upon works that have not entered the public domain. Ron English, the American artist renowned for his parodies of Disney and other characters, was sued by numerous rights-holders. English rightly believed that these big companies later dropped their lawsuits upon realizing that their chances of winning against a famous political activist and staunch supporter of free speech like him would be low.[48] Regardless, the parody exception in copyright law should align with the free speech tradition to safeguard the public's fundamental right to speak through parodic works. American copyright law nonetheless has been strongly influenced by utilitarianism. This section will begin by examining its utilitarian rationale.

From its first enactments of the copyright law in 1790 to the current federal Copyright Act of 1976, Congress has consistently provided an economic incentive to authors by rewarding their creative activities. American courts have tried to balance the rights of copyright-holders and the public with the notion that "[a]n author has a right to quote, select, extract or abridge from another, in the composition of a work essentially new."[49] Fair use developed as a common-law doctrine to help achieve the constitutional goal "to promote the Progress of Science and useful Arts, by securing for limited Times to Authors the exclusive Right to their Writings,"[50] and also to "permit . . . courts to avoid rigid application of the copyright statute when, on occasion, it would stifle the very creativity which that law is designed to foster."[51]

In enacting the Copyright Act of 1976, Congress restated the common-law decisions, which made lawful the otherwise unauthorized, infringing use of copyrighted materials for purposes such as comment and criticism. Under § 102 of the Act, copyright protection extends to "original works of authorship fixed in any tangible medium of expression, now known or later developed, from which they can be perceived, reproduced, or otherwise communicated, either directly or with the aid of a machine or device."[52] The exclusive rights to copyright-holders, as defined in § 106, include the rights "to reproduce the copyrighted work[,]" to prepare derivative works of the original, and to distribute its copies to the public by various means.[53] These rights generally expire seventy years after the author's death.[54] Section 107 of the Act imposes limitations on § 106, providing that the "fair use" of a copyrighted work does not constitute infringement.[55] While fair use explicitly

---

[48] Julie Greicius, *The Rumpus Long Interview with Ron English*, THE RUMPUS (Feb. 4, 2009), http://therumpus.net/2009/02/the-rumpus-interview-with-ron-english/ (last visited Oct. 10, 2010).

[49] Folsom v. Marsh, 9 F. Cas. 342, 344 (C.C.D. Mass. 1841).

[50] U.S. CONST. Art. I, § 8, cl. 8.

[51] Campbell v. Acuff-Rose Music, Inc., 510 U.S. 569, 577 (1994); Stewart v. Abend, 495 U.S. 207, 236 (1990), *citing* Emerson v. Davies, 8 F. Sas. 615, 619 (C.C.D. Mass. 1845).

[52] Copyright Act, 1976, 17 U.S.C. § 102(a) (2006).

[53] *Id.* § 106.

[54] *Id.* § 302(a).

[55] *Id.* § 107.

applies to such uses as criticism, news reporting, teaching or research, the fair use defense is by no means limited to these areas.[56] This doctrine requires a court to balance four factors in determining whether the defendant has made fair use of an original work. First, the court must ascertain "purpose and character of the use," including whether it is for commercial or nonprofit educational purposes.[57] Second, the court must assess the nature of the copyrighted work, particularly whether it is creative or factual.[58] Third, the court must discern "the amount and substantiality of the portion" used in relation to the copyrighted work as a whole.[59] Fourth, the court must consider the effect of the use upon the market or potential market, or the value of the copyrighted work.[60]

A. Pre-Campbell References to Parody

The fair use defense, as emphasized, is not limited to the enumerated purposes in the statute. The first time the Supreme Court reviewed a parody case in the context of fair use was in its 1958 opinion, Benny v. Loew's, Inc., where it affirmed without opinion the Ninth Circuit's holding that CBS's TV burlesque of Loew's film adaptation of the play Gas Light infringed Loew's copyright.[61] On the defendants' argument that parody should be protected under the doctrine of fair use as a form of literary criticism or comment, the Ninth Circuit and the Supreme Court agreed with the District Court for the Southern District of California that the parody in question did not constitute fair use.[62] The Ninth Circuit based its holding upon the principle that "a parodized or burlesque taking is to be treated no differently from any other appropriation."[63] Hence, a stringent standard was set up, according to which only parodic works borrowing very insubstantially from the original would fall safely within fair-use limits.[64]

The Benny decision did not prevent lower courts from ruling for parodists in subsequent decisions. In Berlin v. E.C. Publications, Inc. (1964), the Second Circuit found the book of parodic lyrics in question non-infringing because there was no substantial similarity between these lyrics and the original popular songs.[65] In dicta, the court also outlined the parameters for parody under a fair-use analysis, namely, that the parody does not appropriate a greater amount of the original work than is necessary to "recall or conjure up" the object of his

---

[56]   Id.
[57]   Id. § 107(1).
[58]   Id. § 107(2); see, e.g., Universal City Studios, Inc. v. Sony Corp. of Am., 659 F.2d 963, 972 (9th Cir. 1981), rev'd on other grounds, 464 U.S. 417 (1984).
[59]   Id. § 107(3).
[60]   Id. § 107(4).
[61]   Benny v. Loew's, Inc., 356 U.S. 43 (1958).
[62]   Benny v. Loew's, Inc., 239 F.2d 532 (9th Cir. 1956).
[63]   Id. at 537.
[64]   See id.
[65]   Berlin v. E.C. Publ'n., Inc., 329 F.2d 541 (2d. Cir. 1964).

satire.[66] In addition, without making any semantic distinction between "parody" and "satire," the court held that they are entitled to protection "as entertainment and as a form of social and literary criticism."[67] The lower court in *Berlin*, however, did draw a distinction between "parody" and "satire" based upon the target of their criticism, arguing that the new songs merely "satirized" modern life, and so were not subject to the *Benny* test and qualified as fair use.[68] However, this same court held that a work targeting something or someone external to the underlying work was not fair use, in *Walt Disney Productions v. Mature Pictures Corp* (1975). Here, Disney sought and won a preliminary injunction to prevent Mature Pictures from using *The Mickey Mouse March* as background music in a movie scene depicting the sexual coming-of-age of a group of teenaged boys.[69] The court held that the defendant, by playing the entire song repeatedly, had used much more of the original than was necessary to accomplish any legitimate parodic purpose.[70] Moreover, because this "parody" did not target *the Mickey Mouse March*, its use of the copyrighted material was not fair.[71]

The doctrinal incongruity between *Berlin* and *Mature Pictures Corp.* was resolved by both the Second and the Ninth Circuits in *MCA, Inc. v. Wilson* (1981) and *Walt Disney Productions v. Air Pirates* (1978) respectively. Initially, the District Court of the Southern District of New York in *MCA* found a sexually explicit parody of the World War II-era song *Boogie Woogie Bugle Boy* to be infringing because it targeted not "Bugle Boy," but the sexual mores of the era of which the song was a product.[72] Later on, the same court in *Elsmere Music, Inc. v. NBC* (1980) found that NBC's Saturday Night Live parody of the "I Love New York" advertising campaign was fair use. It cited *Berlin* to allow parodists to use the copyrighted works as a means of criticizing something or someone external to them, and the Second Circuit affirmed.[73] A similar reasoning was then endorsed by the Second Circuit in its opinion in the *MCA* appeal, holding that parodists could borrow from a copyrighted work as a means of criticizing or ridiculing something else, as long as the work also serves a target of criticism or ridicule in its own right.[74] The same rule evolved in *Walt Disney Productions v. Air Pirates*, where the Ninth Circuit did not "regard it as fatal . . . that the 'Air Pirates' were parodying life and society in addition to parodying the Disney characters."[75] The Ninth Circuit added that "[t]o the extent that the

---

[66]   *Id.* at 544, 545.

[67]   *Id.* at 545.

[68]   Berlin v. E.C. Publ'n., Inc., 219 F. Supp. 911, 914 (S.D.N.Y. 1963).

[69]   Walt Disney Prod. v. Mature Pictures Corp., 389 F. Supp. 1397 (S.D.N.Y. 1975).

[70]   *Id.* at 1398.

[71]   *Id.*

[72]   MCA, Inc. v. Wilson, 425 F. Supp. 443, 453 (S.D.N.Y. 1976), *aff'd*, 677 F.2d 180, 189 (2d Cir. 1981).

[73]   Elsmere Music, Inc. v. NBC., 482 F. Supp. 741 (S.D.N.Y. 1980), *aff'd*, 623 F.2d 252 (2d Cir. 1980).

[74]   MCA, Inc. v. Wilson, 677 F.2d 180, 189 (2d Cir. 1981).

[75]   Walt Disney Prod. v. Air Pirates, 581 F.2d 751, 758, n.15 (9th Cir. 1978).

Disney characters are not also an object of the parody, however, the need to conjure them up would be reduced if not eliminated."[76]

B. *The* Campbell *Decision and Its Parody/Satire Dichotomy*

The narrow scope of the parody defense evolved into a parody/satire dichotomy in the Supreme Court's landmark decision, *Campbell v. Acuff-Rose Music, Inc.* (1994). The case arose out of an unauthorized parody of a popular song called "Oh, Pretty Woman," co-authored in 1964 and its publication rights assigned to Acuff-Rose Music.[77] In July 1989, the manager of 2 Live Crew wrote to Acuff-Rose Music, informing them of an intent to create a parody of the song, to fully credit the original authors with authorship and ownership, and to pay the company the statutorily required rate for its use.[78] After Acuff-Rose Music refused to give permission to use the song, 2 Live Crew released a rap version parody of "Oh, Pretty Woman" entitled "Pretty Woman" as part of a commercial album, and acknowledged the original authors and publisher.[79] The lyrics of the first stanza closely paralleled those of the original, but were different for the rest of the song.[80] The music of the parody, closely paralleling the original's, was punctuated with laughter and scraper noises.[81] The parody also directly copied the original's famous bass riff.[82] In June 1990, Acuff-Rose Music sued 2 Live Crew and Luke Skywalker Records in the District Court for the Middle District of Tennessee for copyright infringement, alleging, among other things, that the music of the parody and lyrics of the first stanza were too substantially similar to the original.[83] Claiming that their use fell within the fair use exception of § 107 of the Copyright Act, 2 Live Crew moved for summary judgment.[84]

The District Court for the Middle District of Tennessee, finding 2 Live Crew's song to be a parody which constituted fair use of the original, granted summary judgment for the defendants.[85] The plaintiffs appealed to the Sixth Circuit, which reversed the District Court's decision. Relying heavily upon the Supreme Court's decision in *Sony*,[86] the Sixth Circuit determined that commercial uses of original works are "presumptively unfair."[87] Because 2 Live Crew's use of the copyrighted

---

[76]   *Id.*
[77]   Acuff-Rose Music, Inc. v. Campbell, 754 F. Supp. 1150, 1152 (M.D. Tenn. 1992), *rev'd*, 792. F.2d 1429 (6th Cir. 1992).
[78]   *Id.*
[79]   *Id.*
[80]   *Id.* at 1153.
[81]   *Id.*
[82]   *Id.*
[83]   *Id.* at 1152.
[84]   *Id.*
[85]   *Id.* at 1158–59.
[86]   *Supra* note 58.
[87]   Acuff-Rose Music Inc. v. Campbell, 972 F.2d 1429, 1436, 1443 (6th Cir. 1992), *rev'd*, 510. U.S. 569 (1994).

work was "wholly commercial," the court presumed "a likelihood of future harm" for both the original's and its derivative work's markets.[88]

The Supreme Court finally granted certiorari and unanimously held that 2 Live Crew's new song was a parody and fair use of the original.[89] Led by Justice Souter, the Court determined that a commercial parody can be fair use. Thus, the Court of Appeals properly assumed that 2 Live Crew's song contains parody commenting on and criticizing the original work, but "erred in giving virtually dispositive weight to the commercial nature of that parody by way of a presumption, . . . 'that every commercial use of copyrighted material is presumptively . . . unfair . . . .'"[90] It determined that the first factor of the fair-use test, which concerns the purpose and character of the use, inquires whether the new work supersedes the original or transforms it: "the more transformative the new work, the less will be the significance of other factors, like commercialism, that may weigh against a finding of fair use."[91] Hence, the Court cautioned against "elevating commerciality to hard presumptive significance."[92] Recognizing the social benefits of parody and its "obvious claim to transformative value," the Court offered a means of identifying parody by holding that: "The heart of any parodist's claim to quote from existing material . . . is the use of some elements of a prior author's composition to create a new one that, at least in part, comments on that author's works."[93] Refusing to judge the artistic merits of 2 Live Crew's song, the Court found that it was a parody that criticized and commented on the original.[94]

Here, the Supreme Court also distinguished "parody" from "satire." After concluding that parody can be considered fair use, it added that if the new work "has no critical bearing on the substance or style of the original composition, which the alleged infringer merely uses to get attention or to avoid the drudgery in working up something fresh," then other fair use factors, such as whether the new work was sold commercially, loom larger.[95] It moved on to explain that while a parody targets and mimics the original work, a satire uses the work to criticize something else, "can stand on its own two feet and so requires justification for the very act of borrowing."[96] Apparently favoring parody and devaluing satire, the Court nonetheless tempered its position in a footnote, by stating that if a parody's "wide dissemination in the market runs the risk of serving as a substitute for the original or licensed derivatives," then "it is more incumbent on one claiming fair use to

[88] *Id.* at 1438–39.
[89] *Campbell*, 510 U.S. at 574.
[90] *Id.; citing* Sony Corp. of America v. Universal City Studios, Inc., 464 U.S. 417, 451 (1984).
[91] *Id.* at 579.
[92] *Id.* at 585.
[93] *Id.* at 580.
[94] *Id.* at 582–83.
[95] *Id.* at 580.
[96] *Id.* at 580–81.

establish the extent of transformation and the parody's critical relationship to the original."[97] On the other hand:

> . . . when there is little or no risk of market substitution, whether because of the large extent of transformation of the original work, the new work's minimal distribution in the market, the small extent to which it borrows from the original, or other factors, taking parodic aim at an original is a less critical factor in the analysis, and looser forms of parody may be found to be fair use, as may satire with lesser justification for the borrowing than would otherwise be required.[98]

In his concurring opinion, Justice Kenney took a more dichotomized position by stating that the parody "must target the original, and not just its general style, the genre of art to which it belongs, or society as a whole," a prerequisite that "confines fair use protection to works whose very subject is the original composition and so necessitates some borrowing from it [the original]."[99] He also cautioned courts to be wary of *post hoc* rationalization of just any commercial takeoff as a parody.[100]

The rest of the *Campbell* decision revolves around parody in addressing other factors of the fair-use test. The Court determined that the second factor regarding the nature of the copyrighted work, was "not much help in this case, or ever likely to help much in separating the fair use sheep from the infringing goats in a parody case."[101] Regarding the third factor, the Court held that the parody "must be able to 'conjure up' at least enough of that original to make the object of its critical wit recognizable," while leaving the exact application of this test to future cases.[102] Even though 2 Live Crew's song copied what may be perceived as the "heart" of the original, the Court determined that the "heart" is "what most readily conjures up the song for parody, and it is the heart at which parody takes aim."[103] Hence, the copying was not excessive in relation to the "parodic purpose" of the new song.[104] Concerning the fourth factor, the Court held that it must consider "whether unrestricted and widespread conduct of the sort engaged in by the defendant . . . would result in a substantially adverse impact on the potential market" for the original and

[97] *Id.* at 580, n.14.
[98] *Id.*
[99] *Id.* at 597.
[100] *Id.* at 600.
[101] *Id.* at 586.
[102] *Id.* at 588. It directed lower courts to inquire what else the parodist did besides going to the heart of the original. If a substantial portion of the alleged parody was copied verbatim from the original, and the parodic element added by the defendant is "insubstantial, as compared to the copying," then the third factor will weigh heavily against the defendant. But if the parodist has merely copied some "distinctive or memorable features" in order to "conjure up" the original, and has "thereafter departed markedly from the [original] for its own ends," the copying cannot be said to be "excessive in relation to its parodic purpose." *Id.* at 589.
[103] *Id.* at 588.
[104] *Id.* at 588–89.

licensed derivatives of the original.[105] Commerciality alone therefore does not create a "presumption" of market harm. Moreover, a parody may legitimately suppress demand for the original through its critical function, and only fails this factor when it usurps demand for the original or its derivative works.[106] Because neither Live Crew 2 nor Acuff-Rose Music put forth evidence to address the potential effect of the defendant's work on the market for non-parody rap derivatives of the original, the Sixth Circuit made an "erroneous presumption" that the new song would harm the market.[107] Holding no opinion on whether the new song's repetition of the bass riff is excessive copying, the Court remanded the case to the lower court "to permit evaluation of the amount taken, in light of the song's parodic purpose and character, its transformative elements, and considerations of the potential market substitution."[108]

C. Between the Parody/Satire Dichotomy and a "No Parody" Liberalized Fair Use Standard

The *Campbell* decision helps to preserve the flexible, case-by-case analysis intended by Congress. Nevertheless, the narrow parody defense established in *Campbell* was driven by both utilitarianism and a narrow natural rights perspective towards copyright that privileges rights-holders at the expense of the public.[109] John Tehranian contends that the Court's requirement that the parody targets at least in part the original is founded upon a "propertized" vision of fair use, reducing fair use to a test about necessity and casting it as a privilege and not a right.[110] These conceptualizations of authors' and users' rights thus go against the utilitarian principle on which American copyright law is based. This "propertized" vision of authors' rights and fair use, which prioritizes authors' rights over the public's, no doubt also departs from the natural rights conceptions of copyright and fair use/dealing explained in Part I, according to which copyright accommodates the right to parody. On the other hand, Alfred Yen explains the process in which courts, generally lacking empirical evidence, engage in intuitive cost-benefit reasoning to apply the fair use doctrine.[111] According to the *Campbell* court's reasoning, the harm to the author's incentives caused by the parody is offset by the unique value(s)

---

[105] *Id.* at 590.
[106] *Id.* at 598.
[107] *Id.* at 594.
[108] *Id.* at 589.
[109] Alfred Yen, *When Authors Won't Sell: Parody, Fair Use, and Efficiency in Copyright Law*, 62 U. COLO. L. REV. 79, 87 (1991); JOHN TEHRANIAN, INFRINGEMENT NATION: COPYRIGHT 2.0 AND YOU 41 (2011).
[110] *Id.*
[111] Yen, *supra* note 109.

that it offers the public.[112] Following this logic, a satire that unnecessarily borrows from the original harms the author's incentives without offering any unique value to the public.[113] Hence, both utilitarianism and a narrow natural rights conception of copyright led to the parody/satire dichotomy and the idea that parody and satire are distinct categories.

Over the past decade, courts have, in some instances, developed an increasingly liberal fair use standard, apparently to counter the tightening statutory control over the use of copyrighted materials.[114] To that extent, they downplayed the importance of the parody exception as defined in *Campbell*, or did not even mention this exception when holding that the works were fair uses. One example is the Second Circuit's 2006 decision in *Blanch v. Koons*. Artist Jeff Koons created a series of paintings entitled "Easyfun-Ethereal" for Deutsche Bank and Guggenheim by drawing upon images from advertisements and his own photographs.[115] One piece, called "Niagara," used a photograph produced by fashion photographer Andrea Blanch.[116] Koons borrowed only the woman's legs and feet from Blanch's photograph and pasted them vertically instead of slanting upward as in the original.[117] The Circuit Court held that Koons's use of Blanch's work passed the transformative test, because it did not repackage her expression, but rather used it as "'raw material' in the furtherance of distinct creative or communicative objectives,"[118] which as Koons explained, included providing "commentary on the social and aesthetic consequences of mass media."[119] The Second Circuit downplayed the significance of the parody exception in *Campbell*, stating that "[t]he question is whether Koons had a genuine creative rationale for borrowing Blanch's image, rather than using it merely 'to get attention or to avoid the drudgery in working up something fresh.'"[120]

This liberal view of fair use is also found in *Cariou v. Prince*, a 2013 decision by the Second Circuit. Here, a professional photographer published a book of landscapes and portraits, entitled "Yes, Rasta," which he took while spending time with Rastafarians in Jamaica.[121] A famous appropriation artist then used images from "Yes, Rasta" to create a group of collages called "Canal Zone," by enlarging, tinting,

---

[112] *Id.*

[113] *See id.*

[114] For instance, the 1998 Digital Millennium Copyright Act (DMCA), which was Congress' answer to copyright-holders' concern about piracy on the Internet, authorizes holders to troll and investigate websites, peer-to-peer networks, and other forms of plural networks to detect piracy, and provides Internet service providers with a swift mechanism for dealing with suspected infringement. Amy Lai, *Sailing Toward a Truly Globalized World: WTO, Media Piracy in China, and Transnational Capital Flows*, 18 UCLA ENT. L. REV. 75, 79–82 (2011).

[115] Blanch v. Koons, 467 F.3d 247 (2d Cir. 2006).

[116] *Id.*

[117] *Id.* at 248.

[118] *Id.* at 251, 253.

[119] *Id.* at 253, 254.

[120] *See id.* at 255.

[121] Cariou v. Prince, 714 F.3d 694, 698 (2d Cir. 2013).

collaging, cropping, or painting over these images.[122] The Circuit Court went further than *Koons* by not relying upon the parody definition in *Campbell* and by impliedly throwing a wrench in its parody/satire distinction. It held that fair use requires not that the work comment on the original, but only that it alter the underlying work with "new expression, meaning, or message" to the "reasonable observer."[123] It found that the defendant's uses of the plaintiff's works were fair because they conveyed "new expression" and "new aesthetics with creative and communicative results" distinct from the plaintiff's.[124] It held for the defendant despite his abundant uses of the plaintiff's works, on the grounds that appropriating large portions of the original work is sometimes necessary and there is no rule that fair uses cannot take any more source material than necessary.[125]

In the same year, the Ninth Circuit also adopted this broad view of acceptable fair use by holding that significant copying can be fair as long as the use is creatively transformative. In *Seltzer v. Green Day, Inc.* (2013), illustrator and street artist Derek Seltzer brought claims against rock band Green Day for their use of his image of a screaming face, entitled "Scream Icon."[126] Seltzer used "Scream Icon" as street art and a form of self-identification in his advertisements for his work and gallery shows.[127] Green Day and its concert tour video producer and photographer created a four-minute video that included an image of the "Scream Icon" poster, adding graphic elements to it and using it as a backdrop for one of Green Day's songs ("East Jesus Nowhere") on their 2009–10 national concert tour.[128] The Ninth Circuit cited the Second Circuit's decision in *Cariou* to argue that a transformative use is one that delivers "new expressive content or message."[129] Green Day's use of Seltzer's icon was transformative because it constituted new creative expression and content about religion, even though it made few physical changes to the original and did not comment on it.[130] In addition, the third factor "does not weigh against an alleged infringer, even when he copies the whole work, if he takes no more than is necessary for his intended use."[131] Therefore, Green Day's appropriation of Seltzer's entire icon, which it used to convey a different meaning than Seltzer did, was fair use.[132] By holding that significant copying can be fair use as long as the use is creatively transformative, courts have gone a long way in liberalizing the fair use standard.

---

[122]   *Id.*
[123]   *Id.* at 705–06.
[124]   *Id.* at 708.
[125]   *Id.* at 709.
[126]   Seltzer v. Green Day, Inc., 725 F.3d 1170, 1174 (2d Cir. 2013).
[127]   *Id.*
[128]   *Id.*
[129]   *Id.* at 1177.
[130]   *Id.* at 1176–77.
[131]   *Id.* at 1178.
[132]   The court also reasoned that because the "Scream Icon" was a single image and not "meaningfully divisible," it was not possible to copy part of it. *Id.* at 1178.

The Right to Parody

In *Authors Guild, Inc. v. Google, Inc.* (2015), the Second Circuit expanded upon *Campbell*'s criterion of transformativeness to encompass not only "transformative work" that adds "new expression," but also "transformative purpose" that gives the prior work "new meaning."[133] In 2004, Google began its massive digitization and permanent storage program with the cooperation of the libraries of the University of Michigan and other universities.[134] Over the years, Google has scanned and indexed millions of volumes as the list of participating libraries from around the world has grown.[135] Two class-action suits—one on behalf of publishers, the other on behalf of authors—were brought against Google in 2005 in the District Court of the Southern District of New York.[136] In November, 2013, Judge Chin formally dismissed the lawsuit, by ruling that Google's use of the works qualified was fair use, and Author's Guild appealed.[137] In late 2015, the Second Circuit held that Google's unauthorized digitizing of copyrighted works, creation of a search functionality, and display of snippets from those works were non-infringing fair uses, because the copying was highly transformative, the public display of text was limited, and the snippets did not provide a significant market substitute for the protected aspects of the originals.[138] This public-oriented transformative purpose accordingly justifies the minor losses rights-holders might suffer from uses of their copyrighted works where, as here, the digitalized copies did not serve as market substitutes for the originals.[139,140]

The *Google* case, which expanded *Campbell*'s criterion of transformativeness to encompass both "transformative work" and "transformative purpose," was neither unprecedented nor surprising. In *Bill Graham Archives v. Dorling Kindersley Ltd.* (2006), the Second Circuit held that a biography's reduced-sized complete images of posters of the legendary rock band the Grateful Dead were "transformative" because the biography used the images of the posters as "historical artifacts" to document the band's concerts.[141] This aesthetic/documentary distinction presaged the application of the fair use exception to technological reproductions of copyrighted materials that do not yield new works. In *Perfect 10, Inc. v. Amazon.com* (2007), the Ninth Circuit determined that Google's posting of thumbnail images of the photos owned by an adult entertainment company to provide a searchable index of thumbnails contained benefits outweighing any infringement.[142] In *A.V. ex rel. Vanderhye*

---

[133]   Authors Guild, Inc. v. Google Inc., 804 F.3d 202 (2d Cir. 2015).
[134]   *Id.* at 208, n.3.
[135]   *Id.*
[136]   Authors Guild, Inc. v. Google Inc., 954 F. Supp. 2d 282 (S.D.N.Y. 2013).
[137]   *Id.*
[138]   Authors Guild, Inc. v. Google Inc., 804 F.3d at 218, 229.
[139]   *Id.* at 212–13, 223.
[140]   The Authors Guild appealed to the Supreme Court, which declined to take the case. Corynne McSherry, *Case Closed: Supreme Court Lets Fair Use Ruling Stand in Google Books Litigation,* ELECTRONIC FRONTIER FOUNDATION (Apr. 18, 2016), www.eff.org/deeplinks/2016/04/case-closed -supreme-court-refuses-hear-authors-guilds-challenge-google-books (last visited Oct. 10, 2017).
[141]   Bill Graham Archives v. Dorling Kindersley Ltd., 448 F.3d 605, 615 (2d. Cir. 2006).
[142]   Perfect 10, Inc. v. Amazon.com, 508 F.3d 1146 (9th Cir. 2007).

v. iParadigms, LLC (2009), the Fourth Circuit ruled that the archiving of plaintiffs' papers by the commercial plagiarism detection service, its purpose to detect and discourage plagiarism and therefore unrelated to the papers' expressive content, was fair use.[143] In *Authors Guild v. HathiTrust* (2014), the Second Circuit found that the scanning, digitalization, and permanent storage of full copies of copyrighted books to create a full-text search database and to provide access to the print disabled were transformative fair uses.[144] In light of all these cases, the Second Circuit's decision regarding Google books was almost a certainty.

Undoubtedly, the expansion of the "transformative" criterion to include "transformative purpose" that gives the prior work "new meaning" without adding "new expression" has not been confined to cases where technologies transformed aesthetic works into documentaries, indexes, or databases. Yet the liberalization of fair use standard over the last decade has not negated the importance of a broad parody exemption in copyright law.

D. Substituting a Broad Parody Defense for the Parody/Satire Dichotomy

A broad parody exemption should replace the current parody/satire dichotomy. First, because of the strong tradition of parody in American society, the parody defense should be given a place in copyright law, so as to affirm the public's right to parody and to remind users that to speak through parodies is not the same as appropriating copyrighted works for other purposes.

Second, retaining the parody defense also has another major advantage. Probably due to their belief that "satirical" works are not fair uses or are less fair than parodic ones, the courts in *Koons* and *Seltzer* downplayed and evaded the *Campbell* court's parody/satire dichotomy respectively in holding that the defendants' uses of copyrighted works to target something else were fair. Nevertheless, the parody definition laid down by the *Campbell* court has continued to be followed by courts in recent years.[145] For example, in *Bourne Co. v. Twentieth Century Fox Film Corp.* (2009), the District Court for the Southern District of New York accepted the defendants' parody-of-the-author argument that their song was intended in part to poke fun at Walt Disney's purported anti-Semitism and was fair use.[146] In *Henley v. DeVore* (2010), the District Court held that the senatorial candidate's appropriation of the author's songs in his campaign to target the author's viewpoints more generally was

---

[143] A.V. ex rel. Vanderhye v. iParadigms, LLC, 562 F.3d 630 (4th Cir. 2009).

[144] Authors Guild, Inc. v. HathiTrust, 755 F.3d 87 (2d Cir. 2014).

[145] Some other examples include *Mattel, Inc. v. Walking Mountain Productions*, where the court held that the artist's use of photographs containing the famous "Barbie" doll was fair use, 353 F3d 792 (9th Cir. 2003); and *Burnett v. Twentieth Century Fox Film Corp.*, 491 F. Supp. 2d 962 (C.D. Cal. 2007), where the court accepted the defendants' parody-of-the-author argument that their use of the author's character to ridicule the author's wholesome image was fair use.

[146] Bourne Co. v. Twentieth Century Fox Film Corp., 602 F. Supp. 2d 499, 507 (S.D.N.Y. 2009).

satire, not parody, and therefore was not fair use.[147] Hence, as long as courts choose to follow the *Campbell* court's argument, rather than the liberalized fair use standard created by some recent decisions, they will likely hold that works making transformative uses of originals but without criticizing or commenting on them are not fair.

Further, the expansion of the fair use doctrine to include technological conversions of copyrighted materials for "transformative purposes" in cases like *Google Books, Inc.* may not even benefit parodies. A parody can be created through conventional methods, with or without using new technologies. Unlike the new works in these cases which served documentary, research, and indexing purposes, a parody may not serve a "transformative purpose" that is distinctly different from the original's.

It should be noted that the parody definition in *Campbell* otherwise measures up to the one proposed in Part I. The *Campbell* court did not consider humor to be absolutely essential to a parody.[148] Further, it did not even consider critical intent to be an essential element of parody either. Although "Oh, Pretty Woman" can be said to be critical of the original song "Pretty Woman,"[149] the court stated that the parody "may loosely target an original" as long as the parody "reasonably could be perceived as *commenting on* the original or criticizing it, to some degree."[150] Thus, a work that merely serves as a commentary may qualify as a parody. In addition, the parody defense would not likely be weakened by moral rights claims. When the United States acceded to the Berne Convention, it stipulated that the Convention's "moral rights" provisions were addressed sufficiently by laws covering slander and libel.[151] The Visual Artists Rights Act of 1990 (VARA), which was enacted as a measure sequent to the United States joining the Berne Convention, and which then became part of the U.S. Copyright Code, gives qualifying authors of visual arts the right to "prevent any intentional distortion, mutilation, or modification that would be prejudicial to his or her honor or reputation," among others.[152] These rights are nevertheless subject to the fair use provision.[153] To date, no moral rights claims have been filed against authors of parodies or imitative works based upon visual arts.

---

[147] Henley v. DeVore, F. Supp. 2d 1144 (C.D. Cal. 2010).

[148] The *Campbell* court drew upon the *American Heritage Dictionary*, 510 U.S. at 580, to state that a parody "imitates the characteristic style of an author or a work for comic effect or ridicule." The Eleventh Circuit in *Suntrust Bank v. Houghton Mifflin Co.*, 268 F.3d 1257, 1269 (11th Cir. 2001) chose to bypass the question of whether the work was humorous, considering that it "would always be a wholly subjective inquiry."

[149] The court opined that the contrast between the copying work and the original "can be taken as a comment on the naiveté of the original of an earlier day, as a rejection of its sentiment that ignores the ugliness of street life and the debasement that it signifies." *Campbell*, 510 U.S. at 583.

[150] *Id.* at 580–81, 583.

[151] ROBERTA ROSENTHAL KWALL, THE SOUL OF CREATIVITY: FORGING A MORAL RIGHTS LAW FOR THE UNITED STATES 30 (2010).

[152] 17 U.S. Code § 106A(a)(3)(A).

[153] *Id.* § 106A(a).

Because visual artists' moral rights are restricted by the fair use provision, one can fairly predict that unless the parodic works are defamatory, any moral rights claims would not likely prevail under the current law.[154]

To accommodate the public's right to free speech, the current parody/satire dichotomy in American copyright law therefore only needs to be replaced by a broadened parody defense shielding from liability works criticizing or commenting on something other than the originals. In fact, many scholars contend that the *Campbell* court's distinction between parody and satire, though theoretically impossible, is practically unfeasible. Annemarie Bridy cites Linda Hutcheon, who contends that parody and satire are often "used together" in a single text, and Michael Issacharoff, who observes that it is "difficult at times to unravel satire and parody" in the same work.[155] Bridy thus seeks a better method to classify a hybrid text without resorting to mutually exclusive and misleading definitions of parody and satire, by drawing upon Ziva Ben-Porat's distinction between "indirectly satirical parody" and "directly satirical parody."[156] Bridy argues that the work from which an indirectly satirical parody borrows is not merely used as a means to an unrelated satiric end, but is included to some degree within the scope of its social, cultural or political critique. Thus, an indirectly satirical parody should qualify as fair use.[157] A directly satirical parody, which instrumentalizes the parodied text for a satirical purpose wholly unrelated to the work, has no need to "conjure up" that particular work to serve its satiric ends. As such, it should not be considered fair use.[158]

Bridy's view that there must be some kind of identity between a parodied text and the parody in order for the parody to qualify as a fair use is in fact very similar to the *Campbell* court's holding that a parody must comment "at least in part" on the original author's work. Bruce P. Keller and Rebecca Tushnet contend that distinguishing parody from satire requires precisely the kind of aesthetic and literary judgment that copyright law generally instructs courts not to pass.[159] Clearly, whether a parody is "directly" or "indirectly satirical" is a similar undertaking. Not only does this inquiry involve subjective judgments, but its answer ultimately hinges

---

[154] For example, Geri J. Yonover imagines that Renaissance artist Leonardo da Vinci filed a copyright infringement claim based on the VARA against twentieth-century artist Duchamp, who added a moustache to his replica of Leonardo's Mona Lisa. As Yonover argues, on the fourth factor of the fair use test, Congress notes that expert testimony can show whether the use affects the honor or reputation of the artist. Thus, Leonardo should bear the burden of proof by proffering evidence that Duchamp's replica had done damage to his reputation, one example being a reduction in the sales of his works. *The "Dissing" of Da Vinci: The Imaginary Case of Leonardo v. Duchamp: Moral Rights, Parody, and Fair Use*, 29 VAL. U. L. REV. 935, 1000–01 (1995).

[155] Annemarie Bridy, *Sheep in Goats' Clothing: Satire and Fair Use after Campbell v. Acuff-Rose Music, Inc.*, 51 J. COPYRIGHT SOC'Y U.S.A. 257, 273 (2004).

[156] *Id.* at 275–76, citing Ziva Ben-Porat, *Method in Madness: Notes on the Structure of Parody, Based on Mad TV Satires*, 1 POETICS TODAY 245, 248 (1979).

[157] *Id.* at 276–77.

[158] *Id.* at 275, 277.

[159] Bruce P. Keller & Rebecca Tushnet, *Even More Parodic Than the Real Thing: Parody Lawsuits Revisited*, 94 TRADEMARK REP. 979, 987 (2004).

on the writer's original intent. Tyler T. Ochoa rightly asserts that courts cannot definitively determine an author's intent in writing a particular work, a task which, according to many literary scholars, is "both foolish to attempt and impossible to achieve."[160]

Contending that courts should not have the discretion to make a subjective determination about a parodist's intent, or pass aesthetic judgments on parodic works, numerous scholars hold that parody should be reconceptualized so that it covers a wider range of works. According to Kathryn D. Piele, because copyright law aims to encourage creativity, secondary works should fall under the protection of § 107 as long as they use original copyrighted works to "comedically criticize or comment on anything."[161] Paul Tager Lehr contends that parody should be defined as "an imitation of a work more or less closely modelled on the original, but so turned to produce a ridiculous (or humorous) effect."[162] Sherri L. Burr goes further by emphasizing that courts should make decisions within narrow confines that do not require judgments of parodies' artistic merits, including whether they are comical or not.[163] Hence, Burr rightly argues, parody should be defined as "a work created by one author or group of authors using the work of another with the intent to transform the original work," which "must either educate about, comment on, criticize, ridicule, or make humorous the original work or a social condition."[164]

Undoubtedly, this inclusive exemption would be more responsive to First Amendment free speech principles. Joseph Liu persuasively argues that the fair use doctrine in American law is ill-defined and fails to ease its potential conflict with the First Amendment.[165] Treating satire as fair use would serve to reduce some of the uncertainty created by this doctrine and offer more "breathing space" to free speech.[166] Ochoa aptly notes that asking copyright-holders for permission to use their works for satirical purposes would be seeking their endorsement of the ideas conveyed by the new works.[167] Hence, drawing the parody/satire distinction would allow them to censor satirical opinions with which they disagreed.[168] Lehr illuminates that courts indeed have used the discretion inherent in the current fair-use framework to deny protection to parodies that they found distasteful, and in doing so, have participated in

---

[160]   Tyler T. Ochoa, *Dr. Seuss, the Juice and Fair Use: How the Grinch Silenced a Parody*, 45 J. COPYRIGHT SOC'Y U.S.A. 546, 557 (1998).

[161]   Kathryn D. Piele, *Three Years after Campbell v. Acuff-Rose Music, Inc.: What Is Fair Game for Parodists?* 18 LOY. L.A. ENT. L. REV. 75, 99 (1997).

[162]   Paul Tager Lehr, *The Fair-Use Doctrine Before and After "Pretty Woman's" Unworkable Framework: The Adjustable Tool for Censoring Distasteful Parody*, 45 FLA. L. REV. 443, 477 (1998).

[163]   Sherri L. Burr, *Artistic Parody: A Theoretical Construct*, 14 CARDOZO ARTS & ENT. 65, 75 (1996).

[164]   *Id.*

[165]   Joseph Liu, *Copyright and Breathing Space*, 30 COLUM. J. L & ARTS. 101, 105 (2007).

[166]   *Id.* at 118–19.

[167]   Ochoa, *supra* note 160, at 611.

[168]   *Id.*

censorship.[169] The *Campbell* court attempted to temper the scope of inquiries by stating that "[t]he threshold question when fair use is raised in defense of parody is whether a parody character may reasonably be perceived."[170] Ironically, though, requiring a court to make the judgment as to whether the work is a true parody that qualifies as fair use would give courts practically unfettered discretion to discard distasteful works as infringing non-parodies.[171] Ochoa, Keller and Tushnet even affirm the usefulness of satire, by pointing out that it may provide a "uniquely effective"[172] and/or "broad"[173] social commentary, which may not be achieved by a parody that targets the work alone.

Expanding the scope of the parody defense to include works targeting the originals and those using the underlying works to criticize or comment on something else is preferable to treating both "parody and "satire" as fair uses under copyright law, a method which, in theory, would accommodate the same amount of speech. Not only is the *Campbell* court's definition of parody unnecessarily narrow, but the latter option may not eliminate the flawed parody-satire dichotomy. Although the *Campbell* court's dichotomization of parody and satire is flawed, its description of "satire" as being able to "stand on its own two feet" is indeed accurate: a satire need not draw upon a preexisting work. The *Oxford Dictionary* defines a satire as "a poem or a novel, film, or other work of art which uses humor, irony, exaggeration, or ridicule to expose and criticize prevailing immorality or foolishness, especially as a form of social or political commentary."[174] Although literary scholar Charles A. Knight describes the tendency of satires to parody or imitate other genres or literary models, imitation of preexisting genres or works is not essential to satires.[175] Courts adhering to the propertized conception of fair dealing would determine that satires need not borrow from the originals and less deserving of fair use exemption. Only expanding the scope of parody to cover both parody and satire under the current law would eliminate what courts may perceive to be a lesser category and the flawed parody/satire dichotomy.

E. The Four-Prong Test: Transformativeness and Market Substitution

A broadened parody conception which includes both "parody" and "satire" as defined by the *Campbell* court necessitates a reassessment of the four-prong fair use analysis. Section 107's four-prong test, which requires courts to conduct case-by-

---

[169] Lehr uses several examples, including the *MCA* decision, to show how courts denied fair use protection to what they found distasteful. Lehr, *supra* note 162, at 462–64, 469–70, 476.

[170] *Id.* at 470, *citing Campbell*, 510 U.S. at 582

[171] *Id.* at 471.

[172] Keller & Tushnet, *supra* note 159, at 998.

[173] Ochoa, *supra* note 160, at 611–12.

[174] Oxford English Dictionary, www.oed.com/viewdictionaryentry/Entry/171207 (last visited Oct. 10, 2017).

[175] Charles A. Knight, The Literature of Satire 32 (2004).

case analyses of parodies (or other uses of copyrighted works) that defendants claim to be fair uses of copyrighted works, ferrets out secondary works that do not meet the fair-use standard. Does a parody, by virtue of its nature, qualify as fair use, or does it need to go through the four-prong analysis?

Courts only need to focus on the first and the fourth factors in determining whether a parody is fair use. Although the second factor regarding the nature of the copyrighted work may help courts to determine whether uses other than parody are fair, the *Campbell* court rightly determined that it was "not much help in this case, or ever likely to help much in separating the fair use sheep from the infringing goats in a parody case."[176] The first factor, which requires courts to look at the "purpose and character of the use," is nonetheless important as it relates to the nature of parody. Judge Pierre Leval, in his 1990 seminal article proposing a "transformative" standard for fair use, emphasizes that the fair use doctrine intends to stimulate the "creation of new information, new aesthetics, new insights and understandings" for the "enrichment of society."[177] A parody, by definition, contains criticism and/or commentary.[178] When judging whether the parody is transformative of the original work, courts should lean towards disallowing fair use protection for works that merely repackage the original work so as to "avoid the drudgery in working up something fresh," and allowing protection for works that provide new information, insights, and understandings.[179] Just as courts should not have discretion regarding whether a parody comments on the original work or something else, they should not judge the merits of the new information or insights. On the contrary, whether the new works present information and insights that are not found in the old works is relatively objective and therefore not subject to the whim of individual judges.

The third prong of the analysis, the "amount and substantiality of the use," is an ill-defined factor that draws together the transformativeness issue in the first prong and the market impact in the fourth.[180] Neither did the *Campbell* court provide much guidance on how much copying would be permitted,[181] nor have subsequent decisions, such as those studied in this chapter, agreed on the acceptable amount that the new work can take from the original work.[182] Thus, focusing upon the amount the parodist borrows needlessly brings in a subjective and ill-defined element into the fair use inquiry.[183] Taking the

---

[176] *Campbell*, 510 U.S. at 586.

[177] Pierre Leval, *Toward a Fair Use Standard*, 103 Harv. L. Rev. 1105, 1111 (1990).

[178] *See* Chapter 2.

[179] *Campbell*, 510 U.S. at 580.

[180] *See* 17 U.S.C. § 107(3); *see* Anastasia P. Winslow, *Rapping on a Revolving Door: An Economic Analysis of Parody and Campbell v. Acuff-Rose Music, Inc.*, 69 S. Cal. L. Rev. 767, 822 (1996).

[181] *See Campbell*, 510 U.S. at 586–89.

[182] Anastasia P. Winslow cites Michael Chagares to argue that focusing on the amount taken is "inherently ambiguous" and does not further copyright's goal of promoting the arts, although she focuses on pre-*Campbell* decisions in her argument. Winslow, *supra* note 180, at 806.

[183] *Id.* at 822.

four-prong test as a whole, the ultimate purpose of this factor is to ensure either that a parodist does not free-ride on another's creativity, which is accomplished by the first factor inquiry, or that the parody does not serve as a substitute for the original or its derivatives, which is what the fourth factor is about.[184]

As Part I of this book has emphasized, the market substitution factor is crucial for determining whether parodies (or other uses) are fair uses of the underlying works. The principal consideration in applying the fourth factor of the fair use analysis should be whether the parody would likely interfere with the economic incentives that spur creativity, or, from natural rights perspectives, adversely affect the rights-holder's property interest. As Judge Leval stated, "The market impairment should not turn the fourth factor unless it is reasonably substantial."[185] However, it is highly unlikely that the creation of a parody would ever substantially impair copyright's economic incentive system because, as the Second Circuit noted: "any work of sufficient notoriety to be the object of parody has already secured for its proprietor considerable financial benefit," and "further protection against parody does little to promote creativity, but it places a substantial inhibition upon the creativity of authors adept at using parody to entertain, inform, or stir public consciousness."[186] Anastasia P. Winslow contends that whether one work would substitute for the other is an open-ended inquiry which should be addressed through an objective compar-ison between the two works, by assessing the changes that the parodist has made to the original and the types of audiences that the works favor.[187] This method for assessing the potential adverse impact of the new work on the original's market should apply to both parodies that target the originals and those that criticize or comment on something else.

A more challenging issue is how to assess parodies' potential adverse impacts on the markets for the licensed derivatives of the original works. Winslow persuasively argues that the economic rationale for granting owners control over secondary uses is substantially weakened when they have no objective interest in licensing the derivative uses in question.[188] However, Winslow also points out that it is illogical to include "parodic" derivative works in the same market as "satirical" derivative works: authors probably would not license the former because they target the original works, but would probably license the latter because they target something else (or someone other than the author).[189] Winslow's reasoning is flawed here. As Chapter 2 has explained, it would be wrong to presume that copyright owners or authors are more likely to license

---

[184] *Id.* at 806–07.
[185] Leval, *supra* note 177, at 1125.
[186] Warner Bros. Inc. v. Am. Broad. Co. Inc., 720 F.2d 231, 242–43 (2d Cir. 1983).
[187] Winslow, *supra* note 180, at 807.
[188] *Id.* at 823.
[189] *Id.*

satirical parodies. To better evaluate parodies' potential adverse impacts on the markets for their underlying works' licensed derivatives, courts should assess the likelihoods that the copyright owners would license derivative works targeting the same audiences as the new works do. Only if there are strong likelihoods for this to happen should courts determine that the new works would likely supplant the licensed derivatives' markets and diminish the authors' incentives.

F. *The Parody/Satire Dichotomy's Impact: Three Examples*

The *Campbell* court emphasized that a proper fair-use analysis considers and weighs all of the § 107 factors. Hence, a "parody, like any other use, has to work its way through the relevant (fair use) factors, and be judged case by case, in light of the ends of copyright law"; a satire not targeting the original work can be considered fair use, for instance, when there is little possibility that consumers would view the satire as a commercial substitute, or a small amount of the copyrighted work was used.[190] Yet the parody/satire dichotomy, created by the *Campbell* court and particularly through Justice Kennedy's concurring opinion, has exerted a heavy influence on many subsequent decisions.

Although the Eleventh Circuit rightly held that the parody in *Suntrust Bank v. Houghton Mifflin* (2001) was fair use, the parody/satire dichotomy had a heavy impact on its and the lower court's reasoning. Here, the estate of Margaret Mitchell sued to enjoin publication of Alice Randall's *The Wind Done Gone* on the ground that it constituted an unauthorized derivative work based on *Gone with the Wind*.[191] While the story of *Gone with the Wind* focuses on the life of a wealthy slave-owner during the American Civil War, *The Wind Done Gone* retells the story from the point of view of the African-American slaves during the same time period.[192] The District Court for the Northern District of Georgia initially enjoined publication, accepting the Mitchell estate's argument and rejecting Randall's fair use defense.[193] The Eleventh Circuit, holding that *The Wind Done Gone* was protected by the fair-use doctrine and the First Amendment, reversed the District Court's injunction.[194]

Both courts were heavily influenced by the parody/satire dichotomy. Although the District Court acknowledged that *The Wind Done Gone* has numerous parodic elements, it characterized the novel as a sequel or a satire, the overall purpose of which being to "provide a social commentary on the antebellum South."[195] Hence, the court concluded that it was nothing more than an effort to free-ride on the

---

[190] Campbell, 510 U.S. at 581, 580, n.14.
[191] Suntrust Bank, 268 F.3d at 1259.
[192] Suntrust Bank v. Houghton Mifflin, Co., 136 F. Supp. 2d 1357, 1367 (N.D. Ga. 2001), *vacated*, 268 F.3d 1257 (11th Cir. 2001).
[193] *Id.* at 1385.
[194] Suntrust Bank, 268 F.3d at 1277.
[195] Suntrust Bank, 136 F. Supp. 2d at 1378.

famous novel and "to entertain and sell books to an active and ready-made market for the next Gone with the Wind sequel."[196] The court overlooked the fact that the two novels have more or less the same time frames. Assuming that a sequel means a story that follows the original work, its argument that the new work competed with potential sequels of Mitchell's work was weak. The Eleventh Circuit, though making a speech-friendly decision by holding that Randall's work was fair use, pigeonholed this new work by labeling it as a parody and overlooking what would be known as its "satirical" elements.[197] It described Randall's novel, written from the perspective of a different narrator, as "a specific criticism of and rejoinder to the depiction of slavery and the relationships between blacks and whites in *Gone with the Wind*," and held that its "for-profit status [was] strongly overshadowed and outweighed in view of its highly transformative use of Gone with the Wind's copyrighted elements."[198] By labeling the work a parody, or a "[d]estructive parody" that serves social good by increasing the supply of criticism, it overlooked the fact that Randall's work, which also comments on antebellum South in general, could also be deemed what the *Campbell* court called a satire.[199]

Contrarily, in *Dr. Seuss Enterprises, L.P. v. Penguin Books USA, Inc.* (1997), the parody/satire dichotomy led the court astray. Here, Penguin Books USA, Inc. and Dove Audio, Inc. agreed to publish and distribute a satirical account of the O.J. Simpson trial, entitled *The Cat NOT in the Hat! A Parody by Dr. Juice*, which recounts the events of the trial in simple and repetitive rhyming verse like those in *The Cat in the Hat* by Theodor S. Geisel under the pseudonym Dr. Seuss.[200] Dr. Seuss Enterprises filed suit against the authors and publishers of the parody, claiming that it violated the Copyright Act along with other laws.[201] The District Court of the Southern District of California entered a preliminary injunction against the defendants, holding that the plaintiff had demonstrated a likelihood of success on the merits of its copyright claim.[202] On an interlocutory appeal, the Ninth Circuit affirmed the District Court's rulings.[203]

After the District Court found Penguin's claims that its book critically commented on the original work to be "completely unconvincing,"[204] the defendants, on appeal to the Ninth Circuit, elaborated on its claim that the work was both a satire of the O.J. Simpson trial and a parody of Dr. Seuss' works.[205] However, the Ninth

---

[196]   *Id.*
[197]   *See* Suntrust Bank, 268 F.3d at 1269.
[198]   *Id.*
[199]   *See id.* 1283.
[200]   Dr. Seuss Enter., L.P. v. Penguin Books USA, Inc., 924 F. Supp. 1559, 1561 (S.D. Cal. 1996), *aff'd*, 109 F.3d 1394 (9th Cir. 1997).
[201]   *Id.* at 1561–62.
[202]   *Id.* at 1562.
[203]   Dr. Seuss Enter., L.P. v. Penguin Books USA, Inc., 109 F.3d 1394, 1406 (9th Cir. 1997).
[204]   Dr. Seuss Enter., L.P., 924 F. Supp. at 1569.
[205]   Penguin argued that the work was both a satire and a parody: "The Parody's author felt that, by evoking the world of the Cat in the Hat, he could (1) comment on the mix of frivolousness and moral

Circuit, unable to perceive any parodic element in the work, held that the characterization of the work as a parody was a "post-hoc characterization of the work" that was "pure shtick" and "completely unconvincing."[206] In addition, it quickly concluded that the commercial nature of this "satire" means that "market substitution is at least more certain and market harm may be more readily inferred."[207] In drawing this prompt conclusion, it did not consider all § 107 factors carefully in its fair-use analysis, such as by studying the amount of copying in the defendants' work, or by comparing the original's market and the intended market of the new work.

Another decision that shows the adverse impact of the parody/satire dichotomy is *Salinger v. Colting* (2010). This lawsuit originated from Swedish American author Fredrik Colting's allegedly unauthorized sequel of J.D. Salinger's only novel *The Catcher in the Rye*, which Colting wrote under the pseudonym John David California.[208] Entitled *60 Years Later: Coming through the Rye*, Colting's work describes the adventures of a 76-year-old Holden Caulfield (thinly disguised as "Mr. C"), including his encounter with Salinger, who was transformed into a character in the book.[209] Salinger sought an injunction restraining publication of *60 Years Later* on the ground that it infringed his copyright.[210] The defendants objected, claiming fair use and First Amendment protection.[211] The District Court of the Southern District of New York issued an injunction to enjoin the publication and distribution of the book after finding Salinger was likely to prevail on the merits of the case.[212] On appeal, the Second Circuit affirmed.[213]

The District Court's finding that the disputed work was not a parody of *Catcher* played a key role in its holding against the defendants. It rejected the defendants' claims that *60 Years Later* was a parody of Caulfield and Salinger and concluded that such contentions were "post-hoc rationalizations."[214] While the defendants alleged that the book aimed to examine how Caulfield's uncompromising world-view in *Catcher* led to his misery and alienation from society, the court considered "those effects already apparent

---

gravity that characterize the culture's reaction to the events surrounding the Brown/Goldman murders, (2) parody the mix of whimsy and moral dilemma created by Seuss works such as *The Cat in the Hat* in a way that implied that the work was too limited to conceive the possibility of a real trickster 'cat' who creates mayhem along with his friends Thing 1 and Thing 2, and then magically cleans it up at the end, leaving a moral dilemma in his wake." Dr. Seuss Enter., L.P., 109 F.3d at 1402–1403.

[206] Dr. Seuss Enter., L.P., 109 F.3d at 1402–03.

[207] *Id.* at 1403.

[208] Salinger v. Colting, 264 F. Supp. 2d 250, 253 (2009), aff'd, 607 F.3d 68 (2d Cir. 2010).

[209] Amy Lai, *The Death of the Author: Reconceptualizing 60 Years: Coming Through the Rye as Metafiction*, 15 INTELL. PROP. L. BULL. 9, 25–27 (2010), an analysis based upon a close reading of John David California, *60 Years Later: Coming through the Rye* (2009).

[210] Salinger, 64 F. Supp. 2d 250, 250.

[211] *Id.* at 254.

[212] *Id.*

[213] Salinger v. Colting, 607 F.3d 68 (2d Cir. 2010).

[214] Salinger, 64 F. Supp. 2d at 258.

in Salinger's own narrative about Caulfield."[215] In addition, relying upon the narrow definition of parody, namely that it must target the original novel and its characters, the court rejected the defendants' argument that the book parodies Salinger's reclusive nature and his alleged desire to exercise "iron-clad control over his intellectual property."[216] Accordingly, it was unable to appreciate the transformativeness of 60 Years Later, for instance, its transformation of Salinger into a character that interacts with the protagonist.[217] Thereafter, the court stated rather simplistically that the new book, which was sold for profit, served a commercial purpose, which weighed against a finding of fair use.[218] In an equally simplistic manner, it held that publishing 60 Years Later could substantially harm the market for a Catcher sequel.[219] It did not consider the small likelihood of this market—that Salinger had categorically refused to publish anything for the last half-century of his life, and had never showed any interest in publishing or licensing a sequel to his work or to participate in any potential derivative market.[220]

G. Applying the Broad Parody Exception to Suntrust Bank, Dr. Seuss Enterprises, L.P. and Salinger

A broad parody exception as set out in Part I and this chapter would help to bring the American copyright jurisprudence more in line with its free speech tradition. In particular, the District Court's and the Eleventh Circuit's opposing decisions in Suntrust Bank indicate that in cases where works target both the original and something outside of it, either their "parodic" or "satirical" elements could be emphasized at the expense of the other depending on whether courts want to hold for authors/rights-holders or parodists. A broad definition of parody would facilitate a proper balancing of their interests.

Because The Wind Done Gone combines both "parodic" and "satirical" elements, one may attribute the defendants' victory to fortune as much as to the sound judgment by the Eleventh Circuit. Should parody be redefined to include both "parodic" and "satirical" works, the sound verdict could have been reached more readily and predictably. Rather than relying exclusively on

[215] Id.
[216] Id. at 261.
[217] See id. at 263–67. It should note noted that the District Courts of the Central District of California and the Southern District of New York accepted the "parody-of-the-author" fair use defense in Burnett v. Twentieth Century Fox Film Corp., 491 F. Supp. 2d 962 (C.D. Cal. 2007) and Bourne Co. v. Twentieth Century Fox Film Corp., 602 F. Supp. 2d 499 (S.D.N.Y. 2009) respectively.
[218] Id. at 267–68.
[219] Id.
[220] John Tehranian, Dangerous Undertakings: Sacred Texts and Copyright's Myth of Aesthetic Neutrality, IN THE SAGE HANDBOOK OF INTELLECTUAL PROPERTY 12 (Matthew David & Debora Halbert eds., 2014).

how Randall's work targets slavery and racism in *Gone with the Wind*, the court would have taken a more holistic view towards its commentaries on these issues both within and outside the original text. Once the court had decided that the new work was a parody that did not free ride on the original's creativity, it likely would have put much less weight on, or even ignored completely, the ill-defined third factor and the difficult question of whether it had taken too much from the original.[221] Instead, it would have moved readily on to the fourth prong of the test, to look at whether this parody would supplant the market demand for the original or its licensed derivatives. Regarding this factor, the court held that plaintiffs failed to show sufficient evidence on market substitution, while the concurring opinion stated that the sales of *Gone with the Wind* possibly had grown since *The Wind Done Gone*'s publication.[222] Hence, the court would have asked whether Suntrust Bank would likely license a work similar to Randall's, which criticizes the romanticized portrait in Mitchell's original or, more broadly, such issues as racism. The answer would likely have been negative.

In *Dr. Seuss Enterprises, L.P.*, the Ninth Circuit made an egregious error by holding that because *The Cat Not in the Hat!* criticized society and was not a parody, there was "no effort to create a transformative work with 'new expression, meaning, or message.'"[223] A broad parody exception would not only have disallowed the court to seize upon the "satirical" elements of the work to hold that it was not fair use, but would also have compelled it to recognize that "parodic" and "satirical" elements are often commingled in a single work. As for the third-prong of the test, provided that the court had recognized the work's transformativeness, it would have been more likely to have accepted the defendants' reasoning that copying the Cat's hat and using the image on the front and back covers and in the text had been necessary for comparing Simpson with the cat character and for articulating the intended messages regarding society's fixation on the trial and the "naïveté of the original."[224] Most importantly, it would have studied more carefully the fourth factor: instead of making an improper presumption of market harm based on the commercial nature of the work, the court would have asked whether the parody of the Simpson trial would likely compete in the market with the works

[221]   The Eleventh Circuit could not conclude whether Randall had taken too much from Mitchell's novel in the course of writing her parody. It noted that very little reference was required to conjure up the original, and by taking whole scenes, characters, and even copied some text verbatim, Randall had seemingly taken more than necessary to write her parody. However, quoting language from *Campbell*, the court noted that a parodist must be able to conjure up at least enough of the original to make the objects of critical wit recognizable, which would leave open the possibility that Randall could take more than the bare minimum necessary to create her parody and still be within the bounds of fair use. *Suntrust Bank*, 268 F.3d. at 1271–74.

[222]   *Id.* at 1275, 1281–82.

[223]   *See* Dr. Seuss Enter., L.P., 109 F.3d at 1401.

[224]   *See supra* note 205.

of Dr. Seuss and its authorized licensees. The former was intended mainly for "adults who are devotees of the O.J. Simpson saga or those who desire to see either O.J. Simpson or Dr. Seuss satirized in a creative and merciless manner."[225] The latter chiefly targeted "children and their parents, both as works of humorous entertainment and as educational tools for encouraging reading and the development of moral values."[226] Dr. Seuss Enterprises also would have likely rejected an offer by the defendants to license *The Cat in the Hat* for use, whether to satirize the Simpson case or to parody itself, because both would have been harmful to its image. Therefore, the court would have overruled the District Court's decision and held that the preliminary injunction was improper.

Scholars contend that Salinger's fame and status in the American literary scene likely had an impact on the Second Circuit's decision.[227] John Tehranian even argues that *60 Years Later* is a better example of fair use than *The Wind Done Gone*, hence attributing the court's decision to *Catcher's* being the only novel of Salinger, a beloved American writer.[228] If there is any truth in these opinions, then the court's holding that the defendant's criticism of Salinger's desire to exercise "iron-clad control over his intellectual property" did not make *60 Years Later* a parody merely served as a pretext for its prejudices against the defendant. Should the meaning of parody be broadened to include works that criticize or comment on anything other than the original text, including its author, the court would have had to recognize *60 Years Later* as a parody. Further, the court, recognizing the transformativeness of *60 Years Later*, would have more readily concluded that it in fact had not "taken well more from *Catcher*, in both substance and style, than was necessary for the alleged transformative purpose of criticizing Salinger and his attitudes and behavior."[229] Most importantly, the court would have conducted a more careful inquiry than it did, by asking whether a parody of *Catcher* in the form of *60 Years Later* would likely compete in the market with *Catcher*

---

[225] Ochoa, *supra* note 160, at 608.

[226] *Id.*

[227] Andrew Gilden and Timothy Greene contend that conventionally popular litigants tend to win in fair-use disputes and Salinger's victory was, in large part, due to his legendary status in the American literary scene, as compared to his unestablished and no-name opponent, whose writing was not treated by the court as real art. Andrew Gilden & Timothy Greene, *Fair Use for the Rich and Fabulous?* 80 U. CHI. L. REV. DIALOGUE 88, 99–100 (2013).

[228] Tehranian argues that with respect to the fourth fair-use factor, *The Wind Done Gone* was more damaging to the Mitchell estate's economic interests than *60 Years Later* was to Salinger's, because the Mitchell estate had demonstrated a concrete and manifest interest in entering the market to create derivative works based on *Gone with the Wind*, in sharp contrast to Salinger who had refused to publish anything for the last half of his life or grant licenses to others to create derivatives of his work. In addition, large parts of *The Wind Done Gone* actually retold the story from *Gone with the Wind*, thereby engaging in more actual borrowing, both literal and structural, than *60 Years Later* did. TEHRANIAN, *supra* note 109, at 185–86.

[229] *See* Salinger, 64 F. Supp. 2d at 263.

and its authorized licensees. Because Salinger had never shown any interest in publishing or licensing a sequel to his work or in participating in any potential derivative market, the answer could only have been negative.

III. APPLYING THE PARODY DEFENSE: THE FREE SPEECH DOCTRINE AS THE GUIDING PRINCIPLE

Part I of the book has argued that the broad parody exception or defense should be applied with reference to the free speech doctrine, to ensure that free speech would not be suppressed for the sake or under the pretext of copyright protection. This chapter has explained how a broad parody defense would stimulate creative productions and facilitate the access to knowledge, hence serving the Copyright Act's purpose "[t]o promote the Progress of Science and useful Arts."[230] This last section will argue that to further align the American copyright jurisprudence with its free speech jurisprudence, courts should apply the parody defense—indeed any speech-related fair use defense—with reference to the First Amendment doctrine, by shifting the burden of proof from defendants to plaintiffs and by analogizing copyright to defamation to ensure that non-defamatory works would not be suppressed under the pretext of copyright protection. Courts should also issue money damages instead of injunctions where necessary, so that meaningful expressions would not be banned directly.

A. Shifting the Burden of Proof

In applying the reformed parody defense, courts should shift the burden of proof from defendants to plaintiffs: instead of parodists proving that they have made parodies of copyrighted works, copyright-holders would have to negate fair use by showing that the uses of their works are not parodies. Earlier on, this chapter cites Liu's argument that treating satire as fair use would serve to reduce some of the uncertainty in the fair use doctrine and offer more protection to free speech.[231] There is more to this argument. Because fair use is an affirmative defense in copyright law,[232] Liu argues, courts should carve out more space for free speech by making procedural alterations to the law, so that the copyright-holder would bear the burdens of negating fair use and of establishing real market harm. Ned Snow concurs with Liu and provides further justification for shifting the burden of proof to rights-holders.

Liu rightly compares copyright law to defamation and the intentional infliction of emotional distress—torts that implicate defendants' free speech rights—where

---

[230] U.S. Const. Art. I, § 8, cl. 8.
[231] *See supra* notes 165, 166.
[232] Liu, *supra* note 165, at 101; Ned Snow, *Proving Fair Use: Burden of Proof as Burden of Speech*, 31 Cardozo L. Rev. 1781, 1788 (2010).

courts made procedural changes to ensure that public debates about public figures would remain free, robust, and without the chilling effect of potential liability.[233] In *New York Times v. Sullivan*, the Supreme Court held that the First Amendment required plaintiffs who are public officials to bear the burden of proving that defendants had acted with "actual malice" before they could recover for defamation under state law, rather than defendants proving the truth of their assertions.[234] In subsequent cases, courts applied the standard in *Sullivan* to defamation cases involving not only public officials, but a broader category of public figures.[235] As Liu argues, defamation and copyright laws both seek to protect a private interest that is unrelated to speech.[236] Nevertheless, copyright law's procedural structure contributes to the chilling effect upon free speech by placing the burden of proving fair use on defendants in the same way that defendants in defamation cases bore the burden of proving truth pre-*Sullivan*.[237] Hence, courts should shift the burden of proving fair use in cases that raise free speech interests.[238] After the defendant has raised a colorable speech claim to show that the use is presumptively fair, the burden should then rest on the plaintiff to negate a defense of fair use.[239] In addition, the plaintiff should bear the burden of establishing actual market harm, by coming up with concrete evidence of harm to actual or likely markets, rather than vague claims of harm to as-yet undeveloped markets.[240]

Snow follows Liu's analogy between copyright and defamation laws, but provides further justifications for the shifting the burden of proof by identifying their differences. Snow concedes that the Supreme Court decisions on defamation leave open the possibility that defendants should bear the burden of proving the truth of the allegations if they are directed towards ordinary people, not public figures.[241] He carefully points out that in common law, the burden of proof in defamation rested with the defendant because the substantive principle that any person accused of wrongdoing is presumed innocent until proven guilty suggests that a defamed plaintiff should be presumed innocent of the defamatory accusation until a defendant could prove otherwise.[242] Yet copyright-holders are not accused of wrongdoing. Hence, the innocent-until-proven-guilty principle becomes irrelevant in fair use analyses, and there is no reason that the speech interests of fair users must be sufficiently strong to justify assigning the burden to copyright-holders.[243]

---

[233] Liu, *supra* note 165, 107–18.
[234] Liu, *supra* note 165, at 109; *citing* N.Y. Times, 376 U.S. at 279.
[235] *Id.*; *citing* Gertz v. Robert Welch, Inc., 418 U.S. 323, 335 (1974).
[236] *Id.* at 112.
[237] *Id.*
[238] *Id.* at 115.
[239] *Id.*
[240] *Id.* at 115–116.
[241] *See* Snow, *supra* note 232, at 1798.
[242] *See id.*
[243] *Id.* Snow points out that the "reassignment" or "restoration" of the rights-holders' burden may be achieved through either Congress or the courts. Congress could amend the Copyright Act so that it

Would shifting the burden of proof reduce the incentives of rights-holders? Both Liu and Snow anticipate the objection that strong protection provides incentives for copyright-holders to create expressions and that facing a burden of proof, they would get less incentivized.[244] Yet both of them rightly assert that as a matter of principle, upholding the right to speak is more important than creating an incentive to speak, and a copyright policy must yield to a constitutional right of speech.[245] Assessing the actual impact of shifting the burden to the copyright-holder, both believe that less creation by disincentivized copyright-holders would not likely translate into fewer works in the overall marketplace of expressions and ideas.[246] Snow quotes First Amendment scholar Eugene Volokh to argue that even assuming that some copyright-holders would cease creating were they to bear the burden of proof, the resulting decrease in original works would likely be less than the decrease in fair-use expressions that result from shifting the burden to fair users.[247] Liu likewise contends that a broader scope of third-party use of copyrighted expressions through fair use may in fact lead to more expressions.[248]

Yet neither Liu nor Snow provides any evidence to allay fears that the shift of burden would dampen individual copyright-holders' incentives to create. Other scholars like Julie Cohen and Rebecca Tushnet, who critique the incentive argument by delving into the nature of creative process, provide insights into why such a change in law would not likely affect incentives to create. Cohen describes creativity as "intrinsically ineffable,"[249] arising out of the dynamic interactions between individual creators and multiple factors such as societies and cultures.[250] Tushnet likewise describes the desire to create as "excessive, beyond rationality and free from the need for economic incentive."[251] Many experiences of creativity are accompanied by intense

expressly states that a copyright-holder must prove that a defendant's use is not fair in order to prevail on a claim for infringement. Alternatively, the Supreme Court could undo what it did in earlier decisions without overturning its holdings in those decisions. It could do so by explaining that although fair use is an affirmative defense, a defendant may invoke it merely by pleading it, as opposed to proving it. Lower courts could also restore the burden to copyright-holders without any instruction by the Supreme Court. *Id.* at 1808–09.

[244] Liu, *supra* note 165, at 122; Snow, *supra* note 232, at 1816–17.

[245] Liu, *supra* note 165, at 122; Snow, *supra* note 232, at 1818–19.

[246] Liu, *supra* note 165, at 122; Snow, *supra* note 232, at 1817–18.

[247] Snow, *supra* note 232, at 1817, *citing* Eugene Volokh, *Freedom of Speech and Intellectual Property: Some Thoughts after Eldred,* 44 *Liquormart, and Bartnicki*, 40 Hous. L. Rev. 697, 721 (2003).

[248] Liu, *supra* note 165, at 122.

[249] Julie E. Cohen, *Creativity and Culture in Copyright Theory*, 40 U.C. Davis L. Rev. 1151, 1151 (2007).

[250] Cohen references Roberta Rosenthal Kwall, *Inspiration and Innovations: The Intrinsic Dimension of the Artistic Soul*, 81 Notre Dame L. Rev. 1945 (2006), Justin Hughes, *The personality Interests of Authors and Inventors in Intellectual Property*, 16 Cardozo Arts & Ent. L.J. 81 (1998), and Russ VerSteeg, *Rethinking Originality*, 34 Wm. & Mary L. Rev. 801 (1993). *Id.* at 1151–52.

[251] Tushnet cites, among others, Margaret Atwood's *Negotiation with the Dead: A Writer on Writing,* which suggests that writers write out of compulsion and overflowing desires. Rebecca Tushnet, *Economies of Desire: Fair Use and Marketplace Assumptions*, 51 Wm. & Mary L. Rev. 513, 522–27 (2009).

pleasure and not spurred by incentives like money or reputation.[252] While incentives affect the extent to which some creators could afford to create, their role in creative productions is inflated.[253] Although neither Cohen nor Tushnet mentions the burden of proof, their perspectives should serve to allay concerns over the impacts that shifting the burden of proof from fair uses to copyright-holders will have on the amount of creativity and speech.

One needs to go back to *Suntrust Bank, Dr. Seuss Enterprises, L.P.*, and *Colting* to examine the likely impacts of the shift of burden of proof from parodists to copyright-holders, and to find out that it likely would have encouraged the defendants to produce more parodies without necessarily demotivating the plaintiffs to create. Even if the burden had fallen upon Mitchell, Dr. Seuss, and Salinger to disprove that potential uses by the public were parodies and fair uses of their works, they might not have anticipated such uses by the public when they produced their works. Assuming that they had foreseen that people would parody their works without seeking their permission, it is doubtful whether vague fears that such unauthorized derivatives would diminish their future profits would have dampened their desires to create, or deterred them from writing. On the other hand, should the burden of proving fair use be lifted off parodists' shoulders, the public would be less inhibited in parodying copyrighted works. Publishers, who are frequently joined as co-defendants in these cases, would have fewer doubts about publishing parodies of famous works.

Interestingly enough, after the Eleventh Circuit vacated the injunction on *The Wind Done Gone*, defendant-publisher Houghton Mifflin, apparently fearing that it would lose before the Supreme Court, chose to settle with the plaintiff's estate by making an unspecified donation to Morehouse College, a historically African-American college in Atlanta, Georgia.[254] In exchange, Suntrust Bank dropped the lawsuit.[255] If the burden had been on the plaintiff to negate fair use, rather than on the defendant to prove it, then the latter might not have settled. In cases where the copyright-holders are like Salinger, who had an aggressive record of suppressing the publication of his letters and the adaptation of his work, through legal actions,[256] this shift of burden would be especially welcomed

---

[252] *Id.* at 522.

[253] Tushnet contends that the major fallacy of the incentive theory is its proposition that maximum incentives require maximum control. Regardless of the strength of copyright protection, it is the likelihood of success in the market, a highly unpredictable variable that law can do little to affect, that determines whether new authors reap rewards from their works. *Id.* at 517–18.

[254] 'Wind Done Gone' Copyright Case Settled, Reporters Committee (May 19, 2002), www.rcfp.org /node/92088 (last visited Oct. 10, 2017).

[255] *Id.*

[256] For example, upon learning that the British writer Ian Hamilton intended to publish a biography that made extensive use of letters Salinger had written to other authors and friends, Salinger sued to stop the book's publication. The court in *Salinger v. Random House, Inc.*, 811 F.2d 90 (2d Cir. 1987) ruled that the author's right to control publication overrode the right of fair use.

by writers who contemplate parodying their works and publishers interested in publishing such parodies.

B. Analogizing Copyright to Defamation

Whether the burden of proof falls on plaintiffs or defendants, courts should draw upon the First Amendment principle more directly when applying the parody defense, such as through analogizing copyright to defamation. Courts should assume that the well-known fictional characters, such as those in Mitchell's, Dr. Seuss', and Salinger's works, should be subject to at least as much criticism as public figures.[257] Hence, they should not authorize copyright-holders to exercise censorship over the contents of parodic works in circumstances where similarly situated public figures would not be able to do so.[258] In this way, courts could prevent plaintiffs, especially public figures, from suppressing non-defamatory speech for the sake or under the pretext of copyright protection.

Ochoa offers a remarkable example of how the free speech principle should guide the application of a parody defense, by imagining the plaintiff in *Dr. Seuss Enterprises* as O. J. Simpson.[259] If Simpson sued on the ground that the book was libelous, or that it intentionally inflicted emotional distress upon him, he would have to prove both that the book was false, and that the defendants acted either with knowledge that it was false or in reckless disregard as to whether or not it was false.[260] Yet the Ninth Circuit, by applying copyright law in an overly restrictive manner and without regard to First Amendment values, offered the fictional characters of Dr. Seuss greater protection from comment or criticism than an actual person would enjoy.[261] What the Ninth Circuit should have done was to draw upon the First Amendment doctrine and apply the parody defense in a speech-friendly manner to avoid suppressing criticisms of public figures.[262]

Another example can be made of a parody of George W. Bush's campaign website during a former presidential election, which a political enthusiast set up to relate satirical stories about him.[263] If the Federal Election Commission had not decided not to take action against the man and Bush's presidential campaign had indeed filed suit against him,[264] the court should have determined whether the enthusiast's website properly fulfilled its transformative purpose by criticizing or commenting on

---

[257] See Ochoa, *supra* note 160, at 616.
[258] *Id.* at 617.
[259] *Id.* at 615.
[260] *Id.*
[261] *Id.* at 616.
[262] *Id.* at 617.
[263] Terry M. Neal, *Satirical Web Site Poses Political Test*, WASH. P. (Nov. 29, 1999), www.washingtonpost .com/wp-srv/WPcap/1999-11/29/002r-112999-idx.html (last visited Oct. 10, 2017).
[264] *FEC Takes No Action against Anti-Bush Web Site*, TECH. L.J. (Apr. 20, 2000), www.techlawjournal .com/election/20000420.htm (last visited Oct. 10, 2017).

Bush (or someone else). The court should also have considered whether Bush would have won if he had brought a defamation suit against the enthusiast. By applying the parody exception in a speech-sensitive manner, courts would ensure that the speech interests of parodists would not be impaired or suppressed for the sake or under the pretext of copyright protection.

C. Money Damages in Place of Injunctions

Various scholars note that where courts find that the works will likely displace the original works, instead of issuing injunctions, they should limit remedies to damages in cases involving speech interests, and grant injunctions only where there is strong reason to believe that damages would be inadequate.[265] This would also substantially eliminate prior restraint concerns, currently at issue whenever courts issue preliminary injunctions in copyright cases. Although the prospect of money damages may chill free speech, granting injunctions only where damages are likely inadequate can avoid the outright banning of expressions.[266]

When the Ninth Circuit in *Dr. Seuss Enterprises, L.P.* and the District Court in *Colting* determined that the defendants' works would likely harm the markets of the originals, they should have recognized the values of the works and therefore ordered damages to be paid. By affirming the District Court's order to grant a preliminary injunction prohibiting the publication and distribution of *The Cat NOT in the Hat!*, the Ninth Circuit suppressed the commentary on O. J. Simpson's trial. In *Colting*, the District Court granted Salinger's motion for a preliminary injunction. The Second Circuit vacated the order and remanded the case to the District Court to apply the correct equitable standard for an injunction, according to which the plaintiff must establish that "it has suffered an irreparable injury," that "remedies available at law, such as monetary damages, are inadequate to compensate for that injury," that, "considering the balance of hardships between the plaintiff and defendant, a remedy in equity is warranted," and that "the public interest would not be disserved by a permanent injunction."[267]

---

[265] Liu, *supra* note 165, at 116; *citing* Jed Rubenfeld, *The Freedom Of Imagination: Copyright's Constitutionality*, 112 YALE L.J. 1 (2002); Mark A. Lemley & Eugene Volokh, *Freedom Of Speech And Injunctions In Intellectual Property Cases*, 48 DUKE L.J. 147, 211 (1998); and Tiffany D. Trunko, *Note, Remedies for Copyright Infringement: Respecting the First Amendment*, 89 COLUM. L. REV. 1940 (1989).

[266] Jonathan Fox argues that the copyright-holder and the parodist would be incentivized to work out a licensing arrangement if an injunction is unavailable. If a copyright-holder decides to seek an injunction under the new damages-are-adequate standard and he fails, the parodist would be able to publish the parody and not compensate the copyright-holder. Jonathan M. Fox, *The Fair Use Parody Defense and How to Improve It*, 45 IDEA: INTELL. PROP. L. REV. 617, 646 (2006).

[267] Salinger, 607 F.3d at 77. The Second Circuit followed the Supreme Court's decision in Ebay v. MercExchange, L.L.C., which overruled the longstanding precedent by holding that a patentee is not entitled to a permanent injunction against a patent infringer: "the decision to grant or deny

Colting nevertheless settled with Salinger's estate in 2011, perhaps due to his fear that the plaintiff would take the case to the Supreme Court, and/or the amount of monetary damages would be huge. As per agreement, he must not publish or otherwise distribute his book, its electronic version, or any other editions in the United States or Canada until *Catcher* enters the public domain, although he would be free to sell the book in other international territories.[268] Despite the Second Circuit's decision to vacate the District Court's order of injunction, this settlement meant that the market places, at least those of the United States and Canada, have been deprived of Colting's interesting commentary on both the novel and Salinger the author.

* * *

This chapter has studied the parody/satire dichotomy in American copyright law and how a broadened parody defense would help to bring the American copyright jurisprudence more in line with its free speech tradition. The next chapter will explain why the parody and satire fair dealing exceptions in Canadian copyright law may lead to a potential parody/satire dichotomy and the suppression of expressions falling within the latter category. Hence, compared with the dual exceptions, a broad parody exception would better accommodate the user's right to freedom of expression.

permanent injunctive relief is an act of equitable discretion by the district court, reviewable on appeal for abuse of discretion." eBay Inc. v. MercExchange, L.L.C., 547 U.S. 388, 391 (2006).

[268] Andrew Albanese, *J.D. Salinger Estate, Swedish Author Settle Copyright Suit*, Publishers Weekly (Jan. 11, 2011), www.publishersweekly.com/pw/by-topic/industry-news/publisher-news/article/45738-j-d-salinger-estate-swedish-author-settle-copyright-suit.html (last visited Oct. 10, 2017).

4

Canada's Potential Parody/Satire Dichotomy

"Hey. Everyone's different," says Derek.
"But some are more different than others," says Budge, and they all laugh.[1]

In Canada, the right to freedom of expression is a natural right recognized and safeguarded by the Charter of Rights and Freedoms. The right to parody stems from this natural right. Although the parody and satire categories in the fair dealing provisions of the Copyright Modernization Act 2012 seem to offer broad protection of parodic works, they may create a parody/satire dichotomy, driven by judicial globalization and the meaning of "satire." Accordingly, courts may be less inclined to treat works falling within the satire category as fair dealings, even though they would not compete with the originals or harm their rights-holders' interests. A broad parody exception would serve to bring Canada's copyright system more in line with its freedom of expression jurisprudence.

After discussing the history of freedom of expression and the tradition of parody in Canada, this chapter will review the lack of recognition of a parody defense in Canadian statutes and case law prior to 2012, and explain why the parody and satire exceptions may result in the suppression of expressions falling within the satire category. First, the liberalization of fair dealing by the Copyright Pentalogy in 2012 does not in fact apply to parody cases. Second, the new exceptions may lead to a dichotomy in which satire becomes an inferior category, due to the potential influence(s) of American law and/or the meaning of the word "satire." Although works categorized as satire will pass the first step of the fair dealing analysis, courts may be less inclined to hold that works that do not direct part of their criticism or commentary towards the originals pass the second-stage fairness analysis. A broad parody exception substituting for the dual categories would reduce the potential influence of a propertized conception of fair dealing and possible bias against satire, thus helping courts to properly balance the interests of rights-holders with those of users. Whether narrowly or broadly defined, parodies will likely survive moral rights challenges.

[1] Margaret Atwood, The Heart Goes Last: A Novel 230 (2015).

This chapter will then examine how Canadian courts would be able to overcome the hurdles of applying the Charter to the parody exception to align Canada's copyright system with its freedom of expression tradition and to safeguard the right to parody. A broadened parody exception might create circumstances of "genuine ambiguity," which then would entitle courts to apply the exception by engaging with the Charter to balance the parodists' freedom of expression with the Copyright Act's objectives. Considering the extensive use of the *Salinger* decision in America in the last chapter and a lack of relevant case law in Canada, the last section will employ two hypotheses inspired by *Salinger* to illuminate how courts may engage with the Charter to apply a broadened parody exception.

I. FREEDOM OF EXPRESSION AND THE RIGHT TO PARODY IN CANADA

Like the United States, Canada has upheld freedom of expression as a central value of liberal democracy.[2] Under s. 2(b) of the Canadian Charter of Rights and Freedoms (1982) ("the Charter"), which applies to both the national and provincial governments, everyone has the fundamental freedoms of "thought, belief, opinion and expression, including freedom of the press and other media of communication."[3] Other related freedoms are "freedom of conscience and religion," "freedom of peaceful assembly," and "freedom of association."[4] Section 1 of the Charter provides that these fundamental freedoms are subject "to such reasonable limits prescribed by law as can be demonstrably justified in a free and democratic society."[5] Section 33(1) further provides that Parliament or a provincial legislature may adopt legislation "notwithstanding" the protections of s. 2, by making an express declaration that its action complies with s. 1.[6]

The English common law, being the origin of the Canadian Constitution and free speech tradition, is not especially sympathetic to free speech claimants.[7] Hence, s. 2(b) of the Charter is considered to have brought a fundamental change to the constitutional landscape regarding freedom of expression.[8] The influences of natural law on this freedom are apparent in both the Charter and the Supreme Court of

---

[2] Peter Greenawalt, *Free Speech in the United States and Canada*, 55 L. & CONTEMP. PROBS. 1, 5 (1992).
[3] Canadian Charter of Rights and Freedoms, s. 2(b), Pt. I of Constitution Act, 1982, Sch. B to the Canada Act 1982 (U.K.), 1982, c. 11.
[4] *Id*. s. 2(a)(c)(d).
[5] *Id*. s. 1. R. v. Oakes [1986] 24 C.C.C. (3d) 321, 348 (S.C.C.) established the standard two-prong approach for s. 1 analysis, according to which the state's objective must be of "pressing and substantial concern in a free and democratic society" and the impugned measure must meet a proportionality test.
[6] *Id*. s. 33(1). Although s. 33 in theory authorizes direct legislative overrides of charter rights, Parliament has never invoked this power and provincial legislatures have been equally reluctant to override charter rights. RONALD J. KROTOSZYNSKI, JR., THE FIRST AMENDMENT IN CROSS-CULTURAL PERSPECTIVE: A COMPARATIVE LEGAL ANALYSIS OF THE FREEDOM OF SPEECH 38 (2006).
[7] Kent Roach & David Schneiderman, *Freedom of Expression in Canada*, 61 S. CT. L. REV. 429, 431–32 (2013).
[8] *Id*. at 429; Greenawalt, *supra* note 2, at 6.

Canada's (SCC) decisions. The Preamble of the Charter states that "Canada is founded upon principles that recognize the supremacy of God and the rule of law," while the Charter was inspired by international human rights documents such as the Universal Declaration of Human Rights (UDHR).[9] Like Locke and Rawls, the SCC justified the protection of freedom of expression by describing it as an essential component of democratic self-government.[10] In addition, its endorsement of "the pursuit of truth," "self-fulfillment and human flourishing" as important social values that justify the protection of freedom of expression,[11] as well as a "marketplace of ideas" theory of free speech,[12] are reminiscent of Locke, Kant, and Milton. Further, the SCC described freedom of expression as "the matrix, the indispensable condition of nearly every other freedom."[13] It guarantees that expressive activities constituting speech are "infinite in variety," including "the written or spoken word, the arts, and even physical gestures or acts," and that "all expressions of the heart and mind, however unpopular, distasteful or contrary to the mainstream" are deserving of Charter protection.[14]

Freedom of expression was subject to numerous restrictions in the pre-Charter era for the sake of national security, public morality, and the protection of reputations of individuals. A good example was the sedition law from 1919 to 1936, drafted in response to the general labor unrest in the nation, and based upon the War Measures Act of 1914 that gave broad powers to the federal government to maintain security and order during war or insurrection.[15] This draconian law, long-since repealed, was later replaced by laws criminalizing seditious libel, conspiracy, and intention.[16] Other speech restrictions include prohibitions on obscenity and defamation. The statutory offence of obscene speech first appeared in the 1892

---

9   Chief Justice Dickson, in *Reference Re Public Service Employees Relations Act (Alberta)*, commented that international instruments should be persuasive sources for interpretation and observed that the "Charter conforms to the spirit of the contemporary international human rights movement." [1987] 38 D.L.R. (4th) 161, 182 (S.C.C.).

10   In Dolphin Delivery Ltd. v. R.W.D.S.U., Local 580, Justice McIntyre, writing for the majority, held that "Representative democracy . . . which is in great part the product of free expression and discussion of varying ideas, depends upon its maintenance and protection . . . The principle of freedom of speech and expression has been firmly accepted as a necessary feature of modern democracy." [1986] 33 D.L. R. (4th) 174, 176 (S.C.C.).

11   See the majority opinion in Irwin Toy Ltd. v. Quebec (Attorney General) [1989] 25 C.P.R. (3d) 417 (S. C.C.).

12   The SCC in *R. v. Keegstra* valued the fostering of a vibrant and creative society by the "marketplace of ideas," although, as Krotoszynski rightly notes, this theory was also endorsed in *Erwin Toy*, in which the majority opinion stated that freedom of expression facilitates the "pursuit of truth." R. v. Keegstra [1990] 61 C.C.C. (3d) 1, 78 (S.C.C.); Irwin Toy Ltd., 25 C.P.R. (3d) at 452; KROTOSZYNSKI, *supra* note 6, at 36.

13   R. v. Sharpe [2001] 150 C.C.C. (3d) 321, 342 (S.C.C.).

14   Irwin Toy Ltd., 25 C.P.R. (3d) at 446; *see, e.g.*, Roach & Schneiderman, *supra* note 7, at 429; KROTOSZYNSKI, *supra* note 6, at 19, 33.

15   E.g., *Section 98 Criminal Code*, THE CANADIAN ENCYCLOPEDIA, www.thecanadianencyclopedia.ca/en/article/section-98-criminal-code/ (last visited Oct. 10, 2017).

16   Criminal Code, S.C. 1985, c. C-46.

Criminal Code.[17] In applying this statute, courts adopted the English common law *Hicklin* test, a product of Victorian religious morals and class prejudices.[18] Also under the common law, defamatory statements, whether they target public figures or private individuals, are presumed to be false and malicious and no further proof of harm needs to be shown.[19] Because publishers of defamatory utterances bore the burden of proving their truthfulness or showing that these utterances fell within a limited range of privileged statements, public officials and famous people used defamation law as a means of curbing messages that would impair their reputations.[20]

What reasonable limits are justified in a free, democratic society in the post-Charter era? The War Measures Act was replaced by the Emergencies Act of 1988, which makes no mention of censorship, while the priority given to freedom of expression has made treason and seditious conspiracy charges difficult to sustain.[21] The Anti-terrorism Act, introduced in 2001 in the wake of terrorist attacks on the United States, survived Charter challenge on the ground that violence or threats of violence fall outside the s. 2(b) guarantee.[22] Nonetheless, it was sparingly used.[23] Meanwhile, laws on obscenity and defamation have also become much more speech-friendly. Criminal Code amendments were made in 1959 to introduce a new definition of obscenity that concerns the "undue exploitation of sex or of sex and other characteristics,"[24] and the SCC developed a "community standards of decency" test for obscenity in 1962.[25] Because artistic freedom lies "at the heart of freedom of expression values," the SCC later held that materials offending community standards but containing artistic or literary merits could be excused from criminal prohibition.[26] Concerning defamation law, although the SCC rejected importing into

---

[17] Roach & Schneiderman, *supra* note 7, at 453.
[18] *Id.*
[19] *Id.* at 510.
[20] *Id.*
[21] Barry Cooper, *The Bureaucratization of Treason*, C2C JOURNAL (Mar. 10, 2010), www.c2cjournal.ca/2010/03/whatever-happened-to-treason/ (last visited Oct. 10, 2017), *citing* Carl F. Stychin, *A Postmodern Constitutionalism: Equality Rights, Identity Politics and the Canadian National Imagination*, 17 DAL. L.J. JOURNAL 61, 62 (1994). Stychin argues that "Canadian" has become "an identity open to resignification and intersection through an ever-changing variety of perspectives engaged in a dialogue guaranteed by the Charter." *Id.* at 62.
[22] R. v. Khawaja [2012] 90 C.C.C. (3d) 361, 374–75 (S.C.C.).
[23] Roach & Schneiderman, *supra* note 7, at 499.
[24] *Id.* at 453.
[25] Brody et al. v. The Queen [1962] 32 D.L.R. (2d) 507, 531 (S.C.C.).
[26] In R. v. Butler [1992] 70 C.R.R. (3d) 129, 146, 148–49 (S.C.C.), the SCC held that materials offending community standards are not obscene so long as they satisfy the "internal necessities" or artistic defense test, which requires assessing the materials to determine whether the exploitation of sex is internally necessary to a plot or theme, and does not merely represent "dirt for dirt's sake." In R. v. Sharpe [2001] 150 C.C.C. at 355 (3d), a child pornography case, Justice McLachlin broadened the artistic defense to include all expressions "reasonably viewed as art," not merely those internally necessary to the literary or artistic purpose.

Canadian law the U.S. rule in *New York Times v. Sullivan*,[27] it reasoned that strict liability could be used as "a weapon by which the wealthy and privileged stifle the information and debate essential to a free society."[28] Hence, it established a new defense of responsible communication, available to the defendant in cases where the publication was "on a matter of public interest" and the defendant was "responsible, in that he or she was diligent in trying to verify the allegation(s), having regard to all relevant circumstances."[29]

One thing that distinguishes the Canadian freedom of expression jurisprudence from its American counterpart is its prohibition of hate speech in both pre- and post-Charter eras. Protected by the First Amendment of the U.S. Constitution, hate speech has been prohibited by Canadian criminal law for five decades.[30] The Charter endorses multiculturalism and states that its provisions, including s. 2(b), "shall be interpreted in a manner consistent with the preservation and enhancement of the multicultural heritage of Canadians."[31] The SCC ruled that the guarantee of freedom of expression by the Charter does not extend to "the public and willful promotion of hatred against an identifiable group."[32] In addition, the repeal of the section of the Canadian Human Rights Act prohibiting "hate messages" did not prevent the SCC from reiterating support for provincial human rights code prohibitions on hate speech.[33] Nonetheless, the deliberate publication of statements that

---

[27] The SCC stated that the common law of defamation is not "unduly restrictive or inhibiting" and "complies with the underlying value of the Charter and there is no need to amend or alter it." Hill v. The Church of Scientology a/Toronto [1995] 2 S.C.R. 1130, 1187–88 (S.C.C.).

[28] Grant v. Torstar Corp. [2009] 79 C.P.R. (4th) 407, 424 (S.C.C.).

[29] *Id.* at 441. Chief Justice McLachlin determined that matters of public interest included all variety of subjects in which the public would have "a genuine stake" and which would encourage "wide-ranging public debate." *Id.* at 442.

[30] Criminal Code, S.C. 1985, c. C-46, s. 319 (1) & (2). Parliament followed the Cohen Committee's recommendations by criminalizing the wilful promotion, other than in a private conversation, of racial hatred against certain identifiable groups. Defenses to provide latitude for freedom of expression include truth, reasonable belief in the truth of a matter of public interest, commentary in good faith opinion upon a religious subject, and good faith identification of matters tending to produce feelings of hatred. Furthermore, charges could not be laid without the provincial Attorney General's consent. Roach & Schneiderman, *supra* note 7, at 462.

[31] Canadian Charter, s. 27.

[32] Keegstra, 61 C.C.C. (3d) at 3, 5.

[33] In *Canada (Human Rights Commission) v. Taylor* [1990] 75 D.L.R. (4th) 577, 601 (S.C.C.), Justice Dickson defined "hatred" for the purposes of human rights legislation as referring to "unusually strong and deep-felt emotions of detestation, calumny, and vilification." The speech restriction in the Canadian Human Rights Act was reasonable as it placed its emphasis on the discriminatory effects of hate speech on minorities. *Id.* at 609. In *Saskatchewan (Human Rights Commission) v. Whatcott* [2013] 355 D.L.R. (4th) 383, 414–16 (S.C.C.), Justice Rothstein reaffirmed each of the principal holdings of the Saskatchewan human rights tribunal's holding and Justice Dickson's majority opinion in *Taylor*. It found that the hate speech provision in the Saskatchewan Human Rights Code minimally impaired the impugned right to freedom of expression, but severed the words "ridicules, belittles or otherwise affronts the dignity of" from the Code because such expression was not rationally connected to the objective of reducing systemic discrimination. –

the speaker knows to be false and that might excite prejudices in the recipients is a protected form of expression under s. 2(b).[34]

The Canadian history of censorship has evolved with its freedom of expression jurisprudence.[35] Aside from more extreme forms of censorship imposed during times of war and emergency through the War Measures Act,[36] the Customs Act of 1847 first prohibited the importation of "books and drawings of an immoral or indecent character," conferring power on customs officials to seize materials they deemed to be of such character.[37] Since the SCC liberalized and modernized the obscenity law by developing the "community standards of decency" test and by allowing experts to testify on the merits of impugned literature, barefaced attempts to censor speech have been rare.[38] Limitations on literary expressions have become more difficult to justify in the post-Charter era. Yet customs officials have continued to confiscate materials under the Customs Act, and gay- and lesbian-themed non-obscene materials have been unfairly targeted.[39]

Undoubtedly, parodies that do not pose a threat to national security, contain obscene/defamatory materials, or promote hatred against identifiable groups would not likely be censored in Canada. In fact, parody has contributed significantly to the Canadian literary and cultural scenes since the early nineteenth century.[40] Writers such as Stephen Leacock and Paul Hiber used the parodic form to quest for a cultural identity related to but distinct from those of the old colonial

---

34 In *R. v. Zundel* [1992] 75 C.C.C. (3d) 449, 507 (S.C.C.), Justice McLachlin opined that the fact that the particular content of a person's speech might "excite popular prejudice" is "no reason to deny it protection." "[I]f there is any principle of the Constitution that more imperatively calls for attachment than any other it is the principle of free thought – not free for those who agree with us but freedom for the thought that we hate."

35 Pearce J. Carefoote contends that the banning of Molière's *Tartuffe* in 1694 by Comte de Frontenac, Governor of Québec on the local bishop's advice signaled the birth of censorship. Pearce J. Carefoote, *Censorship in Canada, Historical Perspectives on Canadian Publishing*, HISTORICAL PERSPECTIVES ON CANADIAN PUBLISHING, http://digitalrussell.mcmaster.ca/hpcanpub/case-study/censorship-canada (last visited Oct. 10, 2017).

36 *Id.*

37 Bruce Ryder, *Undercover Censorship: Exploring the History of the Regulation of Publications in Canada*, IN *Interpreting Censorship in Canada* 132 (Allan C. Hutchinson & Klaus Petersen, eds. 2007).

38 In the 1960s, provinces sported their own censorship boards – most of which were later renamed as "classification" boards – which worked to keep undesirable films out of the marketplace. *Censorship*, CANADA'S HUMAN RIGHTS HISTORY, http://historyofrights.ca/encyclopaedia/main-events/censorship/ (last visited Oct. 10, 2017); Carefoote, *supra* note 35.

39 In 1990, Jane Rule's *The Young in One Another's Arms* was seized for obscenity while en route to Little Sisters bookstore. In *Little Sisters Book and Art Emporium v. Canada*, the SCC finally upheld the right of Canada Customs to inspect and seize "obscene" materials, but also criticized them for focusing on materials with gay themes, particularly those imported by gay and lesbian bookstores. Little Sisters Book and Art Emporium v. Canada (Minister of Justice) [2000] 2 S.C.R. 1120, para. 267; *see* Carefoote, *supra* note 35.

40 WILLIAM H. NEW, ENCYCLOPEDIA OF LITERATURE IN CANADA 866 (2002); *Humorous Writing in English*, THE CANADIAN ENCYCLOPEDIA, www.thecanadianencyclopedia.ca/en/article/humorous-writing-in-english (last accessed Oct. 10, 2017).

world.[41] Much more recently, Margaret Atwood used parodies to inquire into issues such as feminism.[42] Unsurprisingly, minorities – Chinese Canadians and First Nations people – have continued to voice their discontents through parodying the Dominion Day (the former name of Canada Day) and the national anthem, respectively.[43] Recently, a Vancouver comedy duo created a fake parodic campaign video announcing Canada's candidacy for President of the United States, after their first parodic video in the 2012 American Presidential Election.[44] Whether as a weapon of critique or a tool of identity construction, parody is vital to freedom of expression. One would imagine that should parodic works get censored or banned for containing unpopular messages, or get seized at the border for similar reasons, organizations involved in anti-censorship advocacies and other activities would rightfully intervene on behalf of their authors.[45]

II. THE RIGHT TO PARODY IN CANADIAN COPYRIGHT LAW

Copyright has posed another hurdle to Canadians' quest for freedom of expression.[46] The lack of a parody exception in copyright law or a proper definition of "parody" by statutes or by courts curtails the right to parody. The Copyright Act of 1921,[47] which came into force in 1924, defined copyright as "the sole right to produce or reproduce the work or any substantial part thereof in any material form whatsoever, to perform, or in the case of a lecture to deliver, the work or any substantial part thereof in public … "[48] Section 16(1)(i), which duplicated s. 2(1)(i) of the Copyright Act 1911 of the United Kingdom, provided that "[a]ny fair dealing with any work for the

---

[41] New, *supra* 40, at 867.

[42] *Id.*

[43] *See, e.g.,* *Humiliation Day*, The Long Voyage: From the Pigtails and Coolies to the New Canadian Mosaic, http://access-cht.ca/chinese-history/fight-for-rights/humiliation-day/?lang=en (last visited Oct. 10, 2017); Connie Walker, *"Oh Kanata!" Video a Twist on Canadian National Anthem*, CBC News (Mar. 18, 2014), www.cbc.ca/news/aboriginal/oh-kanata-video-a-twist-on-cana dian-national-anthem-1.2577697 (last visited Oct. 10, 2017).

[44] *E.g.,* Lauren Sundstrom, *Hilarious Parody Video Wants Canada to Run for U.S. President*, Vancity Buzz (Jan. 28, 2016), www.vancitybuzz.com/2016/01/canada-run-for-us-president-video/ (last visited Oct. 10, 2017).

[45] PEN Canada, established in 1921, campaigns on behalf of writers who are persecuted, imprisoned, or exiled for exercising their freedom of expression. The Writers' Union of Canada, established in 1973, advocates on behalf of published authors, the most notable example being its fight against Bill C-54, an "anti-pornography" measure that threatened literary expression, in 1987. The Freedom of Expression Committee of the Book and Periodical Council was established in the wake of a 1978 attack upon Alice Munro's *Lives of Girls and Women*. Carefoote, *supra* note 35.

[46] David Fewer, *Constitutionalizing Copyright: Freedom of Expression and the Limits of Copyright in Canada*, 55 U. T. Fac. L. Rev. 175, 198 (1997).

[47] Canada's first Copyright Act of 1868 came into force after Canadian Confederation in 1867. Sara Bannerman, *Copyright: Characteristics of Canadian Reform*, in Canadian Copyright and the Digital Agenda: From Radical Extremism to Balanced Copyright 18 (Michael Geist, ed. 2010).

[48] Copyright Act, S.C. 1921, c. 24, s. 3(1).

purposes of private study, research, criticism, review, or newspaper summary"
shall not constitute an infringement of copyright.[49] The fair dealing provisions
were reformed first, by the North American Free Trade Agreement
Implementation Act, 1993, s. 64(1), and second, by An Act to Amend the
Copyright Act, 1997, s. 18.[50] Yet the fair dealing provisions of the Copyright
Act of 1997, encoded in its s. 29–29.2, only contain exceptions for the purposes
of research, private study, criticism, review, and news reporting.[51] It was the
Copyright Modernization Act of 2012 which introduced fair dealing categories
in the form of "parody" and "satire."

A. Parody in Canadian Case Law Prior to the 2012 Reform

Not only did Canada's previous copyright statutes fail to provide for a parody
exception, but Canadian courts also did not consider parody to be a defense to
copyright infringement in enforcing these statutes before 2012. As the following
judicial decisions show, this happened regardless of whether the defendants raised
a parody defense or relied upon other theories to appropriate copyrighted works for
their own purposes, whether the parodic works targeted the originals or something
else, or whether these works served commercial or non-commercial purposes.
Indications by courts that parody might serve as a defense to infringement in some
circumstances were very indirect.

In *Ludlow Music Inc. v. Canint Music Corp.* (1967), the first Canadian case
addressing parody and copyright infringement, the defendant parodied
American singer-songwriter Woody Guthrie's song "This Land is Your Land"
by crafting new lyrics to the old tune to "gently chide … the Canadian
Government and the Canadian people for their alleged feelings of inferiority"
and retitling the song as "This Land Is Whose Land."[52] The song was released
in the year of Canada's centennial.[53] Ludlow Music Inc., unimpressed with the
parody, alleged that "the use of words" were "in bad taste and insulting to the
Canadian public," and that it would "cause incalculable damage to the
Plaintiff and destroy the meaning and acceptance of the song in the minds
of the Canadian."[54] The Exchequer Court of Canada determined that the law
did not authorize the defendants to reproduce the tune of the song even

---

[49] *Id.* s. 16(1)(i).
[50] Giuseppina D'Agostino, Healing Fair Dealing? *A Comparative Copyright Analysis of Canadian Fair
      Dealing to UK Fair Dealing and US Fair Use,* 53 McGILL L.J. 309, 318 (2007).
[51] Copyright Act, S.C. 1985, c. C-42, s. 29.1–2.
[52] Ludlow Music Inc. v. Canint Music Corp. [1967] 51 C.P.R. 278, 290–91 (Ex. Ct.).
[53] *Id.* at 283.
[54] *Id.* In 1959, Ludlow Music Inc. had licensed Guthrie's work for adaptation and distribution in Canada
      via revisions prepared and performed by the Travellers. Ludlow Music Inc. held the rights for this
      authorized Canadian version and the song was to play a prominent part in the centennial celebrations
      of 1967. *Id.*

though the words were substantially different from those of the original.[55] Thus, it granted an injunction restraining the defendants from further sales of the album, deeming it a "proper exercise of judicial discretion to protect property rights against encroachment that has no apparent justification, and, in particular, to protect copyright against what appears to be piracy."[56]

In *MCA Canada Ltd. (Ltée) v. Gillberry & Hawke Advertising Agency Ltd.* (1976), the question of whether a parody constitutes copyright infringement was again addressed by the court. The defendant advertising agency created a parody of the words of the musical work "Downtown," composed by Tony Hatch and made famous by Petula Clark, to its original tune.[57] This time, the purpose was solely commercial: to "extoll . . . the merits of Lewis Mercury, a car dealership located in downtown Ottawa."[58] Justice Dubé of the Federal Court of Canada granted an injunction restraining the defendant from further infringement of "Downtown," and awarded the plaintiff infringement, punitive and exemplary damages.[59]

The court next addressed parody and copyright infringement in *ATV Music Publishing of Canada Ltd. v. Rogers Radio Broadcasting Ltd. et al.*, a 1982 case highly similar to *Ludlow Music Inc.* Here, the defendants made a parody of "Revolution," a Beatles song composed by John Lennon and Paul McCartney, in order to offer as a "commentary on the events preceding the proclamation of the Constitution Act."[60] Justice Van Camp of the Ontario High Court of Justice granted a motion for an interlocutory injunction preventing the defendants from infringing ATV Music Publishing of Canada Ltd.'s copyright.[61] It held that "irreparable harm" must ensue to the plaintiff when the music of a song so well-known was used with other words: "[i]t would be difficult ever again to listen to the original song without the words of the new song intruding."[62]

In *Canadian Tire Corp. v. Retail Clerks Union, Local 1518* (1985), the defendant union, during a strike against a franchisee of the plaintiff which operated a Canadian Tire store, used leaflets with a Canadian Tire logo overlaid with a diagonal line in the manner of international traffic signs indicating "do not enter."[63] The court held

55   The court determined that "Section 2(v) of the Copyright Act recognizes that a musical work may be 'with or without words.'" In addition, "the plaintiff has copyright in the song 'This Land is Your Land' – being the words of the song and the tune of the song considered as a single work." *Id.* at 298.
56   *Id.* at 299.
57   MCA Canada Ltd. (Ltée) v. Gillberry & Hawke Advertising Agency Ltd. [1976] 28 C.P.R. (2d) 52, 54 (F.C.T.D.).
58   *Id.* at 53.
59   *Id.* at 56–57.
60   Graham Reynolds, *Necessarily Critical: The Adoption of a Parody Defence to Copyright Infringement in Canada*, 33 Manitoba L.J. 243, 248 (2009), citing James Zegers, *Parody and Fair Use in Canada after Campbell v. Acuff-Rose*, 11 C.I.P.R. 205, 208 (1994).
61   ATV Music Publ'g. of Canada Ltd. v. Rogers Radio Broad. Ltd. et al [1982] 65 C.P.R. (2d) 109, 115 (Ont. S.C.).
62   *Id.* at 114.
63   Canadian Tire Corp. v. Retail Clerks Union, Local 1518 [1985] 7 C.P.R. (3d) 415, 416–17 (F.C.).

that the defendants were not allowed to use the logo without the permission of the copyright-holder, even if such a use entailed no commercial or financial interest.[64] In *Rotisseries St.-Hubert v. Le Syndicat des Travailleurs* (1986), the defendant union used a parody of the plaintiff's company logo on pamphlets, stickers, and buttons during a labor dispute with the company.[65] In this case, the court directly addressed the legality of parodying copyrighted works.[66] It determined that the reproduction of a substantial part of the protected work constituted a "parody" which, though falling within the scope of s. 2(b), entitled the plaintiff to relief from copyright infringement because the defendants could have expressed their grievances through other means.[67]

The fair-dealing defense was not raised in the foregoing cases. The defendants in *Ludlow Music Ltd.* and *ATV Music Publishing of Canada Ltd.* used a compulsory license defense in their arguments, whereas the defendant in *MCA* alleged that he could not identify the owner of the copyrighted work.[68] The defendants in *Canadian Tire Corp. Ltd.*, on the other hand, claimed a right to freedom of opinion through the design and a freedom to convey information through the logo respectively.[69] In *Rotisseries St.-Hubert Ltee*, the defendants relied upon both s. 2(b) of the Charter and s. 3 of the Charter of Human Rights and Freedoms (Quebec).[70] It was not until 1997 that the Federal Court addressed the issue of whether the fair dealing defense protects parody in *Compagnie Générale des Établissements Michelin-Michelin & Cie v. C.A.W.-Canada et al.*

In a union organizing campaign at CGEM Michelin Canada's Nova Scotia plants, C.A.W. distributed leaflets depicting CGEM Michelin's corporate logo, "a beaming marshmallow-like rotund figure composed of tires" called the Michelin Tire Man (or Bibendum):

> broadly smiling ... arms crossed, with his foot raised, seemingly ready to crush underfoot an unsuspecting Michelin worker. In the same leaflet, another worker safely out of the reach of "Bibendum's" looming foot has raised a finger of warning and informs his blithe colleague, "Bob, you better move before he squashes you". Bob, the worker in imminent danger of "Bibendum's" boot has apparently resisted

[64] *Id.* at 418–21.
[65] Rotisseries St.-Hubert v. Le Syndicat des Travailleurs [1986] 17 C.P.R. (3d) 461, 464–65 (Que. S.C.).
[66] *See id.* at 471–77.
[67] *Id.*
[68] Reynolds cites James Zegers to emphasize that in *Ludlow Music* and *ATV Music*, the compulsory license defense was used. Zeger said: "[u]nder subs. 19(1) of the Act it was not a breach of copyright in a musical recording to make a record of that work provided that records had previously made with the copyright owner's consent and provided that proper notice was given to the owner. s. 19(2) limited s. 19 (1) by prohibiting alteration to copyrighted works recorded pursuant to 19(1) unless the alteration was authorized by the owner. Essentially, s. 19 granted, under certain conditions, a license to make recordings of copyrighted work without the copyright owner's permission." Reynolds, *supra* note 60, at 248 (2009), *citing* Zegers, *supra* note 60, at 208.
[69] *Canadian Tire Corp.*, 7 C.P.R. (3d) at 420.
[70] *Rotisseries St.-Hubert Ltee*, 17 C.P.R. (3d) at 463.

the blandishments of the union since a caption coming from his mouth reads, "Naw, I'm going to wait and see what happens". Below the roughly drawn figures of the workers is the following plea in bold letters, "Don't wait until it's too late! Because the job you save may be your own. Sign today for a better tomorrow."[71]

In response to the plaintiff's copyright and trademark infringements allegations, the defendants argued that their version of Bibendum was a parody: although Canadian Copyright Act does not contain an explicit parody defense to copyright infringement, the category of "criticism" under the fair dealing defense should be interpreted in such a manner that would encompass parody.[72] Justice Teitelbaum of the Federal Court (Trial Division) rejected the union's argument as a "radical interpretation" of the Copyright Act, which would be "creating a new exception to . . . copyright infringement, a step that only Parliament [has] the jurisdiction to do."[73] In addition, he described the logo as "private property," which "cannot be used as a *location* or forum for expression."[74] By substantially reproducing the "Bibendum" design on their union campaign leaflets and posters, the defendants infringed plaintiff's copyrights.[75]

Nevertheless, in two cases that followed the *Michelin* decision, the courts seemed to accept the proposition that parody could serve as a defense to copyright infringement in certain circumstances. One was *Productions Avanti Ciné Vidéo Inc. v. Favreau et al.* (1999), which concerns a television series entitled "La petite vie," a "highly original and very well-known situation comedy" and "probably the most popular series in the history of Quebec television."[76] Copyright owners of the series alleged that Favreau infringed their copyright by producing a pornographic film entitled "La petite vite."[77] The Quebec Court of Appeal concluded that the defense of fair dealing does not lie where the parody is "really the appropriation or use of that work solely to capitalize on or 'cash in' on its originality and popularity."[78] In *British Columbia Automobile Assn. v. O.P.E.I.U., Local 378* (2001), the BC Automobile Association sued its office union for passing off, trademark violation, and breach of copyright by creating a website similar to the Association's and using the Association's trademarks in its domain name and meta tags.[79] Although the union claimed that it copied elements of the website in order to "criticize," the court held that such copying did not constitute fair dealing because the union website did not contain any criticism of the Association's and did not mention its source and

---

[71] Compagnie Générale des Établissements Michelin-Michelin & Cie v. C.A.W.-Canada et al. [1997] 71 C.P.R. (3d) 348, 354 (F.C.).

[72] *Id.* at 377.

[73] *Id.* at 381.

[74] *Id.* at 388.

[75] *Id.* at 397.

[76] Productions Avanti Ciné Vidéo Inc. v. Favreau et al. [1999] 1 C.P.R. (4th) 129, 135 (Que. C.A.).

[77] *Id.*

[78] *Id.*

[79] B.C. Automobile Ass'n. v. O.P.E.I.U., Local 378 [2001] 10 C.P.R. (4th) 423, 429–30 (B.C. S.C.).

author.[80] While "parody" was nowhere mentioned, the court implied that an imitative work criticizing the object of its imitation could serve as a defense to copyright infringement.[81]

In 2002 and 2004, the SCC handed down two landmark decisions that affirmed the limited nature of authors' rights in their works, which need to be balanced against the public's interests in using them. The SCC in *Galerie d'Art du Petit Champlain inc. et al. v. Théberge* (2002), in interpreting the meaning of "reproduction" in the Copyright Act, held that it is important to recognize the creator's rights while "giving due weight to their limited nature."[82] Therefore, "[e]xcessive control by holders of copyrights and other forms of intellectual property may unduly limit the ability of the public domain to incorporate and embellish creative innovation in the long-term interests of society as a whole, or create practical obstacles to proper utilization."[83]

In 2004, the SCC in *CCH Canadian Ltd. v. Law Society of Upper Canada* dramatically shifted the way that copyright defenses should be interpreted. When a group of publishers sued the Law Society of Upper Canada for copyright infringement in providing photocopy services to researchers, the court unanimously held that the Law Society's practice fell within the bounds of fair dealing.[84] Prior to this case, defenses to copyright infringement were seen as limitations on the copyright-holder's exclusive rights and generally interpreted restrictively. Here, Chief Justice McLachlin emphasized the importance of balancing "the public interest in promoting the encouragement and dissemination of works of the arts and intellect and obtaining a just reward for the creator."[85] She clarified that "fair dealing" does not provide "simply a defense" to copyright infringement which removes liability, but instead defines the outer boundaries of copyright and is therefore a "user's right."[86] Citing Law Professor David Vaver, she further noted that "[i]n order to maintain the proper balance between the rights of a copyright owner and users' interests," "[b]oth owner rights and user rights should therefore be given the fair and balanced reading that befits remedial legislation."[87]

Despite these two decisions, a 2009 decision in British Columbia shows the pervasive influence of *Michelin*. In *Canwest Mediaworks Publications Inc. v. Horizon Publications Ltd.* (2008/09), a media company brought an action against the defendants for passing off, trademark infringement, and copyright infringement after they had created a parody edition of *Vancouver Sun* and dropped these mock

---

80   *Id.* at 474–75.
81   *See id.* at 475.
82   Galerie d'Art du Petit Champlain Inc. et al. v. Théberge [2002] 17 C.P.R. (4th) 161, 176 (S.C.C.).
83   *Id.*
84   CCH Canadian Ltd. v. L. Soc. of Upper Canada [2004] 30 C.P.R. (4th) 1 (S.C.C.).
85   *Id.* at 17.
86   *Id.* at 25.
87   *Id.*

copies in the *Vancouver Sun* vending machines.[88] This fake edition reproduced the masthead of the *Vancouver Sun* and contained articles criticizing Canwest newspapers' pro-Israel biases.[89] The plaintiff motioned to strike various elements from the defendants' statement of defense, including paragraphs arguing that parody is a defense to copyright infringement due to the fair dealing exception for criticism in s. 29.1.[90] The court allowed the motion and struck the paragraphs from the statement of claim, citing Justice Teitelbaum's opinion in *Michelin* that parody is not an exception to copyright infringement under the Copyright Act and does not constitute a defense.[91]

B. Calls for a Parody Exception

The need for a parody exception in Canadian copyright law had not escaped the attention of scholars. Writing in 1997, Fewer recognizes parody as an "ancient genre" with tremendous social values and a "time-tested example" of "transformative" and "critical" uses that "often involve authorial creativity and social critique encompassing values at the core of freedom of expression."[92] The narrow scope of the fair dealing defenses in the former Copyright Act fails to encompass the "full range of values" enshrined in freedom of expression.[93] Gendreau contends that copyright law's accommodation of a parody defense can be achieved by judicial action.[94] She attributes the reluctance of courts to apply the Charter to copyright law to the fact that the former is a public law instrument, while the latter is a private law matter, as well as their flawed opinion that copyright law already incorporates freedom of expression values through its internal mechanisms.[95]

Craig's endorsement of a parody defense stems from her belief in copyright's goal of encouraging communicative activities and social dialogues.[96] Courts, she argues, should not import ownership values derived from copyright into an examination of the defendant's communicative activity, "aggrandiz[ing] the respectability and righteousness of the owner while thoroughly undermining the speech interests and communicative efforts of the defendant: elevating property and diminishing speech."[97] She therefore criticizes the SCC for employing a physical analogue as

---

[88] Canwest Mediaworks Publications Inc. v. Horizon Publications Ltd. [2008] 2008 BCSC 1609, para. 1 (B.C.S.C.); [2009] 2009 BCSC 391, para. 2 (B.C.S.C.).

[89] *Id.* at paras. 3–4.

[90] *Id.* para. 1.

[91] *Id.* para. 14.

[92] Fewer, *supra* note 46, at 199–201.

[93] *Id.* at 184.

[94] Ysolde Gendreau, *Copyright and Freedom of Expression in Canada*, IN COPYRIGHT AND HUMAN RIGHTS 21–36 (Paul Torremans ed., 2004).

[95] *Id.* at 28–29, 31–33.

[96] See Carys J. Craig, *Putting the Community in Communication: Dissolving the Conflict between Freedom of Expression and Copyright*, 56 U. TORONTO L.J. 75 (2006).

[97] *Id.* at 85.

an analytic tool in *Michelin,* which "obviated the tangible and intangible divide between physical property and intellectual property," and avoided the appearance of imposing limits on defendants' expressive activities.[98] Her theoretical work, discussed in Part I of this book, does not address the scope of protection that should be accorded to parodic works. By stressing that the law should recognize different forms of copying as expressive activities and the relevance of community in the copyright system, she impliedly endorses a broad parody exception encompassing a wide range of works.[99]

Unlike others, Graham Reynolds lays out an elaborate proposal of a new parody fair dealing exception. He first cites Michael Spence, Margaret A. Rose, and Linda Hutcheon to endorse a broad definition of parody.[100] He also contends that parodies are not necessarily critical and should not be embedded within the "criticism" fair dealing category, which would deny protection to non-critical parodies.[101] He deems it uncertain whether courts would interpret the fair dealing category of criticism liberally to include parody after *CCH Canadian Ltd.,* in view of the court's reliance on *Michelin* to strike the argument that parody is a defense to infringement in *Canwest Mediaworks Publications.*[102] Thus, the Copyright Act should be reformed to include the sixth acceptable "parody" fair dealing category, joining research, private study, criticism, review, and news reporting.[103] This category should entitle individuals to use substantial amount of copyrighted materials without the consent of copyright owners for the purpose of parody, as long as their dealings pass the fairness analysis.[104]

C. The New Parody/Satire Exceptions in the Copyright Modernization Act

The Copyright Modernization Act expands the "fair dealing" doctrine by permitting the use of copyrighted materials to create a parody or satire, provided that the use is "fair."[105] According to the SCC in *CCH Canadian Ltd.,* whether a dealing is fair is a question of fact.[106] The court thus identified six non-exhaustive factors to determine whether a dealing is fair, which are: the purpose of the dealing, the character of the dealing, the amount of the dealing, alternatives to the dealing, the nature of the work, and the effect of the dealing on the work.[107] The new Act was passed only after repeated but failed attempts to reform the law over a period of six years from 2005 to

---

[98]   *Id.* at 92–94.
[99]   See 113–14; Carys J. Craig, *Reconstructing the Author-Self: Some Feminist Lessons for Copyright Law,* 15 J. GENDER, SOC. POL'Y & L. 207, 263–65 (2007).
[100]   Reynolds, *supra* note 60, at 244–46, 250–51.
[101]   *Id.* at 244.
[102]   *See id.* at 258–60.
[103]   *Id.* at 251.
[104]   *Id.* at 252–53.
[105]   Copyright Modernization Act, S.C. 2012, c. 20, s. 29.21.
[106]   CCH Canadian Ltd. [2004] 30 C.P.R. (4th) 1 (S.C.C.).
[107]   *Id.* at 26–29.

2011.[108] Its new "fair dealing" exceptions, lauded by artists and the public at large, seemed to answer the calls for a parody exception.[109]

The new exceptions have nonetheless sparked a mix of reaction – uncertainty, optimism, and skepticism – among lawyers and legal academics. As lawyer and scholar Bob Tarantino notes, in these two exceptions "lies the seed for what will be many years of speculation and debate as Canadian lawyers and potential litigants struggle with the contours of humour."[110] Although parody and satire are now categories of fair dealing, assessing when a given dealing is "fair" using the six factors outlined by the SSC in *CCH Canadian Ltd.* will remain challenging.

In a follow-up essay to his parody proposal, Reynolds is optimistic that the new Copyright Act will offer broad protection for parodies. Without addressing how "parody" and "satire" will be defined by courts, he contends that the two new categories, taken together, will be broad enough to encompass works that target originals as well as those commenting on something else.[111] In addition, the fact that "parody" and "satire" fall within the same section as research and private study in the fair dealing provisions means that they need not be "critical" and can include non-critical works.[112] Reynolds particularly lauds the new law for not requiring the parody to satisfy an "attribution" requirement, which could serve as an artificial barrier affecting its message and/or diminishing its overall impact.[113]

Reynolds' sentiment is mirrored by lawyer and critic Douglas Murray, who contends that because the new statute expressly includes "satire" as a purpose in its fair dealing provisions, Canadian courts will find it difficult to restrict its definition to indirect critiques of the original works while excluding those that target exclusively something else.[114] Andrei Mincov even considers the new law "dangerous" because its new "satire" exception could serve as "an excuse for virtually any unauthorized use of a work that has been modified into or merged with some other

---

[108]   Michael Geist, *Introduction, IN* FROM "RADICAL EXTREMISM" TO "BALANCED COPYRIGHT" 1 (Michael Geist ed., 2010); Peter Nowak, *Copyright Law Could Result in Police State: Critics,* CBC NEWS (June 12, 2008), www.cbc.ca/news/technology/copyright-law-could-result-in-police-state-critics-1.707544 (last visited Oct. 10, 2017).

[109]   *See* Grace Westcott, *The Freedom to Mock,* PEN CANADA (July 10, 2012), http://pencanada.ca/blog/the-freedom-to-mock/ (last visited Oct. 10, 2017).

[110]   Bob Tarantino, *Parody Defence Not Far Away,* Lexology (May 22, 2012), www.lexology.com/library/detail.aspx?g=8e21ff72-411d-473e-9ba8-20e5b1bf870e (last visited Oct. 10, 2017).

[111]   Graham Reynolds, *Parodists' Rights and Copyright in a Digital Canada, IN* DYNAMIC FAIR DEALING: CREATING CANADIAN DIGITAL CULTURE 249 (Darren S. Wershler-Henry, Rosemary J. Coombe & Martin Zeilinger, eds. 2014).

[112]   *Id.* at 248–49.

[113]   *See id.* at 249.

[114]   Douglas Murray, *The Funny Thing about Satire: Parody and Satire Added to Canada's Fair Dealing Defence,* BROADCASTER MAG. 12 (Oct. 2013), *available at* https://issuu.com/glaciermedia/docs/brc_2013oct01 (last visited Oct. 10, 2017).

work."[115] Thus, the exception could justify virtually *any* infringement and serve "no meaningful objective" other than to "make a parody of the Copyright Act."[116]

Michael Geist feels less uncertain that the new categories will offer broad protection for works of parody and satire. He explains that as the number of fair dealing purposes has grown, the first-stage test should now be very easy to meet.[117] A perfunctory first-stage purposes test nonetheless may be followed by a far more rigorous second-stage fairness assessment.[118] Through the study of the "Copyright Pentalogy" (five decisions handed down by the SCC on July 21, 2012 and a few months after the new Copyright Act came into force), Geist further argues that Canada has shifted from a fair dealing to a fair use approach like the one employed in the United States.[119] Although virtually any copying may qualify as "fair use/dealing," whether a particular use is legally "fair" will be determined through a multi-factor analysis.[120].

D. Potential Parody/Satire Fair Dealing Dichotomy

In *Society of Composers, Authors and Music Publishers of Canada, Canadian Recording Industry Association and CMRRA-SODRAC Inc. v. Bell Canada*, one of the five SCC decisions in 2012, the SCC held that *CCH Canadian Ltd.* created "a relatively low threshold for the first step" of the fair dealing analysis, so that "the analytical heavy-hitting is done in determining whether the dealing was fair" in the second step of the test.[121] The Copyright Pentalogy led to much optimism among academics and the public at large. Such optimism is not unwarranted, considering the broadened scope of fair dealing in two of the five cases, *Bell Canada* and *Alberta (Minister of Education) v. Canadian Copyright Licensing Agency (Access Copyright)*. This section will nonetheless argue that the broadened scope of fair dealing does not readily extend to cases involving parodies. It will then explain why the parody/satire dichotomy in American copyright jurisprudence may influence Canadian courts. This, along with a propertized notion of fair dealing and the very meaning of "satire," may lead Canadian courts to consider "satires" inferior to "parodies." Therefore, works within this inferior category may not pass the second-stage fairness assessment, even if they would not likely serve as market substitutes for their originals or their derivatives and would not harm the interests of rights-holders.

---

[115] Andrei Mincov, *New Section 29.21 of the Copyright Act – Good or Bad?* MINCOV L. CORP. (Oct. 15, 2012), http://mincovlaw.com/blog-tag/new%20copyright%20act&page=3 (last visited Oct. 10, 2017).
[116] *Id.*
[117] MICHAEL GEIST, THE COPYRIGHT PENTALOGY: HOW THE SUPREME COURT OF CANADA SHOOK THE FOUNDATIONS OF CANADIAN COPYRIGHT LAW 171, 176–80 (2013).
[118] *Id.* at 159.
[119] *Id.* at 178.
[120] *Id.* at 180.
[121] SOCAN v. Bell Canada [2012] 102 C.P.R. (4th) 241, 250 (S.C.C.).

1. *The Broadened Scope of Fair Dealing in* Bell Canada *and* Alberta (Minister of Education)

In *Bell Canada*, the SCC determined whether online music service providers allowing consumers to listen to free 30–90-second previews for musical works before making purchases constituted fair dealing under the Copyright Act.[122] The Copyright Board held that the previews constituted fair dealing for the purpose of research, and did not amount to copyright infringement.[123] After the Federal Court of Appeal upheld the Board's decision, SOCAN appealed to the SCC. The SCC affirmed that fair dealing must be interpreted broadly, because allowing users to engage in some activities that would otherwise constitute copyright infringement serves to attain "the proper balance" between "protection of the exclusive rights of authors and copyright owners and access to their works by the public."[124]

The SCC determined that the consumers' use of previews of musical works constituted "research" for the purpose of identifying which songs to purchase, which satisfied the first step of the fair dealing inquiry.[125] Moving on to the second-stage fairness analysis, the court determined that the purpose behind the use of the previews was to facilitate consumer research, rather than to replace the songs.[126] With respect to the character of the dealing, the previews could not be duplicated or further distributed.[127] On the amount of the dealing factor, the court, assessing the proportion of the preview in relation to the whole work rather than the aggregate number of previews streamed by consumers, determined that it constituted a modest dealing.[128] Regarding the alternatives to the dealing, previews of songs were "reasonably necessary" to achieve their research purpose.[129] On the nature of the work factor, the court, affirming the desirability of disseminating the music, concluded that the previews facilitated potential consumers' identification of musical works they wanted to buy and the dissemination of these works.[130] Finally, on the effect of the dealing on the work, because the previews were shorter and of lower quality, they would not adversely affect the original songs but would encourage their purchases.[131] Concluding that the Board properly balanced the purposes of the Copyright Act by encouraging the creation and dissemination of works while ensuring fair rewards to creators, the SCC unanimously dismissed SOCAN's appeal.[132]

---

[122]   *Id.* at 245.
[123]   *Id.* at 244.
[124]   *Id.* at 250.
[125]   *Id.* at 247.
[126]   *Id.* at 251.
[127]   *Id.* at 252.
[128]   *Id.*
[129]   *Id.* at 253.
[130]   *Id.* at 254.
[131]   *Id.*
[132]   *Id.*

Carys Craig identifies the inclusion of technological neutrality[133] as a landmark aspect of the Copyright Pentalogy.[134] In *Bell Canada*, Justice Abella explained that this principle "seeks to have the Copyright Act applied in a way that operates consistently, regardless of the form of media involved, or its technological sophistication."[135] In other words, it ensures that the law is applied to create equivalent effects in different technological contexts. Because assuming (or even double-counting) unfairness based on the aggregate volume of digital dealings could effectively weaken or eviscerate the fair dealing defense in an online environment, the SCC determined that the relevant amount in the fair dealing analysis is the proportion of each extract to the whole work.[136] Ensuring that copyright law would not potentially impede the opportunities for greater access afforded by the Internet, this principle helps to facilitate the protection of users' rights articulated in *CCH Canadian Ltd.*[137]

The other decision that broadened the scope of fair dealing is *Alberta (Minister of Education)*, in which the SCC considered whether the photocopying of textbook excerpts by teachers, on their own initiative, to distribute to students as part of course materials was fair dealing pursuant to the new Copyright Act.[138] Because photocopying, which served the allowable purpose of "research or private study," easily passed the first-step purpose analysis,[139] the dispute centered on the Copyright Board's application of the factors in *CCH Canadian Ltd.* in the second-part fairness assessment.

Justice Abella, writing for the majority, focused on only four factors. On the purpose of the dealing, the teachers' instructional purposes were consistent with "research" and "private study" as long as they had no ulterior motive in providing photocopies to their students.[140] Citing *Bell Canada*, the majority also held that the amount of the dealing factor required an examination of the proportion of the short excerpts that the teachers copied in relation to each entire textbook.[141] On the alternatives to the dealing factor, the majority held that photocopying short excerpts was reasonably necessary to achieve the purpose of "research" and "private study" for the students.[142] Finally, regarding whether the dealing adversely affected or competed with the original work, the majority could not see how photocopying short excerpts of complementary texts would compete with the textbook market, or find

---

[133] Carys J. Craig, *Technological Neutrality: (Pre)Serving the Purposes of Copyright Law*, IN COPYRIGHT PENTALOGY: HOW THE SUPREME COURT OF CANADA SHOOK THE FOUNDATIONS OF CANADIAN COPYRIGHT LAW 277 (Michael Geist, ed. 2013).

[134] *Id.* at 277.

[135] *Bell Canada*, 102 C.P.R. (4th) at 253; Craig, *supra* note 133, at 282.

[136] *Bell Canada*, 102 C.P.R. (4th) at 253.

[137] *See id.*; Craig, *supra* note 133, at 281–84.

[138] *Alberta (Minister of Educ.) v. Canadian Copyright Licensing Agency* [2012] 102 C.P.R. (4th) 255 (S.C.C.).

[139] *Id.* at 262.

[140] *Id.* at 262–66.

[141] *Id.* at 272–73.

[142] *Id.* at 273–74.

any evidence of a link between photocopying short excerpts and a decline in text-book sales.[143] The court, in a 5/4 split, held that the Board's finding of unfairness was based on a misapplication of the *CCH Canadian Ltd.* factors.[144] Thus, it allowed the appeal by *Alberta (Minister of Education)* and remitted the matter back to the Board for reconsideration.[145]

Reynolds considers that the SCC adopted a reasonableness standard of review in *Alberta (Minister of Education)*, which shows the "continuing evolution of the SCC's interpretation of the purpose of the Copyright Act . . . to contributing to the development of a robust public domain."[146] Two elaborations by Reynolds are especially noteworthy. When evaluating the alternatives to the dealing factor, the Copyright Board reasoned that educational institutions could "[b]uy the originals to distribute to students or to place in the library for consultation," on the assumption that they could afford to purchase multiple copies of original texts to distribute to students.[147] Reynolds considers this a "curious statement" because the Board noted that the option of purchasing the book is "from a practical standpoint . . . not open to the student."[148] Accordingly, Justice Abella rightly called the Board's suggestion that schools could "buy the original texts to distribute to each student" "a demonstrably unrealistic outcome."[149] In addition, although the Copyright Board failed to deter-mine what factor(s) contributed to the decline in textbooks sales, it concluded that "the impact of photocopies . . . is sufficiently important to compete with the original to an extent that makes the dealing unfair."[150] Justice Abella fairly critiqued the "evidentiary vacuum" in the Board's conclusion that the photocopies had a suffi-ciently detrimental impact on the original.[151] Reynolds aptly concludes that the SCC's decision shows that "fairness is not as discretionary a concept as it seems to be."[152]

The broadened fair dealing in *Bell Canada* and *Alberta (Minister of Education)* does not benefit parody cases. First, creating a parody involves a conscious choice of what work(s) to use and how much to borrow from the work(s). How the principle of technological neutrality can work in the favor of parodists is not clear. If anything, advances in technology have facilitated access to a greater pool of works from which

---

[143] *Id.* at 274.
[144] *Id.* at 259.
[145] *Id.* at 274.
[146] Graham Reynolds, *Judicial Review of Copyright Board Decisions in Canada's Copyright Pentalogy*, IN COPYRIGHT PENTALOGY: HOW THE SUPREME COURT OF CANADA SHOOK THE FOUNDATIONS OF CANADIAN COPYRIGHT LAW 35 (Michael Geist, ed. 2013).
[147] *Id.* at 27; *citing* Statement of Royalties to be Collected by Access Copyright for the Reprographic Reproduction, in Canada, of Works in Its Repertoire, CBD No. 6, para 107 (2009), www.cb-cda.gc .ca/decisions/2009/Access-Copyright-2005-2009-Schools.pdf [*Alberta (Minister of Education)* (CB)].
[148] *Id.* at 28, *citing Alberta (Minister of Educ.)* (CB), *supra* note 147.
[149] *Id.* at 28, *citing Alberta (Minister of Educ.)*, 102 C.P.R. (4th) at 267.
[150] *Id.* at 29, *citing Alberta (Minister of Educ.)* (CB), *supra* note 147, para. 111.
[151] *Id.* at 29–30, *citing Alberta (Minister of Educ.)*, 102 C.P.R. (4th) at 268.
[152] *Id.* at 32.

the user could choose, and the increased availability of alternatives could weaken the fair dealing defense by making the parodying of copyrighted works less justified. It was impractical for schools to purchase multiple copies of original textbooks in *Alberta (Minister of Education)*, hence reasonable for them to copy excerpts of textbooks to the students. Yet it may be far more difficult for users to prove that they had no reasonable available alternatives if the works they parodied are not even the targets of their criticisms or commentaries.

2. The Potential Parody/Satire Dichotomy

The last chapter has argued that the parody/satire dichotomy in American copyright law has led to the erroneous suppression of works that would not otherwise displace the underlying works or harm their authors' interests. The parody and satire categories in Canadian copyright law may lead to a similar dichotomy, because American law may influence how Canadian courts will define "parody" and "satire." In addition, because satire, unlike parody, need not imitate preexisting works, courts that adhere to a propertized conception of fair dealing may be less likely to hold that works categorized as "satires" pass the second-stage fairness assessment, even if they would not likely displace the underlying works or harm their authors' interests.

In the era of globalization, legal problems tend to arise in similar ways, especially in advanced societies and economies.[153] Whereas national governments used to respond to these problems independently of other nations, they now frequently look to one another, leading to the convergence of national laws.[154] Judicial globalization, as part of legal globalization, refers to judicial interaction across borders.[155] While the most active types of interaction can be found in processes like dispute resolution, a more passive and implicit form of interaction occurs in the form of the "cross-fertilization" of national judicial decisions.[156] Judges cite or rely on foreign law and decisions for argumentation and for enriching their legal reasoning.[157] The U.S. Supreme Court, which almost never quotes other courts, has long been the main supplier of ideas and is the most quoted among the foreign courts.[158] According to Justice Kathryn Neilson of the Court of Appeal for British Columbia, due to Canada's Commonwealth background, the presence of both civil and common law systems, and its broad participation in and endorsement of

---

[153]   Ralf Michaels, *Globalization and Law: Law beyond the State*, IN LAW AND SOCIETY THEORY300–04 (Reza Banakar & Max Travers, eds. 2013).

[154]   *Id.*

[155]   Anne-Marie Slaughter, *Judicial Globalization*, 40 VIR. J. INT'L L. 1103, 1103 (2000).

[156]   *Id.* at 1116–19.

[157]   Marta Cartabia & Sabino Cassese, *How Judges Think in a Globalised World? European and American Perspectives*, GLOBAL GOVERNANCE PROGRAMME OF ROBERT SCHUMAN CENTRE FOR ADVANCED STUDIES/EUROPEAN UNIVERSITY INSTITUTE (Dec. 2013), at 3, http://cadmus.eui.eu/bit stream/handle/1814/30057/2013_07-Policy%20Brief_RSCAS_GGP-WEB.pdf? sequence=1&isAllowed=y (last visited Oct. 10, 2017).

[158]   *Id.*

international conventions, judicial use of sources from other jurisdictions has always been an aspect of Canadian jurisprudence.[159] In addition, statistics show that Canadian judges have consistently displayed an interest in American law, even if English law continues to be more influential.[160] Basil Markesinis and Jörg Fedtke note that regarding the reception of American law in Canada, there is "no slavish adoption of its solutions nor, indeed, the opposite, that is, a closing of the eyes towards the large (and sometimes menacing) Southern neighbour, but an opportunity for a genuine dialogue in search for inspiration."[161]

The SCC cautioned against the automatic portability of American copyright concepts into the Canadian arena, given the "fundamental differences" in the respective legislative schemes.[162] Yet Canadian courts have referenced American courts' decisions to lend support to their arguments, to clarify Canadian law, or both. One good example of judicial globalization in the context of copyright is found in *CCH Canadian Ltd.*, in which the SCC drew references to American case law to formulate its standard of "originality." The majority opinion referenced Justice O'Connor's concern in *Feist Publications Inc. v. Rural Telephone Service Co.*, a 1991 decision by the U.S. Supreme Court, that the "industriousness" standard of originality would violate the tenet of copyright law in protecting expressions but not ideas.[163] Under the American standard, a work that originates from an author and is not a mere copy of another work is sufficient to ground copyright.[164] Although many Canadian courts have adopted a low standard of originality, the SCC held that mere labor could not ground a finding of originality, and contributions in terms of skills and judgments are necessary for a work to be "original" enough for copyright protection.[165] By referencing *Feist Publications, Inc.*, the SCC formulated its standard of originality, by holding that an "original" work must be more than a

[159] Justice Kathryn Neilson, *"Judicial Globalization" – What Impact in Canada?* HUTCHEON DINNER (Oct. 21, 2009), at 19, www.brandeis.edu/ethics/pdfs/internationaljustice/ Judicial_Globalization_Neilson_Oct_2009.pdf. Justice Neilson cited Justice Beverly McLachlin, current Chief Justice of the SCC, among other Justices: "This is the Canadian experience—one that has, from the beginning, accepted foreign law as capable of providing useful insights and perspectives. Foreign law is used selectively, where it is relevant to and useful to resolving disputes." *Id.* at 20, *citing* Beverley McLachlin, *Canada and the United States: A Comparative View of the Use of Foreign Law*, THE AMERICAN COLLEGE OF TRIAL LAWYERS NORTHWEST REGIONAL CONFERENCE, ALBERTA (Aug. 8, 2009).

[160] Peter McCormick, *American Citations and the McLachlin Court: An Empirical Study*, 47 OSGOODE HALL L.J. 83, 93 (2009).

[161] SIR BASIL MARKESINIS & JÖRG FEDTKE, JUDICIAL RECOURSE TO FOREIGN LAW: A NEW SOURCE OF INSPIRATION? 84–85 (2006).

[162] Compo Co. v. Blue Crest Music Inc. [1979] 45 C.P.R. (2d) 1, 9 (S.C.C.).

[163] CCH Canadian Ltd., 30 C.P.R. (4th) at 17, *citing* Feist Publ'n. Inc. v. Rural Telephone Service Co., 499 U.S. 340, 353 (1991).

[164] *Id.*

[165] *Id.* at 15–16, 18. The SCC also referenced Tele-Direct (Publications) Inc. v. American Business Information, Inc., 154 D.L.R. (4th) 328 (C.A.), a 1998 decision by the Federal Court of Appeal of Canada. It also cited French law, under which "originality means both the intellectual contribution of the author and the novel nature of the work as compared with existing works," an understanding

mere copy of another work, but need not be creative in the sense of being novel or unique.[166]

Elsewhere, Canadian courts have referenced American statutes and decisions to clarify Canadian law. In *Théberge*, for example, the SCC cited the expansive derivative works provision in American copyright law, along with relevant decisions by the Seventh and the Ninth Circuits, as a contrast to the lack of an explicit and independent concept of "derivative work" in Canadian legislation.[167] Another example is *Michelin*, in which the Federal Court distinguished Canadian fair dealing from American fair use by emphasizing the exhaustiveness of the former and the open-endedness of the latter.[168] In *Bell Canada*, the SCC made good use of the U.S. Supreme Court's decision in *Campbell* to reject SOCAN's argument that the definition of "research" should require the creation of something new. It pointed out that it was not clear whether transformative use was "absolutely necessary" even for a finding of fair use in American law.[169]

Certainly, American statutes and cases have not been the only source of inspiration or guidance for Canadian courts. Markesinis and Fedtke illuminate how Canada's mixed cultural background has "prepared Canadians for an open and multi-cultural approach to law," through a survey of citations by Canadian courts to English as well as other foreign cases.[170] The SCC, for instance, referenced a number of English cases and an Australian case in *CCH Canadian Ltd.*,[171] and both English and New Zealand cases in *Alberta (Minister of Education)*.[172]

Definitions of "parody" and "satire" by the U.S. Supreme Court will provide one source of guidance for Canadian courts to define "parody" and "satire." Canadian courts will also look to the British and Commonwealth jurisdictions. Whereas the New Zealand Parliament has yet to include a parody exception to its law, Australia's Copyright Amendment Act 2006 added "parody or satire" to its fair dealing exceptions to copyright infringement.[173] In 2014, a new fair dealing exception was introduced into British copyright law, which provides that the use of copyrighted material

---

reinforced by the expression *le droit d'auteur* – literally the "author's right" in the French title of the Copyright Act. *Id.* at 16.

[166] See *id.* at 15–18.

[167] Théberge, 17 C.P.R. (4th) at 188–89.

[168] Michelin, 71 C.P.R. (3d) at 379–82.

[169] Bell Canada, 102 C.P.R. (4th) at 249–50, citing Campbell v. Acuff-Rose Music, Inc., 510 U.S. 569, 579 (1994).

[170] MARKESINIS & FEDTKE, *supra* note 161, at 83.

[171] These include Hubbard v. Vosper [1972] 1 All E.R. 1023; Associated Newspapers Group plc v. News Group Newspapers Ltd. [1986] R.P.C. 515; Sillitoe v. McGraw-Hill Book Co. (U.K.) [1983] F.S.R. 545; Beloff v. Pressdram Ltd. [1973] 1 All E.R. 241; Pro Sieben Media AG v. Carlton UK Television Ltd. [1999] F.S.R. 610. The Australian case that was referred to but not followed was Moorehouse v. Univ. New S. Wales [1976] R.P.C. 151 (Aus. H.C.).

[172] These include Sillitoe v. McGraw-Hill Book Co. (U.K.) Ltd. [1983] F.S.R. 545; Univ. London P., Ltd. v. Univ. Tutorial P., Ltd. [1961] 2 Ch. 601; Hubbard v. Vosper [1972] 1 All E.R. 1023. The New Zealand case is Copyright Licensing Ltd. v. Univ. Auckland [2002] 3 N.Z.L.R. 76.

[173] Copyright Act 1968, s. 41A (Aus.).

for the purpose of "caricature, parody or pastiche" would not be infringement.[174] The U.K. Intellectual Property Office defines "parody" as something that "imitates a work for humorous or satirical effect."[175] To date, however, the parody or satire defense has not been invoked in the U.K. or Australia. Assuming that Canadian courts will draw upon American case law to determine how "parody" and "satire" should be defined, its parody/satire dichotomy may impact Canadian decisions.

In addition, Canadian courts will likely reference dictionaries for the meanings of "parody" and "satire." As mentioned, the *Oxford English Dictionary* and the *American Heritage Dictionary* agree on the imitative nature of parody, but do not agree on whether a parody may only target the original, or may imitate the original in order to criticize or comment on something else. Thus, even assuming that Canadian courts are not influenced by American cases, they may still require that a parody direct part of its criticism or commentary at the underlying work.

Works falling within either the "parody" or the "satire" category will pass the first-step purpose analysis. Yet for two reasons, the potential parody/satire dichotomy means that "satires" may not pass the second-step fairness assessment even if they would not otherwise displace the underlying works or harm their rights-holders' interests. First, although the SCC in both *Théberge* and *CCH Canadian Ltd.* affirmed the limited nature of authors' rights,[176] a propertized conception of fair dealing continued to run through many parody cases. This chapter has drawn upon Craig's criticism of the *Michelin* court for employing a physical analogue to obviate the differences between physical property and intellectual property.[177] In fact, the propertized conception of copyright was by no means adopted by the *Michelin* court alone, as semblances of this physical analogue can be found in earlier cases. The court in *Ludlow Music Ltd.* issued an injunction against defendants' parodic song to protect plaintiff's "property rights against encroachment" by the song.[178] The court in *ATV Music Publishing of Canada Ltd.* held that the "intruding" words of the defendants' song caused "irreparable harm" to the plaintiff.[179] These physical analogues led to the *Michelin* court's holding that the plaintiff's "private property" could not be used as "a *location* or forum for expression" by defendant.[180] *Canwest Mediaworks Publications Inc.* – a more recent case – showed the pervasive influence of *Michelin*, by relying on Justice Teitelbaum's opinion to hold that parody does not constitute a defense to copyright infringement.[181]

---

[174] Copyright, Designs and Patents Act, 1988, s. 30A (U.K.).

[175] Intellectual Property Office, *Exceptions to Copyright: Guidance for Creators and Copyright Owners* (Oct. 2014), at 6, www.gov.uk/government/uploads/system/uploads/attachment_data/file/448274/ Exceptions_to_copyright_-_Guidance_for_creators_and_copyright_owners.pdf (last visited Oct. 10, 2017).

[176] Théberge, 17 C.P.R. (4th) at 176; CCH Canadian Ltd., 30 C.P.R. (4th) at 25.

[177] See section I(B).

[178] Ludlow Music Inc., 51 C.P.R. at 301.

[179] ATV Music Publ'g. of Canada Ltd., 65 C.P.R. (2d) at 114.

[180] Michelin, 71 C.P.R. (3d) at 391.

[181] *Canwest Mediaworks Publ'n. Inc.*, paras. 13–14.

Second, even assuming that this recent parody case is a mere outlier, and courts will no longer treat intellectual properties as if they are tangible, physical properties, the fact that a satire, unlike a parody, need not imitate a preexisting work according to dictionaries may still lead Canadian courts to consider dealings in the form of "satires" to be less fair than "parodies."

Hence, courts may use the second-stage fairness assessment to hold that "satires" are not fair dealings of the original works. Four of the fair-dealing factors mentioned in *CCH Canadian Ltd.* are particularly important in illuminating the adverse impacts of a satire category.[182] On the purpose of the dealing, courts will "make an objective assessment of the user/defendant's real purpose or motive" in using the copyrighted work.[183] "Research done for commercial purposes," the SCC stated, "may not be as fair as research done for charitable purposes."[184] On the amount of the dealing, the quantity of the work taken "will not be determinative of fairness, but it can help in the determination."[185] In *Bell Canada* and *Alberta (Minister of Education)*, the SCC assessed the proportions of the originals copied in relation to the whole works.[186] Considering the alternatives to the dealing, courts will determine whether the use of the originals are "reasonably necessary" to achieve the purpose of the satire, and whether there was an "equally effective" alternative as opposed to simply another alternative.[187] Finally, concerning the effect of the dealing on the work, courts will consider whether the dealing will compete with the work.[188] The SCC emphasized that "it is neither the only factor nor the most important factor that a court must consider in deciding if the dealing is fair."[189]

Even assuming that the propertized conception of fair dealing, considered to have informed the *Campbell* decision, now has minimal influence on Canadian courts, the fact that satires need not rely on the imitation of preexisting works may still persuade courts to consider fair dealings in the form of "satire" unfair. On the first factor, although courts will find that fair dealing for the purpose of satire is the "real motive," the commercial nature of some satires may lead courts to hold that their authors are riding the coattails of the originals, thus tipping the scales towards finding that their dealings are unfair.[190] On the second factor, courts may be influenced by the argument in *Campbell*, or even in *Salinger*, that the satirical nature of the works – that they target something other than the originals – does not

---

[182] The four factors studied in this paragraph are the ones identified as useful to highlighting the shortcomings of a satire category and the necessity for replacing parody and satire categories by a broad parody category. The character of the dealing and the nature of the work factors are not useful in fleshing out the adverse effect of categorizing a work as satire.

[183] CCH Canadian Ltd., 30 C.P.R. (4th) at 27.

[184] *Id.*

[185] *Id.*

[186] Bell Canada, 102 C.P.R. (4th) at 252; Alberta (Minister of Educ.), 102 C.P.R. (4th) 255, 272–73.

[187] CCH Canadian Ltd., at 30 C.P.R. (4th) at 28.

[188] *Id.*

[189] *Id.*

[190] *See* CCH Canadian Ltd., at 30 C.P.R. (4th) at 28.

justify extensive copying of the originals.[191] On the third factor, courts may cite *Campbell* to hold that the uses of the originals are not "reasonably necessary" because a satire can "stand on its own two feet" and other alternatives would be "equally effective."[192] Therefore, even if courts find that the satires would not likely compete with the original works, the other factors may lead them to hold that their dealings of the underlying works are unfair.

3. *United Airlines, Inc. v. Cooperstock*

Interestingly enough, the Federal Court provided a broad definition of "parody" in *United Airlines, Inc. v. Cooperstock* (2017), the first decision to consider the scope of the "parody" category of fair dealing since the legislative amendments in 2012. In 1997, Jeremy Cooperstock registered the domain name "UNTIED.com" to create a parody of the official website of United Airlines after the airline company disregarded his serious, polite complaint about its services.[193] Apart from mocking the design and logo on United's actual website, Cooperstock's work reflected public opinions about the company through its complaints page.[194] In 2012, United brought proceedings against Cooperstock in the Superior Court of Quebec and the Federal Court of Canada, the former petitioning to have some senior airline employees' contact information removed from his parody,[195] and the latter alleging copyright and trademark infringements.[196] Cooperstock's motions to dismiss United's application for an injunction were denied by the Superior Court in 2014 and 2016, and the Court of Appeal of Quebec upheld the injunction in early 2017.[197] On June 23, 2017, the Federal Court ruled that the parody website infringed United's copyright and trademarks.[198]

The Federal Court, seeking to find the meaning of "parody" in Canadian copyright law, determined that the words of the legislation must be "read in their entire context and in their grammatical and ordinary sense harmoniously with the scheme of the Act, the object of the Act, and the intention of Parliament."[199] It then referenced *CCH Canadian Ltd.*, in which the SCC emphasized the importance to balance the rights of authors with those of users and the definition of parody by the

---

[191] *See* Campbell v. Acuff-Rose Music, Inc., 510 U.S. 569, 580–81 (1994); Salinger v. Colting, 641 F. Supp. 2d 250, 263–67 (S.D.N.Y. 2009).

[192] *See* Campbell, 510 U.S. at 580–81 (1994); CCH Canadian Ltd., at 30 C.P.R. (4th) at 28.

[193] Ellen Roseman, *United Airlines Fights Legal Battle with Untied Website*, Toronto Star (Nov. 30, 2012), www.thestar.com/business/personal_finance/spending_saving/2012/11/30/united_airlines_fight s_legal_battle_with_untied_website.html (last visited Oct. 10, 2017).

[194] *Id.*

[195] United Airlines, Inc. v. Cooperstock [2014] 2014 QCCS 2430 (QCCS); United Airlines, Inc. v. Cooperstock [2016] 2016 QCCS 4645 (QCCS), *aff'd* [2017] 2017 QCCA 44 (QCCA).

[196] United Airlines, Inc. v. Cooperstock [2017] 147 C.P.R. (4th) 251 (F.C.).

[197] Cooperstock v. United Airlines, Inc. [2017] 2017 QCCA 44 (QCCA).

[198] Cooperstock, 147 C.P.R. (4th) at 295.

[199] *Id.* at 285.

Concise Canadian Oxford Dictionary.[200] It also drew upon the *Campbell* court's narrow definition of parody, and emphasized the need to use it "cautiously considering the differences between fair use in the United States and fair dealing in Canada."[201] It determined that the definition of parody used by the European Court of Justice in *Deckmyn v. Vandersteen* (2014) "is consistent with the ordinary meaning of the term, the purpose and scheme of the fair dealing provisions in the Copyright Act, and the intention of Parliament."[202] Hence, it held that parody should have two basic elements: "the evocation of an existing work while exhibiting noticeable differences" and "the expression of mockery or humour."[203] In addition, Justice Phelan contended that:

> In addition, in my view, parody does not require that the expression of mockery or humour to be directed at the exact thing being parodied. It is possible, for example, for a parody to evoke a work such as a logo while expressing mockery of the source company, or to evoke a well-known song while expressing mockery of another entity entirely.[204]

Although the *Cooperstock* court's definition of parody will very likely be followed by other judges of the Federal Court, it may get appealed and/or not be followed by other courts in the future. Rights-holders may appeal the Federal Court's definition of "parody" by bringing it to the Federal Court of Appeal. If so, the Federal Court of Appeal may look at the definitions of parody in different jurisdictions to determine whether to narrow the scope of the "parody" exception. Should it adopt a narrower definition, it would examine whether the works in question still pass both stages of the test and are fair dealings of the works parodied.

In addition, decisions by the Federal Court are not binding on provincial and territorial courts. One must note that in the *Cooperstock* case, whether or not the law requires the expression of mockery or humor in a parody to be directed at the parodied work would hardly have changed the Federal Court's determination that Cooperstock's parody website, which targeted United Airlines, constituted parody under the law. In fact, the broad definition adopted by the Federal Court made the "satire" exception seemingly redundant. Hence, even though other courts will reference the *Cooperstock* decision, depending on the circumstances of the cases, they may choose to adopt different definitions, and may determine that a parody must direct its part of its criticism or commentary at the original.

Assuming that the future Federal Court follows the *Cooperstock* definition that parody need not target "the *exact* thing being parodied" and can express mockery of "another entity entirely," this definition might not prevent the court from requiring

---

[200] *Id.* at 284–85, 286, 288–93.
[201] *Id.* at 287.
[202] *Id.* at 288.
[203] *Id.*
[204] *Id.*

that the parody's target and the original be connected. *Ludlow Music Inc.*, in which defendants parodied "This Land is Your Land," an American song, to describe Canadian people, is a good example of how a song targeting something else can still have a connection to the original. Although the new song "This Land is Whose Land" targeted Canadian people and not the Americans, the "exact thing being parodied," its mockery of Canada's usurpation of the Aboriginal peoples' lands[205] may be seen as a subtle criticism of the colonialist subtext in the American version (treating "this land" originally belonging to the Indian Americans as "your" – the white settlers' – land). For other examples, whether a connection exists might be difficult to judge. Where the court requires a connection between the parody's target and the parodied work but perceives no connection, it may categorize the work as "satire."

E. Substituting a Broad Parody Exception for the Dual Categories

A broad parody fair dealing exception should substitute for both the "parody" and "satire" exceptions under the current law. This category encompassing works that criticize or comment on the originals and/or something else would serve to reduce any influence of a propertized conception of fair dealing and possible bias against "satires," and further align the Canadian copyright jurisprudence with its freedom of expression jurisprudence. As a result, courts would be less inclined to hold that parodies that otherwise would not compete with the originals are unfair. Hence, a reformed exception would more likely protect users' right to freedom of expression and more properly balance the interests of rights-holders with those of users.

1. When a Broad Parody Exception Probably Matters

The current parody and satire exceptions would not likely lead to the suppression of free expressions where the imitative works unambiguously target the originals or what they represent. Excellent examples include parodies of corporate logos by trade unions in *Canadian Tire Corp. Ltd.* and *Michelin*. Under the current law, the courts would very likely have found that the parodies of Canadian Tire's and CGEM

---

[205]   "The early French had great persistence,
Despite the Indians' combined resistance;
With righteous feeling, they started stealing,
This land that's made for you and me . . ..
This land is your land, this land is my land,
This voyageur and fleur-de-lie-land;
So populate it, then separate it,
This land is made for you and me.
Then came the English and assorted henchmen,
Who started fighting with all those Frenchmen;
All through this bother, they told each other,
This land is made for you and me . . .." *Ludlow Music Inc.*, 51 C.P.R. at 295.

Michelin's logos both fell squarely into the "parody" fair-dealing category and passed the first-step purpose analysis.[206] These parodies of corporate logos would also have passed the second-step fairness assessment easily. On the purpose of the dealing factor, the courts would have held that both logos had served non-commercial purposes of protesting against the companies in the form of parody.[207] Regarding the amount of the dealing and the alternatives to the dealing, the courts would likely have held that using the entire logos had been reasonable for the protests and few other alternatives could have better served such purposes.[208] As for the effect of the dealing on the original work, regardless of how long the parodies had circulated in public, they would not have competed with the companies represented by the logos, even if the protests may have hurt their businesses.[209] Therefore, courts would reach the correct decisions easily, whether the current parody exception is replaced by the more inclusive one.

Whether the current exceptions are replaced by a broad parody exception or not, courts also would not likely hold that imitative works targeting something other than the original but containing little or no criticism or commentary are fair dealings. A good example would be *MCA Canada Ltd.*, in which the advertising agency borrowed the original tune of "Downtown" to advertise its car dealership in downtown Ottawa. Because the imitative work was not satirical, it would have been unlikely for the court to consider it "satire" under the current law, or that it fell within the broad "parody" exception.[210] Even if the court had categorized this work as "satire" or "parody," on the purpose of the dealing, the court would likely have determined that the song offered little or no criticism or commentary, and primarily served the commercial purpose of promoting the car dealership.[211] Regarding the amount of the dealing, using the whole tune would have further tipped the scale towards a finding of unfairness.[212] In addition, the court would have found that the relationship between the song and the car dealership was too tenuous, and that the defendant had had many "equally effective" alternatives to promote its business.[213] Therefore, even though the defendant's work would hardly compete with the original or serve as its substitute,[214] the court likely would have held that its dealing of the original work was unfair, whether a broad parody exception replaced the dual exceptions.

In some cases, the more inclusive parody exception would serve to promote freedom of expression by reducing any influence of the propertized conception of

---

[206] Canadian Tire Corp., 7 C.P.R. (3d) at 416–17; Michelin, 71 C.P.R. (3d) at 354.
[207] *See* CCH Canadian Ltd., 30 C.P.R. (4th) at 27.
[208] *See id.* at 27–28.
[209] *See id.* at 28.
[210] MCA Canada Ltd. (Ltée), 28 C.P.R. (2d) at 54.
[211] *See id.* at 27.
[212] *See id.*
[213] *See id.* at 28.
[214] *See id.*

fair dealing on courts' decisions and/or potential bias against "satires." Good examples would be *Ludlow Music Inc.*, in which the defendants parodied "This Land is Your Land" to create a new song about Canadian people,[215] and *ATV Music Publishing of Canada Ltd.*, in which the defendants parodied the Beatles' song "Revolution" and turned it into a "commentary on the events preceding the proclamation of the Constitution Act" of Canada.[216] As discussed, the former arguably mocked the American version's colonialist assumptions while satirizing Canada for its treatment of First Nations peoples. The latter, which directly commented on Canadian affairs, can be interpreted as an oblique critique of America.[217] If courts had found that they did not clearly target the originals and had put them in the "satire" category, they may have easily used the alternatives to the dealing factor to tip the scale against findings of fair dealings. In addition, considering that both songs had used the entire tunes of the originals to serve both commercial and commentary purposes, the court would easily have held that they were not fair dealings. Contrarily, if a broad parody exception had replaced the parody and satire exceptions, the new songs would have felt squarely within the "parody" category. courts would more likely have held that these new works, though commercial in nature, served the purpose of parody by providing commentaries.[218] Whether or not other reasonable alternatives may have been available to the parodists, their works would not likely harm their markets.[219] Hence, courts would more likely have considered these "parodies" to be fair dealings than if they had been categorized as "satires."

2. The Misapplication of Two Fairness Factors in Cooperstock

The broad parody exception would not prevent courts from holding that parodies are unfair dealings even if they would not compete with the parodied originals or the services they represent. This is indicated by the Federal Court's decision that Cooperstock's website, which it categorized as "parody," infringed the copyright of the airline company. Nonetheless, the court's erroneous decision did not diminish the superiority of a broad parody exception, because it was caused by its misapplication of two important factors in the second stage fairness analysis.

On the purpose of the dealing factor, the court determined that Cooperstock's "real purpose or motive" was to "embarrass," "punish," even "defame" United Airlines for its perceived wrongdoings rather than to engage in parody, because his website "extended too far" the humor and mockery required of parody.[220] Yet Cooperstock's transposition of two of the letters in the word "United" to make

[215]   Ludlow Music Inc., 51 C.P.R. at 290–91.
[216]   Reynolds, *supra* note 60.
[217]   *Id.* at 60.
[218]   CCH Canadian Ltd., 30 C.P.R. (4th) at 27.
[219]   *See id.* at 28.
[220]   Cooperstock, 147 C.P.R. (4th) at 289.

"Untied" the title of his parody website, which suggests the disorder and chaos in the company's services, presented sufficient evidence of his humorous intent to pass any "objective assessment" by the court.[221] Regarding Cooperstock's "real purpose or motive," the court did not specify at what point the element of humor or mockery is "extended too far" so that what was humorous became embarrassing or punitive.[222] Arguably, intents for humor or mockery can go along with other intents in parodies, and they do not cancel out one another. Hence, any embarrassment or even punishment caused by Cooperstock's parody website did not make his humorous or mockery intent or motive less real.

Having wrongly determined that Cooperstock's real purpose or intent was to embarrass or punish the airline company, the court continued to misapply the effects of the dealing factor, holding that Cooperstock's substantial copying of the original website and logo had a harmful impact on United Airlines by defaming it.[223] As the court argued, the parody made customers believe that they were interacting with United Airlines when they were actually interacting with UNTIED.com, and that United Airlines was unprofessional by not responding to complaints.[224] Admittedly, the parody, by evoking the original, may have caused slight confusion at first glance. Yet a reasonable person would soon notice that UNTIED.com was a complaints website that took the form of a parody upon finding, for example, a "complaints database" and disclaimers indicating that it was not the website of United.[225] Regarding the question of whether the parody had any harmful impact on United Airlines or its website, the Federal Court should have followed *CCH Canadian Ltd.*, and asked: did the parody website harm United by competing with it in the airline services market?[226] Although UNTIED.com had been around for 20 years, it existed merely to mock and to criticize, rather than to compete.[227] If the court had correctly applied these two factors, then it would very likely have held that the parody website was fair dealing.

F. Surviving Moral Rights Challenges

While a broad and inclusive parody exception would not shield courts from making erroneous decisions, it is still preferable to the parody and satire exceptions in the current law. Would the moral rights provisions in the copyright statute conflict with a broad parody exception? Interestingly enough, none of the scholars studied in this chapter has addressed the potential conflicts between the moral rights provisions and

---

[221] *See id.*
[222] *See id.*
[223] *See id.* at 292.
[224] *Id.*
[225] *Id.* at 270–71.
[226] *See* CCH Canadian Ltd., at 30 C.P.R. (4th) at 28.
[227] *See* Cooperstock, 147 C.P.R. (4th) at 289; *see also* Roseman, *supra* note 193.

the parody and satire categories. Thus, they seem to imply that parodic (and satirical) works falling within these categories will survive potential moral rights challenges.

The moral rights provisions provide for the author's "right to the integrity of the work and . . . the right, where reasonable in the circumstances, to be associated with the work as its author by name or under a pseudonym and the right to remain anonymous."[228] On the right to integrity, "the author's or performer's right to the integrity of a work or performer's performance is infringed only if the work or the performance is, to the prejudice of its author's or performer's honour or reputation," "distorted, mutilated or otherwise modified" or "used in association with a product, service, cause or institution."[229] In *Théberge*, the SCC held that the author's moral rights are infringed "only if the work is modified to the prejudice of the honour or reputation of the author."[230]

The test for the prejudice to the author's honor or reputation was laid down much earlier in *Snow v. Eaton Centre Ltd. et al.*, a leading case on moral rights in 1982. Here, the defendant had purchased a sculpture of sixty geese from the plaintiff, attached red ribbons around the necks of the geese, and placed them in the shopping center as part of its Christmas decoration.[231] The plaintiff, alleging that the addition of the ribbons made the geese "look ridiculous" and modified his work in a manner prejudicial to his honor or reputation, brought a moral rights claim against the defendant to have the ribbons removed.[232] The Ontario High Court of Justice opined that the words "prejudicial to his honour or reputation . . . involve a certain subjective element or judgment on the part of the author so long as it is reasonably arrived at."[233] Relying upon experts and artists in the field, the court held for the plaintiff and granted the injunction.[234] In *Prise de Parole Inc. v. Guérin, Éditeur Ltée*, the Federal Court of Canada applied the test used in *Snow*, determining that although the defendant's new work was a "clumsy adaptation" of the author's work from the author's "subjective" perspective, this perspective "must be reasonably arrived at."[235] The court found that the author's work was not "distorted to the prejudice of the author's honour and reputation," on the grounds that he had not been ridiculed or mocked by his colleagues or the newspapers, that there was no change in the amount of his public appearances, and that no complaints had been made about the adaptation.[236]

Parodies, whether narrowly or broadly defined, will likely survive moral rights claims of attribution and those that are not defamatory and do not distort the original

---

[228] Copyright Act, s. 14.1(1).
[229] *Id.* s. 28.2(1).
[230] Théberge, 17 C.P.R. (4th) at 171.
[231] Snow v. Eaton Ctr. Ltd. et al. [1982] 70 C.P.R. (2d) 105, 106 (Ont. H.C.J.).
[232] *Id.*
[233] *Id.*
[234] *Id.*
[235] Prise de Parole Inc. v. Guérin, Éditeur Ltée [1995] 66 C.P.R. (3d) 257, 260 (F.C.).
[236] *Id.* at 266.

works in ways that are prejudicial to the honor or reputation of their authors arguably would survive claims to integrity by authors. One must note that the *Snow* decision came down long before the SSC's 2004 decision in *CCH Canadian Ltd.*, which acknowledged fair dealings as "user rights," and the copyright reform in 2012. In addition, attaching red ribbons to the geese arguably did not carry criticism or commentary, or any message other than signaling it as part of the Christmas decoration.[237] According to *CCH Canadian Ltd.*, parodying the author's work would be a "user's right."[238] As emphasized in Part I of the book, parodies, though built upon existing works, are new works. In addition, they almost invariably modify the underlying works to convey messages. Although the *Snow* court indicated that the moral rights of integrity are "not unconstitutional" and are greater than those based on libel or slander,[239] the court in *Prise de Parole Inc.* stressed the objective component of the test by giving weight to the reasonableness standard and by examining whether the new work distorted the original to the prejudice of its author's honor or reputation and caused ridicule or mockery.[240]

In determining whether parodies that modify the underlying works violate authors' moral rights to integrity, future courts therefore will very likely put more weight on the parodists' right to freedom of expression and less on the authors' subjective feelings. Hence, one can reasonably expect courts to find parodies violate neither the attribution rights of the originals' authors, nor their integrity rights as long as the parodies do not defame them.

III. PARODY IN APPLICATION: APPLYING THE CHARTER

The previous chapter has made extensive use of the *Salinger* decision to explain how the parody defense should be applied by courts. The rest of this chapter will discuss the works of David Fewer and Graham Reynolds and their insights into how the Charter right to freedom of expression may be applied to copyright law and the parody exception in particular. Because there is a lack of parody case law in Canada, this last section will also employ two hypotheses inspired by the *Salinger* lawsuit to illuminate how courts may engage with the Charter to apply a broadened parody exception in Canadian copyright law.

A. The Charter Challenges in Copyright Actions

David Fewer's 1997 article examines how copyright law may operate as a form of private censorship when courts preserve the copyright owners' proprietary interests but neglect the public's right to expression guaranteed by s. 2(b) of the

---

[237]   Snow, 70 C.P.R. (2d) at 106.
[238]   CCH Canadian Ltd., 30 C.P.R. (4th) at 25.
[239]   Snow, 70 C.P.R. (2d) at 106.
[240]   Prise de Parole Inc., 66 C.P.R. (3d) at 266.

Charter.[241] When defendants raised a s. 2(b) of the Charter defense to copyright infringements, Canadian courts had rejected the argument out of hand, paying little, if any, consideration of the scope of s. 2(b), or whether the Charter even applies to such cases.[242]

Fewer explores three different ways in which the Charter might be applied to copyright litigation.[243] A major hurdle in applying the Charter to copyright law arises from the black-letter text of s. 32(1), which compels state actors to conform to the Charter, meaning that a litigant must successfully characterize the impugned act as "government action" to successfully raise a Charter claim.[244] Nevertheless, a defendant might characterize any assertion of a right granted under the Copyright Act as government action and invoke s. 2(b) against the federal government's statutory regime, by asserting that Parliament, in granting exclusive rights to copyright owners under the Copyright Act, has trodden upon user rights to freedom of expression guaranteed by s. 2(b).[245] In addition, a defendant might characterize any court order under the Copyright Act as government action, and challenge court-ordered remedies as infringing their freedom of expression.[246] Finally, a defendant might argue for the Charter's application to common law developed around the Copyright Act, on the ground that the jurisprudence under the Copyright Act has developed in a fashion that is incompatible with freedom of expression.[247]

Reynolds, writing almost two decades later, provides an up-to-date account of how the Charter right to freedom of expression might be applied to copyright litigation. Like Fewer, Reynolds identifies the possibility for litigants to challenge the Copyright Act for placing unreasonable limits on their right to expression. He nonetheless points out that such challenges would fail because in *Michelin*, the leading case governing the intersection of copyright and freedom of expression, Justice Teitelbaum concluded that "[t]he Charter does not confer the right to use private property – the Plaintiff's copyright – in the service of freedom of

---

[241] Fewer, *supra* note 46, at 197.

[242] Fewer cites several cases, including The Queen v. James Lorimer & Co. [1984] 77 C.P.R. (2d) 262, 273 (F.C.A.), in which the Federal Court of Appeal dismissed the Charter claim: "If, indeed, the constraints on infringement of copyright could be construed as an unjustified limitation on an infringer's freedom of expression in some circumstances, this is not among them." In Source Perrier (Sociot Anonyme) v. Fira-Less Marketing Co. [1983] 70 C.P.R. (2d) 61, 67 (F.C.T.D.), the court declined to extend the scope of s. 2(b) to the parody, stating that "the most liberal interpretation of 'freedom of expression' does not embrace the freedom to depreciate the goodwill of registered trade marks, nor does it afford a licence to impair the business integrity of the owner of the marks merely to accommodate the creation of a spoof." *Id.* at 176, 210.

[243] Fewer, *supra* note 46, at 213.

[244] *Id.*

[245] *Id.* at 219.

[246] *Id.* at 217.

[247] *Id.* at 217–18; *citing* Dolphin Delivery Ltd., 33 D.L.R. (4th) at 190, 198; R. v. Salituro [1991] 3 S.C.R. 654, 675 (S.C.C.).

expression."[248] Reynolds points out that courts can apply the Charter to common law in limited circumstances. In *Bell ExpressVu*, a 2002 decision, the SCC held that statutory provisions may only be interpreted in light of Charter values in circumstances of "genuine ambiguity."[249] Justice Iacobucci cited Justice Major who, in *CanadianOxy Chemicals Ltd. v. Canada (AG)*, noted that: "[i]t is only when genuine ambiguity arises between two or more plausible readings, each equally in accordance with the intentions of the statute, that the courts need to resort to external interpretive aids."[250] To determine whether circumstances of "genuine ambiguity" exist, courts must determine the intention(s) of the statute and then apply the modern approach to statutory interpretation.[251] Only when the application of this approach results in "differing, but equally plausible, interpretations" may Charter values be used as an interpretive mechanism.[252] In such circumstances, the reviewing court would not simply ask whether there is "existence of justification, transparency and intelligibility within the decision-making process" or "whether the decision falls within a range of possible, acceptable outcomes which are defensible in respect of the facts and law."[253] It would need to ask whether a proper balance has been achieved between the relevant Charter value, or freedom of expression, with the objectives of the Copyright Act.[254]

Reynolds contends that the SCC could also re-conceptualize fair dealing as a stand-alone defense to promote or protect freedom of expression.[255] Aside from drawing references to scholars who have linked the SCC's fair dealing jurisprudence to freedom of expression or to human rights more broadly,[256] he cites Justice McLachlin's holding in *CCH Canadian Ltd.* that fair dealing categories are to be given "large and liberal" interpretations to indicate the embeddedness of s. 2(b) in the SCC's fair dealing jurisprudence.[257] Hence, he foresees that the SCC might in future re-conceptualize fair dealing not only as a limit on copyright-holder's right, or even a "user right," but also as a stand-alone defense to promote or protect freedom of expression.[258]

---

[248] Graham Reynolds, *The Limits of Statutory Interpretation: Towards Explicit Engagement, by the Supreme Court of Canada, with the Charter Right to Freedom of Expression in the Context of Copyright*, 41 QUEEN'S L.J. 1, 44 (2016); *citing* Michelin, 71 C.P.R. (3d) at 388.

[249] *Id.* at 34, 39, *citing* Bell ExpressVu Ltd. Partnership v. Rex [2002] 18 C.P.R. (4th) 289, 308 (S.C.C.).

[250] *Id.* at 39, *citing* Bell ExpressVu Ltd., 18 C.P.R. (4th) at 308.

[251] *Id.* at 39, 40.

[252] *Id.* at 40, *citing* Bell ExpressVu Ltd., 18 C.P.R. (4th) at 320.

[253] *Id.* at 41, *citing* Dunsmuir v. New Brunswick [2008] 291 D.L.R. (4th) 577, 637 (S.C.C.).

[254] *Id.* at 41, 42, *citing* Doré c. Québec (Tribunal des professions) [2012] 343 D.L.R. (4th) 193, 219 (S. C.C.).

[255] *See id.* at 38–39.

[256] Scholars cited include DAVID VAVER, COPYRIGHT LAW 669–72 (2000) and Marcelo Thompson, *Property Enforcement or Retrogressive Measure?: Copyright Reform in Canada and the Human Right of Access to Knowledge*, 4 UNIV. OTTAWA L. & TECH. J. 163 (2007). *Id.* at 38.

[257] *Id., citing* CCH Canadian Ltd., 30 C.P.R. (4th) at 25.

[258] *Id., citing* CCH Canadian Ltd., 30 C.P.R. (4th) at 25.

Fewer's and Reynolds' ideas of applying the Charter to common law so as to bring the Canadian copyright jurisprudence in line with s. 2(b) strengthen the argument of this book. The following hypotheses inspired by the Salinger lawsuit in the United States will show that courts can and should apply the parody exception by engaging with the Charter, and issue damages rather than injunctions where the parodies are held to have infringed owners' rights.

B. Two Salinger-inspired Hypotheses

After publishing his only novel, Salinger led a reclusive life until his death.[259] He became estranged from his wife, and began a number of short-term relationships with younger women, including the 18-year-old Joyce Maynard in 1972.[260] In 1998, to raise tuition for her three children, Maynard sold fourteen love letters by Salinger at an auction to a software entrepreneur and art collector, who later returned the letters to the author.[261] Because of copyright restrictions, the auction house put Salinger's letters on view in a private room under guard, so that they could be seen only by people judged to be prospective buyers.[262]

Let us imagine that a Canadian journalist posing as a prospective buyer had gained access to the letters at the auction, remembered the contents, and later published part of them in the Canadian media. Let us also imagine that Salinger was a Canadian author and the entire incident had taken place in Canada. If Salinger, the copyright-holder of his own letters, had sued the journalist and the media for infringement in a Canadian court, would the defendants have benefited from a fair dealing defense, and could the court have used the Charter to protect the defendants' right to freedom of expression?

If the current Copyright Act had applied to this scenario, defendants could have raised a fair dealing defense by claiming that they had published the copyrighted materials for a news reporting purpose.[263] Nevertheless, under the nature of the work factor, the fact that the letters were both confidential and unpublished might have tilted the scale towards a finding that the dealing was unfair. As the SCC held in *CCH Canadian Ltd.*, "[a]lthough certainly not determinative, if a work has not been published, the dealing may be more fair in that its reproduction with acknowledgement could lead to a wider public dissemination of the work – one of the goals

---

[259]   E.g., *Top 10 Most Reclusive Celebrities*, Time, *available at* http://content.time.com/time/specials/packages/article/0,28804,1902376_1902378_1902428,00.html (last visited Oct. 10, 2017).

[260]   E.g., Dinitia Smith, *J.D. Salinger's Love Letters Sold to Entrepreneur Who Says He Will Return Them*, N.Y. Times (June 23, 1999), *available at* https://partners.nytimes.com/library/books/062399salinger-auction.html (last visited Oct. 10, 2017); Lorri Drumm, *Pittsburgh Woman's Letters from J.D. Salinger Fetch $185,000*, Pitt. Post-Gazette (June 20, 2014), www.post-gazette.com/ae/books/2014/06/19/Pittsburgh-woman-s-letters-from-J-D-Salinger-fetch-150-000/stories/201406190305 (last visited Oct. 10, 2017).

[261]   E.g., Smith, *supra* note 260; Drumm, *supra* note 260.

[262]   Smith, *supra* note 260.

[263]   *See* Copyright Act, s. 29.2.

of copyright law. If, however, the work in question was confidential, this may tip the scales towards finding that the dealing was unfair."[264] Re-conceptualizing fair dealing as a stand-alone defense to promote or protect freedom of expression by the SCC, as Reynolds suggests, have would tilted the scale towards a finding of fairness and protecting defendants' freedom of expression.[265] However, because the "news reporting" provision is straightforward and would not lead to different interpretations for a "genuine ambiguity" to occur, the court could not have applied s. 2(b) of the Charter directly to the provision to ensure the protection of the defendants' freedom of expression.[266]

Now, suppose Salinger published the letters in the form of a book, and a Canadian reader published a new work parodying his love letter series. While the new work could be read as a social commentary on romances more generally, some readers interpreted it as an oblique commentary on Salinger's relationship with Maynard depicted in the original. In addition, the new work contained elements of humor that only a highly sophisticated reader would appreciate. Again, let us imagine that Salinger was a Canadian author who, offended by what he considered a defamatory commentary on his romantic affair as much as by its infringement of his copyright in his own work, realized that he would have little luck winning a defamation lawsuit.[267] He therefore sued the writer and the publisher in a Canadian court for copyright infringement. Could the defendants raise a fair dealing defense, and could the court use the Charter to protect the defendants' freedom of expression?

Obviously, the author and the publisher of the imitative work could raise a parody defense against the author's charge of infringement under Canada's new law. Like the previous scenario, re-conceptualizing fair dealing as a stand-alone defense to promote or protect freedom of expression by the SCC would tip the scale towards a finding of fairness and protecting the defendants' right to free expression through the parody.

What about directly applying the Charter? The court could and should engage the Charter directly when interpreting and applying the "parody" fair dealing provision, in order to prevent the plaintiff from suppressing the defendants' speech. Part I and this chapter have already explained the desirability of a single parody exception. Even assuming that the law provided for this exception in this hypothesis, the statutory language might not have defined "parody" succinctly by describing the whole range of works that it encompasses, or stating that the parodic works need not be humorous. This would likely create a situation of "genuine ambiguity."[268] Because the *Théberge* court held that Canadian copyright law aims

---

[264]   CCH Canadian Ltd., 30 C.P.R. (4th) at 28.
[265]   *See* Reynolds, *supra* note 248, at 38.
[266]   *See id.* at 39–42.
[267]   *See* Torstar, 79 C.P.R. (4th) at 442.
[268]   *See* Reynolds, *supra* note 248, at 39–40; *citing* Bell ExpressVu Ltd., 18 C.P.R. (4th) at 308.

both to "obtain . . . a just reward for the creator to protect authors' rights and to provide incentives for the creation and dissemination of expressive works,"[269] the court would evaluate different conceptions of "parody." A narrower exception would offer more protection of authors' rights, reduce the likelihood that their works would be used against their wishes, and incentivize them to write more. A broader exception would make a larger range of imitative works legal and lead to more works in the market. These "differing, but equally plausible, interpretations" of "parody" would allow the court to engage s. 2(b) of the Charter directly when interpreting and applying the parody provision.[270] Thus, in this hypothesis, the court could and should interpret "parody" liberally to enable the defendant's work to pass the first-step of the fair dealing analysis, even though its critique of Salinger's work and its humorous elements were not very obvious. Because the work, albeit serving a commercial purpose as much as providing a commentary on the original, would not likely compete with the original in its market, the court would likely determine that its use of the original was fair in the second-stage fairness analysis.

Finally, even if the court found that the parody had infringed Salinger's original letters in this hypothetical, it should order a remedy in line with s. 2(b) of the Charter on the ground that the defendants' speech had values. Compared to granting injunctions, which would have suppressed the parodist's speech, money damages would have been far more appropriate to compensate for the estimated losses caused by the parody. In addition, s. 38 of the Copyright Act raises serious concerns by allowing the plaintiff to "recover possession of all infringing copies of that work or other subject-matter, . . . take proceedings for seizure of those copies or plates."[271] To protect the defendants' freedom of expression, courts should avoid granting the plaintiff's request to transfer ownership of the parodic work to him.

* * *

This chapter has argued that a broad parody exception should substitute for the dual parody and satire exceptions to prevent a parody/satire dichotomy and to safeguard the right to parody in Canada. Chapter 5 will turn to the seemingly broad parody exemption in British copyright law, to explain how the right to parody may be threatened by moral rights challenges and will likely be curtailed by a narrow public interest doctrine.

---

[269] Théberge, 17 C.P.R. (4th) at 176.
[270] *See Id.* 40–42, *citing* Doré, 343 D.L.R. (4th) at 219.
[271] *See* Copyright Act, s. 38(1).

5

The (Deceptively) Broad British Parody Exception

I may not agree with you, but I will defend to the death your right to make an ass of yourself.[1]

Imitation is the sincerest form of flattery that mediocrity can pay to greatness.[2]

In the United Kingdom, the right to freedom of expression is protected by the Human Rights Act, 1998. The right to parody was not recognized in the copyright context until the introduction of an exemption "for the purpose of caricature, parody or pastiche" in 2014. This exemption, which does not require that parodies target the original works, appears to be broader in scope than its American and Canadian counterparts, and would seem to bring the U.K. copyright system in line with its freedom of expression jurisprudence. However, the moral rights provisions in the copyright statute potentially conflict with the copyright exception, and British courts might not be able to rely upon a free speech/public interest doctrine in domestic and European laws to safeguard the right to parody.

This chapter will offer an overview of the British freedom of expression jurisprudence and the parodies in its culture. It will then explain why its parody exception, while promising, may not safeguard free expression. The "humor" requirement will not likely become an obstacle, because British humor is broad enough to encompass a variety of contents, styles, and sensibilities. However, this parody exception may come into conflict with and become narrowed by the moral rights provisions. In assessing a parody for fairness, courts can and should prioritize the market substitution factor and place greater emphasis on the nature of the defendant's use factor to protect artistic and/or political expressions.

The last section will examine more closely the reasons that British courts might not be able to apply the parody exception in a way that best serves the public's interest. The public interest doctrine was narrowly circumscribed by the judgment in *Ashdown v. Telegraph Group Ltd.*, a domestic decision. In addition, British courts might not follow the European Court of Justice's decision in *Deckmyn*

---

[1] Oscar Wilde's quote, *in* ALAN HAWORTH, FREE SPEECH: ALL THAT MATTERS 137 (2015).

[2] Oscar Wilde, *Quotes*, GOODREADS, www.goodreads.com/quotes/558084-imitation-is-the-sincerest-form -of-flattery-that-mediocrity-can (last visited Oct. 10, 2017).

v. Vandersteen to balance authors' moral rights with the fundamental right to free-dom of expression after Brexit. Hence, unless *Ashdown* is overruled, or the *Deckmyn* decision continues to be followed post-Brexit, courts could not rely upon this external mechanism to safeguard the right to parody. On the fairness test alone, courts could nonetheless resort to an internal solution to help protect artistic and political speech, by emphasizing the nature of the defendant's use factor. Regarding potential moral rights claims, only if the *Ashdown* decision is overruled, or *Deckmyn* is followed post-Brexit, would courts be able to draw upon a broad public interest or freedom of expression doctrine to ensure that non-defamatory parodies would survive these challenges.

I. FREEDOM OF EXPRESSION AND THE RIGHT TO PARODY IN THE UNITED KINGDOM

In the United Kingdom, freedom of expression is protected under the Human Rights Act, 1998 (HRA), which incorporates most of the substantive provisions of the European Convention on Human Rights (European Convention) into its domestic law.[3] English law, however, has traditionally taken little notice of free-dom of speech.[4] Magna Carta, which retains a potent symbolic power through its recognition of the basic liberties of "freemen of the realm" and the State's obliga-tion to protect them, has been of little practical importance.[5] The Bill of Rights of 1689, which contains specific declarations of rights, only protected freedom of speech of Members of Parliament but not that of citizens.[6] Prior to 1998, British citizens did not enjoy any textual guarantee to freedom of speech, which existed in the form of a residual liberty.[7] Hence, they were free to express an opinion or disclose information only if the expression was not forbidden by legislation or the common law.[8]

In the pre-HRA era, British judges nonetheless had demonstrated a willingness to address free speech claims for many years by relying upon societal traditions to check abuses of governmental powers to restrict the "fundamental human right" to freedom of speech.[9] Thus, they had articulated

---

[3] *See* Human Rights Act, 1998, c. 42.

[4] Eric Barendt, *Freedom of Expression in the United Kingdom under the Human Rights Act 1998*, 84 IND. L.J. 851, 851 (2009); Douglas W. Vick, *The Human Rights Act and the British Constitution*, 37 TEX. INT'L L.J. 329, 330 (2002).

[5] Vick, *supra* note 4, at 337.

[6] *Id.*

[7] *Id.* at 330, 341.

[8] Barendt, *supra* note 4, at 852–53.

[9] RONALD J. KROTOSZYNSKI, JR., THE FIRST AMENDMENT IN CROSS-CULTURAL PERSPECTIVE: A COMPARATIVE LEGAL ANALYSIS OF THE FREEDOM OF SPEECH 187, 197 (2006). *Brind* demonstrates that the absence of a written provision protecting free expressions does not bar consideration of speech interests as either a "right" or a decisional "principle." *Id.* at 197, *citing* R. v. Secretary of State for the Home Department ex p Brind [1991] 1 A.C. 696 (E.W.C.A. Civ.).

a common law right to this freedom.[10] This liberal approach to the freedom of speech, despite the lack of a strong free speech tradition in English law, was particularly obvious during the passage of the HRA in Parliament and the period between its enactment and coming into effect in October 2000.[11]

The HRA marked a shift in the treatment and perception of freedom of expression from a residual freedom to a positive right explicitly recognized by law.[12] Schedule 1, art. 10 § 1 of the HRA, which is identical to art. 10 of the European Convention, provides that "[e]veryone has the right to freedom of expression," including "freedom to hold opinions and to receive and impart information and ideas without interference by public authority and regardless of frontiers."[13] Article 10 § 2 also directly limits its scope, stating that: "the exercise of these freedoms, since it carries with it duties and responsibilities, may be subject to such formalities, conditions, restrictions or penalties as are prescribed by law and are necessary in a democratic society."[14]

Since then, British courts have confidently asserted the fundamental nature of the right to freedom of expression and demanded careful scrutiny of any restriction on this right.[15] In *R. v. Shayler*, the first important free speech case after the HRA came into force, Lord Bingham stated confidently that this fundamental right had been recognized in common law for some time, but was now "underpinned by statute."[16] Another example is the more recent *Laporte* case, in which he compared the common law's approach to freedom of expression, which was "hesitant and negative," with the "constitutional shift" represented by articles 10 and 11 of Sch. 1 to the HRA, whereby freedoms of expression and association became "fundamental rights" and "[a]ny prior restraint on their exercise must be scrutinised with particular care."[17]

The HRA stipulates that the exercise of freedom of expression is limited "in the interests of national security, territorial integrity or public safety, for the prevention of disorder or crime, for the protection of health or morals, for the protection of the reputation or rights of others, for preventing the disclosure of information received in confidence, or for maintaining the authority and

---

[10]   Barendt, *supra* note 4, at 852–53. The classic example is Lord Reid in *Brutus v. Cozens* [1972] UKHL 6, [1973] A.C. 854 (H.L.) (appeal taken from Eng.), which argued that the word "insulting" in the public order legislation should not be construed to penalize the use of offensive language during an anti-apartheid demonstration at Wimbledon.

[11]   Barendt, *supra* note 4, at 853–54.

[12]   *Id.* at 851; Vick, *supra* note 4, at 330.

[13]   European Convention for the Protection of Human Rights and Fundamental Freedoms, art. 10 § 1 (Nov. 4, 1950).

[14]   *Id.* art. 10 § 2.

[15]   Barendt, *supra* note 4, at 854–55.

[16]   *Id.* at 854, *citing* R. v. Shayler [2002] UKHL 11, [2003] 1 A.C. 247, paras. 21–22 (appeal taken from Eng.).

[17]   *Id.*, *citing* R. (on the application of Laporte) v. Chief Constable of Gloucestershire Constabulary [2006] UKHL 55, [2007] 2 A.C. 105, paras. 34, 85 (appeal taken from Eng.).

impartiality of the judiciary."[18] In fact, laws had been enacted throughout the history of England and the United Kingdom to protect national security, including different versions of the Treason Act and the Sedition Act criminalizing disloyalty against the Crown and the nation.[19] Defamation law similarly had a long, though somewhat obscure, history in England.[20] For a long time, English law had put the burden of proving the truth of allegedly defamatory statements on defendants, and had not recognized any general privilege for the press or for anyone else to defame even prominent public figures.[21] Regarding public morality, the 1727 judgment against bookseller Edmund Curl for the publication of *Venus in the Cloister; or, The Nun in her Smock* established obscene libel as an offence under English common law, and became "the first recorded instance of a conviction on grounds of obscenity in the English-speaking world."[22] The 1857 Obscene Publications Act empowered magistrates to order the destruction of offending books and prints.[23] In *Regina v. Hicklin* (1868), Chief Justice Cockburn further interpreted the word "obscene" in this Act to mean a "tendency to deprave and corrupt the minds and morals of those who are open to such immoral influences, and into whose hands a publication of this sort might fall," a standard that made many works of literature – not merely pornographic materials – illegal.[24]

Over the past few decades, the above laws and policies have been replaced by more lenient ones. In some cases, more relaxed laws were enacted long before the HRA. For example, the Obscene Publications Act 1959 introduced a defense of merit on the grounds of "science, literature, art or learning."[25] After the court found that *Lady Chatterley's Lover*, once declared obscene under the *Hicklin* test, had literary merit and its publication was legal, publishers in different media enjoyed far more freedom to publish sexually explicit materials.[26] Much more recently, the Defamation Act 2013 introduced new statutory defenses of truth, honest opinion, and "publication on a matter of

---

[18] HRA 1998, c. 42, Sch. 1, art. 10 § 2.
[19] *See, e.g.,* Treason Act, 1351, c. 2; Treason Act, 1695, c. 3; Treason Act, 1708, c. 21; Treason Act, 1945, c. 44; *Sedition* Act, 1661, c. 1.
[20] The common law action for defamation was established in sixteenth-century England. Reputation was protected by the law – meaningfully, albeit narrowly – from the twelfth to the sixteenth century in local and ecclesiastical courts. LAWRENCE MCNAMARA, REPUTATION AND DEFAMATION 68–79 (2007).
[21] *See, e.g.,* Campbell v. Spottiswoode [1863] 3 B. & S. 769, 777 (Q.B.); Blackshaw v. Lord [1984] 1 Q.B. 42 (E.W.C.A.).
[22] DEREK JONES, CENSORSHIP: A WORLD ENCYCLOPEDIA 311 (2001).
[23] LEORNARD FREEDMAN, THE OFFENSIVE ART: POLITICAL SATIRE AND ITS CENSORSHIP AROUND THE WORLD FROM BEERBOHM TO BORAT 82 (2009).
[24] Regina v. Hicklin [1868] 3 Q.B. 360, 371 (Q.B.); Katherine Mullin, *Poison More Deadly than Prussic Acid: Defining Obscenity after the 1857 Obscene Publications Act (1850–1885)* IN PRUDES ON THE PROWL: FICTION AND OBSCENITY IN ENGLAND, 1850 TO THE PRESENT DAY 19–20 (David Bradshaw & Rachel Potter, eds. 2013).
[25] FREEDMAN, *supra* note 23, at 82.
[26] *Id.* at 83.

public interest," which are especially empowering for the media in expressing opinions about public figures.[27] Certainly, laws that threaten people's speech freedom have continued to be established in the name of national security. An example is the Terrorism Act 2006, which makes it an offence to publish material likely to be understood by members of the public who read or hear it as a direct or indirect encouragement of terrorism or a glorification of terrorism.[28] In 2009, the government nonetheless abolished the offence of seditious libel, which made criticism of the monarch or the government a criminal offence and was used to silence political dissent.[29]

Compared to laws protecting national security and banning obscene and defamatory expressions, laws prohibiting hate speech are relatively recent. With the influx of immigration in the twentieth century, the Race Relations Acts were passed to maintain a multiracial and tolerant society.[30] Later, the Public Order Act 1986 made it an offence to, among other things, use "threatening, abusive or insulting" words, behavior, or written material, with the intent to "stir up racial hatred," or in circumstances where racial hatred is "likely to be stirred up."[31] The Racial and Religious Hatred Act of 2006, in response to terrorist attacks, extends the proscription of incitement to racial hatred to protect "group[s] of persons defined by reference to religious belief or lack of a religious belief."[32] Similarly, the Criminal Justice and Immigration Act 2008, which amended Part 3A of the Public Order Act, makes it an offence to incite hatred on the ground of sexual orientation through the use of words, behavior or written material, public performances, broadcasting programs, or possession of inflammatory materials that are "threatening" and not merely abusive or insulting.[33]

Unsurprisingly, there has been a decline in censorship in Britain on the grounds of obscenity, national security, or potentially defamatory materials over the years. The censorship of printed literature for obscenity is largely a thing of the past.[34] Books and media were banned for national security

[27]   Clive Coleman, *Defamation Act 2013 Aims to Improve Libel Laws*, BBC NEWS (Dec. 31, 2013), www .bbc.com/news/uk-25551640 (last visited Oct. 10, 2017).

[28]   Ian Cobain, *Why Is the Crux of the Incedal Case a Secret? You're Not Allowed to Know*, THE GUARDIAN (Mar. 26, 2015), www.theguardian.com/law/2015/mar/26/erol-incedal-case-secret-trial-terror (last visited Oct. 10, 2017).

[29]   E.g., Index on Censorship, *UK Government Abolishes Seditious Libel and Criminal Defamation*, HUMAN RIGHTS HOUSE (July 13, 2009), http://humanrightshouse.org/Articles/11311.html (last visited Oct. 10, 2017).

[30]   FREEDMAN, *supra* note 23, at 86.

[31]   Public Order Act, 1986, c. 4, s. 18(1).

[32]   Racial and Religious Hatred Act, 2006, c. 1, s. 29(A).

[33]   Criminal Justice and Immigration Act, 2008, c. 4, s. 74; *see Sexual Orientation: CPS Guidance on Stirring up Hatred on the Grounds of Sexual Orientation*, THE CROWN PROSECUTION SERVICE (Mar. 17, 2010), www.cps.gov.uk/legal/s_to_u/sexual_orientation/ (last visited Oct. 10, 2017).

[34]   JOE BROOKER, THE ART OF OFFENCE: BRITISH LITERARY CENSORSHIP SINCE 1971 (1971–THE PRESENT DAY) 205 (2013). The last literary work to be successfully prosecuted under the 1959 Act was Hubert Selby's

reasons,[35] but the censorship of potentially defamatory materials[36] will become increasingly uncommon due to a higher legal standard of what constitutes defamation. However, laws governing hate speech, which have led to the censorship or self-censorship of offensive materials, may continue to restrict freedom of expression. The Criminal Justice and Immigration Act 2008 has not guaranteed the freedom of expressing opinions against sexual minorities even where they are not threatening.[37] Even where the offensive materials are not forbidden by law, unofficial or de facto censorship may occur.[38] In 1989, when the Ayatollah Khomeini pronounced a *fatwa* on Salman Rushdie for his work *The Satanic Verses*, Rushdie went into hiding, while his publishers, fearing violent reprisals, delayed publishing the paperback copy of the book, and some bookstores ceased to stock it, or kept it hidden under the counter.[39] In 2004, Birmingham Repertory Theatre was forced to cancel performances of *Behzti*, which contained a rape scene in a Sikh temple, due to violent protests from the Sikh community.[40]

Hence, the British are entitled to the right to parody, as long as their parodies neither violate the laws on national security, obscenity and defamation, nor constitute hate speech by targeting racial, ethnic, and religious groups or sexual minorities. Indeed, parody has enjoyed a long history in English culture and literature. Whereas the first usage of the term did not appear until the very late sixteenth century, parody as a literary form can be found as early as in medieval England, in what today's literary critics described as the parody or burlesque genre of imitative,

Last Exit to Brooklyn, which was banned as obscene by a jury, but then cleared when this verdict was overturned for technical reasons by the Court of Appeal in 1968. *Id.* at 180.

[35] For instance, *Spycatcher*, written by former secret service agent Peter Wright, as well as newspaper reports of the book, were banned by the British government for their breach of confidentiality during the period from 1985 to 1988. In 1988, Law Lords ruled that the media could publish extracts from the book, on the ground that any damage to national security has already been done by its publication outside of England, but agreed the book constituted a serious breach of confidentiality. *1988: Government Loses Skycatcher Battle*, BBC NEWS, http://news.bbc.co.uk/onthisday/hi/dates/stories/october/13/newsid_2532000/2532583.stm (last visited Oct. 10, 2017).

[36] One example is *Unlawful Killing*, the 2011 British documentary film questioning the circumstances of the deaths of Princess Diana and Dodi Fayed. Ben Child, *Princess Diana Documentary Unlawful Killing Is Shelved*, THE GUARDIAN (July 5, 2012), www.theguardian.com/film/2012/jul/05/princess-diana-documentary-unlawful-killing (last visited Oct. 10, 2017).

[37] For instance, in *Core Issues Trust v. Transport for London* [2013] 22 H.R.L.R. 434, 464 (Q.B.), a Christian charity's attempt to put advertisements on London buses that said "NOT GAY! EX-GAY, POST-GAY AND PROUD. GET OVER IT!" was rejected by the bus company. The court held that advertisements on buses were "highly intrusive" and the plaintiff's ad would "cause grave offence to a significant section of the many inhabitants of London." In addition, it would interfere with their right to respect for private and family life under Article 8(1) of the European Convention, rather than contributing to a "reasoned debate." Finally, the advertisement was "homophobic" and the defendants would have been acting in breach of their equality duty should they allow it.

[38] Brooker, *supra* note 34, at 202.

[39] *Id.* at 201–02.

[40] Sarah Left, *Play Axed after Sikh Protests*, THE GUARDIAN (Dec. 20, 2004), www.theguardian.com/uk/2004/dec/20/arts.religion1 (last visited Oct. 10, 2017).

satirical works.[41] In the Victorian era, such writers as Lewis Carroll, A.C. Hilton, and James Kenneth Stephen gave parody a significant boost.[42] Oscar Wilde parodied different literary conventions to satirize Victorian society.[43] The satirical form of parodies also became associated with both censorship and de-censorship. In 1873, *The Happy Land*, a musical play co-authored by F. Tomline (W.S. Gilbert) and Gilbert à Beckett, parodied Gilbert's earlier work, *The Wicked World*, to criticize its contemporary government.[44] After the actors turned their characters into caricatures of real-life politicians on the opening night of the play, the Lord Chamberlain withdrew the license of the play, before restoring a censored and a much milder version of it.[45] The twentieth century, which saw a loosening of censorship laws and turbulent events like the two World Wars, witnessed a continued trend of using parody to criticize social and political mores.[46]

II. THE RIGHT TO PARODY IN BRITISH COPYRIGHT LAW

The road towards a parody exception in British copyright law was nonetheless a long, bumpy one. Certainly, since the incidents of *The Satanic Verses* and *Behzti*, authors may have felt inhibited from producing parodies that may insult certain groups but that do not constitute hate speech. In addition, topics such as rape and child molestation are generally considered unfit subjects for public expressions of humor.[47] These controversial issues aside, copyright might disentitle British citizens from making parodies. Before 2014, neither British statutory law nor common law

---

[41]   According to the *Oxford English Dictionary*, the first usage of the term in England was found in Ben Johnson's *Every Man in His Humour* in 1598: "A Parodie, a parodie! to make it absurder than it was." Martha Bayless nonetheless discovered its first appearances in medieval England. MARTHA BAYLESS, PARODY IN THE MIDDLE AGES: THE LATIN TRADITION (1997).

[42]   Christian Rutz, *Parody: A Missed Opportunity?* 3 INTELL. PROP. Q. 284, 287 (2004).

[43]   *E.g.*, RUTH ROBBINS, OSCAR WILDE 56 (2011); AMY S. WATKIN, BLOM'S HOW TO WRITE ABOUT OSCAR WILDE 188 (2010); GEORGE ROWELL, THE VICTORIAN THEATRE 1792–1913, A SURVEY 111 (1956).

[44]   Andrew Crowther, *Background of The Happy Land*, THE GILBERT AND SULLIVAN ARCHIVE, www .gilbertandsullivanarchive.org/gilbert/plays/happy_land/background.html (last visited Oct. 10, 2017).

[45]   *Id.*

[46]   One example is the first violent scene in *Clockwork Orange* (1962), Anthony Burgess' highly controversial – albeit never banned – novel, which parodies the terms of debate in the trial on *Lady Chatterley's Lover* and its procedures so as to satirize the motivations of those who based the charge of obscenity on certain words extracted from the book without reference to their overall context. Rod Mengham, *Bollocks to Respectability: British Fiction after the Trial of Lady Chatterley's Lover (1960–1970)*, IN PRUDES ON THE PROWL: FICTION AND OBSCENITY IN ENGLAND, 1850 TO THE PRESENT DAY 265 (David Bradshaw & Rachel Potter eds., 2013).

[47]   In July 2001 a satirical TV program, *Brass Eye*, presented a spoof of the media's hyping of pedophile cases by inveigling celebrities into reciting absurd "facts" such as, "We have footage, too alarming to show you, of a little boy being interfered with by a penis-shaped sound wave generated by an online pedophile." The spoof concluded with a fictional crowd capturing a pedophile and burning him on a 25-foot phallus. The program was met with protests from the distressed public as well as rebukes from government ministers. Freedman, *supra* note 23, at 83–84.

entertained a copyright exception to accommodate parodies, regardless of their subject matters.

A. Thwarted Promises of a Parody Exemption Pre-2014

The earliest English case that implicitly involved a parody defense is *Hanfstaengl v. Empire Palace* (1894).[48] An artist whose paintings had been represented by the *Empire Theatre* in the form of tableaux vivants brought infringement actions against the *Daily Graphic* and the *Westminster Budget* for printing sketches of the tableaux vivants.[49] The court, without addressing whether the sketches offered possible "criticism" of the plaintiff's originals, focused on their purposes and likelihood of substituting for the originals, to determine that they were not the originals' copies or reproductions within the meaning of s. 1 of the Fine Arts Copyright Act, 1862.[50] The court stated that the defendants' copies were "rough sketches, made for a very different purpose and answering a very different purpose, that purpose being, not to give an idea of the plaintiff's pictures, but to give a rough idea of what is to be seen at the Empire Theatre."[51] Because there was "no piracy, actual or intended" and no possibility of confusion, the defendants' sketches were not infringements of the originals.[52]

Although the Copyright Act 1911, like the 1862 statute, also failed to provide for a parody exception, case law in the early-twentieth century continued to imply a parody exception in copyright disputes by emphasizing the amounts of the original works used in the new works. In *Francis, Day & Hunter v. Feldman & Co.* (1914), the copyright-owners of "You made me love you (I didn't want to do it)" alleged that the defendants infringed their copyright by printing, selling, and otherwise disposing of a song called "You didn't want to do it – but you did."[53] The court held that "colourable imitation" means "the reproduction of a work or of any substantial part of it in any material form," and copyright does not extend to phrases, ideas, or methods.[54] Although the defendants' song was based upon the plaintiffs' work, it did not serve as a substitute for the original and did not infringe its copyright.[55]

In *Glyn v. Weston Feature Film Co.* (1916), the court not only focused on the amount of the original work copied but also emphasized the originality of the new work.[56] The author and copyright-owner of the novel *Three Weeks* alleged that the

---

[48] Hanfstaengl v. Empire Palace [1894] 3 Ch. 109 (H.L.); James R. Banko, "*Schlurppes Tonic Bubble Bath*": *In Defense of Parody*, 11 Pa. J. INT'L BUS. L. 627, 634 (1990).

[49] Scenes "presented on stage by costumed actors who remain silent and motionless as if in a picture." [French, "living pictures."] AMERICAN HERITAGE DICTIONARY 1236 (1982). *Id.*

[50] Hanfstaengl [1894] 3 Ch. at 130–32.

[51] *Id.* at 132.

[52] *Id.* at 130.

[53] Francis, Day & Hunter v. Feldman & Co. [1914] 2 Ch. 728 (E.W.C.A.); CATHERINE COLSTON, PRINCIPLES OF INTELLECTUAL PROPERTY 194–95 (1999).

[54] *Id.* at 195.

[55] *Id.*

[56] Glyn v. Weston Feature Film Co. [1916] 1 Ch. 261 (E.W.H.C. Ch.).

defendants' cinematograph films under the title of *Pimple's Three Weeks (without the Option)* reproduced substantial parts of their novel, and demanded, among other things, an injunction to restrain the defendant from selling, letting, or authorizing their public exhibition or otherwise infringing the plaintiff's copyright.[57] The court held that because the amount of the taking was not substantial, the film did not constitute any infringement of the plaintiff's copyright in the novel.[58] The judge further emphasized that "no infringement of the plaintiff's rights takes place where a defendant has bestowed such mental labour upon what he has taken and has subjected it to such revision and alteration as to produce an original result."[59]

The parody defense was raised, addressed, and accepted for the first time in *Joy Music Ltd. v. Sunday Pictorial Newspapers (1920) Ltd.* (1960). The copyright-owners of the popular song "Rock-a-Billy" alleged that the defendant had infringed their copyright by publishing "Rock-a-Phillip Rock!" in a newspaper feature article titled "Rock-a-Philip, Rock! Rock!"[60] The defendant claimed that he had intended to write a parody of the song "Rock-a-Billy" to poke fun at the activities of H.R.H. Prince Philip.[61] The main test to be applied, the court argued, was whether the writer "had bestowed such mental labour upon the material he had taken and had subjected it to such revision and alteration so as to produce an original work."[62] According to the English Copyright Act of 1956, the reproduction of a work for the purpose of a finding of copyright infringement means the reproduction of "a substantial part of the [original] work."[63] Although the defendant's parody had its origin in the song "Rock-a-Billy," it was "produced by sufficient independent new work to be in itself not a reproduction of the words of the original song but a new original work," and therefore did not constitute copyright infringement within the meaning of s. 49(1) of the statute.[64] While the court did not address the plaintiffs' concern that the new song targeted an unrelated figure, it impliedly endorsed a broad definition of parody encompassing works that criticize or comment on the underlying works and/or something else.

In 1983, the Chancery Division of the High Court of Justice nonetheless denied the legitimacy of the parody defense in *Schweppes Ltd. v. Wellingtons Ltd.* by reverting to the substantial use test used in the earlier cases.[65] The plaintiffs held the copyright of their yellow and gold label bearing the word "SCHWEPPES" on their tonic water bottles.[66] They alleged that the defendants had infringed their

---

[57] *Id.*
[58] *Id.* at 269.
[59] *Id.* at 268.
[60] Joy Music, Ltd. v. Sunday Pictorial Newspapers (1920) Ltd. [1960] 2 Q.B. 60 (Q.B.).
[61] *Id.*
[62] *Id.* at 70.
[63] Copyright Act, 1956, c. 74, s. 49(1).
[64] Joy Music Ltd. [1960] 2 Q.B. at 70.
[65] *See* Schweppes Ltd. v. Wellingtons Ltd. [1984] F.S.R. 210 (E.W.H.C. Ch.).
[66] *Id.* at 211.

copyright by selling tonic bubble bath in bottles "bearing two yellow labels which have a very close resemblance indeed to the corresponding labels on the plaintiffs' bottle," the only difference being that "Schweppes" had been changed into "Schlurppes."[67] The defendants, conceding they had taken a substantial part of the plaintiffs' label, relied on the judgment in *Joy Music* to argue that they had labored to make the bottle a parody.[68] The court nonetheless rejected the defendants' defense, pointing out that evidence of sufficient alteration and even originality were beside the point if the resulting work reproduced "a substantial part" of the plaintiffs' work without a license.[69]

In *Williamson Music Ltd. v. The Pearson Partnership Ltd.* (1986), the same court continued to apply the substantial use test to reject the parody defense.[70] Here, the plaintiffs were the copyright-owners of Rodgers and Hammerstein's musical *South Pacific* and the music and lyrics of the song "There is Nothin' Like a Dame."[71] When the defendants advertised the express coach between London and other places in the United Kingdom with a jingle imitating "There is Nothin' Like a Dame," the plaintiffs sued for copyright infringement. The defendants argued that their new song was a parody of the plaintiffs' by showing evidence of the composer's creative effort.[72] The court determined that the only relevant test was the "substantial part test" put forward in the *Schweppes* case: "whether a substantial portion has been taken, not whether a substantial change or addition has been effected."[73] Acknowledging the fact that the parody was not at all "a slavish copy" of the original, it nonetheless relied on expert reports obtained by the plaintiffs stating that the harmony, rhythmical patterns, melodic elements and overall structure of the defendants' song were strongly dependent on the original.[74] It also emphasized that infringement of copyright in music "is not a question of note for note comparison, but of whether the substance of the original copyright work is taken or not," which is "to be determined by the ear as well as by the eye."[75] Because hearing the parody as a whole produced an impression of the original, the test of substantiality was satisfied and the parody constituted infringement.[76]

When the Copyright, Designs and Patents Act 1988 (CDPA) first came into force, fair dealing defenses were limited to the defined purposes of research and private study, criticism and review, and reporting current events.[77] In a more recent case, *Allen v. Redshaw* (2013), which raised the possibility of a parody defense, the court

---

[67] *Id.*

[68] *Id.* at 212.

[69] *Id.* at 212–13.

[70] Williamson Music Ltd. v. The Pearson Partnership Ltd. [1987] F.S.R. 97 (E.W.H.C. Ch.).

[71] *Id.* at 98.

[72] *Id.* at 108–11.

[73] *Id.* at 109.

[74] *Id.* at 109–10.

[75] *Id.* at 108.

[76] *Id.*

[77] Copyright, Designs and Patents Act, 1988, c. 48, ss. 29, 30.

continued to focus on the amount of the original copied.[78] Here, the claimant was an artist, writer and puppeteer who devised with his business partner a stage puppet show called "Mr Spoon on Button Moon," for which he designed its puppets, sets and props and produced numerous drawings and paintings.[79] After Thames Television commissioned a Button Moon television series based upon the stage show, the claimant continued to own the rights in all the underlying artistic works.[80] He sued the defendant for passing off and infringement of copyright in his sale of china mugs, T-shirts, and sweatshirts decorated with a design which copied the Mr Spoon character, the rocket and the button moon.[81] The defendant claimed that he intended to create a "combined parody/joke product" that bore "only a passing resemblance" to the claimant's works and pointed to the "distinct differences which set them apart."[82] The court held that, regardless of the defendant's motives, there is no defense of parody if a substantial part of the claimant's work was copied.[83] Not only did the defendant copy substantial elements of the claimant's original designs, evidenced by "[t]he same or a substantially similar design" on the mug and on the cardboard box in which the mug was presented, but there existed "a causal connection between the parties' respective works," whether the copying was direct or indirect.[84] The fact that the defendant combined the rocket design with the wording of a recycling slogan did not make it a parody of the claimant's designs or entitle the defendant to a parody defense.[85]

B. Calls for a Parody Exception

For a long time, many scholars had called for an explicit parody exception in copyright law. James Banko criticizes the indeterminacy of the substantial use test by pointing out that the meaning of "substantial" is "murky" and that a successful parody may copy a "substantial" amount and still deserve a defense against infringement.[86] Drawing upon American case law, he argues that if the parody causes no economic harm by direct competition, it may not be enjoined.[87] Christian Rutz likewise criticizes the substantial use test, and points out that exemptions of criticism and review in s. 30(1), which require explicit identification and acknowledgment of the original, would not serve as an adequate defense for parody.[88] Rutz

---

[78] See Allen v. Redshaw [2013] 2013 WL 2110623 (P.C.C.).
[79] *Id.* para. 2.
[80] *Id.* para. 3.
[81] *Id.* para. 4.
[82] *Id.* at paras. 21–23.
[83] *Id.* paras. 30–31.
[84] *Id.* paras. 29, 31.
[85] *Id.* para. 30.
[86] James Richard Banko, *"Schlurppes Tonic Bubble Bath": In Defense of Parody*, 11 U. Pa. J. Int'l Bus. L. 627, 652–54 (1990).
[87] *Id.* at 639–41, 654.
[88] Christian Rutz, *Parody: A Missed Opportunity?* 3 Intell. Prop. Q. 284, 285, 289–91 (2004).

proposes a flexible fair use defense in the CDPA, which should apply whether the parody focuses mainly on the work parodied or directs criticism or commentary towards general aspects of life or social values.[89]

Like Rutz, Alina Walsh contends that the requirement in s. 30(1) of the CDPA that the parody acknowledge its source would weaken its ability to amuse the reader or audience.[90] Conceding that the complex nature of parody would make a clear definition difficult, she looks to the American case law for a model to accommodate parody and argues that British courts should opt for a balancing test like the one adopted by American courts.[91] Under this model, courts should look at the way the new work has altered the original, the amount, substantiality, and purpose of its use, and its influence on the market.[92]

Unsurprisingly, all three scholars critique the indeterminacy of the substantial part test. Both Walsh and Rutz contend that a flexible and broad parody exception encompassing both "parodic" and "satirical" works would be a viable solution, and look to the American example for a multi-factor balancing test to determine whether the work would qualify for a parody defense. Banko also impliedly endorses a broad parody exception, by emphasizing that whether the parody infringes the original's copyright should be determined by whether the former directly competes with the latter in the market.

C. Implementing the New Parody Exception in the Copyright Act

In 2006, the Gowers Review of Intellectual Property recommended that the United Kingdom follow Article 5(3)(k) of the Copyright Directive to "create an exception to copyright for the purpose of caricature, parody or pastiche by 2008," pointing out that in the absence of such an exception, the nation was missing out on economic benefits to be derived from innovative forms of transformative creativity.[93] From early 2008 to late 2009, the Intellectual Property Office (UKIPO) launched a two-stage consultation process to seek advice on a new "parody" exception.[94] In 2011, the government began a fresh

---

[89] *Id.* at 296–97.

[90] *See* Alina Walsh, *Parody of Intellectual Property: Prospects for a Fair Use/Dealing Defence in the United Kingdom*, 21 INTELL. CO. & COM. L.R. 386, 388 (2010).

[91] *Id.* at 390.

[92] *Id.*

[93] ANDREW GOWERS, GOWERS REVIEW OF INTELLECTUAL PROPERTY 66–68 (2006), http://webarchive .nationalarchives.gov.uk/+/http:/www.hm-treasury.gov.uk/d/pbr06_gowers_report_755.pdf (last visited Oct. 10, 2017). The then Chancellor of the Exchequer Gordon Brown commissioned Andrew Gowers to lead the review in December 2005, which was published on 6 December 2006 as part of the Chancellor's annual pre-budget report.

[94] UK INTELLECTUAL PROPERTY OFFICE, TAKING FORWARD THE GOWERS REVIEW OF INTELLECTUAL PROPERTY: CHANGES TO COPYRIGHT EXCEPTIONS (2008); UK INTELLECTUAL PROPERTY OFFICE, TAKING FORWARD THE GOWERS REVIEW OF INTELLECTUAL PROPERTY: SECOND STAGE CONSULTATION ON COPYRIGHT EXCEPTIONS (Second Consultation Paper) (2010).

round of consultation in its attempt to remove unnecessary restrictions on the production of parodic works.[95] Its consultative paper published on December 14, 2011 includes various recommendations adopted from the 2011 report undertaken by Ian Hargreaves, Professor of Digital Economy at Cardiff University.[96] At the conclusion of this round of consultation, the government published its 2012 policy statement, *Modernising Copyright*, which declared its intention to follow Article 5(3)(k) of the Copyright Directive, and to introduce a new "fair dealing" exception for "parody, caricature and pastiche."[97] Without such an exception, "the UK may be at a disadvantage on the world stage and ... British broadcasters, production companies, and creators who produce commercially valuable parody works may be inhibited from making the most of their potential."[98]

In the original consultation document of *Modernising Copyright*, the government clarifies that the upcoming legislation would not define the terms "parody," "caricature" and "pastiche," which would bear their ordinary meanings.[99] The response document confirms that "fair dealing" would bear its usual meaning in common law, under the objective test set out in *Hyde Park Residence Ltd v. Yelland.*[100] *Modernising Copyright* highlights three key factors in determining whether a particular dealing with a work is "fair:" first, the degree to which a use competes with the owner's exploitation of the original work; second, the extent of the use and the importance of what has been taken; and third, whether a work has been published or not.[101] The document also explains that if a use "competes with a licensed use and so potentially harms rights holders, it is less likely to be fair dealing, particularly if a licence is easily available on reasonable and proportionate terms."[102] The fair dealing exception would coexist with s. 80 of the CDPA.[103] Respect for moral rights, or the right to object to derogatory treatment, which applies to any dealing that amounts to "distortion or mutilation" of the work or is "otherwise prejudicial to the honour or reputation" of its creator, could be a factor when considering whether a dealing is fair.[104]

---

95 *See, e.g.,* Nick Rose, *The Hargreaves Report,* 22 (7) ENT. L. REV. 201 (2011); Ed Baden-Powell & Jessica Woodhead, *Big Leeks Will Inspire You, but Who Gets the Credit?* 23 (3) ENT. L. REV. 59 (2012).

96 The report concluded that the United Kingdom's inflexible copyright law was stifling innovation and failing to accommodate important contemporary cultural practices, and recommended wholesale changes in the strategic direction of its intellectual property law policy. Rose, *supra* note 95, at 201–02.

97 Ed Baden-Powell & Ed Weidman, *Whose Line Is It Anyway? – New Exceptions for Parody and Private Copying,* 24 (4) ENT. L. REV. 130, 130 (2013).

98 *Id., citing* MODERNISING COPYRIGHT: A MODERN, ROBUST AND FLEXIBLE FRAMEWORK 29 (2012).

99 *Id.*

100 *Id.* at 131.

101 *Id., citing* MODERNISING COPYRIGHT 14.

102 *Id., citing* MODERNISING COPYRIGHT 14.

103 *Id., citing* MODERNISING COPYRIGHT 4.

104 *Id., citing* MODERNISING COPYRIGHT 16, 30.

On October 1, 2014, s. 30A was introduced into the CDPA, providing that "fair dealing with a work for the purpose of caricature, parody or pastiche does not infringe copyright in the work."[105] It was added to the exceptions of "Research and private study," "Criticism or review," and "Reporting of current events," which had been in place since the introduction of the CDPA in 1988.[106] The "parody" exception also contains a provision stating that "to the extent that a term of a contract purports to prevent or restrict the doing of any act which, by virtue of this section, would not infringe copyright, that term is unenforceable."[107] On the whole, the changes to the copyright law, including this exception, have been welcomed, as they brought the legislation closer to the consensus view of other nations.[108] In addition, the parody exception partially addresses the concerns of the scholars discussed: although "fair dealing" is not replaced by American-style "fair use," several factors have taken over the substantial-use test, the most significant one being whether the new work competes directly with the parodied original and harms the interests of the owner(s). However, because "parody," along with "caricature" and "pastiche," is not defined by the statute, the question regarding what works qualify as "parody" is left to debate.

D. Towards a Broad Parody Definition: the UKIPO's Recommendation and the ECJ's Decision in Deckmyn v. Vandersteen

The new parody exception in British copyright law looks more promising than its American and Canadian counterparts as it is broad enough to cover a wider range of works. Neither the parody exception in s. 30A(1), nor the Copyright Directive, defines the key concepts of caricature, parody or pastiche. Yet the UKIPO Guidance not only clarifies that they are intended to bear their ordinary dictionary meanings, but also endorses a broad definition of parody by stating that parody "imitates a work for humorous or satirical effect," without specifying whether it targets the original or an unrelated subject or both.[109] Moreover, it differentiates "parody" from both "pastiche"

---

[105] CDPA, s. 30A; Oyinade Adebiyi, *"Law Imitating Life"*: Will the Day Ever Come? Parody, Caricature and Pastiche, 25(7) ENT. L. REV. 243, 243 (2014).

[106] The provisions for news reporting, criticism and review have now been extended to include "quotation" in general. CDPA, s. 30.

[107] *Id.* s. 30A(2).

[108] *See, e.g.*, Mark Sweney, *UK Copyright Laws to Be Freed Up and Parody Laws Relaxed*, THE GUARDIAN (Dec. 20, 2014), www.theguardian.com/media/2012/dec/20/uk-copyright-law-parody-relaxed (last visited Oct. 10, 2017); Wayne Beynon, *British Comedy Gets the Last Laugh Following Parody Law Reform*, HUFFINGTON POST (Nov. 27, 2014), www.huffingtonpost.co.uk/wayne-beynon/parody-law-reform_b_6230498.html (last visited Oct. 10, 2017).

[109] UK INTELLECTUAL PROPERTY OFFICE, EXCEPTIONS FOR COPYRIGHT: GUIDANCE FOR CREATORS AND COPYRIGHT OWNERS (Oct. 2014), at 6, www.gov.uk/government/uploads/system/uploads/attachment_data/file/448274/Exceptions_to_copyright_-_Guidance_for_creators_and_copyright_owners.pdf (Oct. 10, 2017).

and "caricature,"[110] both of which imitate preexisting works but need not contain any message. Coincidentally, in the same year that the parody exception came into force, the European Court of Justice (ECJ) addressed a number of questions relating to the parody exception under Article 5(3)(k) of the Copyright Directive in *Deckmyn v. Vandersteen*. Affirming that the concept of "parody" must be regarded as "as an autonomous concept of EU law and interpreted uniformly throughout the European Union," it opted for a broad, inclusive definition of parody encompassing works that target the originals and those that comment on unrelated subjects.[111]

In *Deckmyn*, copyright infringement proceedings were brought against Johan Deckmyn, a politician of the far-right Vlaams Belang political party, and the association responsible for the party's funding.[112] At the city of Ghent's new year reception, Deckmyn had handed out calendars with a front cover depicting the Mayor of Ghent throwing coins to citizens appearing to be from diverse religious and ethnic backgrounds.[113] The cover was based upon a famous *Suske en Wiske* comic book *De Wilde Weldoener*, completed in 1961 by Mr. Vandersteen, in which a character in a white tunic throws coins to townspeople.[114] The heirs of the author and its copyright-holders sued Deckmyn and his funding association for copyright infringement in the Belgian courts.[115] The defendants appealed, arguing that the calendar image should fall within the exception for caricature, parody or pastiche under the Copyright Directive, as implemented by Article 22(1)(6) of the Belgian Copyright Act 1994.[116] The plaintiffs argued that the derivative work could not fall within the parody exception because it lacked originality and conveyed a racially discriminatory message.[117]

The Court of Appeal of Brussels, perceiving an absence of consistency in the legal tests for the parody exception, decided to stay the proceedings and refer three questions to the ECJ.[118] The first question was whether the concept of parody is an independent concept under EU law.[119] The second question was whether a parody must satisfy three conditions: displaying an original character, in such a way that the parody cannot reasonably be attributed to the original work's author; intending to provoke humor or to mock, regardless of whether the criticism is directed at the

---

[110] "Pastiche is musical or other composition made up of selections from various sources or one that imitates the style of another artist or period. A caricature portrays its subject in a simplified or exaggerated way, which may be insulting or complimentary and may serve a political purpose or be solely for entertainment." *Id.*
[111] Deckmyn v. Vandersteen [2014] Case C-201/13, para. 15 (ECJ).
[112] *Id.* para. 7.
[113] *Id.* para. 8.
[114] *Id.* para. 9.
[115] *Id.* para. 10.
[116] *Id.* para. 11.
[117] *Id.* para. 12.
[118] *Id.* para. 13.
[119] *Id.*

original work or at something or someone else; and mentioning the source of the parodied work.[120] The last question was whether a work must satisfy other conditions or conform to other characteristics to be classified as a parody.[121]

The ECJ found that, in the interest of a uniform application of EU law, parody should be considered an autonomous concept of EU law.[122] Following the opinion of the Advocate General, it also confirmed that there are only two essential characteristics of a parody: a parody must evoke an existing work, while being "noticeably different" from it, and "must constitute an expression of humor or mockery."[123] The ECJ left it to the national courts of Member States to decide on a case-by-case basis whether a parody is noticeably different from its original and whether it constitutes an expression of mockery or humor.[124] In addition, rights-holders have, in principle, a legitimate interest in ensuring that the work is not associated with a discriminatory message.[125] Hence, national courts must draw their attention to the principle of non-discrimination based on race, color and ethnic origin, specifically defined in Council Directive 2000/43/EC of 29 June 2000, and confirmed, inter alia, by Article 21(1) of the Charter of Fundamental Rights of the European Union.[126] In addition, the objectives of Directive 2001/29 include giving effect to fundamental rights and freedoms and achieving a "fair balance" of rights and interests between rights-holders and users of copyrighted works.[127] The ECJ therefore emphasized that a national court must "strike a fair balance between, on the one hand, the interests and rights of persons referred to in Articles 2 and 3 of that directive, and, on the other, the freedom of expression of the user of a protected work who is relying on the exception for parody, within the meaning of Article 5(3)(k)," in light of all the circumstances of the case.[128]

Will Brexit diminish or negate the influence of Deckmyn on British courts and on how parody is to be defined? Brexit will not change the fact that the parody exception became part of the CDPA and will have been in effect even before Brexit takes place. Insofar as the aim of Brexit is to achieve political independence from the EU institutions, Brexit could mean that the United Kingdom will no longer be subject to the jurisdiction of the ECJ, and ECJ decisions will then cease to be binding on the English courts, unless the United Kingdom agrees to continue to be subject to the ECJ under either the exit agreement or any future agreement.[129] However, assuming

[120] Id.
[121] Id.
[122] Id. paras. 14–17.
[123] Id. para. 20.
[124] Id. paras. 33.
[125] Id. paras. 29–30.
[126] Id. para. 30.
[127] Id. paras. 27, 34.
[128] Id.
[129] E.g., Taylor Wessing, Brexit – the Potential Impact on the UK's Legal System, (June 2016), https://united-kingdom.taylorwessing.com/download/article-brexit-uk-legal-system.html (last visited Oct. 10, 2017); Norton Rose Fulbright, Brexit – UK and EU Legal Framework, (Apr. 2017), www

that one or more cases before Brexit raise(s) the issue of how parody is to be defined, and British court(s) follow the ECJ's decision, post-Brexit British courts will likely pay regard to these decisions and continue to be influenced by *Deckmyn*. Assuming that no cases involving the parody exception are brought in British courts before Brexit, to the extent that its parody exception is modeled upon the Copyright Directive, the ECJ's interpretation of EU law and of the parody exception will likely continue to play some role in English jurisprudence.[130] Finally, even if British courts do not follow *Deckmyn*, they will still likely heed the UKIPO's recommendation and adopt the broad parody definition.

E. The New Parody Exception: "Humor" and Potential Moral Rights Challenges

The parody exception in British law seems to satisfy the demands of the scholars, and brings its copyright system in line with its freedom of expression tradition. Yet there are two potential obstacles to a parody defense. First, while a parody need not be humorous in American or even Canadian law, the UKIPO states that a parody "imitates a work for humorous or satirical effect," and the ECJ ruled that a parody "must constitute an expression of humor or mockery" while evoking an existing work, and be "noticeably different" from it. Because neither the UKIPO nor the ECJ have determined what "humor or mockery" entails, the ECJ having left the matter to the national court, this will create some uncertainty for courts. Second, a parody defense may fail because the work is deemed to violate the author's moral right(s).

1. The "Humor" Requirement

The "humor" requirement should not be difficult to satisfy. "British humor" is a broad concept that encompasses a variety of contents, styles, and sensibilities. Scholars have identified two issues raised by the "humor or mockery" requirement. First, courts may have difficulty in deciding whether parodies are humorous or not, and that the intention of the parodist, not the parody's impact upon the public, should be the relevant yardstick. Sabine Jacques,[131] for example, contends that courts are ill-equipped to predict the public's reactions to a parody, let alone that there are likely a range of reactions towards a parody across different sectors of the public.[132] Requiring national courts to determine whether an alleged infringement is humorous enough could result

---

.nortonrosefulbright.com/knowledge/publications/136975/brexit-uk-and-eu-legal-framework (last visited Oct. 10, 2017).

[130]   Norton Rose Fulbright, *supra* note 129.

[131]   Sabine Jacques, *Are National Courts Required to Have an (Exceptional) European Sense of Humour?* 37 (3) Eur. Intell. Prop. Rev. 134, 136 (2015). *See also* E. Rosati, *Just a Laughing Matter? Why the Decision in Deckmyn is Broader than Parody*, 52 Common Mkt. L. Rev. 511, 518–20 (2015).

[132]   Jacques, *supra* note 131.

in arbitrary decisions.[133] Hence, the ECJ's requirement for humor appears to be workable if it is based upon the parodist's intent to engender humor, which is to be decided on the basis of particular facts by national courts.[134]

The second question concerns the meaning of humor and which standard to adopt. Jacques queries whether the autonomous concept of parody requires courts to develop an objective "European" sense of humor test, given that the ECJ provides no guidance on this matter.[135] Jonathan Griffiths elaborates on the multifaceted nature of "humor," citing as an example a 2015 Belgian case[136] in which artist Luc Tuymans produced a hyperrealistic painting based very closely on Katrijn van Giel's photograph of a prominent Belgian right-wing politician, Jean-Marie Dedecker.[137] When the photographer brought proceedings for copyright infringement, the artist argued that the work was covered by the parody exception in Belgian law.[138] The Belgian court, without making reference to *Deckmyn*, held that the defense did not apply because the artist did not have a humorous intent and that the painting was a mere "reproduction."[139] Griffiths draws upon criticism by members of the artistic community that this judgment made an illegitimate distinction between obvious permissible forms of humor and more referential, post-modern forms of expression.[140] Wondering whether the ECJ meant that "mockery" is a "sub-set" of humor, he argues that the painting's mockery of the politician, which can be understood as a particular type of (derisive) humor, does not fall outside of Article 5(3)(k) of the Copyright Directive.[141] Hence, the Belgian court held wrongly that the parody defense did not apply to the painting.[142]

The requirement that a parody be humorous would not make the parody exception diverge greatly from the broad definition proposed in Part I of the book. Humor has a long and rich history in English literature and culture. Rather than referring exclusively and narrowly to the overly comical or funny, the concept is broad enough to cover a variety of contents, styles, and sensibilities. Good examples of humor can be found in different kinds of irony in medieval English poet Geoffrey Chaucer's poetry and in the speeches of William Shakespeare's witty and comic characters.[143]

---

[133] *Id.*
[134] *Id.*
[135] *Id.*
[136] Jonathan Griffiths, Fair Dealing after *Deckmyn* – the United Kingdom's Defence for Caricature, Parody or Pastiche, IN RESEARCH HANDBOOK ON INTELLECTUAL PROPERTY IN MEDIA AND ENTERTAINMENT 80 (M. Richardson & Sam Ricketson, eds., 2017), *citing* Van Giel Tuymans, Rechtbank van de eerste aanleg [Ct. First Instance of Antwerp], Judgment of the President, Docket no 14/4305/A, 15 January 2015. The case was subsequently settled.
[137] *Id.*
[138] *Id.*
[139] *Id.*
[140] *Id.*
[141] *Id.* at 81.
[142] *Id.*
[143] DON L.F. NILSEN, HUMOR IN BRITISH LITERATURE, FROM THE MIDDLE AGES TO THE RESTORATION: A REFERENCE GUIDE IX–XX (2000).

Other examples abound in the satirical works of eighteenth- and nineteenth-century writers including Alexander Pope, Jonathan Swift, and John Dryden, who ridiculed the world in their attempts to educate the public.[144] From the late nineteenth through the early twentieth century, comedies-of-manners satirizing certain social groups, like Oscar Wilde's works, were published alongside comic fantasies by "benign humorists" like Lewis Carroll, Edward Lear, and Beatrix Potter, who offered a respite from social and cultural problems by writing about imaginary times and places for both children and adult readers.[145] In the "tragicomedies" by twentieth-century writers Bernard Shaw and Henry James, elements of tragedy and comedy are commingled to the extent that the line between the two genres is often blurred or erased.[146]

Today, what is known as "British humor" is a broad concept that often entails ridiculing mundane reality and satirizing the absurdity of everyday life.[147] Although other people and things often serve as targets of humor, self-deprecation is also common.[148] Aside from negative humor, which can take the form of "denigrating," "biting sarcasm," there are positive forms of humor, for instance, jokes "looking on the bright side of life."[149] Whether British courts follow the ECJ decision or not, they will be entitled to draw upon its different conventions to determine whether the work contains "humour."

Whether the parodist's intent, or the parody's impact, should serve as the relevant yardstick can be addressed by looking at the significance that the ECJ and the UKIPO attached to the parodist's freedom of expression. In *Deckmyn*, the Advocate General identified parody as "a form of artistic expression and a manifestation of freedom of expression," or possibly both.[150] The ECJ required national courts to strike a fair balance between the interests of rights-owners and freedom of expression of users who rely on the parody exception.[151] The British government emphasized the social and cultural benefits brought by the parody exception and the necessity to balance the interests of rights-holders and users.[152] Whether or not British courts are bound by the ECJ decision, they should examine the intents of parodists to engender humor, which they can determine by evaluating

[144] Don L.F. Nilsen, Humor in Eighteenth- and Nineteenth-century British Literature: A Reference Guide xv–xvi (1998).
[145] Don L.F. Nilsen, Humor in Twentieth-century British Literature: A Reference Guide 1 (2000).
[146] *Id.* at 3.
[147] Salvatore Attardo, Encyclopedia of Humor Studies 342 (2014).
[148] Roger Dobson, *Joking aside, British Really Do Have Unique Sense of Humour*, Independent (Mar. 9, 2008), www.independent.co.uk/news/uk/this-britain/joking-aside-british-really-do-have-unique-sense-of-humour-793491.html (last visited Oct. 10, 2017).
[149] *Id.*
[150] Deckmyn v. Vandersteen, Opinion of Advocate General Cruz Villalón [2014] Case C-201/13, para. 70.
[151] Deckmyn [2014] Case C-201/13, paras. 27, 34.
[152] *See* UK Intellectual Property Office, Modernising Copyright: A Modern, Robust and Flexible Framework Executive Summary 2 (2012).

the parodies, rather than their impacts on the public, which may be difficult to measure and out of the parodists' control. The appropriate test for the parody exception, therefore, is whether the intent to produce humor is reasonably apparent from the parodic work.

2. The Moral Rights Constraint

That the new parody exception will coexist with the current UK moral rights regime, some have argued, makes it a timid defense to copyright infringement.[153] In introducing the parody defense, the British government emphasized that the moral rights provisions of the CDPA, which would not be amended with the introduction of s. 30A, would provide a valuable constraint on the scope of the new defense.[154] The UKIPO confirmed this.[155] Thus, the author's right of attribution continues to apply, as does his or her right to object to the "derogatory treatment" that amounts "to distortion or mutilation of the work or [are] otherwise prejudicial to the honour or reputation of the author or director."[156] The UKIPO's Impact Assessment document further states that the application of the "integrity right" is intended to "limit the potential for harm to copyright owners caused by this exception" and "potential for any lost sales due to negative reputational effects" of the parody.[157]

Griffiths seeks to resolve the potential conflict between the author's attribution right and the parody exception through the principle of freedom of expression.[158] The CDPA provides a number of exceptions to the attribution right, but no general exception to the right of attribution for parody. However, s. 30A does not require acknowledgement of a parodied work, an omission pointing to the fact that parodies tend only to make implicit, rather than explicit, references to works upon which they are based.[159] Thus, a court confronted with a claim for attribution of an underlying, parodied work might hold that the right to be identified as the author of a work is implicitly satisfied in the case of a parody.[160] In addition, s. 77(8) requires that where an author specifies a pseudonym, initials or some other form of identification in

---

[153] E.g., Alec Cameron, *Copyright Exceptions for the Digital Age: New Rights of Private Copying, Parody and Quotation*, 9 J. INTELL. PROP. L. & PRACTICE 1002, 1006 (2014).

[154] "The Existing moral rights regime will be maintained unchanged, so that creators will be protected from damage to their reputation or image through the use of works for parody." UK INTELLECTUAL PROPERTY OFFICE, *supra* note 152, at 31.

[155] UKIPO, *supra* note 109, at 7.

[156] CDPA, s. 80(2)(b).

[157] UK Intellectual Property Office, *Copyright Exception for Parody: Impact Assessment (IA)* (Dec. 13, 2012), http://webarchive.nationalarchives.gov.uk/20140603102647/http://www.ipo.gov.uk/ia-exception-parody.pdf (last visited Oct. 10, 2017).

[158] Griffiths, *supra* note 136.

[159] *Id.* at 75.

[160] *Id.*

asserting the right to be identified, "the form shall be used," while any reasonable form of identification can be employed in satisfaction of the attribution right.[161] To enable a parodist to get around this requirement, Griffiths argues that courts might rely upon *Deckmyn's* confirmation that parody is protected by freedom of expression and that a requirement for a parody to be accompanied by a heavy-handed acknowledgement of authorship would violate that right.[162]

The CDPA defines integrity right as the right to object to "derogatory treatment" of the work that constitutes "distortion or mutilation" of the work or is "otherwise prejudicial to the honour or reputation" of the creator.[163] The lack of certainty regarding whether the "distortion or mutilation" clause should be treated separately from the "honour or reputation" clause thus creates another potential hurdle for the parody exception. Some courts have supported the interpretation that distortion and mutilation can be treated as individual concepts. One example is *Tidy v. Trustees of the Natural History Museum* (1996).[164] Elsewhere, courts have adopted the idea that "distortion or mutilation" should be considered part of the clause prohibiting damage to the author's honor or reputation. In *Confetti Records v. Warner Music UK Ltd.* (2003), the court determined that s. 80 of the CDPA is intended to give effect to Article 6bis of the Berne Convention (1928), which reads: "to any distortion, mutilation or other modification of, or other derogatory action in relation to, the said work, which would be prejudicial to his honour or reputation."[165] It also reasoned that in the "compressed drafting style" of the British legislature, the word "otherwise" suggests that the distortion or mutilation is only actionable if it is prejudicial to the author's honor or reputation.[166] Therefore, "the mere fact that a work has been distorted or mutilated gives rise to no claim, unless the distortion or mutilation prejudices the author's honor or reputation."[167]

As emphasized throughout Part I and in Chapter 4, a parody often modifies and sometimes distorts or mutilates a copyrighted work, for instance, by rewriting it or part of it or by including new elements. Courts therefore should follow the judgment in *Confetti Records* and consider the distortion or mutilation of the original work to be a violation of the author's integrity right only if it is prejudicial to his or her honor or reputation.

Still, opinions differ as to when a parody might constitute the "derogatory treatment" of a work that is "prejudicial to the honour or reputation of the author or director." Some contend that a parody would not usually be

[161]   *Id.* at 76.
[162]   *Id.*
[163]   CDPA, s. 80(2)(b).
[164]   Tidy v. Trustees of the Natural History Museum [1996] 39 I.P.R. 501 (E.W.H.C. Ch.).
[165]   Confetti Records v. Warner Music UK Ltd. [2003] 2003 WL 21162437, para. 149 (E.W.H.C. ch.).
[166]   *Id.* para. 150.
[167]   *Id.*

prejudicial to the author's honor or reputation.[168] Others claim that an author's integrity rights "are often outraged by a parodic or burlesque treatment of his work"[169] and that "the creation of an express integrity right reinforces the author's armoury against the parodist."[170] Still others claim that the author's integrity right will only be infringed where the parody is "offensive to the spirit of the original work."[171]

To address the potential prejudices to the author's honor or reputation caused by a parody, Griffiths again relies on the freedom of expression doctrine. If the court holds that the parody falls within s. 30A, the parodist can claim that the work is protected by freedom of expression within the framework established in *Deckmyn* to find that the parodist's freedom of expression matters more than the author's allegation that his reputation was jeopardized.[172] Michael Spence contends that freedom of expression trumps intellectual property only if the original texts have been necessary to criticize either them or their authors, because authors may seek redress through laws on injurious falsehood and defamation.[173] Those whose works have been appropriated to comment on something else may claim an integrity right in their works and seek redress through copyright law.[174] Maree Sainsbury, on the contrary, argues that the author's moral rights should not be used to stifle criticism or comment, whether the parody comments on the original or something else, as long as the parodist has not been motivated by malice or excessively critical.[175]

As Chapter 2 emphasized, the public's right to parody would not conflict with authors' moral rights. Griffiths' arguments reconcile the potential conflict between the two sets of rights, as Part I has done. Still, because the British government and the UKIPO both emphasized that the moral rights provisions are intended to place a constraint on the right to parody, and it is possible that British courts will not follow *Deckmyn* after Brexit, moral rights claims by authors potentially narrow what looks like a broad parody exception. This issue will be addressed further in section III of this chapter.

---

[168]   Michael Spence, *Intellectual Property and the Problem of Parody*, 114 L. Q. Rev. 594, 597 (1998), citing Modern Law of Copyright and Designs 99 (Laddie, Prescott & Vitoria, 2d eds. 1985).

[169]   *Id.*, citing Staniforth Ricketson, Law of Intellectual Property 202 (1984). *See also* Staniforth Ricketson, The Berne Convention for the Protection of Literary and Artistic Works: 1886–1986 486 (1987).

[170]   *Id.* at 597, citing G. Dworkin, *Moral Rights in English Law – the Shape of Rights to Come*, 11 Eur. Intell. Prop. Rev. 329 (1986).

[171]   *Id.* at 587, citing Weir, *The Parodist's Nirvana: Droit Moral and Comparative Copyright Law*, 11 (4) Copyright Rep. 1, 26 (1994).

[172]   Griffiths, *supra* note 136, at 77.

[173]   Spence, *supra* note 168, at 612–13.

[174]   *Id.*

[175]   Maree Sainsbury, *Parody, Satire, Honour and Reputation: The Interrelationship of the Defence of Fair Dealing for the Purposes of Parody and Satire and the Author's Moral Rights*, 18 (3) Aus. Intell. Prop. J. 149, 166 (2016).

F. Market Substitution, Amount of Use, and Nature of Dealing

According to British case law, a work that falls within any of the enumerated fair dealing purposes would need to be evaluated according to several fairness factors, including the nature of the work being used,[176] how the original work was obtained,[177] the amount taken,[178] how transformative the dealing is,[179] the existence of commercial benefit,[180] whether the dealing has malevolent or altruistic motives,[181] its potential market impact on the original,[182] and potential alternatives of the dealing.[183] The prioritization of the market substitution factor would enable the parody exception to promote free speech and creativity. More emphasis on the nature of the defendant's dealing would also facilitate the accommodation of artistic speech and expressions related to public affairs.

Griffiths draws attention to *Ashdown v. Telegraph Group Ltd.* (2001), in which the Court of Appeal approved a passage from *The Modern Law of Copyright and Designs*, a leading commentary summarizing the existing British jurisprudence on "fairness."[184] According to this commentary, the most important factor is whether the alleged fair dealing is "commercially competing with the proprietor's exploitation of the copyright work, a substitute for the probable purchase of authorized copies, and the like," whereas the second and third most important factors are "whether the work has already been published or otherwise exposed to the public" and "the amount and importance of the work that has been taken," respectively.[185] Neither the *Ashdown* decision nor the passage touches on parody.

Griffiths persuasively argues that certain aspects of the factor-based fair dealing approach need to be adjusted in order to recognize the particular qualities of parody. Concerning the first factor, any potential licensing market for the parodic use of work should be ignored, and economic loss suffered as a result of a parody's criticism should not militate in favor of the rights-holder.[186] Because a parody draws upon published and recognizable work, the second factor is unlikely to have any

---

[176] Giuseppina D'Agostino, *Healing Fair Dealing? A Comparative Copyright Analysis of Canada's Fair Dealing to U.K. Fair Dealing to U.K. Fair Dealing and U.S. Fair Use*, 53 McGill L.J. 309, 342 (2008), citing Hyde Park Residence Ltd. v. Yelland [2000] 3 W.L.R. 215, para. 40 (dealing with current events).

[177] *Id., citing* Beloff v. Pressdram Ltd. (1972) [1973] 1 All E.R. 241 at 264 (Ch.).

[178] *Id., citing* Hubbard v. Vosper, [1972] 1 All E.R. 1023, 1031 (C.A.).

[179] *Id., citing* DAVID VAVER, COPYRIGHT VOL. 2 522 (1998) [unpublished, archived at Osgoode Hall Law School Library].

[180] *Id., citing* Newspaper Licensing Agency Ltd. v. Marks & Spencer Plc [1999] E.M.L.R. 369 (C.A.).

[181] *Id.* at 343, *citing Hyde Park Residence Ltd.*, para. 36.

[182] *Id., citing Hubbard*, [1972] 1 All E.R. at 1031.

[183] *Id., citing Hyde Park Residence Ltd.*, [2000] 3 W.L.R. 215, para. 40.

[184] Griffiths, *supra* note 136, at 87–90, *citing* Ashdown v. Telegraph Group Ltd. [2001] 44 E.M.L.R. 1003, 1011 (C.A. civ.).

[185] *Id.* at 88, *citing Ashdown* [2001] 44 E.M.L.R. at 1011.

[186] *Id.* at 90.

relevance.[187] Regarding the third factor, courts have recognized that a use is more likely to be unfair if it takes a large amount of a work in absolute or proportionate terms, or if it takes a large or disproportionate part of "important" elements of that work.[188] Because a parody has to evoke a published work, the assessment of the "importance" of the part of a work taken by a parodist may have to be more permissive than it is for some other forms of permitted use, and the taking of the whole of a particular component may have to be held to be fair under s. 30(A).[189]

Griffiths' analysis partially addresses what Alec Cameron and Oyinade Adebiyi consider to be a major concern raised by the UKIPO'S guidance notes.[190] The UKIPO explains that fair dealing in the context of parody permits "use of a limited, moderate amount of someone else's work," and that outright copying of an original work would not be permitted.[191] As an example, it says "[t]he use of a few lines of a song for a parody sketch is likely to be fair, whereas the use of a whole song would not be and would continue to require a licence."[192] The confusion stems from the difficulty in defining and quantifying "moderate." In fact, the CDPA defines "infringement" as the use of "the whole or a substantial" part of a work without permission.[193] Therefore, a new fair dealing exception to infringement, which essentially carves out a dealing or use that is exempted from copyright protection, arguably defeats itself if it is overly restrictive and if it rules out using a "substantial" or qualitatively significant part of the work for the purpose served by the dealing. Because a parody must evoke its underlying work and be "noticeably different" from it, its borrowing – even if qualitatively significant – would not, in the words of Endicott and Spence, "undermine" the original work's "expressive effect."[194]

By comparing "fair dealing" in British law with "fair balance" in EU law, Griffiths sees the need for British courts to depart from the former to accommodate the latter.[195] He explains that in the "fair balance" concept referred to by the ECJ in *Deckmyn*, the goal of a decision-maker is to adjudicate between the funda-mental right of property by rights-holders and the right to freedom of expression by parodists.[196] On the clear hierarchy in the freedom of expression jurisprudence in the European legal order, great significance is attached to political expressions and

---

[187] *Id.* at 89.
[188] *Id.*
[189] *Id.*
[190] *See* Cameron, *supra* note 153; Adebiyi, *supra* note 105.
[191] UKIPO, *supra* note 109, at 5–6.
[192] UK Intellectual Property Office, *Explanatory Memorandum to the Copyright and Rights in Performances (Personal Copies for Private Use) Regulations 2014*, at 8, www.legislation.gov.uk/ukdsi/ 2014/9780111116029/pdfs/ukdsiem_9780111116029_en.pdf (last visited Oct. 10, 2017).
[193] CDPA, s. 16(3)(a).
[194] Timothy Endicott & Michael Spence, *Vagueness in the Scope of Copyright*, 121 L. Q. Rev. 657, 673–74 (2005).
[195] Griffiths, *supra* note 136, at 93–94.
[196] *Id.* at 93.

expression on matters of public interest, and high levels of protection are provided for artistic or creative forms of expression.[197] By contrast, commercial speech does not have an equivalent status.[198] However, a distinction is drawn between expression with a purely commercial purpose, which is accorded a lower level of protection, and expression on matters of general interest, which is strongly protected even where its publication is profit-driven.[199] To accommodate fair balance, British courts conducting the traditional fair dealing analysis therefore would have to place more emphasis on the "nature of the defendant's use," to which they have paid little regard in the past.[200] Whether British courts will follow *Deckmyn* to accommodate the fair balance test or not, they can and should emphasize more strongly the nature of the defendant's use/dealing of the copyrighted work, so as to offer stronger protection for artistic and political expressions.

G. Testing the New Parody Exception

To illuminate how the broad parody exception would help to promote freedom of expression and creativity, as long as courts prioritize the market impact factor and emphasize the nature of the defendant's use, this section will first apply the new parody exception to *Allen* and *Williamson Music*. Let us assume that the court found that the defendant's designs in *Allen*, which copied the plaintiffs' Mr. Spoon character, Rocket, and button moon, contained humor and were parodies of the originals. When it came to the fairness assessment, the fact that the defendant benefited from a market that the plaintiffs could potentially enjoy, along with the substantially copying, would have militated against a finding of fair dealing. Even if the court had emphasized more strongly the nature of the defendant's use factor, it would likely have held that the designs accomplished little other than reproducing the originals and carried little political and/or artistic expression(s). Let us also assume that the court in *Williamson Music* had considered the defendants' advertisement jingle "There is Nothin' Like a Dame" contained enough humor to be a parody. When it comes to the fairness assessment, although the advertisement would not have any impact on the original's market, the court would likely have held that the jingle borrowed too much from the original, a factor militating against a finding of fair dealing. Placing more emphasis on the nature of the defendant's use, the court would likely have held that the jingle had a purely commercial purpose and carried no political and very little artistic expression. In both cases, the parody defense would have been rejected.

Parodic works containing artistic and/or political messages would likely be considered fair dealings under the new law. One example is "Newport State of Mind,"

[197] *Id.*
[198] *Id.*
[199] *Id.* at 94.
[200] *Id.*

a parody of the music video of "Empire State of Mind."[201] The UKIPO's guidance document casts doubt on whether "Newport State of Mind" would meet the requirements of "fair dealing," noting that "although the lyrics of the song and accompanying video were parodied, the underlying music track and arrangement were unchanged."[202] The prioritization of the market substitution and the nature of the defendant's use would likely lead to a different result. Although the parody borrows the music track and arrangement of the original, its new lyrics and video would make it an unlikely market substitute for the original. In addition, should the court emphasize the nature of the defendant's dealing, the parody's artistic expressions would tip the balance towards a finding of fair dealing. Hence, courts may find for parodists in circumstances where parodies combine old music with new lyrics and videos.

Would parodies employing old soundtracks and new videos, such as numerous parodies of Miley Cyrus's Wrecking Ball video, pass the fairness assessment? As the UKIPO comments, "videos consisting of an entirely unchanged soundtrack (unchanged lyrics and music) accompanying a replacement video" would not constitute fair dealing.[203] It is uncertain whether the court would consider a parodic video a market substitute for the original by using a soundtrack identical to it: although people who like the music alone may download the video and be content to listen to the unchanged soundtrack, others who prefer to enjoy also the visual aspects of the video would loath to see a different video accompanying the music. Because the parody uses the entire soundtrack, the court would likely find that it has borrowed too much from the original. Such a video, however, may contain political and/or artistic message(s). Should the court place a heavy emphasis on the nature of the defendant's use factor, there may be a chance, however slight, for it to hold that the work is a fair dealing of the original.

III. APPLYING THE PARODY EXCEPTION: AN EXTERNAL DOCTRINE VERSUS AN INTERNAL SOLUTION

This last section of the chapter will revisit the moral rights issue by explaining how the narrow public interest doctrine in British law will make it difficult to apply the parody exception to in a way that best serves the public's right to free expression. Hence, this section will return to *Ashdown*, in which the Court of Appeal held that copyright is a valid limit on the exercise of freedom of expression. After this decision, scholars criticizing its narrow circumscription of the public interest doctrine

---

[201] "Newport" was directed by the London-based filmmaker M.J. Delaney, and featured London-based actors Alex Warren and Terema Wainwright, who rap and sing in the video respectively. Published on the web on 20 July 2010, the video went viral. By the middle of August 2010, nearly 2.5 million people had watched it on YouTube, which removed it on 10 August after the request by EMI Music Publishing.

[202] UKIPO, *supra* note 157, at 4.

[203] UKIPO, *supra* note 157, at 4.

proposed an alternative approach to fairness which addresses the requirements of the European Convention. This approach was later adopted in *Deckmyn*. However, unless the *Ashdown* decision is overruled by the Supreme Court, or British courts follow the ECJ's decision, they will have to adhere to a narrow public interest doctrine in copyright cases.

A. The HRA and How the Court Should Have Ruled in Ashdown

Under the HRA, legislation "must be read and given effect" in ways that are compatible with the European Convention.[204] Alternatively, courts may declare a provision in an Act of Parliament incompatible with the European Convention.[205] After determining that the right to freedom of expression is at issue, a court should examine whether the restriction imposed by the statute meets the conditions required under the European Convention, art. 10 § 2, according to which the limit on free speech must be prescribed by law and be imposed for a legitimate aim, such as to prevent disorder or to protect health, morals, or the reputation or rights of others.[206] It must also be necessary for that purpose and be proportionate and justified by relevant and sufficient reasons.[207]

In *Ashdown*, the Court of Appeal held that copyright is a valid limit on the exercise of freedom of expression and that the existing statutory defenses within the CDPA, s. 30 were adequate to resolve the dispute between the right to freedom of expression and copyright.[208] The dispute emerged after the *Sunday Telegraph* published a minute written by Paddy Ashdown, the former leader of the Liberal Democrats, of his secret meeting with the Prime Minister on October 21, 1997, several months after the general elections, about his proposal to form a coalition cabinet.[209] Two years after the meeting, Ashdown, upon stepping down from his leadership position, considered the possibility of publishing his memoirs and presented parts of his diaries, including the as-yet-published minute, to several publishers on a confidential basis.[210] The document reached the hands of the political editor of the *Sunday Telegraph*.[211] On November 28, 1999 the *Sunday Telegraph* published three separate items about the minute, including a major story incorporating about a fifth of the minute, either verbatim or in close paraphrase.[212] Ashdown sued the

---

[204]	HRA, s. 3(1).
[205]	*See id.* s. 4.
[206]	ECHR, art. 10 § 2.
[207]	*Id.*
[208]	Ashdown [2001] 44 E.M.L.R. 1003 (C.A. civ.).
[209]	*Id.* at 1003–04.
[210]	*Id.* at 1003.
[211]	*Id.*
[212]	*Id.* at 1003–04.

newspaper for breach of confidence and infringement of copyright, and applied for summary judgment on the copyright claim.[213]

Besides the obvious defenses of fair dealing for the purpose of criticism or review and fair dealing for the purpose of reporting current events and public interest, the *Sunday Telegraph* brought to the court a novel claim, by arguing that the court was obliged, under s. 3 of the HRA, to interpret ss. 30 and 171(3) of the CDPA compatibly with the right to freedom of expression contained within art. 10 of the European Convention.[214] It claimed that the articles in question raised a matter of legitimate political controversy and promoted public knowledge and discussion of those responsible for governing the country.[215] The High Court (Chancery Division), conceding that the Telegraph Group's claim could fall within the prima facie right to freedom of expression under art. 10 § 1, noted that this right was not absolute and was to be balanced with the conflicting interests listed in art. 10 § 2.[216] It held that Ashdown's copyright interest fell within art. 10 § 2 and that the requisite balance between art. 10 § 1 and the conflicting interest covered by art. 10 § 2 was adequately struck by the provisions of the CDPA.[217] It thereby issued a summary judgment on the copyright claim and granted an injunction against further infringement.[218]

The Court of Appeal dismissed the newspaper's appeal. Like the Chancery Division, it held that the existing statutory defenses within s. 30 of the CDPA were adequate to resolve the dispute between the right of freedom of expression and copyright.[219] As a general rule, freedom of expression should have no impact on the regular course of copyright litigation, and only in "rare circumstances" will it come into conflict with the protection afforded by the Copyright Act.[220] It also agreed with the Vice-Chancellor in finding that the CDPA, s. 30(1) (fair dealing for the purpose of criticism or review) did not apply because the minute itself had not been subject to criticism or review.[221] In considering the application of s. 30(2) (fair dealing for the purpose of reporting current events), it found that the *Sunday Telegraph*'s activities could arguably be described as "reporting current events" but could not constitute fair dealing.[222] First, the defendant's publication of

[213] *Id.* at 1004.
[214] *See* Ashdown [2001] 20 E.M.L.R. at 545.
[215] *Id.* at 557–58.
[216] *Id.* at 552–54.
[217] *Id.* at 560.
[218] *Id.* at 555, 561–62.
[219] *Ashdown* [2001] 44 E.M.L.R. at 1010–11.
[220] "Where the subject matter of the information is a current event, section 30(2) of the Copyright Act may permit publication of the words used. But it is possible to conceive of information of the greatest public interest relating not to a current event, but to a document produced in the past. We are not aware of any provision of the Copyright Act which would permit publication in such circumstances, unless the mere fact of publication, and any controversy created by the disclosure, is sufficient to make them 'current events'." *Id.* at 1018.
[221] *Id.* at 1011.
[222] *Id.* at 1024–26.

Ashdown's minute was found to be a commercially competitive use of the work, which has been frequently held to militate strongly against a finding of fair dealing.[223] Second, the minute had not been published prior to its disclosure by the newspaper, another factor which also militated against a finding of fairness.[224] Third, regarding the amount and importance of the work taken, the court determined that the defendant had taken too much of the claimant's "work product."[225] Accordingly, the appeal was dismissed.[226]

The *Ashdown* decision has been heavily criticized for its narrow circumscription of the public interest doctrine and its rigid application of the fair dealing factors.[227] Scholars argue that in light of the HRA's requirements, "fairness" under s. 30 should have been assessed differently. First, courts should consider not only the commercial use of the alleged fair dealing but its overall purpose, and should apply a strong presumption in favor of the defendant where the publication raises issues of legitimate public concern.[228] Hence, the *Sunday Telegraph's* reporting of newsworthy events should have been taken into consideration.[229] In particular, the commercial and non-commercial dichotomy is inadequate in assessing the nature of the dealing.[230] Although the *Sunday Telegraph* had a commercial motivation, the value of newspapers goes beyond mere profits due to the contributions that they make to the public discourse and the marketplace of ideas.[231] In addition, limits placed on the "amount and importance" of the work copied are arbitrary, and the media should be granted a wide margin of discretion concerning the amount of the work that can be used, in order to avoid the potential chilling effect of sanctions for copyright infringement.[232]

It was perhaps no coincidence that the commentators' proposal to widen the scope of a public interest doctrine according to the HRA and the European Convention was incorporated into the ECJ's fair balance test in *Deckmyn*. Regarding the conflict between the right to freedom of expression and copyright, if *Ashdown* is overruled by the Supreme Court, then courts may rely on the external mechanism in the form of a public interest doctrine. Alternatively, should British courts follow the fair balance approach of *Deckmyn*, they can

---

[223] *Id.* at 1025–27.

[224] *Id.* at 1027.

[225] *Id.* at 1027–28.

[226] *Id.* at 1029.

[227] Michael D. Birnhack, *Acknowledging the Conflict between Copyright Law and Freedom of Expression under the Human Rights Act*, 14 (2) Ent. L. Rev. 24 (2003); Christina J. Angelopoulos, *Freedom of Expression and Copyright: The Double Balancing Act*, 3 Intell. Prop. Q. 328 (2008).

[228] Angelopoulos, *supra* note 227, at 339–40.

[229] *Id.* at 342–44.

[230] Birnhack, *supra* note 227, at 33.

[231] *Id.*

[232] Angelopoulos, *supra* note 227, at 343, *citing* Fressoz and Roire v. France, (1999) 5 B.H.R.C. 654, (2001) 31 E.H.R.R. 2.

hold for defendants if their expressions are political and/or artistic in nature. If neither of these takes place, courts may resort to an internal solution by putting more weight on the nature of the defendant's use factor. Accordingly, less emphasis would be placed on whether the uses are commercially motivated or whether large amounts of the original works have been copied.

B. A Harry Potter *Hypothesis*

A hypothesis inspired by British writer J.K. Rowling's *Harry Potter* novels will further illuminate how drawing upon a broad public interest doctrine in applying the parody exception would serve to promote freedom of expression and a robust public sphere. Rowling's fantasy fiction, which has earned her worldwide fame, has not gone without criticism.[233] The naïve world-view of the *Harry Potter* stories, in which the good always defeat the bad, has been criticized.[234] Although her later novels may reveal a more complex and ambiguous vision of the adult world,[235] the similar, good triumphs-over-evil pattern shared by each of the first six books prevails.[236] The seventh and last novel, *Harry Potter and the Deathly Hallows* continues to honor the "ancient convention of closure in all of fairytaledom" by revealing to readers in a section entitled "Nineteen Years Later" that Harry is married to Ginny, and Hermione married to Ron.[237]

Let us imagine a scholar-cum-writer produced a new work, in the form of a sequel, critiquing Rowling's world-view. This "sequel" cited extensive passages from her last novel, rewrote many parts of her story, and incorporated major characters, landmarks, and symbols. This writer had also marketed this critical work as a "sequel" to Rowling's work. Given Rowling's aggressive stance towards what she has considered to be infringements, which has led to numerous legal disputes over the *Harry Potter* series,[238] she might regard the "sequel" as a rip-off and take legal action against the parodist.

---

[233] See, e.g., JACK ZIPES, STICKS AND STONES: THE TROUBLESOME SUCCESS OF CHILDREN'S LITERATURE FROM SLOVENLY PETER TO HARRY POTTER (2001); Mark Harris, *The End of Childhood*, ENT. WKLY. (July 27, 2007), www.ew.com/ew/article/0.20048278.00.html (last visited Oct. 10, 2017).

[234] Jack Zipes points out that each Harry Potter novel begins with the protagonist trapped in "The Prison" of his home, followed by the "Noble Calling" during his most depressive moment, the ensuing "Heroic Adventures," and finally the "Reluctant Return Home." *Id.* at 160. If the books had consisted of a lot of unexpected twists, Zipes argues, they would not have become so popular in a consumerist society. *Id.* at 162.

[235] See, e.g., Benjamin H. Barton, *Harry Potter and the Half-Crazed Bureaucracy*, 104 MICH. L. REV. 1523, 1525–26, 1535 (2006).

[236] See Zipes, *supra* note 233; Harris, *supra* note 233.

[237] See Harris, *supra* note 233.

[238] E.g., John Eligon, *Rowling Wins Lawsuit against Potter Lexicon*, N.Y. TIMES (Sep. 8, 2008), www .nytimes.com/2008/09/09/nyregion/09potter.html (last visited Oct. 10, 2017); Kieren McCarthy, *Warner Brothers Bullying Ruins Field Family Xmas*, THE REGISTER (Dec. 21, 2000), www .theregister.co.uk/2000/12/21/warner_brothers_bullying_ruins_field/ (last visited Oct. 10, 2017).

Due to a lack of precedents concerning literary parodies in British case law, the court might reference decisions by American courts, especially *Suntrust Bank v. Houghton Mifflin Co.* and *Salinger v. Colting.* The British court might determine that the borrowing of Rowling's novel by the new work is comparable to the parody of *Gone with the Wind* in *The Wind Done Gone.* However, like the *Salinger* court, it might also find that the parodist copied too much of Rowling's work and/or that the "sequel," by quoting extensively from the original's important passages, would compete with the original and harm its sales. Should a broader scope for freedom of expression be allowed because British courts follow *Deckmyn* (after Brexit), or the public interest doctrine be broadened because *Ashdown* is overruled, the parodist's freedom of expression would be safeguarded. The court would more likely determine that the parodist's critique of Rowling's original enriched the market place of ideas, and even consider that some negative impact on the profits of Rowling's work should be tolerated. Alternatively, if neither of these happens, the court could rely on an internal mechanism by focusing more strongly on the nature of the defendant's dealing and the parody's artistic and political values.[239] In doing so, it would more likely hold that the parody of Rowling's work constituted fair dealing.

C. Surviving Moral Rights Challenges

While more emphasis by courts on the nature of the defendant's use factor would help parodies to survive the fairness test, only external solutions – a broadened scope of the public interest doctrine with the overruling of *Ashdown*, or a direct engagement with users' right to freedom of expression by following the *Deckmyn* decision – would help parodies to survive potential moral rights claims, and, in the on-going hypothesis, Rowling's moral rights claim against the parodist of her novel.

As discussed, authors may file claims of false attribution against parodists. If an author requests to have the original work identified as his or her own in the parody, the court drawing upon a broad public interest doctrine or directly engaging with the parodist's freedom of expression can argue that the parodist has the right to implicit attribution by evoking the well-known work.[240] Another challenge will arise when the parody gets mistaken for the original work or a new work by the original author. In *Clark v. Associated Newspapers Ltd.* (1998), confusion arose when the defendant published parodies of the plaintiff's published diaries by using the plaintiff's name in the parodies' titles. The court emphasized the significance of ensuring that no confusion arises over the authorship of the parody and that of the original work.[241] An effective parody that avoids using the original author's name in its own title (as is often the case) indeed would lessen the chance of false attribution.[242] Arguably,

---

[239]   See Griffiths, *supra* note 136, at 94.
[240]   See *id.* at 75.
[241]   Clark v. Associated Newspaper Ltd. [1998] R.P.C. 261 (E.W.H.C. ch.).
[242]   Sainsbury, *supra* note 175, at 165.

courts drawing upon a broad public interest doctrine would permit parodists to cite the original titles and original authors' names in ways that would not reasonably lead to false attribution. In the *Harry Potter* hypothesis, a court drawing upon this doctrine would less likely hold that a parody named after Rowling's novel or Rowling infringes Rowling's attribution right.

What about integrity right? As explained, in *Confetti Records*, Justice Lewison stated that it was not at all necessary to read down s. 80 of the CDPA in order to ensure compliance with art. 10 of the European Convention.[243] Because the test for determining whether a work is prejudicial to one's honor or reputation has yet to be standardized, a greater scope for public interest or freedom of expression would mean that expressions that would have been found to violate the author's integrity rights in the past would more likely be considered legal by courts.

While the word "honor" can be subjective, courts in common law jurisdictions have instilled an objective element in it.[244] A "reasonableness" test was considered in *Tidy*, in which Justice Rattee stated that "before accepting the plaintiff's view that the reproduction in the book complained of is prejudicial to his honour or reputation, I have to be satisfied that that view is one which is reasonably held, which inevitably involves the application of an objective test of reasonableness."[245] Referencing *Snow v. Eaton Shopping Centre*, a Canadian case on integrity right, the British judge finally determined that whether a work would pass the test depends on whether its author's reputation would be harmed "in the mind of any reasonable person looking at the reproduction of which he complains."[246]

The reasonableness test nonetheless has not fully evolved with specific objective criteria. In *Morrison Leahy Music Ltd. v. Lightbond Ltd.* (1993), George Michael brought an injunction to prevent the defendants from releasing a sound recording consisting of a medley derived from five of Michael's compositions and interspersed with other music (the "Bad Boys Megamix").[247] The court, granting the injunction, held that taking short snatches of compositions from their original context and playing them in a new context could cause the "distortion or mutilation" of the works and amount to a "derogatory treatment" of the work and a breach of the author's integrity right, a matter of fact to be resolved at trial.[248] In two cases decided after *Tidy*, courts sought to be more objective in their assessments. In *Pasterfield v. Denham* (1998), the court held that expert evidence would be necessary to support the claim of breach of integrity right. Here, the plaintiff alleged that the defendant's alterations to his leaflet's drawings were distortions or mutilations that prejudiced his

---

243 Confetti Records [2003] 2003 WL 21162437, para. 161.
244 Sainsbury, *supra* note 175, at 155, *citing* ELIZABETH ADENEY, THE MORAL RIGHTS OF AUTHORS AND PERFORMERS: AN INTERNATIONAL AND COMPARATIVE ANALYSIS 117 (2006).
245 Tidy [1996] 39 I.P.R. at 504.
246 *Id.*
247 Morrison Leahy Music Ltd. v. Lightbond Ltd. [1993] E.M.L.R. 144 (E.W.H.C. Ch.).
248 *Id.* at 151.

honor or reputation as an artist.[249] The court ruled that the there was a lack of expert evidence. In addition, there was "no suggestion of dishonesty or fraud or any intention to injure" plaintiff, "nor was it foreseeable that the offending words would do so," and it was not sufficient that he was aggrieved by what had occurred.[250] In *Confetti Records* (2003), the defendant altered the plaintiffs' musical work by re-mixing it and including different words that allegedly contained references to violence and drugs.[251] The claim for infringement of integrity right failed because the court failed to infer evidence that the references were in fact "derogatory" and the author made no complaint about the references hurting his reputation or honor.[252]

It is uncertain whether the court in the *Harry Potter* hypothesis would follow *Pasterfield* to require expert evidence, or follow *Confetti* and rely on its own judgment. According to the facts presented in the hypothesis, Rowling might not be able to furnish expert evidence of how her right of integrity had been violated. The latter approach, however, would lead to an uncertain outcome. One might think that the court would not reasonably consider a work that merely articulated artistic and political views of Rowling's novel, and that neither showed any malice nor defamed the original's author, infringed the author's integrity right. Yet even an objective test would not guarantee a decision that would promote freedom of expression.

If the court was able to draw upon a broad public interest doctrine or directly engage with the parodist's freedom of expression, it would less likely consider the parody to be an infringement of Rowling's integrity right. Hence, should the *Ashdown* decision be overruled, or the *Deckmyn* decision be followed, courts could facilitate the role of parody in promoting a robust public sphere.

* * *

The United Kingdom's parody exception may be deceptively broad, despite its apparent inclusiveness. The next chapter will turn to its neighbor France, which, being a Member State of the EU, can draw upon the freedom of expression doctrine in both domestic and European laws to broaden the scope of the right to parody, despite its authorial property-oriented copyright jurisprudence.

---

[249]   Pasterfield v. Denham [1999] F.S.R. 168, 168–70 (Ply. C.C.).
[250]   *Id.* at 185.
[251]   *Confetti Records* [2003] 2003 WL 21162437, paras. 49–61.
[252]   *Id.* paras. 150–60.

6

The Broadening French Parody Exception

The writer as a writer has but one heir – the public domain.[1]

This chapter will look at France, the only civil law jurisdiction in this book, whose copyright system is considered to be more oriented towards the protection of authorial property than its counterparts in other jurisdictions. The French parody exception nonetheless has been liberally interpreted by courts in accordance with the French freedom of expression jurisprudence. French courts have also drawn upon the freedom of expression doctrine in both domestic and European laws to enable parodies to survive moral right challenges. While the British parody exception is deceptively broad, due to the increasing reliance on this doctrine by the French judiciary, the French parody exception is arguably broadening.

The chapter will begin by introducing the right to freedom of expression in France, which is enshrined in its Constitution and protected by its domestic legislation and the European Convention on Human Rights. The right to parody stems from this natural right, which is subject to laws on national security, obscenity, defamation, as well as laws prohibiting hate speech and incitements of or apologies for terrorism. In recent years, France has strengthened its laws combating terrorism, and parodies considered to contain apologies for terrorism and/or incite hatred have been prohibited.

While the French Intellectual Property Code has no equivalent of the American fair use or Canadian/British fair dealing doctrines, it provides for a parody exception that has been broadly interpreted by courts over the past three decades. Courts have also increasingly drawn upon the freedom of expression doctrine to enable parodies to survive moral right challenges. Thus, French courts can and should continue to apply the parody exception by invoking domestic law and/or art. 10 of the European

---

[1] This quote has been widely attributed to Victor Hugo in the context of the *Les Misérables* decision. For example, Kim Willshire, *Heir of Victor Hugo Fails to Stop Les Mis II: France's Highest Appeal Court Allows Modern Sequel to 1860s Masterpiece*, Guardian (Jan. 31, 2007), www.guardian.co.uk/world/2007/jan/31/books.france. Mira T. Sundara Rajan, Moral Rights: Principles, Practice and New Technology 487 (2011).

Convention. Should courts deny parody exceptions for works that would not harm the authors' moral rights and commercial interests, parodists may appeal to the European Court of Human Rights, which would then apply art. 10 to provide more room for free expressions in the form of parodies.

I. FREEDOM OF EXPRESSION AND THE RIGHT TO PARODY IN FRANCE

The French Constitution protects freedom of expression by incorporating the Declaration of Rights of Man and of the Citizen of 1789 (the Declaration).[2] The famous decision of the French Constitutional Council of July 16, 1971 conferred constitutional significance on the Declaration by interpreting its reference in the Preamble of the Constitution as integrating the Declaration into the "bloc of constitutionality" (*bloc de constitutionnalité*).[3] As art. 10 of the Declaration states, "[n]o one may be disturbed on account of his opinions, even religious ones, as long as the manifestation of such opinions does not interfere with the established Law and Order."[4] Article 11 further states that "[t]he free communication of ideas and of opinions is one of the most precious rights of man. Any citizen may therefore speak, write and publish freely, except what is tantamount to the abuse of this liberty in the cases determined by Law."[5]

The Declaration, drafted and passed by the National Constituent Assembly, was, as Part I explains, inspired by the ideals of the American Revolution, as well as by philosophical ideas like the power of reason and knowledge and the sovereignty of the people rather than the monarchy and the Catholic Church. It aimed to protect the "natural and imprescriptible rights" to "Liberty, Property, Security, and Resistance to Oppression" in all humans who are "free and equal" in these rights.[6] A unitary statement inspired by the natural law and appealing to the natural rights of all humans, it arose out of an expanding public sphere during the French Enlightenment and the old monarchy's failure to suppress free speech through its repressive censorship laws and the increasing number of royal censors from the mid-seventeenth-century towards the eve of the French Revolution.[7] The scope of free speech

---

2 La Constitution de la République française [Constitution of the Fifth French Republic Preamble], Oct. 4, 1958 (Fr.).

3 Le Conseil constitutionnel [Const. Ct.] app. no. 71–44 (July 16, 1971) (Fr.); LOUIS FAVOREU, LES GRANDES DÉCISIONS DU CONSEIL CONSTITUTIONNEL 267 (Paris, Dalloz, 10th ed. 1999).

4 La Déclaration universelle des droits de l'homme et du citoyen de 1789 [Declaration of Rights of Man and of the Citizen of 1789], art. 10 (Fr.), www.conseil-constitutionnel.fr/conseil-constitutionnel/english/consti tution/declaration-of-human-and-civic-rights-of-26-august-1789.105305.html (last visited May 11, 2018).

5 *Id.* art. 11, www.conseil-constitutionnel.fr/conseil-constitutionnel/english/constitution/declaration-of -human-and-civic-rights-of-26-august-1789.105305.html (last visited May 11, 2018).

6 *Id.* arts. 1 & 2, www.conseil-constitutionnel.fr/conseil-constitutionnel/english/constitution/declara tion-of-human-and-civic-rights-of-26-august-1789.105305.html (last visited May 11, 2018).

7 Raymond Burn, *Religious Toleration and Freedom of Expression*, IN DALE VAN KLEY, THE FRENCH IDEA OF FREEDOM: THE OLD REGIME AND THE DECLARATION OF RIGHTS OF 1789, 2778–2 (1994); Helena Rosenblatt,

understood and advocated by revolutionaries at the time was nonetheless rather narrow, and the modern concept of free speech as a right to which all people are entitled in their pursuit of truth did not emerge until long after the French Revolution.[8] The Law on the Freedom of the Press of July 29, 1881 (the Law of 1881), which liberalized the press and promoted free public discussion by abolishing the offence of crimes of opinion (*délits d'opinion*), became one of France's foundational laws on freedom of speech, and remains in force to the present day.[9]

Article 55 of the French Constitution binds France to the European Convention on Human Rights (European Convention).[10] The Convention instituted an effective control of compliance with its dispositions through the European Court of Human Rights (ECtHR).[11] While allowing France to limit freedom of expression to a fairly large extent, the ECtHR has found in some instances where French law was too restrictive of free speech. One example was its determination that a French court's conviction of a protester under a provision of the Law of 1881 that prohibits insults to the President of France was contrary to art. 10 of the European Convention.[12] Although the French Constitution and Judiciary are generally less protective of free speech than their American counterparts,[13] the ECtHR has by and

---

Rousseau, Constant, and the Emergence of the Modern Notion of Freedom of Speech, IN ELIZABETH POWERS, FREEDOM OF SPEECH: THE HISTORY OF AN IDEA 133–34 (2011).

[8] Helena Rosenblatt, for example, argues that philosophers including Voltaire and Rousseau tended to favor a two-tiered policy of censorship, under which only the educated and the elite should enjoy freedom of speech, and censorship was necessary to suppress the opinions of the masses in the interest of peace and security. Hence, in the years immediately following the French Revolution, the National Assembly took over the royal government's responsibilities to suppress the flood of ideas in the marketplace. It was not until early 1800, when the modern concept of free speech – as we know it today – began to emerge, through such thinkers as Benjamin Constant. Rosenblatt, *supra* note 7, at 133–64; Lyombe Eko, *New Medium, Old Free Speech Regimes: the Historical and Ideological Foundations of French & American Regulation of Bias-Motivated Speech and Symbolic Expression on the Internet*, 28 LOY. L.A. INT'L & COMP. L. REV. 69, 99 (2006).

[9] La loi du 29 juillet 1881 sur la liberté de la presse [Law on the Freedom of the Press of July 29, 1881], 1881 (Fr.). Lyombe Eko argues that the Law of 1881, which has been amended from time to time, transformed the press from a de facto into a de jure Fourth Estate and marked a turning point in French press history. Eko, *supra* note 8, at 100.

[10] La Constitution de la République française, art. 5.

[11] European Convention for the Protection of Human Rights and Fundamental Freedoms, art. 46 (Nov. 4, 1950).

[12] Affaire Eon v. France, App. no. 26118/10, para. 59 (ECtHR 2013). A protester was prosecuted and found guilty by the French Supreme Court for insulting the French President, an offence under art. 26 of the Law of 1881, by waving a small placard reading "Casse toi pov'con" ("Get lost, you sad prick") as the presidential entourage was about to pass by. The ECtHR determined that "there is little scope under Article 10 § 2 [of the Convention] for restrictions on freedom of expression in the area of political speech or debate and in matters of public interest." This decision led to an amendment of the Law of 1881 that abolished this offence.

[13] Julien Mailland, *Freedom of Speech, the Internet, and the Costs of Control*, 33 INT'L L. & POLITICS 1179, 1184 (2001),*citing* Alexander Meiklejohn, *Testimony on the Meaning of the First Amendment, Address before the U.S. Senate Subcommittee on Constitutional Rights* (1955), http://w3.trib.om/FACT/1st .meikel.html (last visited May 11, 2018).

large interpreted freedom of expression rather liberally to allow the press to communicate ideas and information on matters related to public interest.[14]

A. Laws on National Security/Public Order, Obscenity, and Defamation

As the Declaration states that the law "has no right to defend" actions that are "injurious to society," and acknowledges that some opinions may threaten "the public order established by the Law," the right to free expression is subject to laws on national security and public order.[15] The French Penal Code bans unlawful assemblies and demonstrations and expressions that threaten public order.[16] In addition, France has reacted to each terrorist incident since the 1980s by enacting new laws. In 2012, Parliament adopted Act 2012–1432 to step up sanctions against acts inciting or justifying terrorism on the Internet.[17] In response to the jihadist attacks in Paris in November 2015, it adopted Act 2017–1510 in late 2017 to strengthen internal security.[18] This new law authorizes, among other things, the closure of mosques or other places of worship for a period of up to six months, if preachers are deemed to express ideas or theories that incite violence, hatred or discrimination, provoke the commission of acts of terrorism, or express praise for such acts.[19]

Freedom of expression is subject to laws on obscenity that have liberalized over the years. The idea of the "obscene" did not emerge in French vocabulary until the staging of Molière's play *Dom Juan* in the mid-seventeenth century.[20] In 1791, the word *obscène* appeared for the first time in a French law that forbade the sale of obscene images.[21] In 1819, a law prohibiting "offenses against public and religious morality or against good morals" provided the basis for the censorship of indecent publications, including Baudelaire's *Les Fleurs du mal* and *Madame Bovary*, during much of the nineteenth century.[22] Currently, art. 283 of the Penal Code forbids "l'outrage aux bonnes mœurs," making it an offense to manufacture, distribute, display, or sell any printed matter, writing or drawing deemed to violate public moral standards.[23] Because the law has not established a specific "obscenity" test, in practice mercenary and gross pornography may be outlawed, while works of art and literature, even if considered unsuitable for minors, are usually exempt.[24]

---

[14] *See, e.g.*, Affaire Eon, App. no. 26118/10.
[15] La Déclaration, arts. 5 & 10.
[16] Le Code penal [The Penal Code], 1992, art. 431 (Fr.).
[17] La loi n° 2012–1432 du 21 décembre 2012 relative à la sécurité et à la lutte contre le terrorisme, 2012 (Fr.).
[18] La loi n° 2017–1510 du 30 octobre 2017 renforçant la sécurité intérieure et la lutte contre le terrorisme, 2017 (Fr.).
[19] *Id.* art. L. 227–1.
[20] JOAN DEJEAN, THE REINVENTION OF OBSCENITY: SEX, LIES, AND TABLOIDS IN EARLY MODERN FRANCE 122–23 (2002).
[21] *Id.* at 126.
[22] *Id.*
[23] JONATHON GREEN & NICHOLAS J. KAROLIDES, ENCYCLOPEDIA OF CENSORSHIP 184 (2005).
[24] *Id.*

Article 29 of the Law of 1881 defines defamation as "any allegation or imputation of an act affecting the honor or reputation of the person or body against whom it is made."[25] Article 35 states that the truth of the allegation serves as the only defense to defamation, except if the factual statement concerns the person's private life.[26] In recent years, the Constitutional Council made two further exceptions to prove the truth of the defamatory allegation – those that refer to matters more than ten years old and those that concern a pardoned or expunged criminal record – on the ground that such a burden violates the freedom of expression of defendants.[27] In addition, French jurisprudence has generally recognized a defense of good faith provided that the allegation in question "(i) pursues a legitimate aim, (ii) is not driven by animosity or malice, (iii) is prudent and measured in presentation, and (iv) is backed by a serious investigation that dutifully sought to ascertain the truth of the statement."[28] These criteria have been loosened in recent years by the French Supreme Court or Court of Cassation to avoid an overly burdensome interpretation of the good-faith defense and to comply with the free speech protection required by art. 10 of the European Convention.[29]

B. Laws Prohibiting Hate Speech, Incitements of/Apologies for Terrorism, and Collective Defamation

If the enshrinement of the right to freedom of expression in the Declaration was a product of an expanding public sphere and the fall of the French monarchy, then French laws prohibiting hate speech are the result of centuries of difficult race and ethnic relations.[30] The Law of 1881 was amended in 1972 to prohibit speech intended to "provoke discrimination, hate, or violence towards a person or a group of people because of their origin or because they belong or do not belong to a certain ethnic group, nation, race, or religion," categories subsequently expanded to include gender, sexual orientation or identity, and disability.[31] Later, the law was amended to make the denial of crimes against humanity, as defined by the Nuremberg

---

[25] La loi du 29 juillet 1881, art. 29.

[26] *Id.* art. 35.

[27] Le Conseil constitutionnel [Const. Ct.] no. 2013–319 (June 7, 2013) (Fr.); Le Conseil constitutionnel [Const. Ct.] no. 2011–131 (May 20, 2011) (Fr.).

[28] Scott Grifen, *Out of Balance: Defamation Law in the European Union*, INTERNATIONAL PRESS INSTITUTE, 74 (2015), http://legaldb.freemedia.at/wp-content/uploads/2015/08/IPI-OutofBalance-Final-Jan2015.pdf (last visited May 11, 2018).

[29] In 2008, the French Supreme Court held that a magazine that published an interview on a subject of public importance could not be denied the benefit of good faith simply because the interview subject was motivated by revenge. In 2011, the same Court held that the investigative journalists who conducted a "serious" inquiry into alleged criminal activity by a bank qualified for good faith even if their form of presentation "did not observe necessary prudence and measure." *Id.* at 75.

[30] Eko, *supra* note 8, at 83–98, 104–07.

[31] La loi du 29 juillet 1881, art. 24; Andrew Weber, *Freedom of Speech in France*, LIBRARY OF CONGRESS, Mar. 27, 2015, blogs.loc.gov/law/2015/03/falqs-freedom-of-speech-in-france/ (last visited May 11, 2018).

Charter, illegal, and to prohibit speech inciting or justifying terrorism.[32] Further, the Penal Code forbids any "private defamation" of or "private insult" towards a person or group for belonging or not belonging, in fact or in fancy, to a certain ethnicity, nation, race, religion, sex, or sexual orientation, or for having a disability.[33] It also forbids any "private incitement to discrimination or to hatred or violence" against a person or group on the same grounds.[34]

Due to different interpretations regarding the meanings of legal terms, decisions by French courts could be difficult to predict.[35] In the *Giniewski* case, for example, a historian was convicted of religious defamation by the French Supreme Court for defaming the Christian community by his article in "Le quotidien de Paris" criticizing Pope John Paul II's *Veritatis Splendor*. The ECtHR determined that the article "had contributed to a debate on ... a question of indisputable public interest in a democratic society" and "had not incited disrespect or hatred," and that the conviction constituted a violation of art. 10 of the Convention.[36] In the *Edgar Morin* case, the French Supreme Court held that the publication of an article entitled "Israel-Palestine: the Cancer" in the opinion page of *Le Monde* did not constitute defamation against Jews and Israel because it was "a virulent criticism of Israeli policy" and did not "impute any specific fact likely to be damaging to the honor of or consideration for the Jewish community as a whole on the grounds of it belonging to a nation or religion."[37] In 2015, the same court nonetheless upheld the criminal conviction of twelve pro-Palestinian activists for wearing t-shirts that advocated a boycott of Israel.[38]

Decisions concerning alleged Holocaust denials and apologies for terrorism have shown greater consistency. In *Leroy v. France*, the ECtHR upheld the French Supreme Court's decision that the cartoonist was complicit in his defense of terrorism by publishing a drawing of the attacks on the Twin Towers on 9/11 with the caption, "We have all dreamt of it ... Hamas did it."[39] More recently, the French Supreme Court upheld the Holocaust denial conviction of far-right politician Jean-

---

[32]   La loi du 29 juillet 1881, art. 24; Weber, *supra* note 31.

[33]   Le Code pénal, arts. R624-3, R624-4.

[34]   *Id.* art. R625-7.

[35]   Pascal Mbongo, *Hate Speech, Extreme Speech, and Collective Defamation in French Law*, IN EXTREME Speech AND Democracy 228–30 (Ivan Hare & James Weinstein, eds. 2009).

[36]   Giniewski v. France, App. no. 64016/00 (ECtHR 2006), www.echr.coe.int/echr/ (last visited May 11, 2018).

[37]   La Cour de Cassation, Première chambre civile [Ct. Cassation, 1st Civ. Chamber] app. no. 05–17.704 (July 12, 2006), www.legifrance.gouv.fr/affichJuriJudi.do?oldAction=rechJuriJudi&idTexte= JURITEXT000007055931 (last visited May 11, 2018).

[38]   *E.g.*, Jess McHugh, *Israel Controversy in France 2015: Pro-Palestine Protesters Punishment Upheld for Organizing BDS (Palestinian Boycotts, Divestment and Sanctions)*, INT'L BUS. TIMES (Oct. 25, 2015), www.ibtimes.com/israel-controversy-france-2015-pro-palestine-protesters-punishment-upheld-orga nizing-2155467 (last visited May 11, 2018).

[39]   Leroy v. France, App. no. 36109/03 (ECtHR 2008).

Marie Le Pen for his comment during a 2015 television interview that the Nazi gas chambers were a mere "detail of the history of World War II".[40]

C. Lawful/Unlawful Parodies and the French Parody Tradition

Undoubtedly, potential lawsuits against contentious materials have chilled expressions. Yet expressions that do not violate laws on national security, obscenity, defamation, and hate speech are generally lawful. At present, censorship is administered not only by customs and Internet laws, but also by the Conseil supérieur de l'audiovisuel, which regulates electronic media to protect children and adolescents from materials inappropriate for their age.[41] Efforts to censor and regulate controversial materials that are otherwise lawful have sometimes backfired.[42]

Like other jurisdictions covered in this book, France has a strong tradition of parodies. Thirteenth-century poet Guillaume le Clerc de Normandie's *Roman de Fergus*, for example, parodied the themes of reputation, love and chivalry in various works of Chrétien de Troyes.[43] Another example is *Les Merveilles de Rigomer*, a verse novel by "Jehan," which reinvents and reinterprets familiar characters and motifs of earlier romance literature.[44] Nobel Prize winner Anatole France is renowned for his parodies of fairy tales and folk legends, including his retelling of Charles Perrault's *Bluebeard* in *Les Sept Femmes de la Barbe-Bleue*.[45] The parodic tradition has continued on to the present and can be found in popular culture. *Les Guignols* (formerly *Les Guignols de l'info*), a satirical latex puppet show broadcast on a French television channel since 1988, has parodied political figures and events, both local and international.[46]

Parodies that are not obscene or defamatory, and that do not threaten national security or provoke discrimination, hate, or violence towards a person or a group because of their origin or because they belong or do not belong to specified categories are generally lawful. In 2015, French comedian Dieudonné M'bala M'bala posted "Je me sens Charlie Coulibaly" ("I feel like

---

[40] Pierre Lepelletier, *Les chambres à gaz, «détail de l'Histoire»: Jean-Marie Le Pen définitivement condamné*, LE FIGARO (Mar. 27, 2018), www.lefigaro.fr/politique/le-scan/2018/03/27/25001-20180327ARTFIG00191-les-chambres-a-gaz-detail-de-l-histoire-jean-marie-le-pen-definitivement-con damne.php (last visited May 11, 2018).

[41] GREEN & KAROLIDES, *supra* note 23, at 182.

[42] For example, after the Paris Council set up a working party to establish monthly book lists on which librarians must base their choice of new children's books, librarians, authors and publishers resisted by forming Reject Censorship (Renvoyons la Censure). *Id.* at 184.

[43] SARAH GORDON, CULINARY COMEDY IN MEDIEVAL FRENCH LITERATURE 72–73 (2007).

[44] *Id.* at 85.

[45] Diane Wolfe Levy, *History as Art: Ironic Parody in Anatole France's "Les Sept Femmes de la Barbe-Bleue,"* 4 (3) NINETEENTH-CENTURY FRENCH STUD. 361 (1976).

[46] Waddick Doyle, *No Strings Attached? Les Guignols de l'info and French Television*, IN NEWS PARODY AND POLITICAL SATIRE ACROSS THE GLOBE 39–50 (Geoffrey Baym & Jeffrey P. Jones, eds. 2013).

Charlie Coulibaly") on his Facebook page in the days after the terrorist attack on January 7, 2015, which killed twelve people at the Paris offices of the French satirical newspaper *Charlie Hebdo*.[47] Dieudonné was prosecuted for "incitement of terrorism" and received a suspended two-month sentence, for what appeared to be a gesture of solidarity with the Islamist gunman Amedy Couliby who murdered four Jewish hostages in a kosher grocery store in Paris, apparently in concert with the terrorists who carried out the massacre at *Charlie Hebdo*'s offices two days earlier.[48] Interestingly enough, Dieudonné's response, which was a mash-up of Charlie Hedbo and Amedy Coulibaly, could be deemed a parody of the "Je suis Charlie" slogan and logo, created by French art director Joachim Roncin and adopted by supporters of free speech and freedom of the press after the shooting.[49]

II. THE RIGHT TO PARODY IN FRENCH COPYRIGHT LAW

French copyright is generally considered to be authorial property-oriented.[50] France has historically conceptualized works, products of their authors' minds, as "sites of cultural memory" (*lieux de mémoire culturel*).[51] Hence, intellectual property has served as an instrument for the protection and promotion of French culture, and the author is the "focal point" of intellectual property protection.[52] The equivalent of the word "copyright" in the French language is *le droit d'auteur*, meaning the author's right, which expresses "a two-fold package of intellectual and literary rights that accrue to authors of 'works of the intellect': 1) a patrimonial (economic) right, which

---

47   Laurence Dodds, *Who is Dieudonne, the French Comedian on Trial for Condoning the Charlie Hebdo Attacks?* THE TELEGRAPH (Nov. 25, 2015), www.telegraph.co.uk/news/worldnews/europe/france/ 11387219/Who-is-Dieudonne-the-French-comedian-on-trial-for-condoning-the-Charlie-Hebdo-attacks.html (last visited May 11, 2018).
48   *Id.*
49   Elias Groll, *Meet the Man Who Put the "Je Suis" in the "Je Suis Charlie,"* FOREIGN POLICY (Jan. 19, 2015), http://foreignpolicy.com/2015/01/19/meet-the-man-who-put-the-je-suis-in-the-je-suis-charlie/ (last visited May 11, 2018).
50   *E.g.*, Jane Ginsburg, *"Une chose publicque"? The Author's Domain and the Public Domain in Early British, French and US Copyright Law*, IN COPYRIGHT LAW: A HANDBOOK OF CONTEMPORARY RESEARCH 144 (Paul Torremans, ed. 2007); LYOMBE S. EKO, NEW MEDIA, OLD REGIMES: CASE STUDIES IN COMPARATIVE COMMUNICATION LAW AND Policy 287–89 (2012).
51   Eko explains that French authors have long enjoyed the status of national cultural icons. Under the patronage system in the pre-French Revolution era, authors did not enjoy property or economic rights over their works, but many of them often dedicated their works to well-to-do patrons or well-placed benefactors. Hence, their rights and benefits were often tied to the perspectives and political fates of their benefactors, and their works censored and controlled by either the king, aristocratic patrons, or the Catholic Church. The French Revolution swept away the patronage system of the ancien régime by raising individual property rights to the level of a sacred, inviolable human right. The revolutionary National Assembly further enacted two important author's rights laws – a 1791 law on the theatrical representation of dramatic works, and a 1793 law on the right of publication and reproduction – which laid the cultural foundations of droit d'auteur in France. EKO, *supra* note 50, at 285–87.
52   LYOMBE S. EKO, AMERICAN EXCEPTIONALISM, THE FRENCH EXCEPTION, AND DIGITAL MEDIA LAW 213–14 (2013).

represents the 'pecuniary benefits resulting from the exploitation of an author's right of literary property,' and 2) an intangible 'moral right.'"[53]

Moral right can be described as a "romantic" right of personality that seeks to protect the "unique expression and metaphysical cachet" or "mental signature" of the author on his or her work.[54] Compared to the laws of other jurisdictions in this book, French copyright law puts far greater emphasis on the author's moral right,[55] which is widely agreed to precede his or her economic rights.[56] Even copyright-expired works in the public domain are not absolutely property-free, because the author's moral right is perpetual and can be invoked to protect the integrity of works whose authors have been dead well past the statutory post-mortem period.[57] The significance of moral right in French copyright law carries implications for the scope of its parody exception and the right to parody copyrighted works.

Compared to other jurisdictions in this book, the French copyright system thus gives more priority to authors' natural rights in their works, theoretically leaving less room for the public to parody them. This section will look at the parody exception in the French Intellectual Property Code and its interpretations by French courts. The requirement that a parody contain a "fun" element has been easy to meet, although the scope of the exception was, in some cases, narrowed by the author's moral right. Nonetheless, courts have increasingly drawn upon the freedom of expression doctrine in both domestic and European laws has enabled parodies to survive potential moral right challenges.

A. Statutory Recognition of the Right to Parody

As part of the Continental European civil law system, French civil law is generally based upon codifications and interpretations of general legal rules and principles of law.[58] Although the Intellectual Property Code (the Code) does not have the exact equivalent of American fair use or Canadian/British fair dealing doctrines, it provides for uses that are exempted from copyright protection. Article L122-5 provides that once a work has been disclosed and communicated to the public in any form, the author cannot prohibit a number of actions to be performed on the work, such as analysis and citation for critical and educational purposes and television

---

[53] *Id.* at 213.
[54] *Id.* at 240.
[55] Mira T. Sundara Rajan points out that French courts used the singular term that communicates the unity of the doctrine underlying different types of moral rights, although the legislation converts the term to its plural form. Sundara Rajan, *supra* note 1, at 64–65. André Lucas argues that the singular term is preferable to the plural term. *Moral Right in France: Towards a Pragmatic Approach*, BRITISH LITERARY AND ARTISTIC COPYRIGHT ASSOCIATION, 1–2, www.blaca.org/Moral%20right%20in%20France %20by%20Professor%20Andre%20Lucas.pdf (last visited May 11, 2018).
[56] Sundara Rajan, *supra* note 1, at 60.
[57] Ginsburg, *supra* note 50, at 144.
[58] EKO, *supra* note 52, at 30.

broadcasting.[59] The parody exception first appeared in Law No. 57–298 of 11 March 1957 on Literary and Artistic Property.[60] The relevant provision was codified in Law No. 92–597 of July 1992 on the Intellectual Property Code, and has remained unchanged since then.[61] Article L122-5(4) of the Code recognizes an exception in the form of "parody, pastiche or caricature, taking into account the rules of the genre" ("La parodie, le pastiche et la caricature, compte tenu des lois du genre").[62] Article L211-3 further provides that beneficiaries of neighboring rights (including performers' rights) in the work cannot forbid uses of the work in the form of parody, pastiche or caricature.[63]

The drafter apparently did not intend to limit the types of works that can be used under the parody exception. The term "disclosed works" in Article L122-5 encompasses all types of works that have been disclosed, by publication or otherwise, to the public. Because the Code also does not specify which acts are exempted from protection, the exception covers all acts that are necessary in the context of parody, pastiche or caricature, including the reproduction, public performance, adaptation, and transformation of the protected work. In addition, the Code does not expressly limit the portions of the work that can be used in a parody.

Despite the lack of limits on the types or portions of work that can be used in a parody and the forms that a parody can take, the Code indicates that the right to parody is subject to economic and moral right restrictions. Article L111-1 provides that "[t]he author of a work of the mind shall enjoy in that work, by the mere fact of its creation, an exclusive incorporeal property right which shall be enforceable against all persons."[64] This right "shall include attributes of an intellectual and moral nature as well as patrimonial attributes."[65] On the author's economic right, Article L122-3 states that "[t]he right of exploitation belonging to the author shall comprise the right of performance and the right of reproduction."[66] Article L122-4 also provides that "[a]ny complete or partial performance or reproduction made without the consent of the author or of his (or her) successors in title or assigns shall be unlawful. The same shall apply to translation, adaptation or transformation, arrangement or reproduction by any technique or process whatsoever."[67] Article L123-1 further states that the author "shall enjoy the exclusive right to exploit the work in any form and to derive monetary profit from it," and "on his (or her) death,

---

[59]   Le Code de la propriété intellectuelle [Intellectual Property Code], 1992, art. L122-5 (Fr.).
[60]   Alexandra Giannopoulou, *Parody in France*, COMMUNIA (June 2016), 2, www.communia-association
        .org/wp-content/uploads/2016/06/report-2-parody.pdf (last visited May 8, 2018).
[61]   *Id.* at 4.
[62]   Le Code de la propriété intellectuelle, art. L22-5(4).
[63]   *Id.* art. L211-3.
[64]   *Id.* art. L111-1.
[65]   *Id.*
[66]   *Id.* art. L122-3.
[67]   *Id.* art. L122-4.

that right shall subsist for his (or her) successors in title during the current calendar year and the 70 years thereafter."[68]

The Code provides for these moral rights: attribution (*attribution, paternité*) (Article L121-1), disclosure (*droit de divulgation*) (Article L121-2), integrity (*droit au respect de l'œuvre*) (Article L121-1), withdrawal (*droit de repentir ou retrait*) (Article L121-4), and protection of honor and reputation (*droit à s'opposer à toute atteinte préjudiciable à l'honneur et à la réputation*) (Article L121-7).[69] On the rights of attribution and integrity, Art. L121-1 further provides that the author "shall enjoy the right to respect" for his or her "name," "authorship," and "work." This right, moreover, "shall be perpetual, inalienable and imprescriptible" and "may be transmitted mortis causa to the heirs of the author."[70]

The parody exception in the Code is mirrored by Article 5(3)(k) of the Copyright Directive, which states that Member States of the EU may provide for exceptions or limitations to the reproductive right and right of communication to the public of copyrighted works used "for the purpose of caricature, parody or pastiche." Because France is a Member State of the EU, the following sections will examine how French courts have interpreted "parody" in the Code and applied this exception, as well as the implications of the ECJ's ruling in *Deckmyn* for future cases on this matter.

B. French Case Law on Parody

Judicial interpretations in France, unlike in common law jurisdictions, do not become authoritative legal precedents for subsequent cases.[71] Hence, French judges interpret articles of the Code to arrive at legal decisions in specific cases, and all future cases will be based on fresh interpretations of the Code without reference to prior judicial decisions.[72]

The Code does not provide definitions for the terms "parody," "pastiche," and "caricature."[73] The French Supreme Court distinguished "parody" from the other two, describing "parody" as a genre that allows for the immediate identification of the parodied work, while "pastiche" makes fun of a character through the "caricature" of which he is the author.[74] The High Court of Paris stated that "[a] parody

---

[68] *Id.* art. L123-1.
[69] *Id.* arts. L121-1, 121-2, 121-4, 121-7.
[70] *Id.* art. L121-1.
[71] EKO, *supra* note 52, at 30.
[72] *Id.*
[73] Giannopoulou refers to legal scholars who argue that each term relates to a different genre, which explains why they are distinguished by the law. "Parody" applies to musical works, while "pastiche" and "caricature" apply to literary and graphic works respectively. Giannopoulou, *supra* note 60, at 6; *citing* H. DESBOIS, LE DROIT D'AUTEUR EN FRANCE (1978) and S. Durrande, La parodie, le pastiche et la caricature, *in* MÉLANGES EN L'HONNEUR D'ANDRÉ FRANÇON (1995).
[74] La Cour de Cassation, Première chambre civile [Ct. Cassation, 1st Civ. Chamber] app. no. 85-18787 (Jan. 12, 1988): "qu'il est dans les lois du genre de la première, qui se distingue en cela du

implies the intention of having fun without hurting (the original work)." ("La parodie suppose l'intention d'amuser sans nuire.")[75]

As the following decisions will show, although interpretations by French courts do not become authoritative legal precedents for subsequent cases, they have held that for a work to qualify as a "parody," it must (1) make substantial transformation of a copyrighted work to create a new, distinctive work, and (2) be devoid of the intention to harm the author of the original work by hurting the author's emotions or commercial interests. In addition, courts in many cases have expressly stated that the work must (3) contain humor. Courts generally have not required that a parody, which carries its author's "intention of having fun," contain criticism, or target the original work, its author, or what it represents.

1. Substantial Transformation

As the previous chapters have shown, creating a parody necessitates borrowing elements from and/or adapting a preexisting work. French courts have held that the parody should be distinctive enough so as to avoid confusion over its and the original's identities. In 1988, the assignee of the patrimonial rights of a songwriter alleged that a song titled "Douces transes" constituted an illicit adaptation of the songwriter's "Douce France."[76] The French Supreme Court held that art. 41 of the Act of 11 March 1957 allowed a writer performing a parody or a caricature to reproduce the original music, "so that the parodied work is immediately identified while the travestying of merely the lyrics is sufficient to create a travesty of the work as a whole and prevent any confusion."[77] Hence, the Court determined that "Douces transes" was a lawful parody of "Douce France," even though only the lyrics, not the musical composition, had been changed.[78]

In 1990, the French Supreme Court held that art. 41 of the 1957 Act authorized the author of a pastiche or a parody to borrow and adapt elements of the original work in ways that do not confuse the public. A political party, the Rassemblement pour la République appealed the decision of the lower court that its propaganda placard containing the juxtaposition of two hemistiches borrowed from two different verses of Jacques X's song "Vesoul" "mutilated and distorted" the song and thereby

---

pastiche, de permettre l'identification immédiate de l'oeuvre parodiée, et dans celles de la seconde de se moquer d'un personnage par l'intermédiaire de l'oeuvre caricaturée dont il est l'auteur … "

[75] La Tribunal de Grande Instance de Paris, 3ᵉ chambre, 3ᵉ section [Ct. First Instance of Paris, 3d Chamber, 3d s.] (Feb. 13, 2001), www.legalis.net/jurisprudences/tribunal-de-grande-instance-de-paris -3eme-chambre-3eme-section-jugement-du-13-fevrier-2001/ (May 11, 2018).

[76] La Cour de Cassation, Première chambre civile [Ct. Cassation, 1st Civ. Chamber] app. no. 85-18.787 (Jan. 12, 1988), www.legifrance.gouv.fr/affichJuriJudi.do?idTexte=JURITEXT000007020421 (last visited May 11, 2018).

[77] *Id.*

[78] *Id.*

infringed its author's moral right.[79] The Supreme Court held that the new composition, which "appeared not like the juxtaposition of two extracts but like a unique and exact extract" of Jacques X's song, did not confuse the public with regard to its identity.[80] Hence, it reversed the decision of the lower court.[81]

Substantial, not minor, transformation of the original work is necessary for the parody to be new and distinctive and for the parody exception to be granted. In 2002, the Court of Appeals of Paris denied the parody exception where sound recordings were accompanied by what it determined to be a denigrating audio commentary.[82] Here, a French TV chain published an excerpt of a 1961 song of Jean Ferrat, adding to it a French humorist's audio commentary containing remarks such as "songs like this, I make every day."[83] The Court considered that although the added comments were not "void of some derision," they could not be added to excerpts of a song without the author's authorization.[84]

The parody exception can be used to defend acts of parody where the parodied work is already humorous or where the parodied work is already a parody of another. Léopard Masqué retold the stories of Tintin, the character of a comic series, in the form of ironic jokes on current geopolitical events. The High Court in 2005 rejected the argument of Moulinsart Foundation, the rights-holder of Tintin, that it was impossible to parody a work that was already parodic and humorous.[85] In 2011, the Court of Appeals upheld the lower court's decision on the grounds that the Tintin character's notoriety and the differences between the plots of the parody and those of the original comics ruled out any confusion between them.[86]

2. Trademark Parodies and the Freedom of Expression Doctrine

There is no parody exception in French trademark law.[87] Yet French courts have determined in a number of cases that parodies of trademarks did not constitute trademark counterfeiting and were lawful, by drawing upon the freedom of expression doctrine. This led to French judicial recognition of trademark parodies as

---

[79] La Cour de Cassation, Première chambre civile [Ct. Cassation, 1st Civ. Chamber] app. no. 88-16.223 (Mar. 27, 1990), www.legifrance.gouv.fr/affichJuriJudi.do?idTexte=JURITEXT000007024695 (last visited May 11, 2018).

[80] *Id.*

[81] *Id.*

[82] La Cour d'appel de Paris, 4ᵉ chambre, section A [Ct. App. Paris, 4th Chamber, s. A] (Sep. 18, 2002).

[83] *Id.*

[84] *Id.*

[85] La Tribunal de Grande Instance d'Evry, 8ᵉ chambre [Ct. First Instance of Evry, 8th Chamber] (July 9, 2009), actu.dalloz-etudiant.fr/fileadmin/actualites/pdfs/FEVRIER_2012/CA18f_vr2011.pdf (last visited May 11, 2018).

[86] La Cour d'appel de Paris, 2ᵉ chambre [Ct. App. Paris, 2d Chamber] app. no. 09-19272 (Feb. 18, 2011), www.voxpi.info/wp-content/uploads/2011/03/ARRET-DU-18-FEVRIER-2011.pdf (last visited May 11, 2018).

[87] Eko, *supra* note 52, at 253.

exercises of freedom of expression under domestic and European Community laws.[88]

In 2003, the Court of Appeals of Paris held that the imitation of Compagnie Gervais Danone's trademark on two complaint websites that criticized its business practices and called for the boycott of its products did not constitute infringement. The Court determined that the websites did not aim to offer commercial products or services in competition with Danone's products, and that their references to the registered trademark of Danone were "necessary to explain the political and polemical nature" of the campaign.[89] In addition, their actions were protected under French laws of freedom of expression and therefore were constitutionally protected expressions.[90]

In the same year, the French courts in one of the landmark "Greenpeace affairs" transposed, for the first time, the pan-European freedom of expression standard to French trademark parody law. Here, the Greenpeace campaign used dollar signs to parody the trademark of Esso, the international brand name and trademark of a subsidiary of the multinational oil company Exxon Mobil, in its "STOP E$$O!" online campaign, claiming that the parody was "unconnected to business interests" and protected by the law on freedom of expression.[91] After the High Court of Paris issued a preliminary injunction on the parody website, Greenpeace France took the case to the Court of Appeals, injecting the European Community's freedom of expression law into the proceedings and requesting the Court of Appeals to refer the matter to the European Court of Justice.[92] The Court of Appeals of Paris lifted the preliminary injunction and remanded the case to the High Court for a hearing on the merits.[93] On remand, the High Court determined that the parody of Esso's trademark did not constitute trademark counterfeiting, because the Greenpeace campaign was an environmental protection campaign and would not likely lead to confusion between the "products" of the two parties.[94] Although French trademark law contained no parody exception, the Court said that the imitation of a mark can be justified under the constitutional principle of freedom of expression as long as the public is not confused as to the identity of the

[88] *Id.* at 259.
[89] La Cour d'appel de Paris, 4ᵉ chambre, section A [Ct. App. Paris, 4th Chamber, s. A] (Apr. 30, 2003), www.legalis.net/jurisprudences/cour-dappel-de-paris-4eme-chambre-section-a-arret-du-30-avril -2003/ (last visited May 11, 2018).
[90] *Id.*
[91] La Cour d'appel de Paris, 14ᵉ chambre, section A [Ct. App. Paris, 14th Chamber, s. A] (Feb. 26, 2003), www.legalis.net/jurisprudences/cour-dappel-de-paris-14eme-chambre-section-a-arret-du-26-fevrier -2003-2/ (last visited May 11, 2018).
[92] *Id.*
[93] *Id.*
[94] La Tribunal de grande instance de Paris, 3ᵉ chambre, 2ᵉ section [Ct. First Instance of Paris, 3d Chamber, 2d s.] (Jan. 30, 2004), www.legalis.net/jurisprudences/tribunal-de-grande-instance-de-paris -3eme-chambre-2eme-section-jugement-du-30-janvier-2004/ (last visited May 11, 2018).

author of the communication, and the "polemical usage" of the trademark was "unconnected to business matters."[95]

3. Competing Works and Advertising Parodies

To avoid harming the commercial interests of the author (or the owner), the parody must not compete with the original work in the market. However, it does not follow that uses must be non-commercial to qualify for the parody exception. Case law has clarified that imitations of works for commercial purposes may still qualify for the parody exception.[96]

One example of commercial uses that qualify for the parody exception was the reproduction of the image of "Monsieur PROPRE" (Mister CLEAN) in the form of "Mister QUEEN" accompanied by the humorous text "AXEL is a real Bitch TM by Shampoo for Magic Circle." The Court of Appeals of Paris in 1998 determined that these modifications distinguished the new character from the parodied one, so that there was no risk of possible confusion with the original work.[97] Recognizing that the parody both made fun of the original and carried the commercial purpose to profit from the original character, it upheld the lower court's decision.[98]

Advertising parodies nonetheless dot not qualify for the parody exception, because their goal is not to provoke laughter but to promote a product or a service. In 1997, a court determined that a French magazine's modification of pictures taken from Marcel Pagnol's film did not constitute a parody, because its replacement of the original actors with mannequins wearing fashion clothes and accessories did not contain humor and merely functioned as an advertisement.[99] In 2001, the High Court of Paris determined that the intention of the defendants in imitating the *Femmes* magazine and its website was to promote the Linux operating system to female customers.[100] Hence, the use was not exempted by the parody exception, and prior authorization by the author was necessary.[101]

4. Balancing the Author's Moral Right with the Public's Right to Parody

Because the Code also protects the author's moral right, courts have balanced it with the public's right to laugh and/or mock, taking into account the French tradition of

---

[95] *Id.*

[96] Giannopoulou, *supra* note 60, at 7.

[97] La Cour d'appel de Paris, 4ᵉ chambre, section A [Ct. App. Paris, 4th Chamber, s. A] (Sep. 9, 1998), www.doctrine.fr/d/CA/Paris/1998/INPIM19980537 (last visited May 11, 2018).

[98] *Id.*

[99] La Tribunal de grande instance de Paris, 1ᵉʳ chambre, 1ᵉʳ section [Ct. First Instance of Paris, 1st Chamber, 1st s.] (Apr. 30, 1997).

[100] La Tribunal de grande instance de Paris, 3ᵉ chambre, 3ᵉ section [Ct. First Instance of Paris, 3d Chamber, 3d s.] (Feb. 13, 2001), www.legalis.net/jurisprudences/tribunal-de-grande-instance-de-paris -3eme-chambre-3eme-section-jugement-du-13-fevrier-2001/ (last visited May 2011, 2018).

[101] *Id.*

satire. The doctrine of freedom of expression in both domestic and European laws can serve to expand the scope of the right to parody, including in trademark cases where the parody exception is not generally applied.

In 1977, the High Court of Paris held that cartoons portraying *Peanuts* characters in obscene situations infringed neither the copyright-holder's adaptation right nor the author's moral right of integrity.[102] The court reasoned that as long as the parody is an independent, distinctive piece of work that is clearly not that of the parodied author, the parodist's right to free expression trumps the author's moral right.[103] In 1978, the same court, by the same logic, held that a parody of the *Tarzan* cartoon did not infringe the author's moral right of integrity.[104]

As explained, the parody exception is not found in French trademark law. The High Court of Marseille determined that the parody website "Escroca," a clever play on the word *escroc* (the French slang for "swindler or racketeer") was an unauthorized "quasi-slavish reproduction of the trademark of Escota" that was "not guided by an intention to amuse without causing harm," but was "guided by hateful sentiments whose goal is to denigrate the company [Escota] and damage its reputation."[105] The Court of Appeals of Aix-en-Provence affirmed the holding that the parody exception set forth in the Code was not applicable to trademark law. It added that even if the law of parody applied to trademark law, the intent to harm, sufficiently expressed in the parody website, would have negated the pastiche or parody.[106]

The doctrine of freedom of expression helped to broaden the scope of the right to parody in the second dispute of the Greenpeace cases. Here, Greenpeace France and New Zealand parodied the logo of Areva, a company specializing in nuclear waste treatment, by reproducing it as a pictogram of the symbol of death – a bloodied skull and cross bones – accompanied by the slogan "Stop Plutonium – l'arrêt va de soi" in their online campaign against the company.[107] On the Greenpeace website, Areva's logo was also inscribed on a sickly-looking fish.[108] Greenpeace France stated that its parody was protected expression under the Law of 1881 because it denounced

---

[102] Neil W. Netanel, *Why Has Copyright Expanded? Analysis and Critique*, IN 6 NEW DIRECTIONS IN COPYRIGHT LAW, 32 (Fiona MacMillan, ed. 2007); *citing* the *Peanuts* case, Tribunal de grand instance de Paris (Jan. 19, 1977).

[103] *Id.*

[104] *Id.*; *citing* the *Tarzan* case, Tribunal de grand instance de Paris (Jan. 3, 1978).

[105] La Tribunal de grande instance de Marseille, première chambre civile [Ct. First Instance of Marseille, Première Civ. Chamber] (June 11, 2003), www.legalis.net/jurisprudences/tribunal-de -grande-instance-de-marseille-1ere-chambre-civile-jugement-du-11-juin-2003/ (last visited May 11, 2018).

[106] La Cour d'appel d'Aix en Provence, 2ᵉ chambre [Ct. App. Aix en Provence, 2d Chamber] (Mar. 13, 2006), www.doctrine.fr/d/CA/Aix-en-Provence/2006/INPIM20060711 (last visited May 11 2018).

[107] La Cour de Cassation, chambre commerciale [Ct. Cassation, Commercial Chamber] app. no. 06-10961 (Apr. 8, 2008), www.legifrance.gouv.fr/affichJuriJudi.do?idTexte=JURITEXT000018644102 (last visited May 11, 2018).

[108] *Id.*

the dangerous impact of Areva's activities on the environment.[109] After the High Court of Paris determined that the parody constituted trademark disparagement, Greenpeace appealed the decision to the Court of Appeals, drawing upon the freedom of expression doctrine in art. 10 of the Convention.[110] In 2006, the appellate court determined that the parody was not protected by the Law of 1881, and that by equating all the goods and services of Areva – including non-nuclear industry products – with death, it had disparaged and denigrated these products and services and abused the right of freedom of expression.[111] Finally, in 2008, the French Supreme Court reversed the appellate court's ruling that Greenpeace had abused the right of freedom of expression.[112] However, upholding the appellate ruling that the Greenpeace parody had disparaged and denigrated Areva's products and services, it ordered Greenpeace to pay the costs of the five-year litigation.[113]

In 2014, the French Supreme Court accepted the parody defense in a case involving the creation of "Commissaire Crémèr" in two albums of comics based upon the famous television character "Commissaire Maigret."[114] The Court held that the new character met the condition of humor and did not create a risk of confusion. In addition, it disagreed with the appellants, who alleged that the new character harmed the moral right, including the name and person of the comedian, who became Commissaire Maigret's incarnation in the eyes of the public.[115] The Court determined that the authors of the "grotesque" new character intended not to degrade the original or his interpretation of the original, but to entertain adults and to "take advantage of the mismatch between Commissaire Crémèr's fictitious inquiries and the public's usual interpretation of the broadcast of the television series."[116] Hence, the author's moral right was not impaired by the new work.

In a 2015 decision, the High Court of Paris ruled that Dieudonné's (the author of "Je me sens Charlie Coulibaly") music video clip, based upon the work of Holocaust survivor Barbara, constituted a "hate parody" and did not qualify for the parody exception. The Court noted that the defendant did not seek a humorous effect by

---

[109] La Tribunal de grande instance de Paris, 3ᵉ chambre, 2ᵉ section [Ct. First Instance of Paris, 3d Chamber, 2d s.] (Jan. 30, 2004), www.legalis.net/jurisprudences/tribunal-de-grande-instance-de-paris -3eme-chambre-2eme-section-jugement-du-30-janvier-2004/ (last visited May 11, 2018).

[110] La Cour d'appel de Paris, 4ᵉ chambre, section B [Ct. App. Paris, 4th Chamber, s. B] (Nov. 17, 2006), www.legalis.net/jurisprudences/cour-dappel-de-paris-4eme-chambre-section-b-arret-du-17-novembre -2006/ (last visited May 11, 2018).

[111] *Id.*

[112] La Cour de Cassation, première civile chambre [Ct. Cassation, 1st Civ. Chamber] app. no. 07-11.251 (Apr. 8, 2008), www.legifrance.gouv.fr/affichJuriJudi.do?&idTexte=JURITEXT000018644039 (last visited May 11, 2018).

[113] *Id.*

[114] La Cour de Cassation, première chambre civile [Ct. Cassation, 1st Civ. Chamber] app. no. 13-14.629 (Sep. 10, 2014), www.legifrance.gouv.fr/affichJuriJudi.do?oldAction=rechJuriJudi&idTexte= JURITEXT000029453424&fastReqId=456790894&fastPos=2 (last visited May 11, 2018).

[115] *Id.*

[116] *Id.*

turning "L'aigle noir" ("The Black Eagle"), one of the emblematic songs of the artist, into "Le rat noir" ("The Black Rat"), an injurious animal "common to the anti-Semitic."[117] Instead, the video constituted a "hate parody . . . violating the author's moral right."[118] Thus, the strip scrolling on the video clip and stating "in accordance with the laws this is a parody of the song the black eagle" could not exonerate the author of "Le rat noir" of his responsibility.[119]

C. Humor or "L'intention D'amuser"

As explained, the High Court of Paris stated that parody implies "the intention of having fun." In French, the word "humour" refers to an "English form of gently wry and self-reflexive humor."[120] The word can be interpreted not only as a personality trait or attitude, but also as a general concept of phenomena called the comic, or the French comique.[121] Comique takes many forms. One example is the burlesque, which, derived from the Italian word burla and meaning ridicule or mockery through travesties of older works, became popular in Italy and France during the seventeenth century and was later introduced to England.[122] Other examples include satirical parodies and absurdist dramas, which were popular means to understand and to come to terms with the atrocities in France and throughout Europe at the turn of the twentieth century.[123] Today, the "comique" serves as a light-hearted form of entertainment as much as it embodies an existentialist attitude towards the world.[124]

French courts have not offered a workable definition of "having fun" or "humor." The Court of Appeals did indicate how "Mister QUEEN" was a humorous reworking of "Monsieur PROPRE" (Mister CLEAN), by parenthesizing the synonym of "propre" – "clean" – which rhymes with "queen" in the parody. On the contrary, the Supreme Court did not explain the humor element in "Douces trances," other than its being "a travesty" of "Douce France." Similarly, it did not elaborate on how "Commissaire Crémèr," which it considered to be a parody of "Commissaire Maigret," fulfilled the humor requirement.

It must be noted that the High Court of Paris focused on its author's manifested intention in having fun ("l'intention d'amuser") rather than the effect created by the new work. Where courts have required that a parody must contain humor, they have

---

[117] La tribunal de grande instance de Paris, 3ᵉ chambre [Ct. First Instance of Paris, 3d Chamber] (Jan. 15, 2015).
[118] Id.
[119] Id.
[120] SALVATORE ATTARDO, ENCYCLOPEDIA OF HUMOR STUDIES 78 (2014).
[121] Id. at 305.
[122] French satirist Paul Scarron's Le Virgile Travesti, a burlesque of Aeneid, was highly influential and inspired later burlesques. Id. at 95.
[123] Id. at 308.
[124] Id.

focused on the intentions of the parodists as manifested in the works. For instance, the Courts did not inquire about the effects of "Douces trances," which resembled the burlesques once popular in France, or "Mister Queen," clearly intended to amuse, on their audiences. Unsurprisingly, French courts have seldom denied the parody exception by judging that the disputed works were not funny or funny enough. Imitations of Pagnol's film and the *Femmes* magazine might appear to be exceptions, but the parody defense was denied in both cases on the grounds that the imitations served advertising purposes and did not show any the intention to amuse. Hence, these decisions seem to indicate that a manifest intention to amuse by transforming an old work into a new, distinctive work, but without using the new work for any advertising purpose, would meet the humor requirement. Arguably, even where courts have required a parody contain humor, the legal standard for the "fun" or humor requirement has been low.

D. Reexamining Parody and Moral Right

While French courts have seldom found that works are not comical or funny enough, the fact that the author's moral right is an essential part of French copyright law, and that courts have denied parody claims on the grounds of moral right violations, necessitates a reexamination of the nature of moral right in French copyright law and the threat that this right poses to the right to parody.

Under French law, the authors' rights to integrity of their works entitle them to oppose every use of their works in contexts that denigrate their meanings, even without altering the works themselves.[125] For instance, the High Court of Paris found fault with the utilization of a piece of Jules Massenet's work as the background music for a publicity movie that highlighted the strengths of a building promoter.[126] The same court held that the director's freedom of choosing actors or actresses could not be invoked to trump the moral right of the descendants of playwright Samuel Beckett, who expressed a clear wish not to authorize women to play the characters in his play *Waiting for Godot*.[127]

Nonetheless, courts have reconciled the author's moral right, which is by no means absolute, with competing prerogatives. The French Supreme Court confirmed, for example, that the judiciary can permit alterations by owners to architectural works against their authors' wishes, taking into account the nature, importance, and circumstances of these alterations.[128] Fundamental rights can also trump moral right. The same court ruled in the *Les Misérables* case that freedom of expression

---

[125] Lucas, *supra* note 55, at 4.
[126] La Tribunal de grande instance de Paris, première chambre, 1ᵉʳ section [Ct. First Instance of Paris, 1st Chamber, S. 1] (May 15, 1991).
[127] La Tribunal de grande instance de Paris, 3ᵉ chambre [Ct. First Instance of Paris, 3d Chamber] (Oct. 15, 1992).
[128] La Cour de Cassation, chambre civile 1 [Ct. Cassation, 1st Civ. Chamber] app. No. 90-17.534 (Jan. 7, 1992), www.legifrance.gouv.fr/affichJuriJudi.do?oldAction=rechJuriJudi&idTexte=JURITEXT 000007027431&fastReqId=906611945&fastPos=1 (last visited May 11, 2018).

forbids the author or his heir from objecting to a sequel being created at the end of their exclusive right in the work.[129] Hence, it considered that the Court of Appeals of Paris had infringed art. 10 of the Convention by holding that the sequels to Victor Hugo's novel violated Hugo's moral right.[130]

The foregoing discussion on parody-related cases shows that whether moral right claims were raised, French courts required parodies to be substantially different from the parodied works to the extent that they would not likely lead the public to confuse them with the preexisting ones. The author's right of attribution is therefore protected through this requirement. As for integrity right, altering works that have been disclosed for the sake of parody is authorized by both the Code and the judiciary. New works that are distinct from the preexisting ones on which they are based, as the reasoning in the *Peanuts* and *Tarzan* cases goes, do not violate the authors' integrity rights in their old works. However, the cases involving Massenet's music and Beckett's play indicate that courts may determine that the author's wish not to have his or her work altered, placed in different contexts, or performed in certain ways trump the public's right to parody the author's work.

On the moral right to protect the author's honor and reputation, courts would more likely hold that the author's right has been violated if they determine that the new work is denigrating, hateful, and has put the author's reputation at risk, as in the parody of Escota, which the court considered to have put the company's reputation at stake without contributing to a debate on the environmental issue. In addition, courts would more likely consider that the parody has violated the author's moral right if it has engaged in hate speech by targeting a specific group of people, as in the case where the court denied the parody exception for "Le rat noir" on the ground that it was anti-Semitic.

The *Les Misérables* and Greenpeace cases indicate that courts may draw upon the freedom of expression doctrine in determining whether the parodies have violated the author's moral rights. If courts consider that the parodies offer meaningful critiques of the original works, as in the case of "Commissaire Crémèr," without degrading the originals or their authors or engaging in hate speech, then they may reject the moral right claims and hold for the parodists. This may happen even if the authors had expressed clear wishes not to have their works altered, placed in different contexts, or performed in ways different than how they were originally performed.

---

[129]   La Cour de Cassation, chambre civile 1 [Ct. Cassation, 1st Civ. Chamber] app. no. 05-15.543 (Jan. 30, 2007), www.courdecassation.fr/jurisprudence_2/premiere_chambre_civile_568/arret_n_9850.html (last visited May 11, 2018).

[130]   *Id.*

E. Recent Developments: *The* Deckmyn *and the* Koons *Decisions*

The scope of the parody exception in French law is as broad as that of the scope of its counterpart in the Copyright Directive, as interpreted by the ECJ in the *Deckmyn* decision, where it stated that a parody need not target the original work, and must "evoke an existing work while being noticeably different from it," and "constitute an expression of humour or mockery."[131] The ECJ also held that a fair balance must be struck on a case-by-case basis by the national courts between the interests of the copyright-holder and the freedom of expression of the parodist.[132] The foregoing discussion has shown that French courts had taken a similar approach by drawing upon the freedom of expression doctrine even before the ECJ's 2014 decision.

The most recent decision where the freedom of expression doctrine was invoked took place in 2017. This dispute arose out of Jeff Koons' unauthorized reproduction of photographer Jean-François Bauret's picture *Enfants* to create his china sculpture titled "Naked."[133] Koons asserted a parody defense, which the High Court of Paris declined.[134] Here, Koons claimed that his sculpture should be protected by the freedom of expression enshrined in art. 10 of the Convention, as it transformed "the innocent couple of young children into a new Adam and Eve discovering desire and sexuality by using a small bouquet of flowers as the equivalent of the apple gift offered to Adam and a phallic shape pistil that attracts the eye of the young girl."[135] Critics contend that even though the court did not rule in Koons' favor and instead determined that his appropriation was dictated mainly by his intention to save creative effort, its willingness to evaluate the freedom of expression defense was "indicative of a shift in French copyright law."[136] That courts were willing to consider this doctrine in a number of earlier cases indicates these critics may have overstated the importance of this decision. However, there is no doubt that French courts have continued to draw upon this doctrine in parody cases.

---

[131] Deckmyn v. Vandersteen [2014] Case C-201/13, para. 20 (ECJ).

[132] *Id.* paras. 27, 34.

[133] La Tribunal de grande instance de Paris, 3ᵉ chambre, 4ᵉ section [Ct. First Instance of Paris, 3d Chamber, 4th s.] (Mar. 9, 2017), www.doctrine.fr/d/TGI/Paris/2017/FR8BC336E3CF13037B1CC8 (last visited May 11, 2018).

[134] Marie-Andrée Weiss argues that the French Court interpreted *Deckmyn* incorrectly by stating that Koons did not direct his parody towards Bauret's picture in his sculpture, because the ECJ did not require that a parody target the original work. In addition, even if the Court was correct in interpreting *Deckmyn* as meaning that a work of art does have to parody the work it evokes to benefit from the parody exception, it should have granted the parody exception. *Jeff Koons Parody Defense Fails in French Copyright Infringement Case*, THE 1709 BLOG (Mar. 31, 2017), http://the1709blog .blogspot.ca/2017/03/jeff-koons-parody-defense-fails-in.html (last visited May 11, 2018).

[135] Marion Cavalier & Catherine Muyl, *French Court Finds Jeff Koons Appropriated Copyrighted Photograph that "Saved Him Creative Work."* TRADEMARK & COPYRIGHT L. (May 2, 2017), www .trademarkandcopyrightlawblog.com/2017/05/french-court-finds-jeff-koons-appropriated-copy righted-photograph-that-saved-him-creative-work/ (last visited May 11, 2018).

[136] *Id.*

This section has shown that the French parody exception generally measures up to the standard proposed in Part I of the book, despite the fact that the author's right has been given more weight in the French civil law system than in its common law counterparts, and that it could be narrowed by moral right claims. The last section will take a closer look at the *Les Misérables* decision, where the Supreme Court invoked the freedom of expression doctrine to resolve the conflict between the right to parody and the moral right of integrity. The section will also employ a parody-related hypothesis to further illuminate how French courts can and should resolve moral right claims brought against parodists, as well as the important role that the ECtHR will play in accommodating the right to parody.

III. APPLYING THE FRENCH PARODY EXCEPTION: FREEDOM OF EXPRESSION IN DOMESTIC/EU LAWS AND THE ROLE OF THE EUROPEAN COURT OF HUMAN RIGHTS

By invoking the freedom of expression doctrine in the Law of 1881 and/or art. 10 of the European Convention, courts have safeguarded the right to parody in this authorial property-focused copyright jurisprudence. Should courts fail to grant exceptions for parodies that otherwise would not harm the authors' moral rights or commercial interests, parodists can and should appeal to the ECtHR, which would then apply art. 10 to provide more scope for parodies that are substantially different from their originals and would not likely harm authors' interests.

A. *The* Les Misérables *Case*

In *Sociétié Plon et autres v. Pierre Hugo et autres*, better known as the *Les Misérables* case, the First Civil Chamber of the French Supreme Court held that François Cérésa's sequels of Victor Hugo's *Les Misérables* did not violate the moral right of the author and his estate.[137] Cérésa published *Cosette ou le temps des illusions* and *Marius ou le fugitif* in 2001, 136 years after Victor Hugo's death, and 149 years after the original publication of *Les Misérables*. Hugo's great-great grandson Pierre Hugo and the Society of People of Letters (Société des gens de lettres) brought suit against Plon, the publisher of both books and Cérésa. The plaintiffs alleged moral right infringements.[138] They also argued that the defendants had, for their own commercial benefit, exploited the reputation of Hugo, who had said that he wanted no sequel to his work.[139] In a public statement, the Hugo family also called *Cosette*, coming just months before the 200th anniversary of Victor Hugo's birth, a vulgar commercial exploitation of "an undeniable treasure of universal cultural heritage"

[137] La Cour de Cassation, chambre civile, app. no. 05-15.543.
[138] *Id.*
[139] *Id.*

that should be banned in the name of defending French culture.[140] After the High Court of Paris held that the new works violated Hugo's moral right, the plaintiffs appealed to the Court of Appeals, which upheld the lower court's ruling.[141]

The French Supreme Court overruled the decision by the Court of Appeals, which declared that "there could be no sequel to a work such as *Les Misérables*, which was definitively complete" ("aucune suite ne saurait être donnée à une œuvre telle que *Les Misérables*, à jamais achevée.")[142] The Supreme Court determined, among other things, that all of the author's copyrights had expired in 1957. His estate's monopoly on the right of adaptation had expired with the expiration of copyrights in the work.[143] In addition, the Court of Appeals failed to establish how Hugo's moral right had been violated. The new works did not contribute to "altering the vision of Hugo" ("altéré l'oeuvre de Victor Hugo") or "a confusion as to the origin or the work" ("une confusion sur leur paternité").[144] Finally, drawing upon art. 10 of the European Convention, the Supreme Court found that a decision in favor of the plaintiffs would amount to an excessive limitation on the writer's freedom of creation (*la liberté de création*).[145] On remand, the Court of Appeals held that Cérésa's work did not interfere with Hugo's moral right, and further imputed that Hugo was not hostile to adaptations of his work.[146] This decision nonetheless left open the possibility that a hostile author might have more rights.

Legal scholar Mira T. Sundara Rajan called this a landmark case in which the French Court moved away from a more "subjective" approach towards moral right in earlier cases where courts accepted the author's own and/or his descendant's opinions as sufficient evidence of a violation of the right of integrity, towards a more "objective" proof of damage to an author's reputation.[147] This movement, Sundara Rajan argues, mirrors standards favored in common law countries in relation to reputation-based claims.[148] The freedom of expression doctrine, drawn upon to safeguard the public's freedom to create, no doubt has also served to protect the public sphere and led to an increasingly popular phenomenon of fan creativity developed over the Internet.[149]

---

[140] Alan Riding, *Arts Abroad; Victor Hugo Can't Rest in Peace as a Sequel Makes Trouble*, N.Y. TIMES, (May 29, 2001), www.nytimes.com/2001/05/29/books/arts-abroad-victor-hugo-can-t-rest-in-peace-as -a-sequel-makes-trouble.html (last visited May 11, 2018).

[141] La Cour d'appel de Paris, 4ᵉ chambre [Ct. App. Paris, 4th Chamber] app. no. 2003/06582 (Mar. 31, 2004).

[142] La Cassation de Cassation, chambre civile 1, app. no. 05-15.543.

[143] *Id.*

[144] *Id.*

[145] *Id.*

[146] La Cour d'appel de Paris, 4ᵉ chambre, section B [Ct. App. Paris, 4th Chamber, S. B] app. no. 07/ 05821 (Dec. 19, 2008), www.doctrine.fr/d/CA/Paris/2008/SKC9F8FBDBCDF2CF3148E5 (last visited May 11, 2018).

[147] Sundara Rajan, *supra* note 1, at 62.

[148] *Id.*

[149] *Id.* at 63.

B. Parodying Les Misérables: A Hypothesis

Whereas the disputed works in the *Les Misérables* decision were sequels, the writer could have written a parody of the novel, given the wide-ranging criticisms of Hugo's work, some of which were negative.[150] Imagine that some cynic parodied his novel by retelling the story in a contemporary setting, so as to poke fun at what he or she considered to be its moralistic tone and stereotypical characters, and/or Hugo's faith in the redeeming power of love and compassion. The parodist then got sued by Hugo's heir for violating the author's moral right. How could and should the French court protect the right to parody?

The French court could rely on the freedom of expression doctrine in the Law of 1881 as well as art. 10 of the European Convention. In fact, French courts would also need to comply with the ECJ's ruling in *Deckmyn*. This chapter has explained how French judges' interpretations of the parody exception in the Code have broadened its scope so that it is aligned with that of its counterpart in the Copyright Directive. Applying the parody exception by balancing authors' rights and users' freedom of expression, as the ECJ did, would further serve to widen the scope for free expression in France. As a result, even assuming that the author had expressed a desire against having his work parodied by others, the freedom of expression doctrine would help to broaden the scope for free expressions in the form of parodies, as long as they are substantially different from the originals and do not constitute hate speech.

Should French courts fail to grant exceptions for parodies that otherwise would not harm the authors' moral rights and copyrights (assuming they have not expired), parodists may consider appealing the cases to the ECtHR, which would then determine the cases by balancing the authors' rights protected in art. 1 against the public's right to freedom of expression safeguarded by art. 10 of the European Convention.

Recently, the ECtHR considered these two rights in *Ashby Donald v. France*. Here, three photographers were convicted by a French court of copyright infringement after publishing unauthorized catwalk photographs on a fashion website.[151] The case was appealed to the ECtHR, which, finding that the French Court had already performed the balancing exercise properly, determined that the claimants' art. 10 right to freedom of expression was not infringed by copyright convictions, on the ground that the publication of the photographs were purely commercial and did not contribute to any important topic of public debate.[152] In circumstances where the uses of the photographs were not purely commercial and/or where the parody exception is invoked, the

---

[150] *See, e.g.*, David Hancock Turner, *Les Misérables and Its Critic*, JACOBIN MAG. (Jan. 2013), www .jacobinmag.com/2013/01/les-miserables-and-its-critics (last visited May 1, 2018); Lois Bee Hyslop, *Baudelaire on Les Misérables*, 41 (1) FRENCH REV. 23 (1976).
[151] Ashby Donald and Others v. France, App. no. 36769/08 (ECtHR 2013).
[152] *Id.* para. 43.

ECtHR may well hold for the users.[153] Hence, the ECtHR will play an increasingly important role in cases arising out of the conflict between copyright and free expression.

In this hypothesis, the ECtHR would likely rule that the parody of Hugo's novel, which contributed to debates on the original novel and on social affairs, did not violate the author's moral right. In other cases, whether the parodies have appropriated works that are still copyrighted or those have entered the public sphere, the ECtHR would apply art. 10 to provide more room for free expressions through parodies. If the parodies are distinct from the originals and neither displace the originals nor constitute hate speech, then the ECtHR would likely hold for the parodists on both copyright and moral rights claims.

***

Although French copyright jurisprudence is generally regarded to be more oriented towards the author's rights than its common law counterparts, the freedom of expression doctrine in domestic and European laws has enabled parodic expressions to survive moral right challenges. This doctrine will likely continue to play an important role in French parody cases. Chapter 7 will examine how a parody exception would benefit Hong Kong, where the freedom of expression doctrine has been under constant erosion.

---

[153] Antoine Buyse, *Copyright vs Freedom of Expression Judgment*, ECHR Blog (Jan. 22, 2013), http://echrblog.blogspot.ca/2013/01/copyright-vs-freedom-of-expression.html (last visited May 11, 2018).

7

A Parody Exception for Hong Kong in Crisis

These two characters – *Egao* (惡搞) – expose the superficiality and vulgarity of Hong Kong society, and its general lack of awareness of the "parody" concept . . . Western societies have long tolerated parodies: their politicians know too well that parodists are not stupid.[1]

My anxiety is this: not that this community's autonomy would be usurped by Peking, but that it could be given away bit by bit by some people in Hong Kong. We all know that over the last couple of years we have seen decisions taken in good faith by the Government of Hong Kong appealed surreptitiously to Beijing – decisions taken in the interests of the whole community lobbied against behind closed doors by those whose personal interests may have been adversely affected.[2]

The right to freedom of speech in Hong Kong is protected by both its Basic Law and its Bill of Rights, despite its handover from Britain to the People's Republic of China (PRC) in 1997. Although the right to parody has not been recognized in its copyright jurisprudence, the Hong Kong government's proposal to introduce a parody fair dealing exception was widely opposed by the public. This chapter will ground the significance of a parody exception in Hong Kong's sociopolitical context. It will explain how the exception proposed in this book would serve to align Hong Kong's copyright system with its free speech tradition and promote a critical political culture essential to Hongkongers' self-governance of their home.

This chapter will examine freedom of speech as a right enshrined in Hong Kong laws from its colonial days to the present, as well as the parody tradition in

---

[1] Chip Tsao 陶傑, *Dare to Play* 敢於嬉戲, Sɪɴɢ Tᴀᴏ Dᴀɪʟʏ 星島日報 (Nov. 28, 2011), https://hk.news .yahoo.com/%E6%95%A2%E6%96%BC%E5%AC%89%E6%88%B2-223000150.html (last visited Oct. 10, 2017) (translation by this book's author).

[2] The most quoted statement by Chris Patten (Hong Kong's last and most beloved governor), *in* Edward A. Gargan, *British Governor of Hong Kong Takes a Parting Shot at Beijing*, N.Y. Tɪᴍᴇs (Oct. 3, 1996), www.nytimes.com/1996/10/03/world/british-governor-of-hong-kong-takes-a-parting-shot-at-beijing .html (last visited Oct. 10, 2017).

Hong Kong culture. It will describe the boom in parodies on its social media platforms since its handover to China, and argue that a parody fair dealing exception will serve to promote a critical political culture necessary for Hongkongers' self-governance of their home, besides fostering creative industries, and empowering Hongkongers to thrive in difficult times. Although the public fears that the parody exception in the Copyright (Amendment) Bill 2014 could become a tool for suppressing speech, this chapter will argue that a parody exception, broadly defined to include "parody" and "satire" but clearly distinguished from "caricature" and "pastiche," would serve to bring Hong Kong's copyright system in line with its free speech tradition and enhance the functions of parody in Hong Kong society.

Previous chapters have argued that courts should apply the parody exception with reference to the free speech doctrine. This chapter will explain that while Hong Kong courts should ideally do the same, this external doctrine could not be relied upon to safeguard the right to parody in Hong Kong, given that freedom of speech has been constantly eroded in the territory by both the PRC and the Hong Kong governments. This chapter will therefore look within the Copyright Ordinance for an internal solution – amending the moral rights provisions, especially providing an exception to the author's integrity right to object to derogatory treatment of the work in the form of parody – which would create breathing space for Hongkongers to exercise their right to parody.

I. FREE SPEECH AND THE RIGHT TO PARODY IN HONG KONG LAW

For most of its colonial period, Hong Kong followed the English tradition of residual freedom on free speech.[3] Although there was little provision for free speech, it was tolerated in a "reasonably open society, where the press is free and critical, and academic and artistic freedoms are respected."[4] Thus, this freedom, though not legally guaranteed, was practically available.[5] Its status changed in the years leading to Hong Kong's changeover. Statutory freedom of expression was introduced with the adoption in 1990 of the Hong Kong Bill of Rights Ordinance (BoR), directly

---

[3] Mei-Ning Yan, *Freedom of Expression and the Right of Journalists to Cover Protests and Demonstrations: Hong Kong and Beyond*, 33 H.K. L.J. 613, 624 (2003). The first colonial constitution, the Royal Charter of 1843, and the Letters Patent, Colonial Regulations, and Royal Instructions to the territory's subsequent governors, all ignored this matter. DEREK JONES, CENSORSHIP: A WORLD ENCYCLOPEDIA 1096 (2001).

[4] Peter Hutchings, *Freedom of Speech in Hong Kong and the Problem of "China"*, 8 CARDOZO STUD. L. & LIT. 267, 269 (1996), *citing* Yash Ghai, *Freedom of Expression, IN* HUMAN RIGHTS IN HONG KONG 370 (Raymond Wacks ed., 1992).

[5] *Id.* at 274.

based upon the International Covenant on Civil and Political Rights (ICCPR).[6] Coming into effect on 8 June 1991, it introduced the positive protection of fundamental rights and freedoms into the territory. Article 16 of the BoR on the "[f]reedom of opinion and expression," replicating art. 19 of the ICCPR, states that "[e]veryone shall have the right to hold opinions without interference" and "the right of freedom of expression," which includes "freedom to seek, receive and impart information and ideas of all kinds, regardless of frontiers either orally, in writing or in print, in the form of art, or through any other media of his choice."[7]

The right to freedom of expression became a constitutional right after Hong Kong's handover to China in July 1997. Under the 1984 Sino-British Joint Declaration (the Joint Declaration) and the Basic Law of the Hong Kong Special Administrative Region (the Basic Law), the Hong Kong "way of life" is to be preserved for fifty years after the changeover.[8] Thus, many of the provisions in the Basic Law were designed to reassure the public that life would not change after the handover in 1997 and that Hong Kong would enjoy a "high degree of autonomy" from the PRC government.[9] Article 27 of the Basic Law, which has served as Hong Kong's mini-constitution since the changeover, provides that its residents shall have "freedom of speech, of the press and of publications; freedom of association, of assembly, of procession and of demonstration; and the right and freedom to form and join trade unions and to strike."[10] Moreover, art. 39 stipulates that the ICCPR as applied to Hong Kong shall remain in force and shall be implemented through Hong Kong laws.[11] In other words, the rights and freedoms enjoyed by Hong Kong residents shall not be restricted unless as prescribed by law, and that such restrictions shall not contravene the provisions of the ICCPR applicable to Hong Kong.

---

[6]   Yan, *supra* note 3, at 624; JONES, *supra* note 3, at 1096. The colony had been a signatory party to the
      ICCPR since 1976.
[7]   Hong Kong Bill of Rights Ordinance, 1991, c. 383, art. 16.
[8]   Joint Declaration of the Government of the United Kingdom of Great Britain and Northern Ireland
      and the Government of the People's Republic of China on the Question of Hong Kong, 1984; the Basic
      Law of the Hong Kong Special Administrative Region of the People's Republic of China, 1997, c. 2101
      (Hong Kong Basic Law).
[9]   In particular, art. 8 of the Basic Law provides that the "laws previously in force in Hong Kong law,"
      including legislation, common law, and the rules of equity, shall be maintained so long as they do
      not violate the Basic Law. Article 18 of the Basic Law provides that the Chinese government will
      not legislate for Hong Kong except in limited areas, such as defense, foreign affairs, and other
      matters considered "outside the limits of the autonomy of the Region." Hong Kong Basic law, arts.
      8, 18.
[10] *Id.* art. 27.
[11] *Id.* art. 39.

Through the BoR and the Basic Law, the ICCPR is put into effect in Hong Kong. According to art. 16(3) of the BoR and art. 39 of the Basic Law, the right to freedom of expression is not absolute and is subject to limitations permissible under art. 19(3) of the ICCPR.[12]

A. Laws on Defamation, Obscenity, and Hate Speech

Freedom of expression in Hong Kong is subject to restrictions necessary for the protection of others' reputations. The law on defamation in Hong Kong is governed mainly by common law, under which the burden of proof lies on the defendant rather than on the plaintiff.[13] Public or media discussions of public affairs involving statements of fact have not generally been given the protection of qualified privilege.[14] However, the defense known as "fair comment on a matter of public interest" offers much room for the public and the media to exercise their freedom of speech.[15]

Regarding obscenity, the British government had adopted a hands-off policy for a long time, which led to the circulation of sexually explicit materials of various kinds in a semi-open fashion or underground.[16] In 1987, it finally enacted the Control of Obscene and Indecent Articles Ordinance (COIAO) to exert some control over the publication and display of indecent and obscene articles in the media.[17] This law nonetheless gives vague definitions of what constitute "obscenity" and "indecency,"[18] and attempts to distinguish "obscene" from "indecent," undertaken by the Obscene Article Tribunal (OAT), have fallen short of resolving the wide disparities between public standards of the community and private tastes of individuals.[19] In addition, s. 28 of the COIAO contains the defense of public good, which is available for both indecency and obscenity charges, if the OAT finds that "the publication or display is in the interests of science, literature, art or learning, or any other object of general concern."[20] Similarly, the Film Censorship Ordinance states that in considering whether a film "portrays, depicts or treats cruelty, torture, violence, crime, horror, disability, sexuality or indecent or offensive language or

---

[12] Hong Kong Bill of Rights Ordinance, art. 16(3); Hong Kong Basic Law, art. 39; ICCPR, art. 19.3.
[13] Rick Glofcheski, *Defamation*, IN HONG KONG MEDIA LAW 45–46 (Doreen Weisenhaus, ed. 2014).
[14] Defamation Ordinance, 1924, c. 21, s. 28.
[15] For example, in *Oriental Press Group Ltd. v. Next Publications* [2003] 1 HKLRD 751 (C.F.A.), the Court of Final Appeal held that the dealings in shares in a public company by the vice-chairman of the company was a matter of public interest. A "fair" comment is one which could have been made by an honest person. It must not have been motivated by "malice" and the defendant must have believed it to be true or justified. *Cheng v. Tse* [2000] 3 HKLRD 418 (C.F.A.).
[16] Zhou He, *Pornography, Perceptions of Sex, and Sexual Callousness: A Cross-cultural Comparison*, IN MEDIA, SEX, VIOLENCE, AND DRUGS IN THE GLOBAL VILLAGE 133 (Kamalipour & Rampal, eds. 2001).
[17] Rebecca Ong, *Policing Obscenity in Hong Kong*, 4(2) J. INT'L COM. L. & TECH. 154, 155–56 (2009).
[18] He, *supra* note 16, at 133.
[19] Ong, *supra* note 17, at 156.
[20] Control of Obscene and Indecent Articles Ordinance, 1988, c. 390, s. 28.

behavior," the censor shall take into account "the artistic, educational, literary or scientific merit of the film and its importance or value for cultural or social reasons."[21] Hence, sexually explicit materials have remained bountiful in Hong Kong.[22]

Hong Kong has laws banning hate speech, but their scope is much narrower than their Canadian and British counterparts. Its Equal Opportunities Commission (EOC), established in 1996, is responsible for implementing laws that prohibit discrimination, including the Race Discrimination Ordinance (RDO) and the Sex Discrimination Ordinance (SDO). The former, which has come into operation since 2009, defines "race" as "the race, colour, descent, national or ethnic origin of the person."[23] It prohibits direct and indirect forms of racial discrimination and racial harassment, defined as the engagement in "any unwelcome, abusive, insulting, or offensive behavior constituting a racially hostile environment and causing humiliation or threat."[24] It also prohibits racial vilification, or the public incitement of "hatred, serious contempt for, or severe ridicule of a person because of his/her race."[25] The SDO, enacted in 1995 and last amended in 2013, does not target hate speech or speech that calls for violence against women. Rather, it applies to the employment context and prohibits discrimination in employment on the grounds of sex, marital status, and pregnancy, as well as sexual harassment in employment.[26]

B. Laws on Public Order and a Failed "Anti-subversion Bill"

The colonial period saw the passing of several sedition laws,[27] both to secure peace in the colony and to respond to political turbulence in China and in Taiwan. These laws included the 1907 Chinese Publications (Prevention) Ordinance,[28] the 1914

---

[21]   Film Censorship Ordinance, 1988, c. 392, s. 10(2)(a), (3)(b).
[22]   He, *supra* note 16, at 133.
[23]   Race Discrimination Ordinance, 2009, c. 602, s. 8(1)(a).
[24]   *Id.* cl. 7.
[25]   *Id.* cl. 46. There is no case law on racist speech. To date, the RDO has been invoked once in a case involving alleged racial discrimination against an Indian child by the Hong Kong police. *See* Singh Arjun (by his Next Friend Singh Anita Guruprit) v. Secretary for Justice & Another [2016] HKDC 626 (D.C.).
[26]   *See* Sex Discrimination Ordinance, 1995, c. 480. As of January 16, 2016, the EOC recommended the introduction of legislation to protect lesbian, gay, bisexual and transgender (LGBT) people against discrimination on the grounds of sexual orientation, gender identity or "intersex status." As is the case with sex discrimination, the EOC is more concerned with discrimination in the employment and education contexts than with hate speech towards LGBT people. *See* Equal Opportunities Commission, *Report on Study on Legislation against Discrimination on the Grounds of Sexual Orientation, Gender Identity and Intersex Status* (Jan. 2016), www.legco.gov.hk/yr15-16/english/panels/ca/papers/ca20160215-rpt201601-e.pdf (last visited Oct. 10, 2017).
[27]   JONES, *supra* note 3, at 1097.
[28]   Hualing Fu, *Past and Future Offences of Sedition in Hong Kong*, IN HUALING FU, CAROLE J. PETERSEN & SIMON N.M. YOUNG, NATIONAL SECURITY AND FUNDAMENTAL FREEDOMS: HONG KONG'S ARTICLE 23 UNDER SCRUTINY 221 (2005), *citing* HONG KONG HANSARD 1907 56 (1907).

Seditious Publications Ordinance,[29] the 1938 Sedition Ordinance and Sedition Amendment Ordinance,[30] and the 1951 Objectionable Publications Ordinance.[31] Not only were all of these ordinances seldom invoked, but they were also repealed over the years. The only exception is the Sedition Ordinance, which was last amended in the year of the changeover to limit its scope by requiring "the intention of causing violence or creating public disorder or a public disturbance" on the part of the offender.[32]

Besides sedition laws, the Public Order Ordinance places an additional restraint on free speech and on public assembly. Enacted in 1967[33] following pro-communist riots in the colony, and amended in 1980, its earlier versions required that protesters obtain a license from the police before public gatherings and processions. In 1995, two years from the handover, the Legislative Council (Legco) repealed many provisions to bring it in line with the BoR and the ICCPR, so that protestors would only need to give prior notification to the police.[34] This provoked pressure from the PRC government, which feared that the 1995 amendment would reduce public order regulatory powers of the post-handover Hong Kong government.[35] The latest version of the Ordinance, which came into force on 1 July 1997, strikes a compromise by adopting a procedure halfway between the licensing and notification systems.[36] Pursuant to the new law, the Police Commissioner, after notification by the protesters, can object to the public assembly or procession "only if he reasonably considers that the objection is necessary in the interests of national security or public safety, public order or the protection of the rights and freedoms of others."[37] In addition, the Ordinance confers on the police the power to prohibit the display of "any flag, banner or other emblem" at a public gathering that "is likely to cause or lead to a breach of the peace."[38]

---

[29] *Id.* at 222, *citing* HONG KONG HANSARD 1914 34 (1914).
[30] *Id.* at 224.
[31] *Id., citing* s. 5, Control of Publications Consolidation Ordinance 1951.
[32] *Id.* at 231; Albert Chen, *The Consultation Document and the Bill: An Overview,* IN NATIONAL SECURITY AND FUNDAMENTAL FREEDOMS: HONG KONG'S ARTICLE 23 UNDER SCRUTINY 103 (Hualing Fu, Carole J. Petersen & Simon N.M. Young, eds. 2005).
[33] Before 1967, the law dealing with public order was to be found in the Public Order Ordinance, the Peace Preservation Ordinance, the Summary Offences Ordinance, and in the common law. The 1967 version of the law was a consolidation of various pieces of preexisting legislation. Legislative Council of Hong Kong, *A Note on provisions relating to the regulation of public meetings and public processions in the Public Order Ordinance (Cap. 245)* (2000/2001), at 1, www.legco.gov.hk/yr00-01/english/panels/se/papers/ls21e.pdf (last visited Oct. 10, 2017).
[34] Yiu-Chung Wong, *"One Country" and "Two Systems": Where Is the Line?* IN ONE COUNTRY, TWO SYSTEMS IN CRISIS: HONG KONG'S TRANSFORMATIONS SINCE THE CHANGEOVER 78 (Yiu-Chung Wong, ed. 2004).
[35] PANG-KWONG LI, POLITICAL ORDER AND POWER TRANSITION IN HONG KONG 18081 (1997). On 15 May, the CE Office scaled down the amendments, before the Provisional Legislative Council passed the latest version of the Ordinance.
[36] *See* Public Order Ordinance, 1967, c. 245, s. 14.
[37] *Id.* s. 14(1).
[38] *Id.* s. 3(1).

In 2003, the Hong Kong government's attempt to introduce a national security law, which would have posed further restraints on freedom of speech, failed – at least temporarily. The law was based upon art. 23[39] of the Basic Law, which prohibits "treason, secession, sedition, subversion" against the Chinese government without defining the precise meaning of these words, and empowers and mandates the Legco of the post-handover Hong Kong government to enact laws to define and penalize such actions. After Beijing's reminder of the obligation to enact the law under art. 23,[40] the Hong Kong government released its proposals of the law for a three-month consultation exercise on September 24, 2002 and issued the National Security (Legislative Provisions) Bill on February 14, 2003. Opponents criticized the Bill for its untimeliness and vaguely defined terms such as "subversion" and "sedition," according to which any speech criticizing the Chinese government could be deemed illegal.[41] The Hong Kong government's consistent refusal to listen to the public and its issuance of the Bill only seven weeks after the close of the consultation period fueled a mass protest on July 1, 2003.[42] On 5 September 2003, the Bill was withdrawn, and further public consultation was shelved.[43]

C. Press Freedom and the Right to Parody

If the right to freedom of expression is a natural right guaranteed by the BoR and based upon the ICCPR, then so is the right to parody. Until 1997, Hong Kong had seen less censorship than most East Asian countries.[44] Despite all those seemingly draconian laws during the colonial era, British governors adopted a laissez-faire policy with regards to social and political issues, which led to a free press in the colony from the early years of its establishment.[45] In the countdown to the handover,

---

[39] Article 23 of the Basic Law reads: "The Hong Kong Special Administrative Region shall enact laws on its own to prohibit any act of treason, secession, sedition, subversion against the Central People's Government, or theft of state secrets, to prohibit foreign political organizations or bodies from conducting political activities in the Region, and to prohibit political organizations or bodies of the Region from establishing ties with foreign political organizations or bodies."

[40] Carol Jones, *The Law Wars: Article 23*, IN LOST IN CHINA? LAW, CULTURE AND IDENTITY IN POST-1997 HONG KONG 174 (2015). Writing in 1990, David Clark had already identified art. 23 as problematic, on the ground that it attempted to restrict free political activity, thus contradicting art. 27, which stated that Hongkongers would enjoy freedom of speech, of the press, and of publication. In addition, it prohibited acts of treason, secession, sedition and subversion, the last not known to the common law. *Id.*, *citing* D. Clarke, *Sedition and Article 23*, IN HONG KONG'S BASIC LAW: PROBLEMS AND PROSPECTS 31–32 (1990).

[41] Jones, *supra* note 40, at 175; Chen, *supra* note 32, at 102.

[42] This was the largest protest in history against the Hong Kong government, in which 500,000 people took to the street to demonstrate against art. 23. Carole J. Petersen, *Hong Kong's Spring of Discontent: The Rise and Fall of the National Security Bill in 2003*, IN NATIONAL SECURITY AND FUNDAMENTAL FREEDOMS: HONG KONG'S ARTICLE 23 UNDER SCRUTINY 13, 49 (Hualing Fu, Carole J. Petersen & Simon N.M. Young, eds. 2005); Jones, *supra* note 40, at 173, 177–78.

[43] Chen, *supra* note 32, at 94.

[44] JONES, *supra* note 3, at 1096.

[45] *Id.*

the colonial government further brought the Film Censorship Ordinance in line with the BoR by removing the "damaging good relations with other territories" clause, which had empowered the Censorship Board to ban films raising politically sensitive matters in the past.[46] In May 1996, the British Privy Council ruled that a newspaper that had disclosed details of an investigation carried out by the Independent Commission against Corruption (ICAC) was protected by art. 16 of the BoR.[47] This decision set an important precedent affirming the importance of the BoR as an essential safeguard for freedom of expression and freedom of the press. Despite the political changeover, therefore, Hong Kong should continue to benefit from a free press, and no one – be they Hong Kong residents or foreigners passing through Hong Kong – should be prohibited from voicing their opinions, written or verbal, as long as they are not defamatory, obscene, or discriminatory in nature and do not threaten public order.

The right to parody stems from freedom of expression and freedom of the press. There are examples of parody in traditional as well as modern Chinese literatures and cultures.[48] It would be both difficult and beyond the scope of this chapter to determine whether Hongkongers in general have read the works of particular Chinese authors, some rather obscure, and the extent of Chinese literary and cultural influences on this former British colony. However, there has been no lack of parodies in Hong Kong's popular culture. *Enjoy Yourself Tonight* (1967–94), a popular variety show that aired on Television Broadcasts Limited, the first wireless commercial television station in the territory, became the first mass entertainment show to frequently mock social affairs by parodying songs and performing satirical dramas.[49] In addition, film actor and director Stephen Chow frequently parodied Hollywood and Hong Kong action films and characters in his works.[50]

Hongkongers enjoy the right to draw upon the tradition of parody to voice their opinions, whether through writing, artworks, or performances, as long as their works are not defamatory, obscene, or discriminatory and do not threaten public order. Due to the boom in parodies in Hong Kong's social media over the past two decades, providing for a parody fair dealing exception in its copyright law has nonetheless become urgent.

---

[46] *Id.*

[47] Ming Pao Newspaper Ltd. & Others v. Attorney General of Hong Kong [1996] 6 HKPLR 103 (C.A.).

[48] Herbert Franke describes parodies of funerary texts in Tao Tsung-I's *Cho-keng lu*, published in 1366. Herbert Franke, A *Note on Parody in Chinese Traditional Literature*, 18(2) ORIENS EXTREMUS 242 (1971). Andrew Stuckey offers examples like early twentieth-century writer Lu Xun's short story, "Mending Heaven," a parody of the Chinese origin myth of Nu Wa. ANDREW STUCKEY, OLD STORIES RETOLD: NARRATIVE AND VANISHING PASTS IN MODERN CHINA 17 (2010).

[49] Doris Yu & Zoe Tam, *Humour out of Chaos: How Satire Helps Channel People's Frustrations*, H.K. FREE P. (Mar. 28, 2016), www.hongkongfp.com/2016/03/28/humour-out-of-chaos-how-satire-helps-channel-hong-kong-peoples-frustrations/ (last visited Oct. 10, 2017).

[50] Kin Yan Szeto, *The Politics of Historiography in Stephen Chow's Kung Fu Hustle*, 49 JUMP CUT (2007), www.ejumpcut.org/archive/jc49.2007/Szeto/ (last visited Oct. 10, 2017).

II. THE RIGHT TO PARODY IN HONG KONG COPYRIGHT LAW

Copyright law in Hong Kong has followed to a great extent the English model. The Hong Kong Copyright Ordinance, which became effective after 27 June 1997, is its first purely local copyright law, while the Copyright Act 1956 of the United Kingdom has continued to apply to protect copyrights of works created before June 27, 1997.[51] No cases involving parodies have been brought before Hong Kong courts, and neither has the parody defense been invoked, before or after 1997, according to Hong Kong law databases.[52] Socio-political crises plaguing the territory have led to a boom in parodic works all over its social media over the past two decades, and proposals to introduce a parody exception in its copyright statute.

A. *Fair Dealing in Hong Kong Copyright Law and the Absence of a Parody Defense*

Copyright lawsuits in Hong Kong have largely involved making, possessing and/or distributing allegedly pirated and counterfeit goods. Although wholesale or substantial copying without the owner's permission leads to copyright infringement,[53] fair dealing with a work for the purposes of "research or private study," "criticism, review and news reporting," "giving and receiving instruction," or "public administration," does not constitute infringement under the current law.[54] In determining whether any dealing with a work is fair, the court shall take into account "all the circumstances of the case and, in particular – (a) the purpose and nature of the dealing, including whether the dealing is for a non-profit-making purpose and whether the dealing is of a commercial nature; (b) the nature of the work; (c) the amount and substantiality of the portion dealt with in relation to the work as a whole; and (d) the effect of the dealing on the potential market for or value of the work."[55] Records show that no copyright cases involving parodies have been brought before courts, and a fair dealing defense for the purpose of parody has not been invoked in Hong Kong. Where defendants had copied the logos of plaintiffs' products and faced charges of passing off, copyright and/or trademark infringement(s), they did not attempt to raise a parody defense as defendants in many English and Canadian cases did.[56]

Although a fair dealing parody defense has not been raised in a copyright suit, "parody" has been mentioned in several cases. In two cases, the Courts offered

---

51 The Copyright Ordinance, c. 39, was introduced in Hong Kong in 1973 to supplement and extend the remedies available under the Copyright Act of 1956. The Law Commission of Hong Kong, Reform of the Law Relating to Copyright (Nov. 1993), at iv, www.hkreform.gov.hk/en/docs/rcopyright-e.pdf (Oct. 10, 2017).

52 *See* Hong Kong Legal Information Institute, www.hklii.hk/chi/ (last accessed Oct. 10, 2017).

53 Copyright Ordinance, 1997, c. 528, s. 22(2), (3).

54 Copyright Ordinance, ss. 38, 39.

55 *Id.* s. 38(3).

56 *E.g.*, Tong Wai Man v. Tam Lun Sang [2013] 2013 WL 5915372 (C.F.I.); Leung Ting v. Lee Yun Tim [2008] 2008 WL 654169 (C.F.I.).

descriptions of parody that are highly similar to the legal definition proposed in this book. In *Tong Sai Ho v. Obscene Articles Tribunal* (2008) and *Ming Pao Newspapers Ltd v. Obscene Articles Tribunal* (2008), the Court reviewed the Obscene Articles Tribunal's classifications of a controversial gender/sex column in the student press of a local university and of a well-known Hong Kong newspaper's supplement comment on the student column. Holding that the supplement was a "parody" of the student column, it offered a broad definition of "parody," which, in this case, aimed "to show and invite its readers to reflect on the different attitudes of people to sex and what they considered as deviant sexual behavior," hence serving as "a critique not only of certain attitudes in the society but also of the way the relevant message was conveyed" in the student column.[57] In *Grant David Vincent Williams v. Jefferies Hong Kong Ltd.* (2013), an employee sued his company for terminating his employment over a "Hitler video" incidentally referred to in a daily newsletter that was sent to subscribers without his superior's prior approval.[58] The Court identified the video as a "parody", describing it as an "art form . . . since the Greek and Roman times" in which "the theme or style, or both, of a person's activity are exaggerated or applied to an inappropriate subject for the purpose of ridicule and effect."[59]

Due to the lack of cases in which the parody defense would have been useful, it is no surprise that the defense has not been invoked by defendants. This situation is bound to change in light of the proliferation of parodic works in Hong Kong's social media for almost two decades, which provided a sound rationale for the Hong Kong government to reform its copyright law and to introduce a parody exception.

B. The Proliferation of Parodies, or Egao, in Twenty-First-Century Hong Kong

There are several Chinese terms for "parody," depending on the contexts in which it appears.[60] Literary parodies in the form of unauthorized sequels, like those of Salinger's or Mitchell's works, have yet to be seen in Hong Kong. Its parodies, most frequently found in social media and created by Internet users through editing and remixing existing materials, are commonly referred to as *egao* (惡搞).[61] Literally meaning "making bad" or "evil doing," *egao* is etymologically derived from the Japanese word *kuso-ge*, which describes badly made video games, as well as the

---

57 Tong Sai Ho v. Obscene Articles Tribunal [2008] HKCFI 901, para. 15 (C.F.I.); Ming Pao Newspapers Ltd. v. Obscene Articles Tribunal [2008] HKCFI 899, para. 15 (C.F.I.).
58 Grant David Vincent Williams v. Jefferies H.K. Ltd. [2013] HKCFI 1011 (C.F.I.).
59 *Id.* para. 49.
60 In the context of literary and film criticisms, it is more properly translated as 戲仿 or 滑稽模仿作品, literally meaning "imitation for laughter/ridicule." *See, e.g.,* LINGUEE, www.linguee.com/english-chinese/search?source=auto&query=parody (last visited Oct. 10, 2017); CAMBRIDGE (ENGLISH-CHINESE) DICTIONARY, https://dictionary.cambridge.org/dictionary/english-chinese-traditional/parody (last visited Oct. 10, 2017).
61 *Egao* is Mandarin pinyin. The Cantonese transliteration for 惡搞 is *ngok gaau*.

appreciation of these sub-par games.[62] Around year 2000, *kuso-ge*, brought into Taiwan by young netizens who frequented Japanese websites, soon became an Internet phenomenon and spread to Hong Kong and China.[63] In addition, although the father of *egao* is widely considered to be Stephen Chow, owing to the presence of parodies in his films, it became associated with a wider scope of meanings.[64] It now indicates "an online-specific genre of satirical humor and grotesque parody circulating in the form of user-generated content" fashioned by simple editing tools.[65] Internet forums, Facebook, and YouTube have become highly popular channels for disseminating these amateurish, user-generated parodies.

Although the targets of *egao* have included celebrities, political figures, and private individuals, *egao* has always carried strong connotations of social criticism and has served as a creative outlet for Internet users to express their views on society and politics in their own styles.[66] Unsurprisingly, the explosion of parodies in Hong Kong's social media has been fueled by its social and political turmoil since the political changeover.

At this juncture, it is necessary to pick up where section I left off and return to the large-scale demonstration against art. 23 in 2003. Although the opposition succeeded, the demonstration and its related democratic activities also alarmed both the Hong Kong and the PRC governments.[67] China thus tightened its grip on Hong Kong through various hardline measures,[68] which it supplemented by a "velvet glove" approach through propaganda and other initiatives.[69] The former have enabled the "mainland" ways to continue to seep into Hong Kong, eroding its core values such as freedom of speech, and leading to further protests.[70] Although the latter did improve the territory's immediate economic prospects, they made it more economically dependent on Mainland China in the long run.[71] In short, both

---

[62]   Gabriele de Seta, Egao and Online Satire, IN POP CULTURE IN ASIA AND OCEANIA 228 (Jeremy A. Murray & Kathleen M. Nadeau, eds. 2016); Oliver Jameson, *You've Probably Never Played . . . Ikki*, MINUS WORLD (Feb. 10, 2016), https://minusworld.co.uk/2016/02/10/ypnp-ikki/; Kuso, *Know Your Meme*, http://knowyourmeme.com/memes/subcultures/kuso (last visited Oct. 10, 2017).

[63]   Kuso, *supra* note 62.

[64]   Hoiying Ng, Mo Lei Tau and Egao: Fun and Politics in the Structure of Feeling of Hong Kong Youth, GLOBAL YOUTH CULTURES (Oct. 2, 2014), https://globalyouthcultures.wordpress.com/2014/10/02/mo-lei -tau-and-egao-hong-kong-youth/ (last visited Oct. 10, 2017).

[65]   de Seta, *supra* note 62, at 227.

[66]   Ng, *supra* note 64.

[67]   *Wen Wei Po*, a pro-Beijing newspaper, criticized the democracy movement for turning Hong Kong into a city of "turmoil." Petersen, *supra* note 42, at 52. Mainland politicians used the phrase *fanzhong luangang* (rebelling against China and causing chaos in Hong Kong) to describe the demonstration. Jones, *supra* note 40, at 180.

[68]   Jones, *supra* note 40, at 180–81.

[69]   Examples include arranging visits of the PRC's Olympic athletes and Chinese astronaut Yang Liwei to Hong Kong. *Id.* at 181.

[70]   On 1 July 2004, another half million people took part in a protest against the Hong Kong government, fueled by reports that three popular radio phone-in hosts had resigned due to intimidation by the Chinese authorities. *Id.*

[71]   *Id.*

strategies have made Hongkongers resentful of the "mainlandization" – both political and cultural – of their home.[72]

One of the 2003 initiatives was the Individual Visit Scheme (IVS), a liberalization measure under the Closer Economic Partnership Arrangement, which enabled Chinese tourists to travel to Hong Kong on an individual basis.[73] Implemented also to boost Hong Kong's economy after the Severe Acute Respiratory Syndrome epidemic,[74] which spread from China to Hong Kong and which caused almost 300 deaths in the city,[75] the IVS has been a major cause of Hong Kong-Mainland China conflicts. Despite the dramatic surge in the numbers of Chinese tourists since the IVS, tourism has never made up more than 5 percent of Hong Kong's GDP and Chinese tourism has merely contributed to half of this percentage.[76] Yet many Chinese tourists, whose arrogance and lack of manners have often made newspaper headlines in both Hong Kong and internationally,[77] have continued to act out their "benefactor mentality" or "master mentality" by treating Hongkongers with condescension and disparagement.[78] The daily influx of tourists has affected many Hongkongers' daily lives and made them feel like strangers in their own home.[79] The One Way Permit Scheme, administered by the Chinese government and allowing 150 Mainland Chinese a day to settle permanently in Hong Kong, has further worsened the hegemonic crisis in the city.[80] In 2012, the Hong Kong government implemented a policy that substantially reduced the number of "birth tourists"

---

[72] *Id.*

[73] Daniel Garrett, *Contesting China's Tourism Wave: Identity Politics, Protest and the Rise of the Hongkonger City State Movement*, IN PROTEST AND RESISTANCE IN THE TOURIST CITY 110 (Claire Colomb & Johannes Novy, eds. 2016); *See* Tourism Commission of Hong Kong, *Individual Visitor Scheme*, www.tourism.gov.hk/english/visitors/visitors_ind.html (last visited Oct. 10, 2017).

[74] Garrett, *supra* note 73, at 110.

[75] *E.g.*, Meagan Fitzpatrick, *SARS 10th Anniversary in Hong Kong Brings Vivid Memories*, CBC NEWS (Mar. 18, 2013), www.cbc.ca/news/world/sars-10th-anniversary-in-hong-kong-brings-vivid-memories-1 .1321674 (last visited Oct. 10, 2017); *The SARS Epidemic: China Wakes Up*, THE ECONOMIST (Apr. 24, 2013), www.economist.com/node/1730968 (last visited Oct. 10, 2017).

[76] *Hong Kong: The Facts – Tourism*, GovHK (May, 2016), www.gov.hk/en/about/abouthk/factsheets/docs/tourism.pdf (last visited Oct. 10, 2017).

[77] Amy Li, *Rude Awakening: Chinese Tourists Have the Money, But Not the Manners*, S. CHINA MORNING POST (Dec. 31, 2014), www.scmp.com/news/china/article/1671504/rude-awakening-chinese-tourists-have-means-not-manners (last visited Oct. 10, 2017).

[78] At an interview, a Chinese tourist remarked that "if the Beijing government had not taken care of Hong Kong, it would have died a long time ago!" Another made a similarly condescending remark: "If we do not come to Hong Kong to consume its goods and services, what could you eat (how could you even support yourselves)?" Originally from a Chinese essay by Chi Chi 致知, *Where did the Mainland Chinese' "Benefactor Mentality" Come from?* 大陸人的「恩主心態」從何來, SPARK (Feb. 19, 2014), https://sparkpost.wordpress.com/2014/02/19/%E5%A4%A7%E9%99%B8%E4%BA% BA%E7%9A%84%E3%80%8C%E6%81%A9%E4%B8%BB%E5%BF%83%E6%85%8B%E3%80% 8D%E5%BE%9E%E4%BD%95%E6%9D%A5/ (last visited Oct. 10, 2017).

[79] Garrett, *supra* note 73, at 107, 111–16.

[80] Christopher Yeung, *Is It Time for HK to Say No to the One-way Permit Scheme?* EJ INSIGHT (Aug. 21, 2015), www.ejinsight.com/20150821-is-it-time-for-hk-to-say-no-to-the-one-way-permit-scheme/ (last visited Oct. 10, 2017).

from China, who had been swarming Hong Kong's hospitals and exploiting their medical resources.[81] Nonetheless, the One Way Permit Scheme was considered by many to be a sufficient and effective tool for the Beijing government to change the population mix in Hong Kong and integrate it with China.[82]

The successful opposition to the National Security Bill in 2003 was followed by a short period of optimism among the Hong Kong populace, who began campaigning for democratic reform and universal suffrage in the election of Hong Kong's Chief Executive.[83] In April 2004, the Standing Committee of the National People's Congress of China, pushed too far by the protests, expressly ruled out both universal suffrage in 2007 and a fully elected Hong Kong legislature in 2008.[84] In 2013, law professor Benny Tai initiated the "Occupy Central" campaign to pressure the Chinese government into granting an elec-toral system that "satisf[ies] the international standards in relation to universal suffrage" in the Hong Kong Chief Executive Election in 2017.[85] The originators of the campaign, as well as the student groups which played a part of it, adopted and adhered to the principle of non-violent civil disobedience of Martin Luther King.[86] After a week-long boycott of classes by students who were frustrated at Beijing's decision to rule out fully democratic elections for Hong Kong, the "Occupy Central" movement commenced on September 28, 2014.[87] It ended that December, with the founders surrendering themselves to the police and announcing their plan to extend the spirit of the movement through community work and education.[88]

Since the beginning of this century, creating online parodies has become a popular way for Hong Kong netizens to vent their anger over the Chinese and

---

[81]   Emily Tsang, *Mainland Women Gatecrashing Hong Kong's Maternity Wards, 3 Years after CY Leung's "Zero-quota" Policy*, S. China Morning Post (Apr. 24, 2016), www.scmp.com/news/hong-kong/health-environment/article/1938268/mainland-women-gatecrashing-hong-kongs-maternity (last visited Oct. 10, 2017). The birth tourism phenomenon began after the 2001 case *Director of Immigration v. Chong Fung Yuen*, in which the Court of Final Appeal held that a boy born in Hong Kong to two Mainland parents neither of whom was a Hong Kong resident was entitled to the right of abode.

[82]   Yeung, *supra* note 80.

[83]   Article 45 of the Basic Law states that there shall be "gradual and orderly progress" in the method of selecting the Chief Executive and that the "ultimate aim" is selection "by universal suffrage upon nomination by a broadly representative nominating committee in accordance with democratic procedures." Hong Kong Basic Law, art. 45. In the last quarter of 2003, the Hong Kong government, as part of its effort to regain public support, seemed prepared to discuss democratic reforms. Petersen *supra* note 42, at 55–56.

[84]   *Id.* at 58–60.

[85]   *Occupy Central with Love and Peace, Occupy Central with Love and Peace: Manifesto* (Jan. 2, 2013), http://oclp.hk/index.php?route=occupy/book_detail&book_id=11 (last visited Oct. 10, 2017).

[86]   *See id.*

[87]   *Occupy Central Urges Hong Kong Protesters to Retreat*, BBC News (Dec. 2, 2014), www.bbc.com/news/world-asia-china-30288543 (last visited Oct. 10, 2017).

[88]   *Id.*

the Hong Kong governments as well as uncivil and ill-mannered Mainlanders.[89] A music video, titled "Locusts World" (蝗蟲天下) and created by a group of netizens who frequented Hong Kong Golden Forum, was posted on YouTube in 2011. Borrowing the music of Cantonese pop song "Under Fuji Mountain" by Hong Kong popular singer Eason Chan, the parody contains new lyrics mocking tourists, new immigrants, and pregnant women from China for corrupting the former colony by ignoring public hygiene, robbing and stealing resources, and driving up prices of property and other commodities.[90] It describes Mainlanders with such conduct as locusts: scenes of locusts darkening the sky, ravaging farmland, and devouring crops alternate with news photographs of Mainland children urinating and defecating on Hong Kong's streets and public transport, Mainlanders selling counterfeit goods in the city's black markets, and small businesses closing due to rent hikes.[91] Early 2012 saw a series of escalating Hong Kong-Mainland China conflicts, leading to the disparaging description of Hongkongers as "dogs" by a professor at Peking University, in response to their accusations of Mainland visitors eating food on Hong Kong's subway train.[92] Soon after that, a group of Hongkongers published a full-page advertisement in a popular tabloid, *Apple Daily*, which shows a locust overlooking Hong Kong's skyline.[93] With a headline screaming "Hong Kong people have had enough!" the advertisement demands that Chinese tourists, immigrants, and birth tourists respect Hong Kong culture, and implores the Hong Kong government to prohibit birth tourism.[94] This further

---

[89] de Seta, focusing primarily on *egao* in Mainland China, explains that *egao* has served as a weapon for Chinese Internet users "to participate in a burgeoning online civil society," "to channel grassroots creativity and to vent widely shared discontents." de Seta, *supra* note 78, at 229.

[90] *See* SuperBillionLearn, *Locusts World* (蝗蟲天下) MV, YOUTUBE (Feb. 1, 2012), www.youtube.com /watch?v=GZ-AFS1QJNM (last visited Oct. 10, 2017).

[91] *See id.*

[92] *E.g.*, Jonathan Watts, *Chinese Professor Calls Hong Kong Residents "Dogs of British Imperialists,"* THE GUARDIAN (Jan. 24, 2012), www.theguardian.com/world/2012/jan/24/chinese-professor-hong-kong-dogs (last visited Oct. 10, 2017).

[93] Sources say that over 800 people donated more than HK$100,000 through a fund-raising campaign on Facebook and Hong Kong Golden Forum to get the cost covered. *E.g.*, *About That Hong Kong "Locust" Ad . . .*, WSJ (Feb. 1, 2012), https://blogs.wsj.com/chinarealtime/2012/02/01/about-that-hong-kong-locust-ad/ (last visited Oct. 10, 2017).

[94] The full translation of the text in the advertisement is as follows:

> "Do you want Hong Kong to spend HK$1,000,000 every 18 minutes raising children of parents who are both non-residents?
> Hong Kong people have had enough!
> Because we understand that you are victimized by poisoned milk powder, we've tolerated your coming over and snapping up milk powder;
> Because we understand that you have no freedom, we've received you on your "free trip" to Hong Kong;
> Because we understand that your education system lags behind, we've shared our educational resources with you;
> Because we understand that you don't read traditional Chinese, we've adopted crippled Chinese characters."

popularized the locust metaphor and inspired more locust-themed parodic songs on YouTube.[95]

Hong Kong's Chief Executives, none of whom are elected through universal suffrage, along with principal government officials and pro-establishment legislative councilors, have also been the main targets of online parodies. Leung Chun-ying (known as C. Y. Leung), the highly unpopular Chief Executive from 2012 to 2017, has been criticized for his hypocrisy, insensitivity, and alleged corruption since he took up his position.[96] Unsurprisingly, parodies containing his images swarmed Hong Kong's social media while he was in office. In one example, Leung's image was photoshopped onto the protagonist's in the movie poster of *The Wolf of Wall Street* (2013). Because one of Leung's nicknames is "Wolf," a pun on his last name alluding to his cunning personality, the poster aptly carries the new title, "The Wolf of Government House."[97] Another popular target has been Carrie Lam, former Chief Secretary for Administration and current Chief Executive, who justified her decision to run in the 2017 Chief Executive Election by claiming that "God" had called on her.[98] One parody has Lam's image photoshopped into a Christian art picture portraying heaven, accompanied by the ancient proverb: "Those whom God wishes to destroy, he first makes mad," to express strong public sentiments against Lam's pro-Beijing stance and fears that she would make an even worse leader than her predecessor. Regina Ip, former Chief Secretary for Security who tried to push the National Security Bill in 2003, also ran for the Chief Executive position. Her catchy blue and red campaign logo carried the slogan "Win Back Hong Kong," in which

"*[In simplified Chinese]* Please respect our local culture when you come to Hong Kong; if it were not for Hong Kong you'd be all screwed."
[We] strongly demand that the government revise the 24th clause of the Basic Law!
Stop the endless invasion of Hong Kong by non-resident pregnant women from Mainland China!"
[Translation by this book's author.]

95   *See, e.g.,* ChunYip Tang, *The Locusts Medley of HK Golden* (高登蝗蟲金曲大串燒), YOUTUBE (May 20, 2014), www.youtube.com/watch?v=L4VtqIInENo (last visited Oct. 10, 2017); Lucifer Chu, *Locust Attacks* (進擊的蝗蟲), YOUTUBE (July 1, 2013), www.youtube.com/watch?v=JZ2KPGLlvhE (last visited Oct. 10, 2017).

96   *E.g.,* Keith Bradsher & Chris Buckley, *Hong Kong Leader Reaffirms Unbending Stance on Elections,* N.Y. TIMES (Oct. 20, 2014); Kris Cheng, *Failure to De-colonise "Caused Many Problems" for Hong Kong, Says Former Beijing Official,* H.K. FREE P. (Sep. 21, 2015); Raymond Yeung & Kimmy Chung, *Hong Kong Leader CY Leung Accuses Lawmaker on Panel Probing HK$50m Payment of Prejudice,* S. CHINA MORNING POST (May 17, 2017), www.scmp.com/news/hong-kong/politics/article/ 2094644/cy-leung-should-have-made-revisions-hk50-million-payment (last visited Oct. 10, 2017); Ying-Kit Lai, *CY Leung Admits Liability for Illegal Structures,* S. CHINA MORNING POST (Nov. 23, 2012), www.scmp.com/news/hong-kong/article/1089352/cy-leung-admits-liability-illegal-structures (last visited Oct. 10, 2017).

97   *See "Why Is "Internet Article 23" Likely to Pass?* REAL H.K. NEWS (Dec. 7, 2015), https://therealnewshk .wordpress.com/2015/12/08/why-is-internet-article-23-likely-to-pass/ (last visited Oct. 10, 2017).

98   *E.g.,* Kris Cheng, *Newly Elected Carrie Lam Reiterates God Called Upon Her to Run, as She Begins Forming Cabinet,* H.K. FREE P. (Mar. 30, 2017), www.hongkongfp.com/2017/03/30/newly-elected -carrie-lam-reiterates-god-called-upon-run-begins-forming-cabinet/ (last visited Oct. 10, 2017).

a red heart appeared above the letter "i" where the dot should be.[99] Scoffing at the pro-Beijing politician's purported goal to "put Hong Kong back on the right track," a netizen parodied her slogan and logo by changing the words to "Die Back Big Six" (a literal translation of the vulgar Cantonese expression "get your ass back to the Mainland and die" 死番大陸) and substituting a skeleton head for the dot in "Die."[100]

Hongkongers certainly have not shied away from parodying Xi Jinping, President of China, especially during the "Occupy Central" movement. Examples included images of Xi holding a yellow umbrella against the background of protest sites in Hong Kong, which went viral over the Internet, and life-size cardboard figures created from such images which were placed at many protest sites.[101] These were based upon a photograph of Xi captured by the state-run Xinhua News Agency during his trip to Wuhan in July 2013 to oversee the construction of a dam.[102] The photograph, which won China's top photojournalism prize, shows Xi standing in the rain, holding a large black umbrella, and talking to the engineers. The presence of the umbrella made it a handy target for Hong Kong protesters. Although the yellow ribbon was initially chosen as symbol of the campaign,[103] after participants used their umbrellas to defend themselves against tear gas and other violent acts by the police, the umbrella – the yellow one in particular – became a fresh symbol of the movement and the spirit of resistance.[104] The original photograph was deemed typical of the political propaganda by the state-run media to push a grass-roots image of a president who cares about ordinary people in China.[105] By turning the umbrella's color to yellow, parodists fashioned a powerful weapon to satirize his authoritarianism and his "behind-the-scene," despotic control of the former colony.

Without a doubt, the trend of using parodies by Hongkongers to articulate their views, vent their frustrations, and participate in the civil society will continue. Because many of these parodies borrow substantially from their originals, conflicts

[99]   See image at https://upload.wikimedia.org/wikipedia/commons/thumb/e/ea/Win_Back_HK_Logo .svg/1280px-Win_Back_HK_Logo.svg.png (last visited Oct. 10, 2017).

[100]   See image at https://io.wp.com/hkjam.com/wp-content/uploads/2016/12/sketch-1481878217678.png? fit=1200%2C675 (last visited Oct. 10, 2017).

[101]   Ellie Ng, *Chinese President's Umbrella Becomes Occupy Central's Favorite Meme*, H.K. FREE P. (Oct. 24, 2014), www.hongkongfp.com/2014/10/24/xi-jinping-yellow-umbrella-political-meme/ (last visited Oct. 10, 2017).

[102]   Jackson Connor, *Photo Of President Xi Jinping Holding Umbrella Wins China's Top Photojournalism Prize*, HUFFINGTON POST (Oct. 23, 2014), www.huffingtonpost.com/2014/10/23/xi-jinping-umbrella -photojournalism-prize-chinese-president_n_6035944.html (last visited Oct. 10, 2017).

[103]   Jasmine Coleman, *Hong Kong Protests: The Symbols and Songs Explained*, BBC NEWS (Oct. 4, 2014), www.bbc.com/news/world-asia-china-29473974 (last visited Oct. 10, 2017).

[104]   Rishi Iyengar, *6 Questions You Might Have about Hong Kong's Umbrella Revolution*, TIME MAG. (Oct. 2014), http://time.com/3471366/hong-kong-umbrella-revolution-occupy-central-democracy- explainer-6-questions/ (last visited Oct. 10, 2017).

[105]   Ng, *supra* note 101.

between netizens' right to freedom of expression and the owners' right in their intellectual property are foreseeable.

C. Justifying a Parody Exception in the Hong Kong Context

One might argue that a fair dealing exception in the form of parody would not be necessary. If the rights-holders of "Under Fuji Mountain," the photograph of Xi Jinping, the "The Wolf of Wall Street" poster, and various artworks were to bring copyright claims against those who parodied their works, the latter might be able to rely upon the existing defense of "criticism" under the current law.[106] However, it is uncertain whether the courts would consider parodies, the critical message(s) of which are not always explicit, to be criticism. As Part I has argued, the right to parody is a universal right, essential to democratic governance, that should be accommodated by the copyright law of every jurisdiction. A parody exception is especially vital to Hong Kong for three related reasons. First, it would help to promote a critical political culture crucial to self-governance and enhance Hong Kong's reputation as "the window on China." Second, it would encourage creativity in a city striving to make its creative industries a major economic force. Third, making and appreciating parodies empowers Hongkongers to thrive in difficult times.

As a former British colony situated in Southern China, Hong Kong has long enjoyed a vibrant and independent media and a unique position as a window into Mainland China.[107] Both local and foreign journalists have made use of its unique geopolitical position and strong legal protections for freedom of expression to report on news from Hong Kong, China, and the greater Asia region.[108] However, under the former colonial regime, and a general lack of social and political turmoil, Hong Kong did not begin to develop a critical political culture until after its handover to China.[109] If Hongkongers are to successfully govern Hong Kong, it is necessary to foster a critical political culture while enhancing its position and reputation as a "window on China."[110]

The years leading to the handover already saw a rising trend of self-censorship by its print media.[111] Some newspapers began hiring Mainland Chinese journalists with close ties to the Chinese Communist Party, while some outspoken writers who were

---

[106] Qili Xu, for example, argues that there is no need for a new fair dealing exception in the form of parody. Qili Xu, *Copyright Protection in the Digital Age: A Tripartite Balance*, 45 H.K. L.J. 751, 781 (2012).

[107] *Threatened Harbor: Encroachments on Press Freedom in Hong Kong*, PEN AMERICAN CENTER (Jan. 16, 2015), www.pen.org/sites/default/files/PEN-HK-report_1.16_lowres.pdf (last visited Oct. 10, 2017).

[108] *Id.*

[109] Peter Yu, *Digital Copyright and the Parody Exception in Hong Kong: Accommodating the Needs and Interests of Internet Users*, Journalism & Media Studies Centre, University of Hong Kong (Jan. 2014), at 6, https://jmsc.hku.hk/revamp/wp-content/uploads/2014/01/jmsc_hku_submission.pdf (last visited Oct. 10, 2017).

[110] *See id.*

[111] JONES, *supra* note 3, at 1098.

critical of the PRC government lost their newspaper columns.[112] Local television stations heavily invested in China's emerging media market removed controversial talk shows and shelved sensitive documentaries.[113] Self-censorship also occurred in higher educational institutions. In 1997, the most liberal university in the territory, under the leadership of its new vice-chancellor, refused to reappoint a well-qualified law professor who was critical of China's human rights record and its interventions in Hong Kong's internal affairs.[114]

As expected, the problem of self-censorship has only become more severe after the handover. Chris Patten, the last and most popular governor of Hong Kong, once revealed that his anxiety over Hong Kong's future was "not that this community's autonomy would be usurped by Peking, but that it could be given away bit by bit by some people in Hong Kong."[115] Hong Kong's autonomy has not been given away by pro-China politicians alone, as revealed by the mounting pressure on Hong Kong journalists by media companies to censor sensitive information, the increasingly pro-government stance by TVB, the only free-to-air terrestrial television broadcaster in Hong Kong, and the continual erosion of academic freedom at different school levels.[116]

It is not only media organizations and academic institutions that have exercised self-censorship. In January 2015, a pro-establishment supporter fired off a letter to Puma, the sportswear company, about an entrant number on a runner's t-shirt in a photograph that Puma posted on its official Facebook page ahead of the annual Standard Chartered Hong Kong Marathon. The supporter complained that the random-looking number "D7689" was a thinly-veiled, profane insult to Hong Kong's then-Chief Executive.[117]

---

[112] *Id.* at 1098–99.

[113] *Id.* at 1099.

[114] *Id.*

[115] Gargan, *supra* note 2.

[116] Jeffie Lam, *Self-censorship "Common" in Hong Kong Newspapers, Say Journalists*, S. CHINA MORNING POST (Apr. 23, 2014), www.scmp.com/news/hong-kong/article/1495138/press-freedom-hong-kong-low-level-journalists-study-finds?page=all (last visited Oct. 10, 2017). TVB was given the uncomplimentary nickname, "Chinese Centralized Television Broadcasts" (in short, CCTVB) for their increasingly pro-government stance. Rebecca Wong, *How and Why Hong Kong's Press Downplayed the "Umbrella Movement"* of 2014, FREE SPEECH DEBATE (Mar. 10, 2015). One example of the continual erosion of academic freedom was Hong Kong University's "covert attempts" to pressure HKU researcher Robert Chung into discontinuing his public opinion polls about the Chief Executive and his government in 2000. JONES, *supra* note 3, at 1101. In 2016, a school body overseeing around 40 secondary and primary schools issued a new code of conduct stating that its teachers and staff are "absolutely not allowed to distribute messages containing a political stance either on the school's communication platforms" or on their personal platforms. Young Wang, *New Conduct Code from Hong Kong School Body Po Leung Kuk Stops Teachers Posting Politics*, S. CHINA MORNING Post (Oct. 25, 2016), http://yp.scmp.com/news/hong-kong/article/104687/new-conduct-code-hong-kong-school-body-po-leung-kuk-stops-teachers (last visited Oct. 10, 2017).

[117] "D7" in Cantonese sounds like the word "fuck". "689" was the number of electoral college votes it took for Chief Executive Leung Chun-ying to get elected in 2012 – slightly over half of the 1,200-member election committee that represented vested interests rather than the Hong Kong voting

The apology by Puma's global chief executive, who called it "a very unfortu-
nate issue" that they did not identify on the spot, and the rapid take-down of
the photograph, reflected the eagerness of some corporations, including global
ones, to pander to the pro-establishment camp and the Hong Kong government
by censoring anything that might cause them embarrassment and displeasure.[118]
Within a short time, parodies of "D7689" flooded the social media. Protection
of parodies through the copyright regime would encourage Hongkongers to
participate in politics by expressing their views on different platforms.[119] This
would counteract the impacts that self-censorship has had on free speech and
enhance Hong Kong's reputation for free speech and free press.

A parody exception would also help to foster creativity in Hong Kong, which has
been striving to turn its cultural and creative industries into major economic force.
Due to its lack of natural resources, the territory has served as a financial hub for
many years. Since the turn of the twenty-first century, the government has emphasized that creative thinking and high-tech innovation should play an important role
in its industrial development and education policies.[120] Although copyright protection is important to the successful development of the creative sector, creating an
exception for parody would remove unnecessary restrictions on parodic productions
and reduce administrative costs incurred in obtaining copyright clearances.[121] This
in turn would help to nurture new creative talents and enrich the cultural and
entertainment industries.[122]

The saying that art offers a beacon of hope to people who live in dark times is
perhaps clichéd. Arts have been created in times both good and bad, and great
works of art alone do not redeem bad realities.[123] Nevertheless, creating and
appreciating art works helps people to engage with reality, to reach out, and even to
fight.[124] If the 2016 U.S. Presidential Election result has made some Americans,
who elect their President every four years through universal suffrage, turn to art for

population at large. The number has been used as a nickname for Leung to satirize his lack of popular
mandate to rule Hong Kong and the lack of legitimacy of the voting system. *E.g.*, 689,
THE ENCYCLOPEDIA OF VIRTUAL COMMUNITIES IN HONG KONG, http://evchk.wikia.com/wiki/689 (last
visited Oct. 10, 2017).

[118] Samuel Chan, *Puma Apologises for "D7689" Hong Kong Marathon Photo Targeting CY Leung*,
S. CHINA MORNING POST (Jan. 26, 2015), www.scmp.com/news/hong-kong/article/1692371/claws-out
-puma-apologises-d7689-hong-kong-marathon-photo-targeting-cy (last visited Oct. 10, 2017).

[119] THE ENCYCLOPEDIA OF VIRTUAL COMMUNITIES IN HONG KONG, *supra* note 117.

[120] *See* Chief Executive Tung Chee Hwa, *The Policy Address*, 1998, 2001, www.policyaddress.gov.hk
/pao1/high_e.htm (last visited Oct. 10, 2017); www.policyaddress.gov.hk/pa98/english/high.htm (last
visited Oct. 10, 2017).

[121] Yu, *supra* note 109, at 9.

[122] *Id.* at 10.

[123] David Berry, *Art Can Be a Beacon of Hope or An Explanation of the World, but Whether It Can Shape
It in Dark Times IS Uncertain*, NATIONAL POST (Dec. 2, 2016), http://nationalpost.com/entertainment/
art-can-be-a-beacon-of-hope-or-explanation-of-the-world-but-whether-it-can-shape-it-in-dark-times-is
-uncertain (last visited Oct. 10, 2017).

[124] *See id.*

solace,[125] then Hongkongers, the vast majority having no say in electing their Chief Executive, have all the more reason to treasure creative art as a means to thrive in difficult times. Thus, greater protection for parodies would well serve Hong Kong society, many members of which have felt disgruntled with both the local and the PRC governments, by empowering them not only to create parodies to vent and/or to profit, but also to seek comfort in times of social and political unrest.

D. Copyright (Amendment) Bills 2011 and 2014

The introduction of the parody exception by the Hong Kong government nonetheless caused uproar among Hongkongers, who suspected that it was politically motivated and would serve as a weapon to curb free speech under the pretext of copyright protection. The Copyright (Amendment) Bill 2011, introduced by the Commerce and Economic Development Bureau & Intellectual Property Department in consultation with the Bills Committee, had already sparked controversies by introducing an exclusive technology-neutral "communication right" of the copyright owner to protect copyrighted materials in a digital environment.[126] According to ss. 31(3) and 118(8C), in determining whether any distribution, or "communication," of an infringing copy "is made to such an extent as to affect prejudicially the owner of the copyright," the court may take into account "all the circumstances of the case and, in particular – (a) the purpose of the distribution; (b) the nature of the work, including its commercial value; (c) the amount and substantiality of the portion copied (in relation to the work as a whole) that was distributed; (d) the mode of distribution; and (e) the economic prejudice caused to the owner of the copyright as a consequence of the distribution, including the effect of the distribution on the potential market for or value of the work."[127]

Bill 2011 did not contain a provision exempting parody or other derivative works from criminal or civil liability. Hence, a person would be criminally liable for infringement by "communicating" a copy of an infringing parody to the public in the course of trade or business or to such extent as to affect prejudicially its copyright owner.[128] Due to the diverse views on Bill 2011 during its examination in the LegCo, particularly regarding its failure to include a parody exception, the

---

[125] E.g., Megan Garber, *Still, Poetry Will Rise*, THE ATLANTIC (Nov. 10, 2016), www.theatlantic.com/entertain ment/archive/2016/11/still-poetry-will-rise/507266/ (last visited Oct. 10, 2017); Marsha Lederman, *Seeking Solace in the Power of Art in a World Turned Upside Down*, THE GLOBE AND MAIL (Nov. 11, 2016), https:// beta.theglobeandmail.com/arts/seeking-solace-in-the-power-of-art-in-a-world-turnedddd-upside-down/arti cle32818390/?ref=http://www.theglobeandmail.com& (last visited Oct. 10, 2017).

[126] Copyright (Amendment) Bill 2011, cll. 13, 51, www.legco.gov.hk/yr10-11/english/bills/b201106033.pdf (last visited Oct. 10, 2017).

[127] *Id.* cll. 27, 51.

[128] *See id.*

Bureau withdrew it and issued a consultation paper in 2013 to seek further opinions from the public on the treatment of parody.[129]

The 2013 paper clarifies the current status of parodies under the Copyright Ordinance, explaining that they do not constitute copyright infringement if they incorporate only the ideas of the underlying works, reproduce insubstantial parts of them, incorporate substantial parts after obtaining authorization from the copyright owners, or incorporate those in the public domain with expired copyrights.[130] Furthermore, parodies do not constitute infringement if their incorporations of underlying copyrighted works fall within the fair dealing exceptions, while those falling outside of these cases may attract civil liability for copyright infringement.[131] In addition, those who distribute copies of infringing parodies to the public in the course of trade or business, or to such an extent as to affect prejudicially the copyright owner, may be criminally liable.[132] However, in reality it would seem unlikely for the distribution of a copy of an infringing parody to be considered "to the extent as to affect prejudicially the copyright owner," because parodies generally target different markets from those of the underlying works and are therefore unlikely to displace demands for them.[133] The consultation paper does suggest that the law may consider introducing a fair dealing exception for parody based on the approaches in Australia, Canada and the UK, under which the distribution and communication of parody would not incur any civil nor criminal liability as long as the qualifying conditions of the exception are met.[134]

The Copyright (Amendment) Bill 2014 introduced a new s. 39A stating that "[f]air dealing with a work for the purpose of parody, satire, caricature or pastiche does not infringe any copyright in the work."[135] In determining whether a dealing is fair, the Court would take into account the overall circumstances of a case, including the following factors: "the purpose and nature of the dealing," including whether the dealing is for a non-profit-making purpose and whether the dealing is of a commercial nature, "the nature of the work," "the amount and substantiality of the portion dealt with in relation to the work as a whole," and "the effect on potential market for or value of the work."[136] To allay public anxiety, the legislation would also clarify the criminal liability for causing prejudice to the copyright owner, this Bill

---

[129] Commerce and Economic Development Bureau & Intellectual Property Department, *Treatment of Parody under the Copyright Regime Consultation Paper* (2013), www.gov.hk/en/residents/government/publication/consultation/docs/2013/Parody.pdf (last visited Oct. 10, 2017).

[130] *Id.* para. 12.

[131] *Id.* para. 14.

[132] *Id.* para. 15.

[133] *Id.*

[134] *Id.* para. 32.

[135] Copyright (Amendment) Bill 2014, cl. 19, www.gld.gov.hk/egazette/pdf/20141824/es32014182421.pdf (last visited Oct. 10, 2017). The other newly added purposes include commenting on current events, quotation, giving educational instruction (especially for distance learning), facilitating daily operations of libraries, archives and museums, and media shifting of sound recordings.

[136] *Id.*

provided that the Court "may take into account all the circumstances of the case;" and in particular, "whether economic prejudice is caused to the copyright owner as a consequence of the communication, having regard to whether the communication amounts to a substitution for the work."[137]

The proposed exceptions of "parody, satire, caricature or pastiche" of Bill 2014 were based upon Western models, which the Bills Committee and the Bureau consulted throughout the drafting processes. Considering that the parody exceptions in the Western jurisdictions have been regarded as a big step forward in liberalizing fair use or fair dealing, the negative criticisms towards the Bill by Hongkongers may seem mind-boggling.

E. Netizens' Fears of the Two Bills

Netizens nicknamed both Bills "Internet Article 23," after art. 23 of the Basic Law that led to the introduction of the controversial National Security Bill in 2003.[138] Regarding Bill 2011, they reasoned that the authorities could use the unspecified circumstances of communication and the term "prejudicially" to mean whatever they want them to mean by reference to the non-exclusive list of statutory criteria in s. 118(8C), and in doing so, hold parodists criminally liable for their works.[139] Furthermore, the criminal provisions would entitle the government to bypass copyright owners to prosecute on their behalf those distributing parodic works or sharing other people's parodic works on the Internet.[140] Thus, the new law would become a powerful political tool to suppress free speech.[141] Some even compared it to book-burning during the Qin Dynasty and the Cultural Revolution of China.[142] In 2011 and 2012, numerous protests were initiated by netizen groups as well as legislators of pan-democratic groups, although these protests were much smaller in scale than those triggered by the National Security Bill in 2003.[143]

The fear that Bill 2011, if passed into law, would function as a tool for suppressing free speech is not unwarranted. Its failure to provide for a parody exception and its

---

[137] Id. cl. 57.
[138] Badcanto, Hong Kong Copyright (Amendment) Bill 2011 Criminalises Parody and Uploading/Posting of Unauthorised Copyrighted Materials Including News Articles/AFP's Misleading Report on Hong Kong Copyright Amendment (Apr. 27, 2012), https://badcanto.wordpress.com/2012/04/27/hong-kong-copyright-amendment-bill-2011-criminalises-parody-and-posting-of-unauthorised-coy righted-materials-including-news-articles/ (last visited Oct. 10, 2017).
[139] Id.
[140] Ricky Chan, Intellectual Property Department of Hong Kong: Withdraw Copyright (Amendment) Bill 2011 (online petition), www.change.org/p/intellectual-property-department-of-hong-kong-withdraw -copyright-amendment-bill-2011-3 (last visited Oct. 10, 2017).
[141] Id.; Badcanto, supra note 138.
[142] Badcanto, supra note 138.
[143] E.g., Netizens Protest Internet Article 23 網民遊行反網絡23條, APPLE DAILY 蘋果日報 (Dec. 5, 2011), http://hk.apple.nextmedia.com/news/art/20111205/15862730 (last visited Oct. 10, 2017); Netizens Petition against Internet Article 23 網民請願反網絡23條, APPLE DAILY蘋果日報 (May 21, 2012), http://hk.apple.nextmedia.com/news/art/20120521/16354818 (last visited Oct. 10, 2017).

lack of specificity would lead to a law far more draconian than its foreign counter-parts. For example, in the United States, criminal copyright infringement requires that the infringer act "for the purpose of commercial advantage or private financial gain."[144] In Canada, criminal copyright infringement involves commercial activities such as the sale or rental of copyrighted materials.[145] Because Bill 2011 did not define "prejudicially," and "economic prejudice" is only one kind of prejudice, nothing would prevent the court from finding parodists of the Cantopop song "Under Fuji Mountain" criminally liable, as long as the copyright-owners could convince the court that they have been "prejudicially affected" by its parody, "Locusts World."[146] Even assuming that courts interpret "prejudicially" to refer solely to the parody's economic impact on its underlying work, the threshold of "more than trivial economic prejudice" is both vague enough to cause uncertainty and low enough to make parodists whose works have merely caused unsubstantial damages to their authors criminally liable.[147] Criminalizing the parodying of copyrighted works would also mean that the government, or even private citizens who feel troubled by the political messages in the parodies, could bring criminal suits against parodists.[148] Furthermore, even though creating parodies for non-commercial pur-poses, unlike large-scale piracy, may not be criminalized, the fear of civil liability, due to the lack of a civil exemption for parody, would be sufficient to discourage parodies and chill free speech.

One criticism of Bill 2014 was that its exceptions for "parody, satire, caricature or pastiche" do not include a provision restricting contractual terms from overriding or limiting such exceptions.[149] Hence the Bill did not offer consumers and businesses sufficient clarity and certainty.[150] Moreover, one legislator argued that it should adopt the U.S. legal principle of "fair use," as opposed to the Hong Kong model of "fair dealing," so that even a use falling outside of the prescribed purposes can be fair, as long as it is consistent with several "fairness" factors.[151]

The concern that the Bill's lack of a provision restricting contractual terms that circumvent copyright exceptions would enable businesses to ban the making of parodies is reasonable. Requesting that the Bill adopt fair use nonetheless would lead to a revamping of Hong Kong's copyright regime.[152] In fact, the inclusion of a parody exception would have been a huge step forward in liberalizing the regime. When introducing Bill 2014, the government

---

[144] Copyright Act, 1976, 17 U.S.C. § 506(a) (U.S.A.).
[145] Copyright Act, R.S.C., 1985, c. C-42, s. 42.1. (Can.).
[146] *See* Badcanto, *supra* note 138.
[147] *See id.*
[148] *Id.*
[149] Stuart Lau, *Hong Kong Copyright Bill Explained: Why Are People So Concerned about This?* S. China Morning Post (Dec. 9, 2015), www.scmp.com/news/hong-kong/politics/article/1888931/hong-kong-copyright-bill-explained-why-are-people-so (last visited Oct. 10, 2017).
[150] *Id.*
[151] *Id.*
[152] *Id.*

applied the new law to several hypothetical cases on its website, including rewriting the lyrics of an existing song and capturing copyrighted images, in its attempt to dispel confusion and allay anxiety.[153] It clarified that if rewriting lyrics falls within the existing or proposed scope of exceptions, such as for the purposes of criticism and review, commenting on current events or parody, and meets the fairness conditions, it would incur no civil or criminal liability.[154] Hence, parodic songs like "Locusts World" would not likely attract any liability. Similarly, capturing copyrighted images would incur no civil or criminal liability so long as they fell within the existing or proposed scope of exceptions and met the relevant qualifying conditions. Thus, using copyrighted images, like movie posters and campaign logos, to mock political figures would very likely be legal.

It would be fair to say that with the shelving of Bill 2014 in early March 2016, Hongkongers lost the opportunity to have their right to parody enshrined in law. Because the exception would provide a boost to the territory's cultural and creative industries, unless the bill is reconsidered by a new legislature in the next term, Hong Kong may suffer in the long run. Undoubtedly, the proposed fair dealing exception in Bill 2014 can be improved.

F. Undistinguished Genres in a "Parody" Exception?

Bill 2014 did not offer definitions of "parody," "satire," "caricature," or "pastiche." The "Keynote" document accompanying the Bill on the government's website cites the *Concise Oxford English Dictionary* (12th edition, 2012) in a footnote, defining "parody" as "an imitation of the style of a particular writer, artist or genre with deliberate exaggeration for comic effect" or as "a travesty;" "satire" as "the use of humour, irony, exaggeration, or ridicule to expose and criticize people's stupidity or vices" or as "a play, novel, etc. using satire"; "caricature" as "a depiction of a person in which distinguishing characteristics are exaggerated for comic or grotesque effect;" and "pastiche" as "an artistic work in a style that imitates that of another work, artist or period."[155] The Bills Committee was well aware of the difficulty in defining "parody." A report that accompanies Bill 2011, after surveying the status of parody in the copyright statutes of various jurisdictions, describes "parody" as a broad term "used loosely for referring to a wide range of materials created by netizens that have adapted or modified existing copyright works for sharing and

---

[153] See Intellectual Property Department, *The Government of HKSAR, Copyright (Amendment) Bill 2014: Frequently Asked Questions*, www.ipd.gov.hk/eng/intellectual_property/copyright/Q_A_2014 .htm#q6 (last visited Oct. 10, 2017).

[154] *Id.*

[155] Intellectual Property Department, The Government of HKSAR, *Keynote to Copyright (Amendment) Bill 2014*, n. 1, www.ipd.gov.hk/eng/intellectual_property/copyright/Keynote_2014_e.pdf (last visited Oct. 10, 2017).

dissemination on the Internet."[156] As such, it is "often associated or used interchangeably with 'satire,' 're-mix,' 'caricature,' 'mash-up works,' 'derivative works,' etc. to describe a variety of online materials created for different purposes."[157]

To date, almost no scholarly voices have been heard regarding the meaning and scope of "parody" in the context of Hong Kong's copyright reform. The exception is Peter Yu, who contends that the statute should not distinguish among the four genres by providing definitions for them.[158] Yu concedes that the lack of clarity in the Ordinance could lead to overzealous criminal prosecutions and would cost netizens who face prosecutions before the available definitions are made by courts a huge amount of time, effort, and resources regardless of whether they would prevail in the end.[159] He nonetheless argues that "standards that are intended to provide *floors* to benefit the public could easily be turned into *ceilings* to cause public harm."[160] Accordingly, "supposedly helpful definitions seeking to provide guidance to internet users could end up backfiring on them by creating *harmful* limits on otherwise legitimate, commonplace user activities."[161]

Yu also recommends that the phrase "parody, satire, caricature and pastiche" be replaced by "parody, satire, caricature, pastiche or other similar or related purposes," the language proposed by the Irish Copyright Review Committee.[162] Unsurprisingly, he also advocates for the law to include an exemption for UGC (user-generated contents). Arguing that much of the content generated by Internet users would not be covered by an exception for parody, satire, caricature, or pastiche, he proposes a new exception for PNCUGC (predominantly noncommercial user-generated content) similar to the one Canada recently adopted.[163] This new exception would cover such examples as the uploading of a home video showing a child's performance of a Cantopop or Mandopop song which, being neither a parody nor satire, would constitute the unauthorized communication of a copyrighted work to the public and open the child performer to civil and criminal liabilities for copyright infringement.[164] Because Hong Kong has no plan to introduce a fair use provision, Yu argues, the PNCUGC exception would be necessary to accommodate a huge

[156]   Commerce and Economic Development Bureau & Intellectual Property Department, *Copyright Exception for Parody* (Oct. 2011), para. 16, www.legco.gov.hk/yr10-11/english/bc/bc10/papers/ bc101122cb1-385-4-e.pdf (last visited Oct. 10, 2011).
[157]   *Id.*
[158]   Yu, *supra* note 109, at 15.
[159]   *Id.*
[160]   *Id.*, citing Dan L. Burk & Julie E. Cohen, *Fair Use Infrastructure for Rights Management Systems*, 15 Harv J. L. & Tech. 41, 57 (2001).
[161]   *Id.*
[162]   *Id.* at 16.
[163]   *Id.* at 17.
[164]   *Id.* at 22.

variety of transformative works that do not compete with the underlying ones and to shield their creators from liabilities.[165]

G. In Defense of a Broad, but Not-Too-Broad Parody Exception

Not distinguishing among the four genres in the "parody" exception, as Yu recommends, may pose problems. If Hong Kong's copyright system has largely followed the British utilitarian tradition, then Bills 2011 and 2014, which aim to offer greater protection for copyrighted works in a digital environment, were inspired by a narrow conception of natural rights that prioritizes rights-holders' interests over those of users. Should the government return to this issue and redraft the bill in the next legislative term, it should propose to substitute a broad parody exception for "parody" and "satire" to reduce the potential prejudicial effect of "satire" and thereby discourage courts from treating "satire" as a form of dealing that is less fair than "parody." The law should also distinguish parody from both caricature and pastiche. This would prevent courts from imposing unfair standards on these two genres, both theoretically and practically different from parody, and would help to educate the public about the significant role of parody in generating a vibrant political discourse and countering self-censorship.

1. Broadening "Parody" to Include "Parody" and "Satire"

An inclusive parody category, clearly defined as encompassing works targeting the originals and those criticizing or commenting on something else, should replace the two fair dealing categories of "parody" and "satire" in Bill 2014. In fact, the government's document, by defining "parody" as "an imitation of the style of a particular writer, artist or genre with deliberate exaggeration for comic effect," does not restrict the genre to "target" parodies and apparently includes what are known as "weapon" parodies.[166] This definition nonetheless lacks clarity. The document also defines "satire" as "the use of humour, irony, exaggeration, or ridicule to expose and criticize people's stupidity or vices."[167] Because "satire" is made redundant by an inclusive parody exception, it should be omitted.

Keeping both "parody" and "satire" and not defining them in the statute would likely pose problems, as courts may determine that using a work for the purpose of "satire" is less fair than for the purpose of parody. Yu notes the frequent distinction made between "parody" and "satire" in *Campbell*, namely, "[p]arody needs to mimic an original to make its point," whereas "satire can stand on its own two feet and so requires justification for the very act of

---

[165] *Id.* at 26.
[166] *See* Intellectual Property Department, The Government of HKSAR, *supra* note 155.
[167] *Id.*

borrowing."[168] He argues that this distinction was made only in the context of *Campbell*, and it is problematic to hold that parody is more likely to be protected than satire.[169] Yet the parody exception has remained untested in all jurisdictions whose laws the Bills Committee consulted, except the United States and Canada. Hong Kong courts, in seeking to interpret the scope of "parody" and "satire," would likely consult the governmental document indicating that a "satire" need not invoke any existing work.[170] Courts may also reference American and Canadian cases. While they may rely on the Federal Court of Canada's recent decision to define parody broadly, nothing would stop them from drawing upon American case law. Therefore, unless a well-defined and inclusive parody category replaces "parody" and "satire," the flawed parody/satire dichotomy or the propertized conception of fair dealing may impact their judgments. After holding that works are "satires" on the ground that they criticize or comment on something else, Hong Kong courts may determine that when works borrowing too much from their originals for satirical purposes, it is not fair dealing, even though they would not likely cause any economic prejudice to the originals' authors by displacing demands for their works.

The parodies discussed in this chapter can illuminate how a broad, well-defined parody exception would help courts to properly balance rights-holders' interests with those of users and bring Hong Kong's copyright system more in line with its free speech tradition. Of all the parodies described in this chapter, only those of Regina Ip's campaign logo and President Xi's photograph target the underlying works. The former targets Ip's pro-Beijing stance by turning her slogan "Win Back Hong Kong" into "Die Back Big Six," whereas the latter targets Xi's hypocrisy and despotic control of Hong Kong by turning the umbrella into a symbol of protest against both the Hong Kong and the PRC governments. The others target something else. "Under Fuji Mountain," for instance, was given new lyrics and a new title, "Locusts World," to satirize the conduct of Chinese tourists and immigrants in Hong Kong. If parody and satire remain two different categories, the court may categorize "Locusts World" as a "satire" that can stand on its own rather than as a vaguely defined "parody," and hold that "Locusts World" has used too much of "Under Fuji Mountain" to serve its satirical purpose. On the contrary, replacing the "parody" and "satire" categories by the proposed parody exception would reduce any potential influence of "satire" or a propertized conception of fair dealing on the courts. Focusing on whether these parodies have served as market substitutes for the originals, courts would more likely hold for the parodists and less likely suppress their right to freedom of expression.

---

[168] Yu, *supra* note 109, at 16–17.

[169] *Id.* at 17.

[170] *See* Intellectual Property Department, The Government of HKSAR, *supra* note 155.

2. Distinguishing "Parody" from "Caricature" and "Pastiche"

The law should also distinguish parody, a vehicle for criticism or commentary, from caricature and pastiche, neither of which needs to contain any criticism or commentary. In doing so, the law would avoid two potential pitfalls: requiring that these two genres carry messages as parodies do, and offering an overly broad and vague definition of parody so that it encompasses caricature and pastiche. Providing for a well-defined parody would also help to facilitate its role in Hong Kong society.

The *Oxford English Dictionary* defines caricature as "[a] picture, description, or imitation of a person in which certain striking characteristics are exaggerated in order to create a comic or grotesque effect."[171] Although elements of caricature are found in ancient Greek and Roman arts and in the allegorical arts of the medieval period, caricature is generally regarded to have been invented by Italian painters Annibale and Agostino Carracci, before it evolved into a mode of political discourse in France and England in the seventeenth and eighteenth centuries respectively, and became an important element in American social and political satires in the twentieth century.[172] Yet the term "caricature," derived from the Italian word *caricare* (meaning to load or to exaggerate), refers simply to a loaded portrait that exaggerates the subject's features.[173] Hence, despite its heavy presence in social and political commentaries, a caricature need not serve any critical or commentary purpose.

Political caricatures, which were abundant in colonial Hong Kong, have continued to flourish over the past decade. John Tsang, former Financial Secretary of Hong Kong and a candidate in the 2017 Chief Executive Election, is well liked by Hongkongers. Many of his caricatures do not contain overt political messages.[174] This is not true for former Chief Executive C. Y. Leung, whose caricatures have almost always contained disparaging messages. In a number of them, fangs are added to his mouth and a pair of horns to his head, to make him resemble a demon.[175] Assume that the law recognized exceptions for the purposes of parody,

---

[171] Intellectual Property Department, The Government of HKSAR, *supra* note 155, *citing* OXFORD ENGLISH DICTIONARY (12th ed. 2012), https://en.oxforddictionaries.com/definition/us/caricature (last visited Oct. 10, 2017).

[172] EDWARD LUCIE-SMITH, THE ART OF CARICATURE 21, 33, 51, 99–116 (1981).

[173] "As the French synonym, *portrait charge*, indicates, a caricature is a loaded portrait. A 1773 complaint against the caricature-drawing Marquess of Townshend maintained that the loaded portrait aimed "[w]ith wretched pencil to debase/Heaven's favorite work, the human face,/To magnify and hold to shame/Each little blemish of our frame.'" Deidre Lynch, *Overloaded Portraits: The Excesses of Character and Countenance*, IN BODY AND TEXT IN THE EIGHTEENTH CENTURY 127 (Veronica Kelly & Dorothea von Mücke, eds. 1994).

[174] *See* images at www.clsa.com/special/fsi/2017/images/john.jpg (last visited Oct. 10, 2017); https://i.pinimg .com/736x/15/d7/d6/15d7d6236e921bb7125cf5d51d05a759–caricatures.jpg (last visited Oct. 10, 2017).

[175] *See* images at http://static6.businessinsider.com/image/4ff1a1996bb3f7bd72000000/hong-kong -protest-burning.jpg (last visited Oct. 10, 2017); www.hrichina.org/sites/default/files/2014_10_10_occu py_hk_art_01.jpg (last visited Oct. 10, 2017).

caricature and pastiche and provided clear definitions of these genres. If the caricatures of Leung and Tsang were modeled on copyrighted photographs and the rights-holders sued the caricaturists, the authors of Tsang's caricatures could argue that they had used the materials for the purpose of caricature, while the authors of Leung's could rely on both the caricature and the parody exceptions. A law that did not distinguish parody and caricature or provide clear definitions for them might lead to two results. Caricatures of Leung might easily meet the definition of parody, while those of Tsang might not. Certainly, courts could also vaguely define "parody" as an umbrella term so that caricatures would fall within this category. Nonetheless, a law distinguishing the two would serve to emphasize, rather than diminish, the expressive purpose of parody and facilitate its role in generating a vibrant political discourse.

The law should also distinguish parody from pastiche, which, like caricature, need not serve any critical or commentary purpose. Derived from the Italian word *pasticcio*, which denotes a pâté of various ingredients,[176] this concept travelled to France in the seventeenth century, where it acquired the name "pastiche."[177] The *Oxford English Dictionary* defines pastiche as "an artistic work in a style that imitates that of another work, artist or period,"[178] whereas critics such as Linda Hutcheon and Mary A. Rose describe postmodern pastiche as "imitation without critical commentary" and as repetition "without difference."[179] Examples of pastiche are abundant in cinema, literature, and others, including Steven Soderbergh's *Kafka* (1991), which assembles the motifs and characters in Franz Kafka's works in a contemporary revolutionary scenario,[180] Milan Kundera's *Immortality* (1990), which sets up imaginary encounters between famous figures,[181] and Franciscus Ankoné's homage to art deco designer Erté in a multi-page presentation of models in French fashion in the *New York Times Magazine*.[182]

Public figures are seldom simply pastiched in Hong Kong media. The rare pastiches, notably those involving John Tsang, further illuminate the importance for the law to distinguish parody from pastiche. Tsang is nicknamed "Uncle Pringles" for his trademark moustache, which reminded people of the brand character of Pringles, the American brand of potato snack chips. Playing on this resemblance, some netizens created pastiches by photoshopping a can

---

[176] Ingeborg Hoesterey, Pastiche: Cultural Memory in Art, Film, Literature 1 (2001).
[177] *Id.* at 2.
[178] Intellectual Property Department, The Government of HKSAR, *supra* note 155, *citing* Oxford English Dictionary (12th ed. 2012), https://en.oxforddictionaries.com/definition/pastiche (last visited Oct. 10, 2017).
[179] Hoesterey, *supra* note 176, at 121.
[180] *Id.* at 78.
[181] *Id.* at 88.
[182] *Id.* at 107.

of Pringles bearing its brand character into Tsang's photographs.[183] Other netizens adorned the Pringles character with a pair of glasses to make him resemble Tsang more closely and added "John Tsang" to the bottom of his face.[184] Imagine that the law provided clear definitions of parody and pastiche, and the copyright-holder of the Pringles character sued the authors of these works. Although the mere juxtaposition of Tsang's image with the Pringles character may be an attempt to endear Tsang to the public, this remix arguably does not carry any criticism or commentary, and might not qualify as a parody. Thus, those who simply photoshopped a can of Pringles into the photographs would find the pastiche exception useful, whereas those who modified the Pringles character could comfortably rely on the pastiche and/or the parody exception. By distinguishing parody from pastiche, the law would avoid imposing an unfair standard on pastiches by requiring that they contain criticisms or commentaries like parodies do. It would also educate the public about the expressive purpose of parody, and facilitate its role in Hong Kong society.

3. The Likely Low "Humor" Bar

As explained in Part I, a parody need not be humorous. Assuming that the law, like the explanatory note to Bill 2014, requires a parody to contain humor, courts would not likely set a high bar for this requirement. First, the meaning of "humor" has never been addressed by Hong Kong courts. Hence, courts may simply follow the social consensus regarding its meaning. The creative and witty uses of symbols and puns to satirize the Hong Kong government and the Chief Executive in pro-democracy protests and television shows have been lauded as "humorous" by the media.[185] Courts would easily find that the parodies discussed in this chapter, which all show their authors' creativity and wittiness, or attempts at creativity and wittiness, meet the humor requirement.

Second, courts may look to the decisions of foreign jurisdictions, many of which have not defined humor either and/or have cautioned courts against evaluating whether a work is "humorous." In *Deckmyn*, for example, neither the Advocate General nor the ECJ defined "humor."[186] The ECJ held that national courts should have broad discretion in determining whether a work is

---

[183] See image at http://vignette1.wikia.nocookie.net/evchk/images/5/55/542853_10200258924251319_11880
36266_n.jpg/revision/latest?cb=20130301172144 (last visited Oct. 10, 2017).

[184] See images at https://4.bp.blogspot.com/-Agh97KrYJS4/WErCPxK1M9I/AAAAAAAABl8/
cFnUkqCa2YU9Yuf25qIHFxQk_ltjS7_oQCLcB/w1200-h630-p-k-no-nu/John%2BTsang.JPG (last
visited Oct. 10, 2017).

[185] See e.g., Yu & Tam, *supra* note 49; Isabella Steger & Edward Ngai, *In Hong Kong, a Democracy March with a Sense of Humor*, WSJ (July 2, 2014), http://blogs.wsj.com/chinarealtime/2014/07/02/in
-hong-kong-a-democracy-march-with-a-sense-of-humor/ (last visited Oct. 10, 2017).

[186] See Deckmyn v. Vandersteen [2014] Case C-201/13, para. 33 (ECJ); Deckmyn v. Vandersteen, Opinion of Advocate General Cruz Villalón [2014] Case C-201/13, para. 68 (ECJ).

a parody, and by implication, whether the work contains humor.[187] The Advocate General also stated that humor can be mixed with other intentions, and "extreme seriousness" "may underlie a humorous expression."[188] In *Campbell*, the U.S. Supreme Court cautioned courts against evaluating a parody's success, and by implication, the funniness of its jokes.[189] Therefore, even if the new law requires that a parody should contain humor, the parodies commonly found in Hong Kong's social media, like those examined in this chapter, would easily pass muster.

Clearly, the Hong Kong government has had no plan to substitute American-style fair use for fair dealing as Yu recommends. Yet fair dealing exceptions in forms of parody, caricature and pastiche, as long as they are clearly defined and correctly interpreted, should partially make up for the relative lack of flexibility of fair dealing. Provided that courts pay attention to the market substitution factor (whether the works would cause substantial economic prejudices to the originals' owners), they would be inclined to consider derivative works that would not likely displace demands for their originals to be fair dealings.

III. APPLYING THE PARODY EXCEPTION: FROM AN UNRELIABLE FREE SPEECH DOCTRINE TO MORAL RIGHTS EXEMPTIONS

Part I and the previous chapters have argued that to align the copyright systems with the free speech traditions of these jurisdictions, courts should apply the parody exception by drawing upon the free speech doctrine, so that controversial but lawful expressions would not be suppressed for the sake or under the pretext of copyright protection. Chapter 5 on the United Kingdom has also illuminated how a narrowly circumscribed public interest doctrine in the British copyright jurisprudence may not help parodies to survive moral rights claims by authors. This section will illuminate how the external freedom of expression doctrine cannot be relied upon to safeguard the right to parody in Hong Kong, given that this freedom has been constantly attacked since the changeover and will likely continue to shrink in the years to come. It will explore a solution internal to the copyright statute: providing an exception to the author's integrity right to object to derogatory treatment of the work in the form of parody, so as to provide more space for Hongkongers to exercise their freedom of expression through parodies.

---

[187] *Deckmyn* [2014] Case C-201/13, *supra* note 186, para. 33.

[188] *Deckmyn*, Opinion of the A.G. [2014], *supra* note 186, para. 68.

[189] Campbell v. Acuff-Rose Music, Inc., 510 U.S. 569, 582 (1994), *quoting* Yankee Publ'g. v. News Am. Pub'g., Inc., 809 F. Supp. 267, 280 (S.D.N.Y. 1992) ("First Amendment protections do not apply only to those who speak clearly, whose jokes are funny, and whose parodies succeed.").

A. An Unreliable External Doctrine

The appeal to freedom of expression and freedom of the press by Hong Kong courts in copyright claims is not unprecedented.[190] Courts should apply the parody exception with reference to this core principle. For example, they may follow the ECJ's example to prioritize the artistic and/or political values of parodies over rights-holders' interests. They may also follow Liu's suggestion, discussed in Chapter 3 and analogize copyright infringement with defamation, to ensure that controversial materials that are not defamatory would not be banned. However, because this core freedom has been constantly assaulted since the changeover by both the PRC and the Hong Kong governments, it could not be relied upon as an external doctrine to safeguard the right to parody.

Section II of this chapter has examined examples of self-censorship engaged by Hong Kong's media and business organizations. Unsurprisingly, efforts at censorship have also been undertaken by the PRC government, which has repeatedly violated the Joint Declaration by going against its "One country, two systems" principle and curtailing Hongkongers' freedom of speech since the early days after the changeover. One example took place in 1999, when Cheung Man-Yee, then Director of Broadcasting of the Radio Television of Hong Kong (RTHK) (a governmental organization) and a staunch defender of press freedom, was removed from her position after inviting Taiwan's official representative in Hong Kong to deliver a short speech in a program defending the view that Taiwan is an independent nation.[191] Given its strong reaction to the speech, the PRC government was believed to have requested Cheung's removal.[192] A year later, the Hong Kong Cable Television's interview of the Vice-President Elect of Taiwan's second presidential election, who advocated for Taiwan's independence and sovereignty, continued to trigger strong reactions from Beijing and pro-CCP groups in Hong Kong.[193] The PRC government warned Hong Kong journalists about their responsibility "to uphold the integrity and sovereignty of the country and not to advocate 'two states' theory and independence of Taiwan," which it considered to have "nothing to do with press freedom."[194]

A much more recent and blatant example of the PRC government attacking freedom of expression in Hong Kong involved the abduction of five booksellers from a Hong Kong bookstore selling controversial books that criticized President Xi. Late 2015 saw a series of "kidnapping" incidents, one taking place in Hong Kong, in which agents from its central investigation team arrested the booksellers and

---

[190] Wong Wing Yue Rosaline v. Next Media Interactive Ltd. & Others [2017] HKCFI 269 (C.F.I.). The Court weighed the plaintiff's right to privacy and copyright in her photographs, obtained and published without her consent by a media company against freedom of the press. Finding for the company, it refused to issue a disclosure order requesting it to disclose the sources of the photographs.
[191] Wong, *supra* note 34, at 22–23.
[192] *Id.*
[193] *Id.* at 23–24.
[194] *Id.* at 23.

detained them in China.[195] On the arrest of one victim, China's foreign ministry claimed that because he had broken Chinese laws, the Chinese authorities across the border were within their rights to handle his case.[196] Nonetheless, publishing and distributing materials that criticize public figures is legal in Hong Kong.[197] The PRC government therefore lacked legal grounds to arrest or detain the book-sellers, let alone bypass legal procedures in its secret arrest of one bookseller.[198]

Apparently, these violent acts by the PRC government have not directly affected Hong Kong's freedom of expression jurisprudence. The most important judicial decision banning political speech has been *HKSAR v. Ng Kung Siu and Another* (1999), in which the Final Court of Appeal upheld the conviction of two individuals for desecrating the Hong Kong flag and the Chinese flag, on the grounds that flag desecration is not legal and there are other protest methods.[199] This decision, which outraged democrats and free-speech activists, became a handy tool for pro-China commentators to advocate even more stringent laws banning opinions disfavored by the Chinese government. Examples are views held by "localist" groups, formed after the civil disobedience movement, that Hong Kong should enjoy more political and cultural autonomy from China, or even become an independent city-state.[200] The PRC government views any talks of "independence" (which includes auton-omy) as illegal, while the Hong Kong government declared that to "advocate independence" is against the Basic Law.[201] Pro-China commentators thus drew

195   E.g., Elizabeth Joseph & Katie Hunt, *Missing Hong Kong Bookseller: I Was Kidnapped by Chinese "Special Forces,"* CNN (June 16, 2016), www.cnn.com/2016/06/16/asia/china-hong-kong-booksellers/index.html (last visited Oct. 10, 2017); Tony Cheung & Phila Siu, "Outrage Expressed in Hong Kong over Missing Bookseller, but No Answers Forthcoming," S. CHINA MORNING POST (June 7, 2016), www.scmp.com/news/hong-kong/law-crime/article/1977002/outrage-expressed-hong-kong-over-miss-ing-bookseller-no (last visited Oct. 10, 2017). Five men associated with the publishing house in Causeway Bay disappeared one after another, beginning in October 2015. The first victim vanished from Pattaya, Thailand. Three others went missing while they were in Mainland China. The last one disappeared from Hong Kong in December 2015. Four of them were later allowed to return to Hong Kong, while one still remains detained. Lam Wing-kee, one of the former, disclosed to the media how he was abducted, blindfolded and handcuffed by secret agents in October 2015.
196   Cheung & Siu, *supra* note 195.
197   *Id.*
198   *Id.*
199   HKSAR v. Ng Kung Siu & Another [1999] HKCFA 10 (C.F.A.). Flag desecration was legal in colonial Hong Kong. The Chinese law banning flag desecration was incorporated into Hong Kong law as the National Flag and National Emblem Ordinance in 1997, as required by Annex III of the Basic Law. In addition, the Regional Flag and Regional Emblem Ordinance, also enacted in 1997, bans the desecration of the Hong Kong flag.
200   Some "localist" groups seek greater political and cultural autonomy from China. Others demand independence and the formation of a city-state. Alissa Greenberg, *A Year after the Umbrella Revolution, Calls for More Autonomy, Even Independence, Grow in Hong Kong,* CNN (Sep. 27, 2015), http://time.com/4049700/hong-kong-independence-occupy-umbrella-localist/ (last visited Oct. 10, 2017).
201   Suzanne Pepper, *Treason or Free speech? Talk of Independence Touches a Sensitive Spot,* H.K. FREE P. (May 9, 2016), www.hongkongfp.com/2016/05/09/treason-free-speech-talk-independence-touches-sensitive-spot/ (last visited Oct. 10, 2017).

upon the *Ng Kung Siu* case to point out that the exercise of freedom of expression ought to be subject to the overriding principles of "one country, two systems" and national unity, and given the lack of legislation expressly prohibiting or criminalizing the advocacy of Hong Kong independence, time is ripe for Hong Kong to reconsider enacting relevant legislation under art. 23 of the Basic Law.[202]

Although the National Security Bill was shelved in 2003, due to the civil disobedience movement in 2014 and the rise of "localist" groups, national security legislation once again emerged as an important topic in the 2017 Chief Executive Election. Carrie Lam, the new Chief Executive, vowed to take "a leading and proactive role" in passing the legislation, although the government must create the right social conditions for legislation.[203] In fact, only a day after she pledged to unite a divided society as the city's new Chief Executive, the Department of Justice ordered the arrest and prosecution of the leaders and key participants in the 2014 protests.[204] While the Department of Justice issued a statement denying any political consideration in its action, scholars attributed the timing of the arrests to the former Chief Executive's (or Beijing's) attempt to make the new Chief Executive adopt a hardline approach towards current and future protests.[205] Therefore, Lam will likely coordinate with the PRC government to create an increasingly suppressive environment, whether the national security legislation will be enacted or not.

Freedom of speech in Hong Kong has not been threatened merely by the prospect of a national security law under art. 23, but also by the Hong Kong government's proposal to amend the current discrimination law to prohibit "discriminatory" speech targeting Mainlanders, after a series of "anti-locusts" street protests in Hong Kong's tourist districts in early 2014.[206] The Race Discrimination Ordinance prohibits discrimination on the basis of "the race, colour, descent, national or ethnic origin of the person."[207] Because the Equal Opportunities Commission takes the

---

[202]   *E.g., id.*; Eliza Chan, *Hong Kong Should Reconsider Enacting Article 23 Legislation to Nip Support for Independence in the Bud*, S. CHINA MORNING POST (Apr. 18, 2016), www.scmp.com/news/hong-kong/politics/article/2082375/occupy-leaders-told-they-face-prosecution-day-after-carrie (last visited Oct. 10, 2017).

[203]   Carrie Lam, *We Connect: Connecting for Consensus and a Better Future (Manifesto for Chief Executive Election 2017)*, at 7, http://wpadmin2017.carrielam2017.hk/media/my/2017/01/Manifesto_e_v2.pdf (last visited Oct. 10, 2017); Kang-Chung Ng & Jeffie Lam, *Hong Kong Leader Carrie Lam Calls for National Security Law Push, but No Clear Time Frame*, S. CHINA MORNING POST (July 3, 2017), www.scmp.com/news/hong-kong/politics/article/2101093/hong-kong-leader -carrie-lam-calls-national-security-law-push (last visited Oct. 10, 2017).

[204]   Chris Lau & Joyce Ng, *Occupy Leaders Arrested and Charged a Day after Carrie Lam Wins Hong Kong Chief Executive Election*, S. CHINA MORNING POST (Mar. 27, 2017), www.scmp.com /news/hong-kong/politics/article/2082375/occupy-leaders-told-they-face-prosecution-day-after-carrie (last visited Oct. 10, 2017).

[205]   *Id.*

[206]   Jennifer Ngo, *Hong Kong May Amend Its Race Hate Law to Protect Mainland Visitors*, S. CHINA MORNING Post (Feb. 20, 2014), www.scmp.com/news/hong-kong/article/1432229/hong-kong-may-amend-its-race-hate-law-protect-mainland-visitors (last visited Oct. 10, 2017).

[207]   Race Discrimination Ordinance, s. 8(1)(a).

position that Mainlanders and Hongkongers should not be differentiated by race and nationality, it is currently reviewing the Ordinance and seeking to address what it considers to be discrimination within the same racial and national group.[208] Yet the locust metaphor, though rude, is not hate speech or an ethnic slur, because it targets the behaviors and manners of some Mainlanders, rather than Mainlanders as a demographic group.[209] A renowned scholar and social commentator aptly compares this metaphor to "Wall Street Crooks," used to describe Wall Street bankers who profit illegally and at the expense of their clients, arguing that both are condemnatory but not discriminatory.[210] Rather than outlawing the metaphor, the government therefore should discourage rude behavior from both Mainlanders and Hongkongers. Its attempt to amend the law to protect the feelings of Mainlanders reveals that it privileges a harmonious Hong Kong–China relationship over Hongkongers' right to free speech, and is ready to chip away at this core, cherished freedom in the former colony to maintain a superficial, fragile harmony.

Because freedom of expression has been continually eroded and will continue to shrink in post-handover Hong Kong, it would become an unreliable external doctrine for safeguarding parodists' freedom of expression even with the introduction of a parody fair-dealing exception. In 2014, Beijing issued a white paper on the "one country, two systems" formula, stating that Hong Kong judges have a "basic political requirement" to love their country.[211] This "patriotism" requirement was widely interpreted to mean being "supportive of and cooperating with" the Beijing and Hong Kong governments, which would erode Hong Kong's judicial independence.[212] Although this requirement has not yet been imposed on Hong Kong judges, this is further evidence that the freedom of speech doctrine cannot be relied upon to safeguard Hong Kong people's right to parody copyrighted works in a jurisdiction where this very freedom is constantly threatened.

B. *Moral Rights Exemptions and Breathing Space*

Because freedom of expression is under continual erosion in Hong Kong, where the judiciary may not be immune to corruption, internalizing the freedom of expression

---

[208] Ngo, *supra* note 206.

[209] At an open consultation by the EOC, a representative of Local Press, an internet media outlet, pointed out that condemning something wrong is a "moral right:" "If a Hongkonger shouted 'locust' in the face of a Mainlander after seeing him poo, would he be subjected to punishment?" Amy Nip, *Should It Be Illegal to Call Someone "Locust"? Protection for Mainlanders Dominates Law Debate*, S. China Morning Post (Aug. 10, 2014), www.scmp.com/news/hong-kong/article/1570269/it -discrimination-say-locust-protection-mainlanders-dominates-debate (last visited Oct. 10, 2017).

[210] Joseph Lien 練乙錚, *Discrimination against "Locusts"* (「蝗蟲」歧視．Mao神．WhatsApp的 「1%」) (Feb. 24, 2014), https://forum.hkej.com/node/110482 (last visited Oct. 10, 2017).

[211] *E.g.*, Peter So, *Judges Don't Need to Be Patriots, Says Former Top Judge Andrew Li*, S. China Morning Post (Aug. 15, 2014), www.scmp.com/news/hong-kong/article/1573867/judges-dont-need-be-patriots -andrew-li?page=all (last visited Oct. 10, 2017).

[212] *Id.*

doctrine by having courts place a heavier emphasis on the nature of the defendant's dealing factor, a solution described in Chapter 5, would not help to provide more room for artistic and political speech. However, amending the moral rights provisions in the Copyright Ordinance would be a good internal mechanism to provide more room for free speech by shielding parodists from moral rights claims by authors. Yu suggests that if a fair dealing exception is to be introduced to exempt parodies from both civil and criminal liabilities for copyright infringements, corresponding changes should also be made to the moral rights provisions.[213] At present, s. 91(4) of the Ordinance provides exceptions to the author's (or director's) (attribution) right to be identified as the author or director of the copyrighted work,[214] whereas s. 93 further includes exceptions to the author's (or director's) (integrity) right to object to derogatory treatment of the work.[215] The Ordinance should be amended to include corresponding parody exceptions, so that the author would give up the right to be identified as the author/director of the parody's underlying work, and the right to object to derogatory treatment of that work in the form of parody.[216] Yu justifies the former exception by pointing out the challenge of including sufficient acknowledgements in certain parodies.[217] He also explains that the latter exception would help to protect parodists from legal action by disgruntled authors who feel that the parodies have caused them embarrassment, emotional pain, or loss of "face."[218]

Interestingly, Bill 2014 only introduced a corresponding exception to the attribution right to be identified as the author or director of the copyrighted work.[219] Because it did not include an exception to the author's or director's integrity right to object to derogatory treatment of the work in the form of parody, parodists' anxieties over potential integrity right claims could chill their speech. The question is whether a narrowly-defined "derogatory treatment" would better attain this balance. Arguably, because a narrow definition of "derogatory treatment" of the original work would hinge on whether the parody defames the author or causes the author emotional distress, the author's integrity right could be addressed by related laws and the integrity right provision could be eliminated altogether.

This solution would entitle parodists to express their opinions about politicians or others through parodies while being shielded from moral rights claims alleging that they have subjected copyrighted works to derogatory treatments through their parodies. Examples from the earlier discussion include appropriating the Chief Executive Carrie Lam's image and the Christian art picture in a parody to condemn her arrogance, and parodying politician Regina Ip's election logo to express

---

[213] Yu, *supra* note 109, at 19–21.
[214] Copyright Ordinance, s. 91(4).
[215] *Id.* s. 93.
[216] Yu, *supra* note 109, at 20–21.
[217] *Id.* at 20.
[218] *Id.*
[219] Copyright (Amendment) Bill 2014, cl. 51.

contempt for her. Each of these examples constitutes a "fair comment in a matter of public interest" and defames neither the target nor the author. If the parody defames the underlying work's author – who may also be the target of the parody – the author and/or the target could bring a defamation suit against the parodist. Whereas Chief Executives may not sue citizens for defamation in their public capacity, if a parody mocking a politician asserts a false statement of fact or opinion that shows "malice," then the politician or the underlying work's author who is also likely affected would be able to sue the parodist for defamation. Hence, providing for exceptions to the author's moral rights, especially the integrity right to object to derogatory treatment of the work in the form of parody, would make room for freedom of speech without sacrificing the rights of copyright owners or authors.

***

In both the United Kingdom and Hong Kong, the free speech doctrine could not be relied upon as an external mechanism to safeguard the right to parody copyrighted works. In the U.K., courts can rely upon the nature of the defendant's use factor to provide more room for political and artistic expressions. For Hong Kong, an internal solution – eliminating the author's integrity right to object to derogatory treatment of the work in the form of parody – would provide more room for parodies, as freedom of speech continues to decline in the territory.

Conclusion

If names be not correct, language is not in accordance with the truth of things. If language be not in accordance with the truth of things, affairs cannot be carried on to success.[1]

This book has shown that the right to parody is a natural right in both the free speech and the copyright contexts. It has also addressed the scope of protection that copyright law should provide to this right. Whether copyright is considered a natural right like speech freedom, or a conventional right established to incentivize the production of creative works, it should give way to the right to parody copyrighted works, provided that the parodies would not harm the interests of rights-holders by displacing market demands for their works. The fundamental nature of free speech calls for a broad parody exception in copyright law, and the prioritization of the market substitution factor. Not only would the broad exception not harm the interests of rights-holders, but it also would not conflict with authors' moral rights.

The previous chapters have discussed how the proposed parody exception would help to bring the copyright systems of the five subject jurisdictions, driven by utilitarianism and/or a narrow conception of natural rights prioritizing the rights of copyright owners, in line with their free speech jurisprudences. This broad parody definition should replace the narrow defense set up by the U.S. Supreme Court, which has been used by lower courts to suppress valuable parodic works that would not likely compete with the copyrighted originals. This broad exception should also replace the parody and satire fair dealing exceptions in Canada's copyright statute, as it would help to diminish any impact of a propertized conception of fair dealing, and properly balance the interests of rights-holders and users.

The parody exception in British copyright law encompasses a broad range of works. Nonetheless, the moral rights provisions in its copyright statute potentially stifle free speech, while a narrowly circumscribed public interest doctrine will prevent courts from applying the exception in ways that best serve the public's speech interests. On the contrary, French courts have not only interpreted its

---

[1] CONFUCIUS, ANALECTS, bk. XIII, ch. 3, verses 4–7 (tr. James Legge, IN CONFUCIAN ANALECTS: THE GREAT LEARNING, AND THE DOCTRINE OF THE MEAN 263–64 (1971)).

statutory parody exception quite broadly, but have continued to broaden its scope by drawing upon the speech doctrine in both its domestic law and the European Convention on Human Rights.

Lastly, the book has examined the parody exception in Hong Kong's Copyright (Amendment) Bill 2014. Chapter 7 has explained that a broad parody exception should replace "parody" and "satire," but be distinguished from "pastiche" and "caricature" in the Bill. A broad and properly defined parody exception, together with an exception to the author's integrity right to object to derogatory treatment of the work in the form of parody, can help to facilitate the role of parody in the former British colony, where free speech has been continually eroded since its handover to China.

✳ ✳ ✳

The much-cited, perhaps clichéd, saying by Shakespeare goes: "What's in a name? That which we call a rose/ By any other name would smell as sweet."[2] Names could be arbitrary and their relationships with the things that they represent could be tenuous and even non-existent. Would parody serve its legal function if it were known by any other name? On a related note, if the most crucial factor that determines the fairness of the use or dealing is whether it would substitute for the underlying work or its derivatives in the market and harm the interests of the rights-holder, is the "parody" exception or defense truly necessary in copyright law? From a practical standpoint, a parody exception would be necessary for jurisdictions in which fair dealing tests are adopted, because a work must fall within an exception before it can proceed to the fairness analysis. Further, the book has described the ancient origins of parody, its long traditions in different cultures, and its significant role in delivering criticisms and commentaries vital for the pursuit of truth, democratic governance, and self-realization. So much is carried in the word "parody." Hence, the exception or defense should be known by no other name than "parody," to educate the public about the role of parody and to foster the parodic tradition. Names, after all, carry tremendous power.

---

[2] WILLIAM SHAKESPEARE, ROMEO AND JULIET, Act 2, Scene 2, 46–47 (1597), www.folgerdigitaltexts.org /html/Rom.html#line-2.2.0 (last visited Oct. 10, 2017).

Index